Mexico
Dilemmas of Transition

Edited by
Neil Harvey

The Institute of Latin American Studies,
University of London
and
British Academic Press
London • New York

Published in 1993 by
The Institute of Latin American Studies,
University of London
and
British Academic Press
45 Bloomsbury Square
London WC1A 2HY

175 Fifth Avenue
New York
NY 10010

British Academic Press is an imprint of I.B.Tauris

In the United States of America
and Canada distributed by
St Martin's Press
175 Fifth Avenue
New York
NY 10010

A CIP record for this book is available from the British Library

Library of Congress catalog card number available
A full CIP record is available from the Library of Congress

ISBN 1-85043-514-6

Printed and bound in Great Britain by
WBC Limited, Bridgend, Mid Glamorgan.

Mexico

Dilemmas of Transition

CONTENTS

LIST OF CONTRIBUTORS

Neil Harvey is a Visiting Assistant Professor at Brown University and the University of Connecticut. He was a Research Fellow at the Institute of Latin American Studies, London in 1989–92, where he published a research paper *The New Agrarian Movement in Mexico, 1979–1990* (1990). For the period 1990–2 he received funding from the Economic and Social Research Council to investigate changes in state-peasant relations in Mexico since 1982.

Alan Knight is Professor of the History of Latin America, Oxford University and a Fellow of St Antony's College, Oxford. He was formerly C. B. Smith Sr. Professor of Mexican History at the University of Texas at Austin. He is author of numerous works on Mexico, including *The Mexican Revolution* (2 vols., 1986) and *US-Mexican Relations, 1910–1940* (1987).

Silvia Gómez Tagle is a Researcher and Lecturer in the Centro de Estudios Sociológicos at the Colegio de México. She has written several articles on Mexican elections and politics and compiled a statistical compendium of electoral data entitled *La Estadística de la Reforma Política* (1990). She also co-ordinated a national research project on the mid-term elections held in August 1991.

John Gledhill is Senior Lecturer in Anthropology at University College London. He has published extensively on Mexico in English and Spanish including the monograph *Casi Nada: a Study of Agrarian Reform in the Homeland of Cardenismo* (1991). A revised and up-dated version of this book has also been published in Spanish by the Colegio de Michoacán.

Mónica Serrano is a Researcher and Lecturer in the Centro de Estudios Internacionales at the Colegio de México. She obtained a

D.Phil from St Antony's College, Oxford in 1991 for her thesis on nuclear non-proliferation treaties. She was a Research Fellow at the Institute of Latin American Studies, London, in 1990–91 where she has published a research paper, *Common Security in Latin America: the 1967 Treaty of Tlatelolco* (1992).

Nigel Harris is Professor of Development Planning at University College London. He is author of numerous works on politics and development, including *Of Bread and Guns: the world economy in crisis*, *The End of the Third World*, *National Liberation*, and has edited the book *Cities in the 1990s: the challenge for developing countries*.

Michael Heller is a Lecturer in the Politics of South-East Asia at the School of Oriental and African Studies, London. Since 1990 he has been carrying out comparative research on public policy and government–business relations in South-East Asia and Latin America. In 1990 he completed a doctoral thesis at Sussex University on Mexico's telecommunications policy.

Paul Haber is an Assistant Professor in the Department of Political Science at the University of Montana. In 1991 he submitted his doctoral thesis on 'Collective Dissent in Mexico: the Politics of Contemporary Urban Popular Movements' to the Department of Political Science at Columbia University. He has also written several articles on Mexico's urban popular movements.

Ann Varley is a Lecturer in Georgraphy at University College London. She has co-authored, with Alan Gilbert, *Landlord and Tenant: Housing the Poor in Urban Mexico* (1991) and has published widely on illegal settlements and land tenure regularization in Mexico.

Sergio Zermeño is a Researcher in the Instituto de Investigaciones Sociales at the Universidad Nacional Autónoma de México. He has written many articles on Mexican politics and social movements. He is author of *México–una democracia utópica: el movimiento estudiantil de 1968* (1978), and co-editor of the volume *Movimientos Sociales en México* (1991).

Ilán Bizberg is a Researcher and Lecturer in the Centro de Estudios Internacionales at the Colegio de México. He has written widely on labour issues in Mexico, including two books *La Clase Obrera Mexicana* (1986) and *Estado y Sindicalismo en México* (1990).

Sylvia Chant is a Lecturer in the Department of Geography at the London School of Economics. She is author of *Women and Survival* *in Mexican Cities: perspectives on gender, labour markets and low-income households* (1991) and co-author, with Lynne Brydon, of *Women in the Third World: gender issues in rural and urban areas* (1989). She has also edited *Gender and Migration in Developing Countries* (1992).

LIST OF ACRONYMS

ARENA	Alianza Renovadora Nacional
AURIS	Instituto de la Acción Urbana e Integración Social
BANAMEX	Banco Nacional de México
BANRURAL	Banco Nacional de Crédito Rural
CAM	Consejo Agrarista Mexicano
CANACINTRA	Cámara Nacional de la Industria de Transformación
CAP	Congreso Agrario Permanente
CAU	Convenio de Acción Unitaria
CCC	Central Campesina Cardenista
CCE	Consejo Coordinador Empresarial
CCI	Central Campesina Independiente
CCU	Central Campesina Unitaria
CD	Corriente Democrática
CDP	Comité de Defensa Popular
CECVYM	Coalición de Ejidos Colectivos de los Valles Yaqui y Mayo
CEESP	Centro de Estudios Económicos del Sector Privado
CFE	Comisión Federal de Electricidad
CFE	Comisión Federal Electoral
CIOAC	Central Independiente de Obreros Agrícolas y Campesinos
CMHN	Consejo Mexicano de Hombres de Negocios
CNA	Consejo Nacional Agropecuario
CNC	Confederación Nacional Campesina

CNOP	Confederación Nacional de Organizaciones Populares
CNPA	Coordinadora Nacional Plan de Ayala
CNPI	Coordinadora Nacional de Pueblos Indígenas
CNTE	Coordinadora Nacional de Trabajadores de la Educación
COCEI	Coalición Obrera Campesina Estudiantil del Istmo
COCU	Comisión Organizadora del Congreso Universitario
CODUC	Comisión Organizadora de la Unidad Campesina
COFIPE	Código Federal de Instituciones y Procedimientos Electorales
CONAMUP	Coordinadora Nacional del Movimiento Urbano Popular
CONASUPO	Compañía Nacional de Subsistencias Populares
CONCAMIN	Confederación de Cámaras Industriales
CONCANACO	Confederación Nacional de Cámaras Nacionales de Comercio
CONPA	Congreso Permanente Agrario
COPARMEX	Confederación Patronal de la República Mexicana
COR	Confederación Obrera Revolucionaria
CORETT	Comisión para la Regularización de la Tenencia de la Tierra
CREA	Consejo Nacional de Recursos para la Atención de la Juventud
CROC	Confederación Revolucionaria de Obreros y Campesinos
CROM	Confederación Regional Obrera Mexicana
CTM	Confederación de Trabajadores de México
DGDT	Dirección General de Desarrollo Tecnológico
DICONSA	Distribuidora de CONASUPO
FDCCH	Frente Democrático Campesino de Chihuahua
FDN	Frente Democrático Nacional
FESEBES	Federación de Sindicatos de Empresas de Bienes y Servicios
FIDEURBE	Fideicomiso de Interés Social para el Desarrollo Urbano de la Ciudad de México
FOMERREY	Fideicomiso para el Fomento Metropolitano de Monterrey

FONACOT	Fondo Nacional para el Consumo de los Trabajadores
FONAFE	Fondo Nacional de Fomento Ejidal
FPI	Frente Popular Independiente
FPTyL	Frente Popular Tierra y Libertad
FRAP	Fuerzas Revolucionarias Armadas del Pueblo
GATT	General Agreement on Tariffs and Trade
IMSS	Instituto Mexicano del Seguro Social
INDECO	Instituto Nacional para el Desarrollo de la Comunidad y de la Vivienda
INFONAVIT	Instituto del Fondo Nacional para la Vivienda de los Trabajadores
INI	Instituto Nacional Indigenista
INMECAFE	Instituto Mexicano del Café
LFOPPE	Ley Federal de Organizaciones Políticas y Procesos Electorales
LP	Línea Proletaria
MAP	Movimiento de Acción Popular
MAR	Movimiento Armado Revolucionario
MAS	Movimiento al Socialismo
MNCP	Movimiento Nacional de los Cuatrocientos Pueblos
MNPA	Movimiento Nacional Plan de Ayala
MUP	Movimiento Urbano Popular
NIC	Newly Industrializing Country
OCEZ	Organización Campesina Emiliano Zapata
OIR–LM	Organización de Izquierda Revolucionaria-Línea de Masas
PAN	Partido de Acción Nacional
PARM	Partido Auténtico de la Revolución Mexicana
PCDP	Partido del Comité de Defensa Popular
PCM	Partido Comunista Mexicano
PDM	Partido Demócrata Mexicano
PECE	Pacto para la Estabilidad y el Crecimiento Económico
PEMEX	Petróleos Mexicanos
PFCRN	Partido del Frente Cardenista de Reconstrucción Nacional
PMS	Partido Mexicano Socialista
PMT	Partido Mexicano de los Trabajadores

PND	Plan Nacional de Desarrollo
PNR	Partido Nacional Revolucionario
PPS	Partido Popular Socialista
PRD	Partido de la Revolución Democrática
PRI	Partido Revolucionario Institucional
PRONASOL	Programa Nacional de Solidaridad
PRT	Partido Revolucionario de los Trabajadores
PSD	Partido Social Demócrata
PST	Partido Socialista de los Trabajadores
PSUM	Partido Socialista Unificado de México
SAHOP	Secretaría de Asentamientos Humanos y Obras Públicas
SARH	Secretaría de Agricultura y Recursos Hidráulicos
SCT	Secretaría de Comunicaciones y Transporte
SECOFI	Secretaría de Comercio y Fomento Industrial
SEDUE	Secretaría de Desarrollo Urbano y Ecología
SIPRO	Servicios de Información Procesada
SME	Sindicato Mexicano de Electricistas
SNTMMSRM	Sindicato Nacional de Trabajadores Mineros, Metalúrgicos y Similares de la República Mexicana
SPP	Secretaría de Programación y Presupuesto
SRA	Secretaría de la Reforma Agraria
STPRM	Sindicato de Trabajadores Petroleros de la República Mexicana
STRM	Sindicato de Telefonistas de la República Mexicana
TELMEX	Teléfonos de México
TRICOEL	Tribunal de lo Contencioso Electoral
UCEZ	Unión de Comuneros Emiliano Zapata
UGOCM	Unión General de Obreros y Campesinos de México
UGOCP	Unión General Obrera Campesina Popular
UNORCA	Unión Nacional de Organizaciones Regionales Campesinas Autónomas
UNTA	Unión Nacional de Trabajadores Agrícolas
UPEZ	Unión de Pueblos Emiliano Zapata
UU	Unión de Uniones Ejidales y Grupos Campesinos Solidarios de Chiapas

PREFACE

Can economic liberalization in developing countries be made compatible with democratization? This has become an important issue in Mexico and Latin America, where increasing social polarization threatens to undermine democratic advances in the political sphere. Earlier forms of state intervention have become increasingly ineffective in guaranteeing social order. Similarly, the ideological elements which gave varying degrees of cohesion to national, inward-orientated development have lost their unifying capacity. In the past, demands arising from social inequalities were mediated through various forms of limited parliamentary democracy, state clientelism, welfare policies, nationalist discourses, co-option and coercion. Without suggesting that these mechanisms will no longer be used, we can say that their effectiveness is declining, both in providing concrete solutions to specific problems and in asserting the authority of state institutions across national territories. In the current context of economic and cultural globalization, moreover, they appear as obstacles to democratic development.

Two very different forces conspire against state-led accumulation and redistribution. On the one hand, transnational capital increasingly demands political and institutional guarantees of stability for long-term investment. Social order (leaving aside its inequalities) is seen as a comparative advantage and this is a function which still pertains to national governments in most of the world. On the other hand, new democratic movements in civil society demand respect for a wide range of citizens' rights and an end to clientelistic and paternalistic forms of political control. Social equality is seen as a necessary step in rebuilding a more just form of social order. Naturally, the meaning of democracy differs between the two, between liberal and radical versions of political reform.

In the case of Mexico, however, both these projects, and the groups that support them, face a state-party (the Partido Revolucionario Institucional – PRI) which has monopolized the privileges of political power for over six decades. Naturally, there are sectors of the party and state bureaucracy which are reluctant to change. Nor is the problem limited to the PRI. For many years, opposition forces and pressure groups (of both left and right) have been accustomed to negotiating their demands with the state and have contributed to the longevity of clientelism and co-option. Democratization in Mexico, whether liberal or radical, will therefore require changes in how those forces deal with the state; that is, in their political practices.

The central dilemma for the Mexican regime is that an authentic commitment to democratization would mark the end of the state-party system and open up the possibility that groups opposed to economic liberalization might take power. Instead, reforms are made to bolster the position of the PRI and, with it, the long-term commitment to economic modernization and integration along neoliberal lines. Alliances with leading business groups (domestic and foreign), sectors of opposition parties, religious bodies and leaders of public opinion are similarly designed to provide a stable political environment for the successful restructuring of the economy. This may be more accurately described as a conservative transition rather than a democratic one.

Whether this strategy can achieve consensus amid the continuing social crisis depends, to a large extent, on the political responses of the opposition parties and movements. In short, the political character of Mexico's transition is not predetermined but reflects shifts in the balance of forces. Nor is it homogeneous since it varies between sectors and regions. The chapters in this book present different aspects of economic, political and social change in Mexico which reveal some of the dilemmas of that country's transition. We hope that they will be useful in reflecting not only Mexican dilemmas but those of other countries facing the challenges of an increasingly interdependent world.

The chapters that follow were originally presented in the research seminar on contemporary Mexico at the Institute of Latin American Studies, London, during 1989 and 1990. The majority were presented at a special workshop entitled 'Mexico in transition: elements of continuity and change', held at the Institute in May 1990. I would like to thank the following institutions which gave financial assistance for the workshop: the British Council (Mexico City), the Nuffield Foundation, Intermex Bank, the Mexico and Central America Section of the Foreign and Commonwealth Office, and the Institute of Latin American Studies. I greatly appreciated the support of Professor Leslie Bethell and Tony Bell in organizing the workshop and the copy-editor at The British Academic Press for carrying out such a professional job on the original manuscript. I also thank all those who participated for their enthusiasm and commitment to the Institute's Mexican Studies programme. I am grateful to the Economic and Social Research Council (ESRC) for a research grant held between 1990 and 1992 which enabled me to carry out the editing and proof-reading stages. Finally, my sincere thanks to Wendy for her constant encouragement and patience and to Alhelí for the joy she has brought in these first few steps of life. To them I dedicate this book.

Neil Harvey
Institute of Latin American Studies, London
May 1992

THE DIFFICULT TRANSITION:

Neoliberalism and Neocorporatism in Mexico*

Neil Harvey

The direction of political change in Mexico has attracted much attention in recent years. What was once seen as a predictable and stable political system became the arena for new tensions and conflicts. The onset of economic crisis coincided with and, in part, led to the emergence of a new governing élite of young technocrats, the independent mobilization of a new business class finding political expression in the Partido de Acción Nacional (PAN), the growth of grassroots popular movements and the unification of the left around the presidential candidacy in 1988 of Cuauhtémoc Cárdenas. All these developments implied a serious erosion of corporatist ties between state and society which had underpinned Mexican stability since the 1930s. They also paved the way for a transition to a new political system, although the direction of change remained unclear.

The chapters in this book address the nature of Mexico's transition in the 1980s by focusing on the challenge of political and economic reform. As many observers have noted, the latter appears to have proceeded at a faster pace than the former. Is it the case that democratic change is being subordinated to the preservation of stability and the pursuit of an exclusionary economic strategy? In the economic sphere reform is geared to making Mexico internationally competitive through increased efficiency and productivity. The rapid changes introduced by the administration of Miguel de la Madrid since 1982 have been continued by that of Carlos Salinas de Gortari

* I would like to thank Joe Foweraker and Mónica Serrano for their comments on an earlier draft version of this introduction.

since December 1988. Nevertheless, modernization policies have been resisted by some sectors of the state bureaucracy and by popular sectors whose living standards have fallen dramatically in the past decade.

The picture which emerges is of a highly contested transition in which the government hopes to contain popular demands for democratic change through a successful economic project and a gradual restructuring of its relations with civil society. Yet such a strategy, designed to allow a selective political opening to those groups which do not directly challenge the majority of the ruling Partido Revolucionario Institucional (PRI) in Congress nor the principles of the government's economic policies, confronts a generalized demand for greater participation in decisions which affect the country's future. If the system fails to open up to such pressure its economic reforms will appear as impositions and lack the consensus necessary to make them politically viable. The regime would then need to rely on more authoritarian means to implement its policies, further undermining the struggle for democratic change.

An earlier attempt to discern the alternative political futures for Mexico raised similar questions. In their introductory chapter Cornelius, Smith and Gentleman (1989) ask what set of political structures will replace the previous system, how rapid the change will be and how conflictual will be the transition. They conclude by summarizing five possible scenarios for political development, defined as immobilism, political closure, modernization of authoritarianism, partial democratization and full democratization from below.[1] Evidence since 1988 appears to show that some aspects of several of these scenarios are present. In general, we may talk of 'political closure' towards the Partido de la Revolución Democrática (PRD), of the 'modernization of authoritarianism' in the restructuring of the control of the electoral system by the PRI and of 'partial democratization', mainly to the benefit of the PAN. 'Immobilism' has been avoided by the PRI–PAN alliance around electoral reform, the reduction of foreign debt payments under the Brady Plan[2] and the lack of effective alternative economic strategies from both PAN and PRD. Needless to say, 'full democratization from below' has been restrained by each of the above practices.

This combination of elements is postponing democratic solutions to Mexico's political, economic and social problems. In the past 60 years élite preferences for authoritarian solutions could contain or repress the resistance of a heterogeneous and deeply fragmented civil society. This is no longer the case. In the early 1990s authoritarianism confronts a widespread demand for democratic political participation, a demand for a new relationship between state and society.

This demand cuts across ideological barriers to embrace both left and right, although its precise meaning and implications differ between social groups and political organizations. But it is undeniable that the presidential elections of 1988 marked a watershed in Mexican politics. As Salinas himself put it on the day after the polls, the era of a 'virtually one-party system' in Mexico had ended, giving way to a period of 'intense political competition'. Most commentators argue that the change is irreversible and that there can be no return to the *status quo ante*. As Silvia Gómez Tagle argues in Chapter 2, one of the main obstacles to a democratic transition is the reluctance of the PRI to share power in a new political and social environment. The social changes of the past decades, accelerated by the economic crisis of the 1980s, have created a new society whose democratic demands imply the radical restructuring of the ruling party and the political system. Yet the overriding concern for the government appears to be how to maintain the PRI as the dominant party, without provoking widespread unrest.

Among those who have tried to draw parallels from other cases, Cammack is most assertive in arguing that the political reform initiated in 1977 is as inherently contradictory for the PRI as the liberalization process was for the ruling ARENA party in Brazil: any attempt to regain credibility through political reform tends to undermine the ruling party's monopoly over resources and its authority in determining how they are distributed (Cammack, 1988). A consequence of this reluctant liberalization is the increasing centralization of presidential power and the distancing of the president from the party. The re-affirmation of presidentialism since 1988 suggests a compromise solution to the problem of regaining credibility for the electoral system. However, hopes that the spectacular interventions of Salinas might rub off on the PRI's fortunes did not materialize until the mid-term federal elections in August 1991. Although the PRI has recuperated areas it lost in 1988, most notably in the November 1990 municipal elections in the state of Mexico, the dominant trend has been towards abstentionism (Romero Miranda, 1990: 17).[3] At first sight, then, it appears that the obstacles to democratization lie with traditional local bosses. To be sure, these are loath to accept the imposition of PRI candidates from the centre (as was seen in Baja California in 1989), or to see themselves sacrificed for the sake of allowing room to the opposition (as Fidel Velázquez complained in 1988). But for Cammack the real problem lies elsewhere, in the basic incompatibility between democratization and the maintenance of single party monopolization of resource allocation. This position is most clearly echoed here by Gómez Tagle.

The slow pace of political reform in Mexico is also due to the role of business élites and their ambivalent attitude towards democratic transition. In Brazil, Uruguay and Argentina, business discontent with state economic mismanagement contributed to the push for democratization (Gillespie, 1990). Yet in Mexico the record of the PRI in assuring long-term stability played a crucial part in dividing and tempering business opposition soon after the 1982 bank nationalization. New radical business groups began to take a more active political role in opposition to the government with the formation of the Businessmen's Co-ordinating Council (Consejo Coordinador Empresarial, CCE) in 1975. Yet their commitment to democratic reform has always been linked to their assessment of the advantages of political change for their economic interests. At the same time, the limitations of democratic reform are accompanied by a restructuring of corporatist linkages between state and sectors of civil society. This process may provide social groups with new spaces for negotiation but they continue to be subordinated to broader economic policy. New forms of representation may be sectorally limited and unable to articulate the demands of temporary, casual workers. I would therefore like to focus on four main tensions of the Mexican transition which form the basis of discussion in this book: reform of the electoral system and the maintenance of political stability; the nature of economic reform; the ambiguities of social concertation (*concertación*); and the implications of neoliberal policies for achieving political representation. I conclude by summarizing the central characteristics which differentiate the Mexican transition in the light of recent moves towards democratization in Latin America.

Stability as a strategy of containment: the limits to political reform?

In Mexico the reforms of 1977 and 1986 helped preserve the PRI as the ruling party while making limited openings to the opposition. One of the reasons often invoked for the slow pace of reform is the fear of provoking instability. In times of economic crisis and, most recently, the highly charged political atmosphere of 1988–90, any attempt to go too far in opening up the system may provoke a crisis of governability. In Chapter 1 Alan Knight remarks that the political élite has traditionally distrusted opponents and alternative policies. There is a fear that a weak PRI would inevitably open the way for the type of political immobilism and violent confrontations witnessed in Argentina and Peru. Democratization is thus made conditional on guarantees of stability, since, as Knight reminds us, for the ruling party 'the memory of past turbulence dies hard'.

Yet the assumptions behind ungovernability are debatable. Certainly, as Whitehead (1981) argued, the political leadership was acutely aware of its own fragility even prior to the debt crisis. Deep social and economic inequalities provided ample ground for spontaneous acts of rebellion, something which many foreign observers failed to take into account. The much-vaunted stability of the Mexican political system tended to mask a rather weaker regime and its own fear of an ungovernable civil society.

However, the political mobilization of most popular groups since 1982 has shown a remarkable adherence to the existing legal and institutional channels. Where violent clashes have occurred they have tended to be isolated incidents, themselves provoked by allegations of electoral fraud. In this sense the PRI appears to be more trusting of the PAN than it is of the PRD. The PAN's victory in Baja California in July 1989, coinciding with widespread allegations of fraud against the PRD in Michoacán, can be partly interpreted in this light. For ruling groups in Mexico, and for the Bush administration, faith in the Salinas presidency appears to come before a political opening to the centre-left.

Ironically, the failure to provide such an opening has contributed to instability, although it may be argued that this remains highly localized. Certainly, Michoacán is not Mexico and, as Gledhill argues in Chapter 3, the fragmented nature of the opposition helps perpetuate PRI rule. Yet a more consensual form of hegemony can only be achieved through clean elections, something which the PRI and the government continue to resist. As Roger Bartra has commented, the problem of governability now appears to reside in the state rather than in civil society (1989:83):

> One of the few achievements that the PRI can still point to, though with questionable pride, is the disquieting fact that social

> tranquillity has persisted in Mexico despite the severe economic crisis that began in 1982. Every day, however, more Mexicans come to suspect that this tranquility is the result of generalised, tolerant, democratic tendencies in civil society rather than of the hegemonic power of revolutionary nationalism, and that the Mexican state is, in fact, the final redoubt of 'México bronco', ready to break the peace, if necessary, to preserve traditional revolutionary nationalism.

Although the technocratic élite which has risen to prominence since 1976 would not identify itself with revolutionary nationalism, it knows it must share power with entrenched interests for whom the myth of the revolution has provided élite cohesion and long-term political stability. Attempts to initiate democratic reforms are inevitably resisted by local and regional bosses who raise the spectre of instability. For Knight, the state in Mexico has periodically shifted emphasis between securing stability and directing change, between Hapsburg and Bourbon styles of government. The current transition therefore appears to resemble the latter, favouring deep social and economic reforms in the face of opposition, not only from popular groups but also from traditional élites. In the past, reformist governments, independently of their ideological and political projects, have come up against local indifference or opposition. Through negotiated concessions and the privatization of bureaucratic agencies, the stability of the state has been reproduced at the expense of the envisaged reforms.

This conclusion contrasts with most accounts which stress the systematic subordination of regional *cacicazgos* (informal power structures) to the central government. For this reason, its implications for our understanding of the current transition are of great importance. Allegations of electoral fraud in the provinces since 1988 suggest that local power groups are far from subordinated to reform-minded technocrats. On the contrary, it may be the case that economic liberalization requires a degree of political control which only the existing party machine can provide. It is not inconceivable that, just as in the past, clientelism and patronage remain the regime's most reliable mechanisms to secure compliance with its policies. Varley, for example, suggests that clientelism rather than administrative rationality will continue to mediate the regularization of urban landholdings (Chapter 9).

The concern with stability was also central to the PRI's promotion of the 1990 electoral reform law, the Código Federal de Instituciones y Procedimientos Electorales (COFIPE). The new law stipulated that a first place party receiving 35 per cent of the vote in federal elections would be assured a majority of seats in the Chamber of Deputies (251 of 500). For each percentage point over 35 per cent, an additional two seats would be allocated. Writing prior to the mid-term elections of August 1991, Gómez Tagle (Chapter 2) observed that this clause was designed to preserve PRI dominance in Congress. The 61 per cent polled by the PRI was thus translated into 320 of the 500 seats. In addition, the PRI benefited from the President's prerogative in proposing magistrates to the Federal Electoral Institute. Despite some positive changes, such as the increase in resources to parties, the PRI continued to control the electoral system. As a result, the ruling party's strategy of containment continued to confront the widespread demand for democratic elections.

The implications of COFIPE are especially serious for the PRD, which opposed its ratification in July 1990. Moreover, as Gledhill shows for the case of Michoacán, the obstacles facing the *neocardenista* movement are formidable.[4] Most obviously, it has failed to develop a competing hegemonic project of its own and has instead directed its energies towards the electoral sphere. This is partly understandable given the heterogeneous origins of the PRD and the difficulties of turning a broad popular coalition into a political party with aspirations to government. Yet the task of building a popular base of support among social movements has in part been neglected as efforts are made to defend electoral gains.

Nevertheless, *neocardenismo* also contains several elements which may be decisive in shaping the direction of the Mexican transition: it possesses a symbolic importance in providing a sense of empowerment and dignity to people previously resigned to passive acceptance of the *status quo*; it is able to unite the popular aspirations and organizations of a fragmented society around a common demand for social justice and respect for the rule of law; the strength of *neocardenismo* may not be enough to re-direct the government's macro-economic strategy, but it may well blunt the neoliberal project and force important concessions from the state. In short, the outcome of the current transition is unlikely to correspond to a purely ideological interpretation of neoliberalism. Rather, it is more likely to reflect the divisions within the state and those existing between the regime and its political opponents.

The problem of ungovernability can therefore be seen as the decreasing capacity of the regime to meet popular demands and institutionalize their political expression. What appears to be true is that Mexican society is no longer governable by the traditional forms of PRI control. That is, society can only become governable through new forms of mediation and representation. The limited and selective process of democratization in the 1980s may not prove sufficient to this task in the long term.

Economic reform and export-led growth: a closed debate?

The overriding concern with stability tends to cloud other issues, specifically the regime's economic project. The problem of transition involves more than the restructuring of the political system to ensure more democratic channels for the expression of dissent. Dissent is not only directed at authoritarianism but also at economic and social policies. Restructuring the system of interest representation may do little to change macro-economic policies and decision-making processes concentrated in what Zermeño calls the regime's *núcleo duro* (central core), consisting of the president, his economic cabinet and advisers. In short, any serious moves towards a more open, democratic system would also involve a critique of the current economic strategy and its consequences for the majority of the population. It appears that neither Mexico's political élite nor the US government is willing to contemplate tinkering with economic policy, which, like governability, takes precedence over democracy. Significantly, as Serrano notes in Chapter 4, attention of US policy makers has shifted away from Mexico's internal politics to issues of immigration, drug-trafficking and the Free Trade Agreement. Washington's support for Salinas's economic reforms leads it to be silent over violations of political rights. At the same time, shifts in Mexican foreign policy towards a greater concentration on relations with the United States reflects the regime's more general concern with assuring increased access to the US market.

Yet if economic reform lacks consensus within society, if decisions are made at the top without meaningful consultation with all political forces, then the perceived benefits of such reform will be limited. Additionally, the scope of political reform will inevitably be conditioned by dominant economic interests. In this respect it is worth considering the implications of neoliberalism for Mexico's political system.

Private-sector pressure for political opening has been closely linked to its attack on the traditionally central role played by the state in directing economic policy. Since the mid-1970s a more robust and well-organized business class has been able to exploit the fiscal crisis of the Mexican state by asserting its own agenda for economic restructuring. This offensive has been particularly marked since the bank nationalization of 1982 as the government of Miguel de la Madrid moved to regain the confidence of entrepreneurial groups. If in previous decades the latter accepted a limited role in economic policy-making, in the 1980s they sought to establish greater leverage over government. The generally favourable response of the de la Madrid administration to private-sector concerns was not a mere conjunctural strategy but represented a decisive shift in the balance of forces in Mexican society in favour of private capital, and particularly those leading fractions of capital linked to finance, manufacturing exports and multinational companies.

At the forefront of this new offensive was the CCE with several of its affiliated organizations: the National Confederation of Chambers of Commerce (CONCANACO), the Employers' Confederation of the Mexican Republic (COPARMEX), the National Agricultural Council (CNA) and the Mexican Businessmen's Council (CMHN) (Luna, Tirado and Valdés, 1987; Escobar, 1987). The political strategy of most business groups was not, however, to break with traditional forms of negotiation with the state (Woldenberg, 1988:197–200). Such a break was feared when some leading entrepreneurs rallied around the PAN in Sonora, Nuevo León and Chihuahua, but the extent of the damage for the government was limited by its acquiescence to demands for a decreasing role of the state in the national economy. The PAN appeared to attract business support for very immediate ends, as another arm with which to press for economic reform. As Maxfield argues (1989:216):

> The bank nationalization spurred a small group of entrepreneurs to take direct action against the regime. Their political activity in the PAN and civic groups is couched in terms of support for political opening – for democracy – but its real stimulus is their hope that it will afford the private sector greater control over economic policy.

This shift has negatively affected many small and medium-sized businesses, which had traditionally been protected by state subsidies and import controls but were now exposed to the winds of international competition. The liberalization of trade has benefited those entrepreneurs in a position to increase their international competitiveness. At the same time the contraction of the internal market in the 1980s meant that production became primarily geared towards exports and a small wealthy élite of Mexicans. In the late 1970s and early 1980s the concentration of capital in a relatively small number of dynamic firms was assisted by preferential access to foreign loans. This pattern has been accentuated since 1982 as the reconversion of industry towards export-led growth has proceeded steadily. Only a small number of firms has enjoyed the financial leverage to embark on modernization while most have been squeezed by the unavailability of affordable credit.

The de la Madrid government, eager to regain the confidence of bankers affected by the 1982 nationalization, allowed a parallel financial market to develop. Yet the increasing activity on the stock market, while stemming capital flight, was not translated into capital investment due to a general lack of confidence in the national economy. Wealthy investors found a haven from the crisis in speculation while investment stagnated. The concentration of capital was clearly illustrated by the exclusion from the stock market of all but the top two hundred firms. In the context of a crisis-ridden nationalized banking system and a selective club for only the wealthiest of private investors, small capitalists and the social sector were hit by the increasing cost of credit. Similarly, government moves to reduce the public-sector deficit and open up the country's market to international competition have tended to hurt small and medium-sized firms, such as those organized by the National Chamber of Manufacturing Industry (CANACINTRA). The political consequence has been the emergence of a critical current within CANACINTRA which has voiced its opposition to the PRI. The Salinas government has, however, been undeterred in following the neoliberal path and has successfully consolidated support from the leading factions of the capitalist class.

The rise of big business in Mexico has profound implications for the country's transition. While pushing a rapid economic reform package of privatization, deregulation and trade liberalization, the dominant class factions are hostile to thorough political reform. They, like the US government, see Salinas and the PRI as their best guarantors of private profit and political stability. As such, their political aim is to keep the *neocardenista* movement in check while welcoming an opening to the PAN. The latter can act as a safety valve for disenchanted small capitalists without affecting the global economic strategy of the government.[5]

The emergence of a new business class also raises the question of who will benefit from increasing integration to the US economy and the proposed Free Trade Agreement. As Harris argues in Chapter 5, the post-war trend of capitalist economies is towards global accumulation through increased trade. Until 1982 Mexico sought to defy this trend through protection of domestic capital, resulting in the enrichment of individual company directors but not in the efficiency of their firms (at least by international standards).

As a result, the recent boom in manufactured exports could only benefit a small proportion of Mexican firms. In contrast to the newly industrializing countries (NICs) of South-east Asia, most of national capital was in a poor financial position to reconvert inefficient and unproductive industries and increase their participation in global capitalism. As we have noted above, credit became extremely expensive after the debt crisis broke and the banks were nationalized. Private financial institutions were limited to the most dynamic firms but declining confidence in the national economy left only two ways open to investors: speculation and exports. The latter required a political decision on behalf of the government to adopt neoliberal policies and a long-term commitment to maintain them. The falling revenue derived from the export of primary commodities such as oil added extra weight to this position. Non-oil exports grew rapidly in the 1980s and displayed an increasing level of specialization and technical sophistication.

Harris argues that the government has traditionally been slow to exploit the country's comparative advantages, thereby hindering potential growth sectors from increasing their share in the world market. Primary among its advantages is the border with the USA, the world's largest importer. The example of increased trade in heavy goods such as vehicle engines illustrates the capacity of the country's exporters to increase their competitiveness. According to Harris, the fear among Mexicans regarding national vulnerability to external demand should be tempered by a more detailed analysis of specific sectors of the economy. Thus, the type of produce or service and market location are crucial variables which make generalizations hazardous. Furthermore, the two countries already experience a degree of interdependence which has removed most restrictions, except those imposed on labour. We can assume that this level of integration will be deepened by the proposed Free Trade Agreement. Mexico, with its large and predominantly young workforce would be in a good position to exploit US demand for manufactures and services.

Yet, given the structure of state–business relations outlined above, the possibilities for international competitiveness have tended to be concentrated in a relatively limited number of export-oriented firms. Smaller firms may provide exporters with inputs and services, thereby increasing employment and contributing to a reactivation of the domestic economy, but they will be subordinated to investment decisions beyond their control. Perhaps such linkages are the most attractive option for domestic entrepreneurs who can no longer expect state support for internationally uncompetitive products. If this is so, criticism from small and medium-sized entrepreneurs is likely to become less of a general attack on the government's economic strategy, fragmenting instead into specific claims regarding particular sectors of the economy.

At the same time, the potential for greater degrees of local integration with export-oriented firms, which Harris sees as a possible solution to unemployment, is hindered by low levels of education and training, and inadequate infrastructure. Given the decline in both public and private investment in these areas in the past decade, the strategy of export-led growth has only benefited those firms with access to foreign technology, inputs and markets. Consequently, economic reform in Mexico cannot limit itself to providing favourable conditions for large companies linked to multinationals; it must instead be geared to improving local employment opportunities, education and training.

However, the practical shortcomings of economic reform have received less attention than the political wrangles which it has caused within the government bureaucracy. The latter has been the site of conflicts between so-called nationalists and neoliberals which have been expressed around ideological positions rather than more substantive issues and concrete proposals.

As Heller argues in his detailed study of telecommunications policy (Chapter 6), the biggest obstacle to economic reform, as with political reform, is those who enjoy the privileges of state bureaucracy. An ideological defence of the public versus the private sector may, in some cases, be nothing more than an opportunistic device to protect cronyism, clientelism and corrupt practices. Traditional forms of state intervention are held to be incompatible with the modernization project of the young technocrats who came to dominate policy-making during the administration of Miguel de la Madrid. In this way, another dilemma of the transition is revealed: state power brokers are responsible for the implementation of the very reforms which are designed to undermine their own positions and privileges. As has often occurred in the past with rural 'caciques' and party 'dinosaurs', state functionaries have sought to survive by bending the new rules to their own advantage. In the rural sector, local-level bosses and functionaries are also an obstacle to reform initiatives which aim to incorporate new peasant movements into policy-making processes (Gordillo, 1987); similarly, traditional union barons such as *La Quina* confronted the government with a nationalist rhetoric which only served to protect the power and privilege of a corrupt union leadership (Loyola Díaz, 1990a). Such strategies have played into the hands of the technocrats by discrediting public ownership to such an extent that privatization and 'reform from above' can be presented as the only desirable alternatives. This leaves out of the equation the role of social and political organizations which struggle for a more democratic and open debate on economic reform through full consultation and negotiation.

Heller's analysis should therefore alert us to two things: we need to look at what lies behind the appearance of an ideological schism between nationalist and neoliberal projects. It can be argued that neither project is mutually exclusive, at least for functionaries in charge of implementing reforms. For example, in telecommunications policy the same official may act as both nationalist and liberalizer according to immediate personal interests; second, we need to carry out research at the micro-level of policy implementation rather than rely on what may be misleading general statements regarding the nature of the transition. In Heller's words, we need to 'unpack the dynamics of power in micro-political settings such as government–business and intra-bureaucracy relations'. The implications of such intra-state struggles, both for the provision of goods and services and for the democratization of policy-making, should not be underestimated. If, as in the case of telecommunications, decisions regarding reform are contested solely within tight bureaucratic boundaries, then the likely result will be a misleading and short-sighted dispute between respective proponents of public versus private ownership. A more meaningful and intelligent debate, which includes the proposals of unions and social movements, may produce a more negotiated process of change and thereby avoid both old-style patronage and imposition of reform from above. However, as already noted, the political conditions for such a debate do not yet exist.

Restructuring state–society relations: the role of social concertation

Popular demands for democratic forms of participation in Mexico have tended to find expression outside the electoral arena. In the past decade new popular movements have fought for greater space and autonomy from the PRI and its affiliated confederations (Foweraker and Craig, 1990). At the same time the shift towards neoliberal policies of economic modernization necessarily implied a distancing between the government and its traditional corporatist allies. As a result, new forms of state–society relations have been emerging which, under the Salinas administration, have become known as *concertación*. As the essays by Harvey (Chapter 7) and Haber (Chapter 8) show, the strategy adopted by Salinas towards independent peasant and urban popular movements has rested crucially on a policy of concertation. By opening up new areas for grassroots participation, the government has sought to regain credibility in the aftermath of the 1988 elections. In several regions this strategy has also isolated popular movements from the PRD as demands are negotiated through the direct intervention of the president. This new terrain of negotiations appears to be competing with the traditional corporatist arrangements between the government and the leaders of PRI-affiliated organizations. Yet the extent to which the Salinas administration is willing to sacrifice political control for modernization is an open question as the limits to *concertación* become apparent. For example, in rural areas, alongside the policy of *concertación* there has also been the use of violence against leaders and supporters of independent peasant movements. Fourteen regional peasant leaders were killed between December 1988 and November 1990. Similarly, agricultural policy may leave some room for manoeuvre for autonomous producer groups (such as those organized by the Unión Nacional de Organizaciones Regionales Campesinas Autónomas, UNORCA), but the general tendency is in the opposite direction: privatization of the social sector and support for private agro-exporters. The failure of the government to assure clean elections in rural districts constitutes another limit to concertation.

Likewise, in urban areas the government has moved swiftly to negotiate the demands of popular groups which have mobilized independently of the PRI. The most important case, which appears to have set a precedent for the policy of *concertación*, was the response of the authorities of the federal district to the demands of victims of the 1985 earthquake. Eckstein has shown how, following a mass movement led by independent organizations, the then head of SEDUE, Manuel Camacho Solís, called all groups to sign the Democratic Accord for Housing Reconstruction (1990:234):

> In signing the agreement, groups agreed, in effect, to work with and not against the state. The accord therefore cleverly brought groups 'into line', and put an end to 'popular' protests. In this way, the *convenio* is consistent with long-standing inclusionary corporatist state–society relations in Mexico.

Since 1988 the government has continued to deploy a strategy designed to depoliticize the demands of popular movements through the signing of new *convenios de concertación*. As Haber shows in his essay on the Comité de Defensa Popular (CDP) of Durango, the PRD has been effectively marginalized by the process of negotiations between the federal government and local popular groups. The political importance of the Programa Nacional de Solidaridad (PRONASOL) is that it establishes a direct relationship between petitioning groups and the presidency, bypassing other forms of intermediation such as political parties. Ironically, this not only contributes to a legitimization of the president at the expense of the PRI, but also leads to a concentration of presidential power, something which had been widely criticized as a crucial element in the 1982 crisis.

Government technocrats emphasize the need to overcome bureaucratic and political obstacles to efficiency in service provision. In this way the establishment of new relations with grassroots movements may serve as a pact against local bosses who now feel threatened from both sides. Yet, as Varley argues in Chapter 9, the regime is unlikely to surrender political control at the local level in favour of administrative rationality. The use of clientelism and patronage is likely to continue under new guises, possibly with an even greater degree of centralization as the president attempts to gain leverage over potentially disruptive officials in local and regional bureaucracies.

Neoliberalism and neocorporatism

It appears that the nature of political accommodation between the state and popular movements has changed in the 1980s. Whereas opposition groups were obliged previously to affiliate to official organizations, the state now respects a degree of local autonomy in exchange for acquiescence over the government's broader economic policies. This type of relationship can be seen as neocorporatist in character. Without broader political change, the depoliticization of demands and the incorporation of new groups and leaders into the negotiation process has a limited impact on the simultaneous centralization of power in what Zermeño (Chapter 10) calles the *núcleo duro* (central core) of the regime. According to Zermeño, the *convenios de concertación*, PRONASOL and the co-optation of prominent intellectuals provide a smokescreen for the exclusionary economic strategy promoted by the de la Madrid and Salinas governments. The *núcleo duro* is surrounded by a set of formal political institutions (for example, parliament, official union confederations, special tripartite committees) where the integrated sectors of Mexican society find some limited room to express dissent. Beyond this arena the excluded majority is engaged in everyday struggles for survival in conditions of anomie, social disorder and the absence of effective political representation.

Similar tendencies towards neocorporatism have emerged in the relationship between the state and organized labour. Bizberg shows in Chapter 11 how economic modernization has implied the rapid erosion of the Confederación de Trabajadores de México (CTM) as a political actor within the traditional corporatist pact. The incompatibility between corporatism and modernization may not reside in the alleged inefficiency of the former, but rather in the demand of the latter for greater flexibility inside the workplace and outside, in the contracting of non-unionized, temporary labour. At the same time, the tendency towards greater flexibility may require greater degrees of worker participation in decisions affecting the labour process. However, this would run counter to the traditionally centralized control over workers and require a dismantling of the hierarchical structure of the CTM. Instead it appears that, as with rural and urban social movements, a new terrain for negotiation has been opened up, one which, nevertheless, remains firmly subordinated to the economic policies of the government.

The desire to impose modernization from above was made clear by the spectacular arrest of the corrupt leadership of the oil workers union in January 1989. Tensions between union bosses and the *técnicos* in government during the 1980s came to a head when the former withdrew their traditional electoral support for the ruling PRI in the 1988 presidential elections. As a result many oil workers voted not for Salinas but for Cárdenas. This was, however, only one of the reasons why Salinas decided to move against the union's secretary of social works and moral leader, Joaquín Hernández Galicia (*La Quina*) and its secretary general, Salvador Barragán Camacho. Of equal importance was the fact that their power was seen as an obstacle to the modernization policies favoured by the new administration. These policies included a partial break up of Petróleos Mexicanos (PEMEX) through the privatization of some areas of petrochemical production and the contracting out of infrastructure works to private competition. The union leadership had reacted strongly to these policies, not out of ideological commitment to nationalism and state control of strategic industries, but simply out of personal interest in maintaining the privileges and power which they had built up in alliance with the state between 1946 and 1982.

The record of the Salinas government in dealing with corrupt union leaders is uneven and responds more to the administration's economic programme than to a concern with union democratization. In general, where unions oppose economic restructuring the regime has sought to replace existing leaders with more amenable ones, as in the case of the oil workers. Where union bosses have supported the introduction of neoliberal policies, the regime has backed them, regardless of the protests from rank-and-file members, as happened with the Ford workers at the Cuautitlán plant in 1990. Here the national executive committee of the CTM-affiliated Union of Ford Workers failed to support the local branch's economic demands and the struggle for reinstatement of workers who had been dismissed due to strike action. In January 1990 CTM thugs at the service of the national leadership attacked the local dissidents at the plant, killing one and injuring several others (Vásquez, 1990a). The minister of labour, Arsenio Farrell Cubillas, refused to intervene in defence of the victims of CTM aggression. The local branch finally decided to leave the CTM for the rival Confederación Obrera Revolucionaria (COR) which, although affiliated to the PRI, also supported a strike by workers of the Modelo brewery in February 1990 which was similarly repressed. The following month the COR established the Frente Sindical en Defensa de los Derechos Laborales y la Constitución. This project, aimed at defending the constitutional rights of labour unions, also received support from the PRD and university workers. However, just as the PRD has faced official intransigence in the electoral arena, so has the new Frente Sindical in its struggle to defend the constitutional rights of workers. The Ministry of Labour has been instrumental in this strategy as it has refused to recognize strikes called by independent unions or by democratic currents within official unions.

Between a newly compliant CTM and the independent but marginalized Frente Sindical, a third type of unionism has made progress in recent years and may represent a more likely arena for democratic change in state–labour relations. The emergence of leaders of democratic currents in the national unions of teachers, electricians and telephone workers has been able to take some advantage of internal disputes within the government or adapt to new economic realities.

The resignation, at the request of Salinas, of Carlos Jonguitud from his position as lifelong leader of the national teachers' union in April 1989 was hailed by some as another *quinazo* (in the style of the spectacular removal of the oil union boss, *La Quina*). In this case, however, the president was confronted by a well-organized movement which had led a decade-long struggle for union democratization: the Coordinadora Nacional de Trabajadores de la Educación (CNTE). The result has been an uneasy pact between the imposed leadership of Elba Esther Gordillo and the leaders of the democratic current. The former has had to distance herself from the legacy of Jonguitud and has been forced to open up some spaces of union representation to the CNTE.[6] These can be considered concrete gains, although the more radical groups in CNTE insist that Gordillo does not represent a meaningful break with Jonguitud. The transition cannot be an easy one, given the past history of repression against the CNTE and the difficulties of securing and maintaining democratic advances. However, it appears to be the only path open since more confrontational tactics, as seen in Michoacán in late 1989, have only hardened the government's position (Hernández, 1990).

A similar process of negotiation has been evident in the Electricians' and Telephone Workers' Unions (SME and STRM). Both have sought to avoid direct confrontation with the government and have instead developed alternative proposals for modernization which aim to provide greater protection of their members' interests. The Salinas government has shown interest in this new unionism since it is neither controlled by the corrupt bosses which cause the PRI electoral damage, as in the case of *La Quina*, nor by opposition parties of the left. More important is the fact that it emphasizes accommodation rather than confrontation with the government's economic policies. Such a strategy is, of course, not without its costs. Leaders of both SME and STRM have had to negotiate the dismissal of hundreds of workers, but they argue that through negotiations they won respect for collective contracts, the guarantee of full redundancy payments and the setting up of new retraining programmes.[7] In April 1989, the leaders of SME and STRM, Jorge Sánchez and Francisco Hernández Juárez, called for the construction of a new confederation in order to strengthen this new type of unionism. In April 1990 six unions, including electricians and telephone workers, formed the Federation of Unions in Goods and Services Companies (FESEBES) (Méndez and Quiroz, 1990).

Its declaration of principles reveals a more pragmatic stance which nevertheless upholds basic rights. It states that FESEBES: will fight for a new unionism without the anti-democratic practices of traditional PRI-controlled unions; will promote full participation of workers in political, social and work-related changes; emphasizes the need to become a force capable of proposing concrete, intelligent alternatives and ready to agree on strategies between members. FESEBES also declared that it would fight for wage increases, defend the right to strike and respect the political autonomy of all members.

In sum, state–labour relations in Mexico are being restructured in different ways, ranging from the imposed compliance of the CTM, to the independent struggle in defence of constitutional rights and the possibility to use new arenas of *concertación* in defence of workers' interests. However, each of these developments appears to be subordinated to the government's economic project due to the absence of an effective alternative from opposition parties. The unions organized in FESEBES may contribute to the protection of only a limited sector of labour, given that privatization and restructuring tend to imply an increased reliance on temporary, short-term employment of non-unionized workers. The dominant scenario for Mexican workers instead appears to be one of exclusion from collective-bargaining arrangements. This point is forcefully made by Zermeño for the urban sector, while Gledhill similarly notes the expansion of a rural underclass of unemployed youth. In this respect Sylvia Chant's essay (Chapter 12) provides a detailed account of household survival strategies and the particular impact of the economic crisis on the employment of female workers. The cases she describes in Querétaro may reflect more general processes of social change and highlight some of the negative implications for the next generation of young female workers. In the 1980s, women's participation in the labour force helped families survive the impact of the crisis, but the extent to which household resources can be stretched may have reached its limits. In this sense Chant confirms the findings of earlier studies and, in doing so, raises the important question of the capacity of the Mexican economy and the state to provide the conditions for a more dignified existence than one of continual hardship. The fragmented and temporary nature of modern employment tends to impede forms of collective action which might demand greater degrees of security and welfare.

Conclusions

The partial and selective nature of democratization in Mexico appears to place it firmly within the broad Latin American experience of the 1980s. For example, Ethier concludes from her synthesis of recent literature on democratization in Latin America and Southern Europe that transitions have been élite-initiated and controlled; are limited to formal political democracy rather than intended to implement structural change; have been achieved through negotiations among dominant groups; and are precarious due to the weak social consensus that they enjoy (Ethier, 1990:18). In Mexico, such limitations are equally apparent, although it may be argued that the transition is a consequence of popular pressure from below, rather than a purely intra-élite affair, a phenomenon which may be equally applicable to the Southern Cone and Brazil. Nevertheless, as Zermeño argues, there is a strong tendency towards 'bureaupolitics' within élite circles which limits the extent of democratization in Mexico.

The main difference of the Mexican transition is that the political élite has successfully maintained the confidence of the leading entrepreneurial group. The policies of the de la Madrid administration, which have been continued by Salinas, avoided confrontation and instead presented the private sector with the opportunity for achieving greater participation in world trade, taking particular advantage of proximity to the US market. Unlike most of its Latin American counterparts, the Mexican political leadership displays confidence in its project for international integration and the achievement of its medium-term goals for economic recuperation. This stands in stark contrast to the constant need for crisis management in Brazil and Argentina, where political élites have been unable to represent the diverse interests of a fragmented bourgeoisie.[8]

The regime's confidence is helped by the opposition's lack of alternative macro-economic policies which can command popular support. The PRD has so far shown itself unable to provide convincing alternatives and, partly for this reason, it has not consolidated the support given to Cárdenas in 1988. Although electoral fraud and repression of its militants have contributed to its defensive position, the absence of a unifying economic project is a clear obstacle to the PRD's future development.

The most likely scenario now appears to be a consolidation of the technocratic élite in government and the continued attempt to contain and co-opt opposition. Needless to say, such a transition has little to do with democracy and everything to do with the restructuring of the economy. Democratic advance will continue to be slow and is likely to be concentrated in the corporative rather than the electoral arena. The opening up of new political spaces through social concertation should be seen as a concrete gain of popular pressure for democratic participation. Several popular movements have used the opportunity to secure solutions to the material demands of their members. As a result, new forms of representation have emerged independently of the existing party system (UNORCA, FESEBES, CDP) which offer some voice to popular sectors. However, this limited democratization of the corporative arena is made at the expense of a deeper process of democratization in the electoral arena. It tends to exclude the poorer, unorganized sectors of the population, for whom the economic strategy offers little comfort. The Mexican regime has responded with a re-affirmation of presidential power, backed by the considerable presence of the mass media, PRONASOL and a number of intellectuals. Such a neo-populist strategy has sought to reconstitute social consensus for the regime, leading, in the short term at least, to the effective containment of opposition movements.

However, this apparent success for the regime conceals a more unstable set of relationships between the state and sectors of civil society. The decomposition of earlier forms of social organization may give way to emergent structures through which new terms of negotiation with the state can be established. On the other hand, it may be the case that even larger numbers of people have been uprooted from their home communities, depend increasingly on seasonal employment and migration, and are deprived of any effective form of representation. In these conditions, the regime's attempts to appeal to 'the people' (from the Salinas campaign slogan of 'Let Mexico Speak' to the constant calls for concertation and solidarity) are partial substitutes for a more thorough process of democratization and a more widely acceptable economic strategy.

Notes

1. 'Political closure' implies the increasing recourse to coercion as events escape the control of the authorities. Such a response would be costly for the regime's internal unity, and destabilization would frighten off private investment. For these reasons, it is not a feasible scenario for a regime committed to attracting investment.

   'Modernization of authoritarianism' would involve a remodelling of existing corporatist arrangements through a new set of alliances, with the goal of retaining the PRI's monopoly of power.

   'Partial democratization' would mean a transition to a system similar to the Indian Congress Party model, whereby opposition parties are allowed periodic victories in the provinces, without affecting the ruling party's majority at the national level.

   'Immobilism' refers to a situation where no one faction in the ruling party is able to impose its will on the other, leading to a bitter internal struggle.

   Finally, 'full democratization from below' would result from the peaceful transformation of the political system, led by a pluralistic civil society which the regime is unable to contain (Cornelius *et al.*, 1989:36–45).
2. In 1989 the US Treasury Secretary Nicholas Brady put forward a new initiative which called on creditor banks to forgive part of the Third World debt and provide new money for debtor countries committed to free market reforms. In February 1990 Mexico became the first country to sign a debt-reduction agreement under the Brady Plan. As a result, external debt fell from around US$ 97 billion to US$ 93 billion in early 1990.
3. Abstentionism in municipal and state elections after July 1988 averaged almost 70 per cent. This trend was apparently reversed by the results of the August 1991 federal congressional elections. According to official figures, abstentionism fell from the 52 per cent registered in 1988 to just 34 per cent. At the same time, the PRI staged a remarkable recovery by polling 61 per cent of the vote, winning 290 of the 300 electoral districts

for congressional deputies and 31 of the 32 Senate seats. Hundreds of irregularities were denounced by opposition parties and the results continued to lack credibility. Fraud became much more difficult to prove, however, due to the PRI's use of more modern techniques in voting manipulation. What is clear is that the high profile assumed by Salinas in the campaign did have an important effect in regaining popular support for the PRI. This was possible due to the massive publicity given to the Programa Nacional de Solidaridad (PRONASOL), the government's anti-poverty programme set up at the initiative of Salinas in December 1988.

4. *Neocardenista* refers to the political coalition movement which emerged in 1988 in support of the presidential candidacy of Cuauhtémoc Cárdenas, now leader of the PRD. This movement draws part of its inspiration from the nationalist and populist regime of the father of Cuauhtémoc, General Lázaro Cárdenas, which governed Mexico from 1934 to 1940.
5. During the business–PAN offensive in 1983–8, the largest groups almost always tended to support the PRI. This was in response to its strategy of opening up more spaces for the leaders of big business. These saw that to stand as PAN candidates in elections could have counter-productive effects for their interests (Tirado, 1990:56).
6. The CNTE has won recognition for the democratically elected representatives of Branches 7 (Chiapas), 9 (Federal District) and 22 (Oaxaca). In 1990 two posts on the national executive committee of the union were won by representatives from branches supporting the CNTE.
7. Negotiations between TELMEX and the union have not, however, solved the problem of job insecurity faced by female switchboard operators. A new project to modernize operations has been discussed without their participation, raising fears that their jobs are not so safe as those of other workers (Vásquez, 1990b:71).
8. Panizza argues that, in the Argentine case, this failure of leadership has been revealed by 'the dramatic acceleration of political time . . . from the four years which it took for Alfonsín to fall from his pedestal as prophet of democratic millenarianism ("a hundred years of democracy", "with democracy the people eat") to the six months in which Menem has fallen from prophet of a new beginning ("Follow me, Argentina, get up and go forward") to Pied Piper of a procession to nowhere' (Panizza, 1990:13). Very few people expect Salinas to meet the same fate.

Part I

STATE AND POLITICAL REFORM

1 · STATE POWER AND POLITICAL STABILITY IN MEXICO

Alan Knight

Mexico is in crisis. That, at least, is a common contemporary refrain. However, it is hardly a new one. Analyses of Mexico in the period under discussion have been notably crisis-prone (Ross, 1982: 17–18). Books have been written detailing earlier crises (Contreras, 1985); Judith Adler Hellman titled her 1970s' political analysis *Mexico in Crisis* (Hellman, 1978). Informed analysts, looking back on the crises of yesteryear, debate long and hard which, in fact and in retrospect, were real crises, or ruptures, and which were presumably false alarms. Since 1982 the alarm bells have hardly stopped ringing. But, as we enter the 1990s and the period of recent crisis approaches double digits, we might pause to consider how long a crisis must endure before it ceases to be a crisis (true, E. H. Carr wrote of a 'twenty-year crisis', just as historians debate the 'general crisis of the seventeenth century'); before, that is, people become deaf to the alarm bells and learn to live amid crisis – which, in a phenomenological sense, would imply the end of the crisis itself.

It may be that, in the economic sphere, this has happened and is happening. The touted date of 1982 denotes the oil price collapse and the major financial crisis which it triggered in Mexico. Since then the problems of inflation, falling incomes, government deficits, the international (and internal) debt have dominated national politics and policy-making. Without remotely implying that they have been solved, it can be suggested that they have proved, so far, broadly manageable. Inflation has been dramatically reduced; debt payments have been modestly curtailed; non-oil exports have been boosted; the government has avoided bankruptcy and met its obligations. Of course, there has also been a sharp fall in living standards (opinions differ as to how sharp). The 1988 presidential election also produced a surprisingly powerful challenge from the left, which has been followed up by regional challenges, at least in certain states (Michoacán, Guerrero). But the net political effects of the post-1982 economic crisis still remain conjectural. It is arguable that the economic worst is over and that, external factors permitting, growth will be greater in the early 1990s than it was in the late 1980s. Furthermore, while the administration faces a reinvigorated, but factious, political opposition, that opposition has hardly produced a successful economic alternative. PAN economic policies are indistinguishable from the PRI's (or vice versa, as you prefer), while the PRD, a vocal and often effective critic of the political corruption and chicanery of the PRI, has failed to offer a convincing economic package. Voters, it seems, do not believe that the opposition possesses the secret of economic success (Cornelius, Gentleman and Smith, 1989: 16); their votes are premised on negative sentiments of political disgust more than positive hopes of economic betterment. To put it differently, they are sceptical about easy economic answers (in which respect they are a good deal more realistic than their US counterparts).

The economic travails of the 1980s, albeit more protracted and severe than those of the early 1930s, have not yet provoked a comparable political reaction. In terms of historical comparison they may better parallel that severe fall in real wages which affected Mexico after 1940, which was not reversed until 1946, and which was not finally overcome until the late 1960s (Bortz, 1988). That process excited labour unrest and protest, notably in the late 1940s; but the Alemán regime perfected the *charrazo*[1] as a means to maintain control and to head off concerted syndical resistance, which might in turn have provoked a political shift to the left (as in 1932–5). Similarly, *campesino* resistance to the marked deceleration of the agrarian reform and the degeneration of the *ejido* (peasant holding) was countered by the familiar combination of co-option and repression. It is true that during the 1940s falling real wages were offset by relatively high levels of employment and changing occupational structures, both of which alleviated the condition of wage-earners. But it is only with hindsight that we will, perhaps, be able to evaluate the importance of such countervailing factors today: remittances from the US, *maquiladora* (assembly plant) employment, the burgeoning black economy, including the drug trade. Very likely, future economic historians will chart a sustained fall in living standards in the 1980s which exceeded that of the 1940s. My point is that wage-earners have in the past experienced a sequence of lean years which did not translate automatically into successful popular mobilization and political insurgency.

The political thunderclap of 1988 is a different matter. Certainly it signalled a new political reality: a PRI president elected with barely a plurality of the popular vote; the validity of his election widely impugned; a Congress possessed of a sizeable opposition block. The thunder has rumbled on, with the PRI relinquishing its first gubernatorial palace in Baja California, and with the electoral opposition making gains, or crying fraud, in numerous municipalities in the centre-west. While this represents a novel situation, we should again be careful about casual use of the term 'crisis'. Michoacán is in crisis, but not the country. After a local crisis in 1985–7, the PRI has bounced back in Chihuahua; the obstacles to creating and sustaining a powerful party of the left remain formidable (some obstacles are of the PRI's making, some are indigenous to the left). I think that, with the limited hindsight we enjoy, we should probably conclude that the (post-1982) economic crisis has been endured (and somewhat mitigated) to the extent that it is no longer 'critical'; and that the (post-1988) political crisis remains an open question, one that might be resolved in a number of ways, several of them involving the continued dominance of the PRI (Cornelius, et al. 1989: 33–44). Needless to say, these views are meant to be objective assessments, not subjective preferences, and they may stand in need of instant revision.

These are also the views of an historian and they embody, no doubt, the historian's preference for long-term perspectives and suspicion of immediatism. In other words, when commentators have regularly discerned crisis and imminent collapse, and no less regularly have been proved wrong, the historian tends to equate cries of crisis with cries of wolf; at the end of that celebrated tale, of course, the real wolf appeared and devoured the sheep, just as, one day, Mexico will no doubt experience a transforming crisis, as it did in 1910–20. This is not to say that Mexico is unchanging, since (forgive the cliché) change has been a constant feature of Mexican society since the revolution, and before. Rather, it is to note that brisk social change has not translated into fundamental political transformation; that the phenomenon of the party–state, claiming the mantle of the revolution and headed by a powerful president, has proved remarkably enduring throughout the 70 eventful years since the armed revolution ended.

This raises the central question of this chapter, which should shed some light on the reasons for the longevity of the Mexican political system and on the challenges which it faces today. How has that political system managed to survive despite the massive changes (demographic, economic, international) which Mexico has experienced since the revolution? And does an analysis of its survival to date suggest how, in the future, it might be sustained – or subverted?

The Mexican state

I take as the central question the relation of the state to civil society. The theoretical literature on the state is voluminous and increasing; I do not pretend to command it and I look to those more familiar with the theory to amend my argument. As a historian, seeking to understand the passage of events in twentieth-century Mexico, I would offer a three-fold analysis of the state, which focuses on: (a) *definition*: what do we mean when we refer to the state? (b) *function*: what role does the state, however defined, play? and (c) *strength*: how 'strong' is the state, especially in terms of its capacity to influence or transform society?[2]

Definition

First, we need to clarify what the state is, or was. In practical terms, that means reaching some agreement on whether the state is to be equated with the central government, with governmental agencies in the country at large, or, broadening the scope even further, with more diffuse forms of political domination. The first equation (state = central government) seems both arbitrary and excessively narrow, yet analyses of the Mexican state, especially of its 'rise', seem to rely heavily on this assumption. In these analyses, the 'rise of the state' or 'the strength of the state', which I will address later, usually mean the rise or strength of the centre, of the central government in Mexico City, above all of the executive. The state is said to be strengthened when, for example, central government powers expand at the expense of local or regional political authorities (that is, even if the outcome is a *redistribution* rather than a net *increase* in political authority or political domination *in toto*). This question relates to the distribution of power within the different arms of government. However, the very definition of government can be contentious. It is well known that, in Mexico, formal and informal political power are not coterminous. *Caudillos* and *caciques* have wielded immense power independent of their formal positions. Here I am not talking simply of diffuse influence of the kind that, for example, captains of industry might possess within capitalist societies; I mean effective, authoritative power, of the kind that states wield, but also of the kind that *caudillos* like Saturnino Cedillo wielded in their particular fiefs, even when they held no formal political office, or that Calles enjoyed as *jefe máximo*, not president, between 1928 and 1934–5 (Ankerson, 1984; Falcón, 1984).

While at the national level this disjunction between formal and informal political power has attenuated over time, the same is less true at the regional or local level. State bosses and cliques, like the Atlacomulco group in the state of Mexico, still wield great influence, to the extent that incumbent governors are neither autonomous political actors nor the representatives of a party or a broad constituency but rather representatives of a tight clientelist network, which links regional élites to the central government (Arreola Ayala, 1985: 7–26). Local bosses and cliques also remain important, manipulating without necessarily assuming formal political office, of which more anon (Martínez Saldaña, 1976:117, 140; Schryer, 1980:107). In addition, there exists a barrage of parastate agencies which embody ample political power, which, in other words, exercise political control over people and, to varying degrees, respond to grassroots political demands. These would include the official unions, the CTM, the other sectoral components of the PRI, the Ejidal Bank, CONASUPO, the Secretaría de Recursos Hidraulícos, and the numerous politico-economic agencies created to benefit the disadvantaged (for example, INI or IMSS) or to regulate production (for example, INMECAFE), institutions which have been generically described as examples of 'bureaucratic' or 'white collar' *caciquismo* (Martínez Saldaña, 1976:108; Gándara, 1976:253; Schryer, 1980:110; Purcell and Purcell, 1980:203; Bartra, 1990). Although these institutions may be distinct from the state as narrowly defined – formally, they may be party or syndical organizations, or agencies of economic regulation – that distinction is, in practice, hollow and formalistic.

Nor are such institutions wholly new, although their number and size have certainly grown in recent decades. In the wake of the agrarian reform of the 1930s, for example, the Ejidal Bank became a crucial source of patronage and control (Benjamin, 1989:211–14). The *indigenista* movement spawned another set of power-holders. Chiapas' Departamento de Acción Social de Protección Indígena, complained a Federal Labor Inspector in 1935, would be better entitled El Departamento de Explotación Indígena (Rodríguez Cabo, 1935). Typically, entrenched local élites successfully cannibalized these new institutions. Pseudo-*indigenistas* 'laid in wait for Federal initiatives . . . in order to give an apparent display of support and then subsequently to prostitute them and convert them into simple instruments of political gain'.[3] My point is not that these agencies invariably represent forms of top-down control, unresponsive to popular demands or interests; that could be debated in particular cases. Rather, it is the simple point that they represent important political resources and that, in any discussion of the state and its relations to civil society, they must be brought into the equation on the state side.

Function

This initial point, to which I shall return, is obviously and intimately linked to the second, that is the function of the state. Again, there is a massive literature which I will not attempt to review. For some, the state serves as a direct agent of class power ('the executive committee of the ruling class'); for others, state power reflects class interests, albeit in a less direct fashion. The state may assume a degree of autonomy, but it cannot break free of its class moorings. A variation on this theme sees the state as rationalizing the conflicts and contradictions of capitalism; that is, serving the broad interests of capitalism without succumbing to immediate capitalist control (Hamilton, 1982:9). Further along the spectrum, the state may be seen as possessing ample autonomy: it controls and moulds civil society as it sees fit ('Bonapartist' is a favourite label; 'Stalinist' would be historically more appropriate). Alternatively, the state may be seen as the neutral arena within which diverse interests conflict and compete; and/or, it may be minimally defined as the agency which possesses a monopoly of violence within a given territorial unit: a definition which is neat but which, like many neat definitions, is historically unhelpful and, more important, begs several important questions, for example whether monopolistic violence is deployed legitimately, or merely coercively. With this last, Weberian, definition we come full circle and find ourselves back with the formalistic and descriptive concept of the state defined in terms of its supposed monopoly of violence, its effective control of police and army, its denial of 'illegal', that is non-state, violence. The limitations of such definition for a society like revolutionary Mexico, where violence, both political and non-political (the line is often hard to draw), has been endemic, do not need labouring.

Formalistic definitions aside, the more important question of the state's function(s) remains. Paraphrasing Therborn, what does the state do when it rules? The answer suggested here relates to Mexico – it is not meant to be a universal theory – and it relates specifically to Mexico in the 80 years since the 1910 Revolution. Even during that period, the function of the state, I will argue, tended to change; in other words, it is necessary to tailor the theory, whether classical Marxist, bonapartist, liberal-pluralist, or whatever, to the historical period/problem and not to assume a perennially and ubiquitously valid perspective. Also, it is necessary to remember that the state embraces a range of actors, and should not be reduced only to the central government.

First, the Mexican state was never a simple agent of class or sectoral interests. Sometimes it threw its weight behind one class or sector, antagonizing the others. But it always maintained a degree of detachment and, furthermore, its recruitment patterns gave it not only a distinct identity, but also a certain corporate *esprit* (Smith, 1979). Even when it leaned to the popular classes (for example, under Cárdenas and, to a lesser degree, under Echeverría) it did not install workers and peasants in the ministries and statehouses; nor, even when it proved most indulgent to Mexican business, did it systematically recruit entrepreneurs or admit private enterprise into the party as a formal bloc.[4] Towards foreign capital, too, the state has proved historically ambivalent, albeit, since 1940, broadly favourable (Bennett and Sharpe, 1985:259). The political bureaucracy, in other words, has constituted a discernible group, possessed of its own collective interests and shared background.

To the extent, therefore, that it did not represent, and its members were certainly not recruited from, a single class, what were its common aims or functions? Here, it is useful to distinguish between, on the one hand, shifting projects, which, in turn, reflect the broader class liaisons of the state at different periods, and, on the other, more enduring state interests, that is, interests peculiar to the state, as against any particular social group, which remained relatively constant despite shifts in project or policy. Projects and policies changed appreciably over time. The political bureaucracy of the 1930s entertained a blueprint for Mexico which was very different from that of the 1950s, still more that of the 1980s. Analyses which assume continuity, and which yoke Mexico's post-revolutionary history to the rise of capitalism or, worse, the rise of the state, tend to be excessively bland and teleological (Knight, 1985). This chapter rejects statolatry and questions the notion that the Mexican state reveals 'embedded orientations', that is, consistent *policy* positions, dating back to its post-revolutionary genesis (Bennett and Sharpe, 1985:43–4, 250). If such orientations do exist, they are so general (for example, the defence of sovereignty, the pursuit of economic development), and capable of such varied implementation, that they offer little by way of explanation; some blueprints, furthermore, required aggressive state intervention and activism, while some implied a more relaxed, hands-off approach. These shifts, crucial to any discussion of state–civil society relations in the period, do not correlate neatly with conventionally defined radical and conservative administrations. State intervention could come from both the left and the right.

Nevertheless, even those administrations content to conserve the *status quo* and to avoid excessive meddling and conflict retained a degree of state autonomy. They did not reflect passively the social balance of power, nor did they constitute a neutral arena of pluralist competition. In other words, the state always played the part of a distinct actor, possessed of its own interests and identity. This commonality of interests and identity could, to a marked degree, transcend major policy differences and thus tended to be strikingly durable over time. The Mexican political class (that is, those grouped in and around the PRI) displayed a marked group loyalty, or élite 'self-discipline' (Purcell and Purcell, 1980:204). This was evident in Cárdenas' tacit support for a regime which systematically dismantled much of the *cardenista* project, even when, in 1952, a loosely *cardenista* coalition challenged that regime (Pellicer de Brody, 1977); and, again, following recurrent *destapes*, (unveiling of presidential candidates) in the relative quiescence of disappointed candidates (Purcell and Purcell, 1980:205). It could be argued that this couplet of collective loyalty and individual self-abnegation derived from the 'élite settlement' of 1929 and that the first major example came with Calles' acquiescence in Cárdenas' seizure of effective power in 1935–6 (Knight, 1990a). To argue that the state's 'initial [1920s] orientations set the character of the Mexican state and [thereafter] restricted all but marginal changes in orientation [sic]' is to exaggerate continuity; to conclude, on this basis, that 'only if the state were captured and reconstituted by new classes could major changes in orientation be expected' is to ignore significant policy shifts which have occurred, for example in the 1930s, notwithstanding a marked continuity in state formation and composition (Bennett and Sharpe, 1985:44; cf. Purcell and Purcell, 1980:195, 198).

This phenomenon of collective loyalty or élite discipline would seem to obey three main causes. First, loyalty had a distinctly prudential quality: it paid off, it received its due reward, while disloyalty increasingly brought severe sanctions. A series of military rebellions failed, the last significant one in 1929, the year of the creation of the PNR. The praetorian route to power, successful for the last time in 1920, was closed off. Presidential candidates who adopted too belligerent a tone, as Amaro did in 1939, suffered as a result (Medina, 1978:100–106). Defeated candidates who flirted with rebellion, as Vasconcelos did in 1929 and Almazán in 1940, were soon reminded that this was no longer 1910, and that the rule of the party was stronger, more institutional, more durable, than the rule of Don Porfirio had been (Krauze, 1976:273–8). In addition, according to the new civilian institutional politics of the 1930s, it made sense to work within the party and the state, rather than to try to build countervailing forces outside, as Cárdenas realized to his advantage and regional *caudillos* like Tejeda and Cedillo learned to their cost (Fowler Salamini, 1978:108–17). More recently, while disappointed presidential aspirants who broke with the party in order to mount independent challenges, for example Padilla in 1946 and Henríquez Guzmán in 1952, performed creditably in terms of votes, they earned the strenuous opposition of their erstwhile party colleagues and risked entering a political wasteland. It remains to be seen whether Cuauhtémoc Cárdenas and Porfirio Muñoz Ledo will follow suit. On the other hand, disappointed aspirants who bit on the bullet and accepted their disappointment stoically, and even some renegades who returned to the fold, received a political pay-off (Purcell and Purcell, 1980:205; Pellicer de Brody, 1977:41). The *político quemado* may rise, Phoenix-like, from the ashes, so long as he (and it usually is a he) displays contrition and submission. Needless to say, the rewards of loyalty and the sanctions for overt dissent affected all sections of the political class, not just the top élites; in the case of Henriquismo, the élites got off more lightly than the rank-and-file. With the continued enjoyment of political power, of course, go certain tangible material rewards, at all levels (Vélez-Ibáñez, 1983:81). Disloyalty hurts the pocketbook as well as the psyche.

To this prudential and instrumental loyalty must be added a certain prescriptive and normative allegiance to the revolution, to the great formative and folkloric ideological construct which dominates the landscape of twentieth-century Mexican politics. No doubt many party activists genuinely believe in the historic mission and redemptive role of the revolution (this is a hunch more than a proven conclusion; see, for example, Esponda de Torres, 1982:27–30; Carmona Amorós, 1982:40–43). To some extent, they have a right to do so since, according to several criteria, the revolution has brought Mexico certain benefits. (Different adherents will, of course, stress different benefits, and some of the benefits, such as political stability or national independence, are non-material and hard to quantify.)

Members of the political élite entertain a profound suspicion of both political opponents and political alternatives. A surrender of power by the PRI would, of course, incur severe psychological and material losses for its ruling members, who cling to power out of individual, familial and collective self-interest. But they no doubt also believe that such a surrender would blight Mexico's future and jeopardize the gains of the revolution. Power would gravitate towards the clerical right, the historic enemy of the 1920s and 1930s, or to the radical left, the subversive stirrers of the 1960s; or it would simply dissipate, threatening Mexico's prized political stability, leading to a condition of stalemate or, worse, civil dissension along the lines of Argentina or Peru. The country, in other words, would become ungovernable, as it had been for some 60 years after independence. The memory of past turbulence dies hard: to advocate internal competition between PRI presidential aspirants is to threaten a return to the praetorian struggles of the 1920s (Carmona Amorós, 1982:40; Whitehead, 1981:29). The regime, as one *político* put it, does not want to 'create any more Zapatas' (Purcell and Purcell, 1980:202). There is evidence, too, that this fear of upheaval, of the 'Hobbesian potential of Mexican society', is not confined to incumbent élites. In Jalapa in the 1960s, at least, 'civic order [was] one of the most highly prized commodities' (Fagen and Tuohy, 1972:136). No president, no administration and no political generation would wish to go down in history as those who lost the revolution, who squandered its political inheritance, who chose surrender or invited chaos.

These factors lend the state – the state of the revolution and of the PRI – a distinct cohesion and *esprit de corps*. Major policy divisions can be papered over by appeals, often tacit, to party/revolutionary loyalty. Conversely, major breakaways incur the stigma of *lèse*-PRI. As this parallel suggests, loyalty to the revolution and to the party of the revolution, what we might call revolutionism, acts analogously to patriotism: it is prudent, moral, and safe to support one's party, right or wrong; equally, revolutionism, with its claim to an overriding higher cause, can easily become the last resort of scoundrels. This cohesion, however, is most cogent at the national level, less so at the local or regional levels. It seems exaggerated to speak of a 'rigid discipline' affecting local party cadres, not least because PRI party cadres are, to some extent, ghostly armies (cf. Purcell and Purcell, 1980:195). In the provinces, especially in the rural hinterland, the PRI tends to be colonized by powerful élites, and the party serves more to represent entrenched local interests than to rivet the power of a detached centralized organization on local society (Martínez Saldaña, 1976:88–106; Gándara, 1976:242–72; Schryer, 1980:105). One consequence is a certain political fluidity, as local politics reflect shifts in social status and economic power. In the *municipios*, splits, alliances, coups and feuds thrive to a degree unknown in national politics since the 1920s; conversely, the imperatives of party loyalty are less compelling (Martínez Assad, 1985).

Strength

A consideration of the definition and the function of the state leads to a third, final, and familiar question, that of the strength of the state. It is easy to find recent analyses which interpret Mexico's post-revolutionary history in terms of the onward and upward progress of the state. Let one egregious example stand for the entire genre: 'the State is the connecting thread (*hilo conductor*) of our history, the synthesis of what is "rational" and significant; in it, with it, or against it, are also to be found our limits as a civil society'.[5] Such analyses necessarily stress the constant enhancement of state power which this process entails and which culminates in the contemporary Mexican nation, legendarily strong, stable, centralized and corporatist (Purcell and Purcell, 1980:194; Knight, 1985:11; Spalding, 1981:141). Even analysts who incline more to an agent theory, linking state to class/sectoral interests, attach obvious importance to the power of the state, its greater or lesser capacity to serve the class/sectoral interests it represents. Certainly, the issue of state power must be addressed. The strength of the state cannot, however, be read off, in positivist fashion, from certain basic indicators, suggestive though these may be. The economic role of the state may have expanded; the political and technical bureaucracy may have burgeoned; military revolts may be a thing of the past, and so on. But the significance of these roughly measurable trends is not as obvious as sometimes imagined.

The alleged rise of the state may in fact involve a redistribution rather than a net enhancement of political power; or it may involve an optical illusion: the organs of the central state appear to grow, but they are in fact cannibalized by local élites and interests. In the first instance, power is redistributed, but not necessarily augmented; in the second, even the redistribution may be illusory. Regional *caudillos*, the booted and spurred warlords of the 1920s, have vanished. The traditional cacique, too, has probably weakened; but in many regions, including sprawling urban areas like Ciudad Nezahualcoyotl, the cyclical production of *caciques* or *caciquitos* goes on; and the ranks of caciquismo have been reinforced by 'white collar caciques', bosses in the big federal agencies, for example (Vélez-Ibáñez, 1983:88, 134, 144, 187; Bartra, 1990). Though formally representatives of the central government, *caciques* may also serve the interests of local élites, even in defiance of their notional sociopolitical function. In Chiapas, programmes of *indigenismo* (development for Indian communities) and agrarian reform, formally designed to empower the poor and weaken local élites, were progressively perverted and appropriated by the élites themselves: over time, the state again became 'informally allied with landowners' (Benjamin, 1989:204, 214, 221, 224–6). Federal agencies entering the jealous world of Los Altos (de Jalisco) were similarly appropriated, as was the official party (Martíñez Saldaña, 1976:78–9, 108; Gándara, 1976:245, 253). In other words the local impact of a burgeoning party, state, or federal bureaucracy was heavily determined by local interests and power structures 'the informal structures of power in rural Mexico directly determine who exercises formal control of political posts' (Schryer, 1980:105; Martínez Vázquez et al., 1985:177, 182–5; Fox and Gordillo, 1989:136–7). And not just in the countryside. Even in the teeming conurbation of Mexico City petty local caciques can stymie the efforts of the central authorities: 'in some of these areas . . . neither municipal, nor state, nor federal political control has been effectively instituted' (Vélez-Ibáñez, 1983:90). Perhaps for this reason, inputs of federal resources do not necessarily appear to purchase support for the central government (Salinas de Gortari, 1982).

Even where the power of the central government has been dramatically augmented, where, that is, the dialectical relationship between political centre and periphery has been decisively and not just ostensibly tipped in favour of the former, it is not always clear that this enhancement of central power involved an equivalent enhancement of total political power. Citizens may suffer, or enjoy, less political subordination under the new modern centralized state than they did under the old traditional decentralized one. The governors and *jefes políticos* of Porfirio Díaz's day exercised formidable power in their immediate localities, as did their minions in dependent municipalities (Knight, 1986,1:15–32). The *caciques* and *caudillos* of the revolution also enjoyed ample arbitrary powers. Saturnino Cedillo ran San Luis as his personal fief for 20 years; during that time no vigorous civic opposition of the kind which, under the guise of Navismo, affected San Luis in both the 1950s and the 1970s was allowed to prevail (Ankerson, 1984; Martínez Assad, 1985; Márquez, 1987). In southern Mexico, too, the political hegemony of the plantocracy, although challenged, remained formidable down to the 1930s. Were the civic and popular movements of 1920s Chiapas operating in a freer, less controlled political environment than their 1970s or 1980s counterparts? Federal agencies are appreciably stronger now than they were then – to that extent the state has grown stronger – but, in part, such agencies offer both opportunities for popular mobilization and counterweights to entrenched local élites (Harvey, 1988, 1990). Highland Chiapas without federal intromission might resemble highland Guatemala more than it already does; and are Guatemalan Indians less politically repressed than their Chiapaneco counterparts? In other words, the growth of central government power may offer strategic space for popular movements; it may result in a lightening of arbitrary local political power (Martínez Vázquez et al., 1985:192).

Finally, discussions of the alleged strength/weakness of the state must also take into account the question of function, of which the state may be loosely said to possess two: that of acting upon civil society, achieving goals set either autonomously or at the behest of powerful social groups; and that of surviving and reproducing itself. The first function relates to the shifting state projects, the second to the state's ongoing commitment to survival and self-reproduction. (This distinction would not, of course, be acceptable to those who see the state purely and simply as an agent of class interests.) These two functions are often antithetical. Aggressive social engineering policies may jeopardize the stability and survival of the state. On the other hand, stability and survival may be best served by policies that are cautious, limited, and unprovocative. Strength, measured in terms of effective, authoritative action, may not correlate with stability, that is, the survival and self-reproduction of the state over time. Traditional (for example, feudal) states tended to be weak, yet often stable over time. Twentieth-century fascist states were strong in terms of their political and economic powers but inherently unstable. The distinction, obvious enough, is important because the two attributes are sometimes conflated. A state, like the Mexican, is deemed strong because it is stable, that is, it has survived and reproduced itself over two generations. Its stability is evident (it is easier to establish criteria of political survival and self-reproduction than of political strength); but it is not evident that this stability derived from or stood as proof of the strength of the state. Consider the counter-examples of South America: Chile, Uruguay, Brazil and, above all, Argentina. Their record since the 1950s has hardly been one of unblemished stability. Yet it could be argued that, for example, the Argentine state is, in important respects, a strong state: it controls a large slice of the economy and handles large transfer payments; it has both mobilized a dependent working-class movement and inflicted a brutal repression on Argentine society. In 1965, for example, government revenue as a proportion of GNP was around 30 per cent in Brazil, 26 per cent in Chile, 19 per cent in Argentina, but only 10 per cent in Mexico (Hansen, 1974:84). The Mexican state played a significant role in economic development, but its commitment to education and social security, which might be considered appropriate indices of social engineering and constituency-building, was relatively parsimonious, certainly prior to the 1970s (Hansen, 1974:85; Looney, 1985:10–11; Bennett and Sharpe, 1985:28, 49–50). In part, we may conclude, the Argentine state has been unstable precisely because it wields such ample powers and its instability, in turn, has encouraged the ample, arbitrary use of state power, whether coercive or populist.[6]

Habsburgs and Bourbons

In the Mexican case, too, I believe there has been a historic trade-off between strength and stability, with the latter enjoying a higher priority than in the South American cases, especially during the phase of *desarrollo estabilizador*, roughly 1950–70. However, even in Mexico, relative priorities have shifted over time, hence they require some brief historical analysis. In order to expedite the analysis, let me develop a terminological distinction introduced elsewhere (Knight, 1990b). Given a constant trade-off between strength and stability, let us call governments which favour active intervention in civil society Bourbon and those which incline to stability and systems-maintenance Habsburg. These are not, of course, random labels, but reflect the broad historic reality of the two dynastic periods of the country's colonial history. Where the Habsburgs delegated power, deferred to powerful corporate interests, notably the Church and, to some extent, the Indian communities, and achieved a substantial measure of social stability, consensus even, the Bourbons favoured more aggressive policies of state-building and economic development. To these ends they attacked vested interests (the Church, especially the Jesuits; the Indian communities; the Mexico City merchants' guild); they sought to replace a ramshackle patrimonial administration with an efficient bureaucracy; they squeezed tax revenue from the colony; they dragooned labour; and, when they encountered popular resistance, they readily resorted to repression. While the Habsburg regime lumbered along for two centuries, relatively immune to major upheavals, the Bourbon era was tense, conflictual, and relatively shortlived, lasting at best some 50 years.[7] The Bourbons sought, with some success, to control civil society more thoroughly than their predecessors. Under their rule, New Spain became a more taxed, more administered, more repressed society. It also became a more fractious and rebellious one, hence the great popular upheaval of 1810. It is impossible to say whether the Bourbon state and project would have survived if the Napoleonic invasion of Spain had not triggered a political and imperial crisis; there are grounds for thinking that both were inherently flawed and risk prone. However, the main point underlying this terminology is that Bourbon governments entertain visions of change, seek to transform civil society, and strive to enhance and exert their interventionist political powers.

They appear as strong governments in two senses: they augment the powers of government (taxes rise, the bureaucracy swells, repression increases); and they try to coax and pummel civil society into new shapes. They are, in other words, activist, interventionist, *dirigiste* regimes. As such, they offend not only popular groups, but also certain élite vested interests. Needless to say, these two manifestations of strength are closely linked. The powers of government are enhanced in order to achieve the desired social transformation. If Bourbon regimes are successful, they demonstrate their capacity, their strength, by transforming society. Often, however, the build-up of state power provokes popular and élite opposition, which in turn stymies the state and aborts the great transformation. Opposition may take the form of outright revolts or, more often, of devious evasion, of insidious internal subversion. While the former are often popular in character, the latter is the preferred strategy of powerful groups, jealous of their local or corporate interests and hostile to the pretensions of a reformist bureaucratic state, that is, central government. Historically, such élites have shown a remarkable capacity to subvert political reforms and administrative rationalization. They have used a variety of methods: bribery, corruption, co-option, nepotism, methods which, inverting James Scott, we might term the 'weapons of the strong'. In consequence, the great Bourbon transformation may emerge as a spatchcocked compromise, a messy stalemate between state and civil society, or, in some circumstances, it may end in outright revolt.

Habsburg regimes, on the other hand, follow Walpole's dictum: *quies non movere* ('let sleeping dogs lie'). They do not entertain such grand visions of social transformation; they are content with limited controls and limited, fiscal benefits; they govern according to some prudential notion of consensus, using repression in selective fashion. In consequence they may seem feeble, creaking, inefficient (*obedezco pero no cumplo*, 'I obey but do not carry out', was the celebrated motto of Habsburg colonial administrators). It is important to stress that the consensus which the Habsburgs encouraged was a skewed consensus in which the opinion and interests of powerful privileged sectors counted the most; and Habsburg government sought to avoid conflict with these sectors. In this sense, Habsburg government mirrored colonial Mexican society, with its inherent class and ethnic inequalities, more than it sought to change it. Although, like all colonial regimes, the Habsburg state necessarily possessed a degree of relative autonomy, it was more of an agent state than its Bourbon successor, which, in contrast, strove for, and achieved, a greater degree of autonomy. For that reason, however, the Habsburg state proved both more durable and less contentious.

We can therefore envisage the Habsburg and Bourbon types of regime occupying opposite ends of a political continuum:

Habsburg	Bourbon
state mirrors society	state moulds society
agent state	relatively autonomous state
modest state project	ambitious state project
systems-maintenance	social engineering
qualified consensus	divisiveness

Bourbon projects: Porfiriato to revolution

While derivative of colonial society, these labels can be applied to the national period equally well. There is a consensus among historians of different persuasions that Mexico's mid-nineteenth century liberals stood in the Bourbon tradition; that they sought to revive the policies of modernization, to use a handy but slippery portmanteau term, which the Bourbons had inaugurated. Confounded by civil war and foreign invasion, the Juarista liberals passed the political baton to Porfirio Díaz, whose neo-Bourbon project proved more successful, at least for a generation. Like the Bourbons, Díaz was keen for state-building and economic development, and he used a combination of incentives and repression (*pan o palo*) to achieve these ends. But, like the Bourbons, Díaz found that he had to rely excessively on traditional political mechanisms, caciquismo, above all, if he was to bring peace, stability, centralization of power and economic development. The cacique served as the necessary bridge between a formally liberal regime and an objectively authoritarian society (Guerra, 1985, 2:309–13). Despite this flaw, which revolutionary regimes would replicate, the Porfiriato did witness major economic advances, which were logically coupled with major social tensions. The regime sought to boost exports, to create an economic infrastructure, to integrate Mexico into the world division of labour. In all this, it succeeded; in the economic realm, we might say, Díaz proved more Bourbon than the Bourbons.

Was the Porfiriato a strong state? Historians differ, in regard to both (tacit) definitions and empirical evidence. Under Díaz, government revenue rose, albeit not dramatically in real per capita terms (Guerra, 1985, 1:278), as shown in Table 1.1. Thanks in part to the telegraph and railway, the Porfirian regime managed to centralize power to an extent unknown in post-colonial Mexico, but centralization did not take the form of a national bureaucracy, still less a national party. Political authority remained highly personal, arbitrary and cacical, hence it proved vulnerable to the succession crisis of 1910. The Porfiriato then failed the classic test of state self-reproduction, that is, the capacity to transfer power over generations. Instead, it remained a personalist regime, dependent on the whims and, more important, the longevity of its eponymous creator, Porfirio Díaz. Meanwhile, rapid economic change engendered sharp social tensions. As befitted a Bourbon-style state, the Porfiriato spurred social change and centralized power (albeit its state-building proved to be excessively

Table 1.1 Evolution of Government Revenue during Porfiriato

	Beginning of Porfiriato (Base year 1877–8)	End of Porfiriato (1910–11)
1 Population	100	160
2 Federal revenue, current pesos	100	537
3 Federal revenue, deflated	100	226
4 Federal + state revenue, current pesos	100	471
5 Federal + state revenue, deflated	100	198
6 Per capita [3]	100	141
7 Per capita [5]	100	124

personalist and fragile). Both processes incurred strenuous opposition, on the part not only of socially aggrieved peasants, but also of politically dissident middle-class and provincial élites (Knight, 1986, 1, chs 2, 3). These disaffected groups, furthermore, lacked institutional channels of protest. The courts no longer mediated peasant grievances, as they had during the colony; and the *camarilla* politics of the Porfiriato denied both the representation of the middle classes and the circulation of élites. Like its Bourbon predecessor, the Porfiriato simultaneously stoked the fires of discontent and sealed the escape valves of political mediation. Similarly it succumbed to a social revolution, exactly a century after the 1810 insurgency.

After a decade of political and social turmoil, the Sonoran dynasty began a successful reconstitution of the Mexican state in the 1920s. Recent analyses have stressed the state-building accomplishments of the revolutionary regime. They point to the record of stabilization (no successful coups after 1920), of centralization (as Mexico City triumphed over the fractious provinces), and of enhanced state power (the growth, in particular, of federal agencies and resources). For some, the revolutionary state assumes the grand proportions of a Bonapartist regime, which moulds a malleable civil society. The state is highly autonomous and powerful; citizens, like the Cristeros, who stand in its way are ground under (Meyer, 1976). The new party, the agrarian reform, the nascent labour confederations and the education drives are all essential instruments for the advancement of state power. The revolution, in terms of its functional outcome, becomes a great engine of political centralization and state-building, a Tocquevillean or Skocpolian revolution.

I have argued against this view elsewhere (Knight, 1985). Let me recapitulate a couple of arguments, linking them to the three categories of discussion introduced above. First, analyses of state-building tend to focus heavily on the central government. Much is made of the centre's defeat of regional *caudillos*, exemplified by Cárdenas' ouster of Cedillo. That represented an important shift in the distribution of power, to be sure. But whether it involved a net enhancement of political power, of the state's control of citizens and social groups, is another matter. The growth of peasant organizations and labour unions/confederations, many linked to the regime and official party, is also of key importance. But, again, this did not involve the baptism of political babes. Peasants, who comprised the great majority of Mexico's population, did not inhabit a political no-mans-land prior to the revolution; rather, they lived in subjection to landowner, cacique, magistrate and priest. Landowners and caciques may or may not have held formal political office, but they certainly enjoyed ample political powers. They controlled the state governorship and the *jefaturas* (prefectures), they rigged the fiscal system, they handled political patronage, they could rely on the forces of repression, the army and the *rurales* (rural police). The Church, of course, represented an alternative source of authority, formally distinct from the state. But the Church's contribution to the maintenance of political order and hegemony was important. In regions like west-central Mexico where, as the Cristiada showed, organized Catholicism was most strongly entrenched, the Church was a palpably political institution: priests organized communities, provided education, moulded public opinion, and chanelled social activities (González; 1972). By the 1900s the Church was actively involved in worker and peasant mobilization; after 1910 it pioneered youth organizations, trade unions, a successful but short-lived political party and a variety of other lay associations. To the extent that the Church represented a distinct political force, it sometimes struggled with the state (roughly, 1913–40) and sometimes co-existed with it (1876–1913, and again after 1940). In the last 50 years, as conflict gave way to detente, the Church remained a powerful factor in politics, both nationally and locally. It opposed national educational policies it disliked; it allied with local élites whom it favoured, whether in Jalisco or Chihuahua; and it gave (qualified, ambivalent) support to ecclesiastical base communities (Loaeza, 1988: ch. 6; Martínez Saldaña, 1976: 107–8, 133–4; Gándara, 1976: 247–8; Aziz Nassif, 1985: 93–5; Concha Malo *et al.*, 1986). The Church, like the cacique, is by no means a spent political force. Conversely, state centralization has far from eliminated countervailing centres of power. It is not only difficult to measure the strength of the state, especially the central state, as against countervailing, and often underestimated, political forces (local élites, clerics, caciques); at times it is hard even to distinguish the one from the other.

This brings us back to the second consideration, that of the function of political power, as deployed in revolutionary Mexico. Here, protagonists of the Leviathan state adopt different positions. For some, the burgeoning revolutionary state is highly autonomous, a Bonapartist engine of domination which could act in complete independence of social groups (Córdova, 1973:322). According to one such formulation, the Mexican state effectively creates the country's national bourgeoisie (Bennett and Sharpe, 1985:39–40, 49). Proponents of the agent theory, on the other hand, see the state as representing powerful class interests, which are causally and chronologically anterior to the state. Usually, it is the bourgeoisie whose interests are so represented; and radical administrations, such as Cárdenas', merely disguise bourgeois hegemony beneath pseudo-radical discourse (Anguiano, 1975). Ostensibly radical measures such as the agrarian reform serve to deliver the peasantry, bureaucratically bound hand and foot, into the clutches of the bourgeois state.

In my view, the revolutionary state of the 1920s and 1930s was neither a potent Leviathan, a maker of society and social classes, nor a simple agent of the bourgeoisie. As regards the central government, the state enjoyed a measure of autonomy and conceived ambitious plans of social transformation: it aspired to be a Bourbon state, as its Porfirian predecessor had. It sponsored mass organizations (CROM, CTM, CNC, PNR, PRM); it pioneered, first cautiously, then dramatically, a major land reform; it combated the most powerful foreign enclave, the oil sector; and it sought to use education to weaken the power of the Church, to enhance nationalism and, finally, to inculcate socialism. These were bold Bourbon policies. They did not respond to any clear class interest. True, the Sonoran regime favoured capitalist agriculture and industry, and it never fundamentally questioned Mexico's role in the world division of labour. But the Sonoran state was far from being the executive committee of a bourgeois ruling class, and this was not because Mexico lacked a recognizable bourgeoisie (cf. Haber, 1989, ch. 5; Saragoza, 1988). Landowners, businessmen, and, of course, the Church hierarchy, were leery of

Sonoran policy; come the 1930s, they were downright hostile to *cardenismo*. Meanwhile, as the central state battled against regional particularism, it necessarily combated powerful regional and local élites: the plantocracy of the south; the Catholics of west-central Mexico; the industrial bourgeoisie of the northwest. Conversely, it espoused popular causes, most obviously (but not uniquely) in the 1930s. Obregón backed Carrillo Puerto in Yucatán; Calles supported Vidal in Chiapas, Tejeda in Veracruz. Agents of the federal government, notably the military, repressed agrarian movements in some regions – General Guadalupe Sánchez, of Veracruz, was notorious – but aided them in others, for example, Jalisco (see Craig, 1983:100–102).

The conclusion to be drawn is not simply that post-revolutionary Mexico was complex, variegated, and thus resistant to categorization in terms of crude theories of state formation and action, all of which is true. It is also that, while the revolutionary state's goal of survival and self-reproduction was achieved, its more sweeping sociopolitical project encountered major obstacles and often failed. The presumed success of the revolutionary state, which in turn may serve as an indicator of its strength, thus depends a good deal on which function of the state is being evalutated. The armed revolution sired a regime which entertained an ambitious Bourbon project, manifest in the 1917 constitution. The regime sought to transform society, albeit according to shifting revolutionary priorities. Calles and Cárdenas, the two principal architects of the state, disagreed a good deal in regard to policy. But they agreed that the state should play a central role in ordering society and both felt a profound, and prudential, loyalty to that body. The society they sought to transform, however, was ridden with class, regional, ethnic and ideological conflicts. The notional conclusion of the armed revolution (in 1917 or 1920, or whenever) merely transferred the arena of conflict from battlefields in the *sierras* and *selvas* to statehouses, ministries, *sindicatos*, *barrios*, pulpits and boardrooms. We may gloss Clausewitz and say that politics, during the 1920s and 1930s, was in many respects the continuation of the revolutionary war by other means. No one class or class coalition enjoyed hegemony; hegemony was being fought over, both nationally and locally. That, more than anything, was what the Cristero War was all about. Viewed in all its myriad regional and institutional variations the revolutionary state reflected this complex pattern. It bolstered landlord rule in some regions while it attacked it in others. In some places it co-existed with the Church, in others it sought to extirpate Catholicism (compare San Luis and Tabasco). It collaborated with foreign capital in respect of mining and battled with it over petroleum. In some regions it was staffed by rising young radicals (Múgica in Michoacán, Tejeda in Veracruz); in others, conservative local élites successfully colonized it, assuming revolutionary offices, titles and slogans while preserving their local political hegemony (Schryer, 1980, ch. 4; Benjamin, 1989: 149–52).

As this picture suggests, the relationship between state and civil society was complex and tense, hence it was capable of important twists and turns. During the mid-1920s, the agrarian reform quickened, the CROM increased in strength, and both the Church and the oil companies became the targets of government policy. By the late 1920s, however, Calles had retreated and the proponents of conservatism seemed to gain the upper hand. But with the onset of the depression and the successive political crises of Obregón's assassination and the Calles–Cárdenas confrontation, radical reform again dominated the agenda (at the national level; states and regions did not uniformally follow these shifts). Nor did these shifts reflect any seismic upheaval in the country's class structure which, though changing, tended to do so in gradual, geological fashion; rather, they were political shifts, reflecting changing fortunes in the struggle for the revolutionary inheritance. The agrarian bourgeoisie, as we may loosely term them, benefited from Callista conservatism but soon after fell victim to *cardenista* radicalism. Conversely, popular movements of the left, including independent labour unions, peasant leagues and the Communist Party, suffered under Calles and rebounded under Cárdenas. Between 1920 and 1940, we may say, the battle for hegemony went on, nationally, regionally and locally. The (central) state gradually augmented its powers. But it was not clear to what ends those powers would be deployed, hence the state did not serve as the faithful representative of a specific class interest. The state was the object of class, as well as regional and ideological, contestations. It did not control the struggle, nor did any one class or sector capture the state. Meanwhile, as the (central) state grew stronger, it developed both a collective ethos and a barrage of mechanisms which fortified its power and smoothed its self-reproduction. Cuartelazos became increasingly risky and feeble.

It would be gross exaggeration, however, to depict the revolutionary state of the 1920s and 1930s as a lumbering Leviathan, dominating civil society. Its defeats were as noteworthy as its victories. During the 1920s it fought the Church to a stalemate and more than once it backed down in the face of oil company intransigence. In the 1930s it espoused a socialist education programme which incurred widespread hostility and indifference; the *maestros rurales*, sometimes depicted as swaggering Cromwellian major-generals, were few, feeble and less feared than fearful, especially when they were young women pitched into a rough rural locality (Vaughan, 1990). Rather than tyrannizing a cowed countryside, they had to contend with *campesino* indifference, landlord and clerical aggression and primitive, poverty-stricken conditions. Meanwhile, the official party became, in many instances, a vehicle for local élites, who saw that the preservation of their interests was best served by opportunistic conversion to the revolution, rather than quixotic opposition. The revolutionary state's transforming powers proved to be quite limited. For all its Bourbon pretensions, it found, like its Bourbon predecessors, that civil society was recalcitrant, that radical initiatives were often blunted, ignored, or cannibalized.

The revolutionary state managed to win its battle for survival and self-reproduction, leaving a legacy of political stability rare in Latin America. It developed more muscle: federal expenditure grew, in real terms, by 93 per cent between 1910 and 1930 and a further 79 per cent between 1930 and 1940; the per capita increases were 77 per cent and 51 per cent (Wilkie, 1973:22–24). Public administration employees, as a percentage of the economically active population, rose steeply between 1910 and 1930 (Grindle, 1977:189). In part, of course, the Mexican state followed trends towards enhanced state power which were evident throughout much of the world. The revolution helped do for Mexico what the First World War did for Europe.[8] However, when it deployed that muscle in attempts to change society, it experienced mixed results. The agrarian reform was its greatest transforming accomplishment, but the reform depended on a combination of widespread popular mobilization, spanning 1910–40, and of a distinct economic conjuncture, the depression of the early 1930s. It represented a special case, 'the exception which proved the rule of accumulation, which governed the totality of economic activities' (Warman, 1976:284). The oil nationalization, too, derived from the autonomous mobilization of the petroleum works. These major reforms therefore represented combinations of state policy and profound social pressure; the strength of the revolutionary state depended on its harnessing of relatively autonomous social forces. More thoroughly top-down reforms, like the socialist education programme, proved abortive. The Mexican state, in other words, required the leverage of social mobilization and support if it was to enact major reforms; it could not change society by unilateral state fiat alone and, when it tried, it usually failed.

The return of the Habsburgs

After the 1940s, a significant shift occurred. In crude terms, the battle for political hegemony was won and lost, hence the period of disputed hegemony came to an end. The crucial and under-researched 1940s witnessed this transition, which I shall discuss briefly in conclusion. In defiance of chronology, however, I want first to outline the post-1940s project, which, according to the dynastic terminology being used here, implied a distinctly Habsburg relationship between state and civil society. In the years after the Second World War the Mexican state was consolidated on the basis of a new programme, which stressed private enterprise over collective ownership, capital accumulation over redistribution, social control over representation, marginalization over encouragement of the left, urbanization over rural development. The state still retained a measure of autonomy, and was not reduced to the executive arm of the bourgeoisie. On occasions, the state infringed the interests of the private sector, or alarmed its sensibilities. But it paid a heavy political price, in terms of protests, lobbying, capital flight, when it did so and policies seen as hostile to business tended to flounder (Maxfield and Anzaldúa, 1987; Spalding, 1981; Looney, 1985:57–8, 89–90). The state also sought to regulate transnational capital, which it did with some success, but policy was cautious and, in some respects, geared to the benefit of Mexican private capital (Bennett and Sharpe, 1985). In general, therefore, the broad contours of policy were remarkably favourable to the private sector: taxes were low, *de facto* protection was high, the relative returns to labour and capital favoured the latter, and both agrarian reform and union militancy were curtailed.

As a result, the muscle which the state had built up during the turbulent 1920s and 1930s was now exercised for different purposes. Bourbon projects of radical transformation were shelved. The socialist education programme was wound up; Avila Camacho pioneered a detente with the Church which subsequent administrations sustained (Kennedy, 1971:81–91). Both the private sector and the expanding middle class were conciliated, with practical benefits and rhetorical pats-on-the-back. For some 30 years, until the political reform relaxed state control in the late 1970s, the radical left was discreetly but effectively debarred from electoral competition and mainstream political participation. The CTM choked off independent unionism. Of course, civil society was never wholly controlled or manipulated: the sequence of social movements which affected Mexico, even during the heyday of the *pax priísta*, stands as a testimony to the state's limited capacity (Knight, 1990b). The crucial thing was that unlike its counterparts in much of Latin America the Mexican state survived and prospered. It withstood the challenges of both left and right, of war, boom, recession, inflation and urbanization.

For this reason it has sometimes been deemed a strong state. But, I repeat, strength can mean several different things. First, in terms of survival and self-reproduction the Mexican state has out-performed all its Latin American counterparts and offers the only example, bar the Soviet Union, of a revolutionary regime, that is a regime born of social revolution, that has lasted longer than the alotted human span – which, in other words, has managed to nurture some three successive political generations. It has, of course, outlasted the spurious 'revolutionary' regimes of Eastern Europe, as well as the Congress Raj in India, which probably offers a more apposite parallel than Eastern Europe. Second, in terms of its fiscal and economic powers, the Mexican state, especially during the stable 1950s and 1960s, was relatively weak, compared, say, to the Brazilian or Argentinian states (Hansen, 1974:66–8, 84–5). The relative size of public-sector administrative employment actually fell during the 1950s (Grindle, 1977:189). Conversely, it was during the phase of declining legitimacy (roughly, the 1970s and after) that government economic powers grew and began to reach South American levels (Looney, 1985:8–13, 57–8). Under Echeverría and López Portillo government spending soared, yet this did not make their administrations any stronger, any more popular, legitimate or authoritative, compared to those of their predecessors. Indeed, the expansion of the state sector seems to have generated factionalism and bureaucratic infighting, rather than effective and incisive government (Purcell and Purcell, 1980:218–19). As the federal bureaucracy waxed, one analyst argued, presidential power waned (Spalding, 1981:155). Currently, both trends seem to have been reversed. 'State-shrinking' now accompanies a reassertion of presidential power. As Salinas, whose doctoral research appeared to prove that government spending did not necessarily buy support or bolster legitimacy, recently declared: 'The scale (dimension) of the state, of itself, is not sufficient to determine its greater or lesser capacity or effectiveness in meeting social demands . . . Our problem has not been a small, weak, state, but a state which, by virtue of its burgeoning size, made itself weak' (Salinas, 1982; 1990a:30).

If power is divorced from positivist indices, for example the size of the federal budget, and measured, impressionistically, to be sure, in terms of the state's capacity to deploy authority and exact compliance, the question of function is again crucial. I have suggested that the revolutionary regime of the 1920–40 period displayed a Bourbon desire to transform society; that it succeeded to the extent that it harnessed powerful social forces, but that in many respects it failed. Between *c.* 1940 and 1970, and especially during the 1950s and 1960s, the regime of the PRI tended to shelve Bourbon blueprints and to operate along more Habsburg lines. That is to say, while it never relinquished relative state autonomy, while it embarked recurrently on projects of state intervention, and while it always retained a measure of genuine legitimacy, it nevertheless governed in the interests of the powerful sectors of society. It followed 'a decision-making process and style that favor[ed] the *status quo*'; and this would apply to 'activist' and 'consolidating' presidents alike (Purcell and Purcell, 1980:220, 222). In other words, this Habsburg political approach was a relatively constant, even structural, feature of state–civil society relations during the era of *desarrollo estabilizador*; it did not reflect mere presidential temperaments.

This approach involved taking the path of least social resistance. To the extent that society is riven with conflicts, of course, no policy is universally acceptable and most policies incur opposition in certain sectors. The rule of the PRI, however, tended to penalize the weak and to protect the strong; it cosseted business, milked the peasantry and collaborated with caciques. It did not do so in blatantly authoritarian fashion: it did not systematically smash trade unions and leftist political parties; it did not silence political dissenters; it did not abdicate civilian power to the military or prosecute extensive dirty wars. It sought instead to conciliate certain aggrieved popular sectors, while ensuring that this conciliation did not radically upset the dominant patterns of political subordination and capital accumulation. Thus, organized labour (a minority of the working class) received some perks and protection; there were sporadic spurts of land reform and occasional ousters of unpopular caciques, *pour encourager les autres*.

A barrage of parastate agencies controlled and placated the peasantry, often acting in connivance with local élites. When conciliation failed, repression was not wanting. But repression tended to be selective rather than indiscriminate. In short, during the heyday of *desarrollo estabilizador*, the PRI governed Mexico along Habsburg lines, favouring corruption, conciliation and the protection of vested interests over ambitious political intervention and social engineering. As the Purcells argue, the regime of the PRI was something of a 'balancing act', involving a complex series of bargains, deals and trade-offs; within this regime, ideology was at a discount (administrations could accommodate a range of ideological positions); but socio-economic power was at a premium. In other words, the balancing act did not entail a neutral mediation of social interests: 'those groups in society that are the most politicized and most privileged exact more from their leaders than those that are less highly politicized and poorer' (Purcell and Purcell, 1980:195, 202, 225–6). With this went a marginalization of political extremes and a degree of genuine consensus, which embraced even groups who were not obvious beneficiaries of the system. 'There is,' Fagen and Tuohy noted in Jalapa, 'a shared investment in the existing regime that transcends class and group boundaries and interests'; however, the legitimacy which this shared investment implied was inert rather than active, based on prescription as much as sentiment. It was, the authors explain, 'a legitimacy that is much closer to a passive acceptance of the inevitable than to an intense belief in essential rightness' (Fagen and Tuohy, 1972:125, 136, 139). Such legitimacy was evident in the classic Habsburg practice of political petitioning, of addressing paternalist authorities in deferential style in the hope of limited redress: 'after ritual voting the most common political activity in Jalapa . . . was "going to an official to seek help"' (Fagen and Tuohy, 1972:161).

Transitions

The transition from Bourbon to Hapsburg styles requires some further clarification. If the revolutionary regime of the 1920–40 period is deemed Bourbon, and its 1950–70 successor Hapsburg, how and why did the change come about? Such a clarification is particularly relevant since the post-1970 period of crisis also appears to carry the hallmark of transition. In other words, the closest historical parallel to the contemporary crisis may be found in the transitional 1940s (see Loyola Díaz, 1990b).

The revolutionary state's efforts to transform society in the 1920–40 period were the product of specific circumstances, the legacy of the revolution and the world depression in particular. This combination conjured up both the social movements and the political ideology which, especially in the 1930s, underwrote *cardenismo*. However, *cardenismo* enjoyed limited success, especially in the longer term. By 1938 the *cardenista* project/coalition was losing momentum; by 1940 it was in retreat; and by 1946 it had been largely liquidated. Both internal and external trends were responsible. Some were conjunctural: the backlash against Cárdenas which was evident in the growth of the right, both clerical and secular; the petroleum expropriation and the onset of the Second World War, which conspired to dampen domestic class conflict and to produce a certain nationalist ralliement.

More important, structural changes now affected the Mexican political economy. Agrarian reform broke up the old *haciendas*, pushing capital into commerce and industry while establishing agriculture on a two-tier footing: the subsistence *ejido* and capital-intensive, often exporting, agribusiness. Industry also flourished, benefiting from import substitution, the deepening of the domestic market and a degree of government assistance, even from the Cárdenas administration. The war gave a further boost to industrialization and yoked the Mexican economy to that of its northern neighbour. Although the post-war years (1946–52) witnessed considerable economic upheaval, by the early 1950s Mexico had entered its phase of *desarrollo estabilizador*, which would last some two decades. On the ideological front, meanwhile, the touchstones of *cardenismo*, that is, agrarian reform, economic nationalism, syndicalization and state intervention, were progressively abandoned or subordinated to new priorities. Economic collaboration with the US was seconded by political and military collaboration, and the new wartime relationship was carried over into the era of the Cold War. Mexico was never an ardent cold warrior, it is true; subsequent policy in regard to Cuba, Chile and Nicaragua bespoke a degree of independence and nationalism in the country's foreign policy. But anti-communism flourished domestically (it encouraged Church–state detente) and the removal of communists from the unions was paralleled by the marginalization of *cardenistas* and Lombardistas in the later 1940s and 1950s.

As this proscription of the left suggests, the incumbent regime was no passive spectator of events. While the profound shifts taking place in Mexican society – urbanization, industrialization, capital accumulatin – were far more than the result of government policy, policy certainly hurried them along. Where Cárdenas had thrown the weight of the central government judiciously and selectively behind workers' and peasants' movements, his successors took the easier course and leaned the other way.[9] They reduced the power of the unions, especially the powerful and independent industrial unions (railwaymen, oil-workers, later electricians), resorting to the *charrazos* of the late 1940s, the repression of 1958–9 and 1976. They curtailed the influence of the CTM within the party and bolstered that of the CNOP. Meanwhile, they coddled business, conciliated the Church and collaborated with provincial élites. In 1946, the year of Alemán's inauguration, the local oligarchy recovered political control of the Los Altos region of Jalisco, and in the Sierra Alta de Hidalgo 1948 marked the beginning of a new form of 'bureaucratic caciquismo', a civilian alliance of the PRI and the rural bourgeoisie (Martínez Saldaña, 1976:15, 70–71; Schryer, 1980:107–11).

The switch from Bourbon to Habsburg styles thus reflected the basic fact that, by the 1940s and 1950s, the country was a flourishing capitalist society, possessed of a growing bourgeoisie and a state which generally, but not invariably or obsequiously, pandered to the interests of that bourgeoisie, above all because the logic of indistrialization and development seemed to require it (Looney, 1985:27, 36). The Bourbon efforts of pre-1940 were relinquished; they were the product of an earlier time, of an older, more rural, more revolutionary society. Even in the 1930s, when times were propitious, Cárdenas had encountered formidable obstacles. By the 1950s, times had changed, the obstacles were now insurmountable, and *cardenismo*, along with its political legatees *lombardismo* and *henriquismo*, was something of a spent force. Cities like Jalapa became 'depoliticized communities' (Fagen and Tuohy, 1972:139).[10] Meanwhile, capital accumulation forged ahead, powered by import substitution. Businessmen, however critical of *priísta* populism, operated within a favourable environment; local élites continued to colonize the PRI or, in some cases, found that they could leave sordid politics to party hacks, concentrating their energy and resources on business and the bottom line (Schryer, 1980:138). Politics, in typical Habsburg style, depended on *camarillas* (cliques), clientelism and conservatism, the latter implying that 'at moments of uncertainty, incumbents and aspirants tend to respond in ways dictated by the high value placed on maintaining the system and the *status quo*' (Fagen and Tuohy, 1972:26). Survival and self-reproduction took priority over rational reform and efficiency. Political reformers, like Madrazo, got short shrift from the PRI machine, Hansen's *cosa nuestra* (Hansen, 1974:ch.5). Economic reformers did not necessarily fare much better, notwithstanding the rise of the celebrated 'technocrats' (Bennett and Sharpe, 1985:262). At the national level, analysts discerned 'vicious bureaucratic infighting', overlapping and competing authorities and 'bureaucratic enclaves' which successfully blocked coherent policy (Purcell and Purcell), 1980:218–19; Spalding, 1981:149). The sexennial upheaval, however conducive to the circulation and satisfaction of élites, obstructed long-term socio-economic planning (Grindle, 1977:168–9). At the municipal level, too, rational technocratic planning was subordinated to short-term politics and clientelism: 'maintaining the system [had] priority over planning for development and patronage over expert performance' (Fagen and Tuohy, 1972:28).

In terms of its primary goals, survival and stability, the regime succeeded. The state in its Habsburg incarnation between around 1950 and 1970, was therefore stable, but not necessarily strong. Its strength remained conjectural and untested, since it was seeking less to achieve a purposive transformation of society than to control and contain relatively autonomous processes of change, processes associated with capital accumulation, import-substitution industrialization, and urbanization. Inasmuch as those changes strongly favoured privileged groups, which we may crudely label the bourgeoisie, the Mexican state now reflected, even represented, bourgeois interests to a substantial degree. It bought stability by deferring to those interests, by subtly subordinating others and by abandoning ambitious projects of reform.

The final implication of this argument is that the post-1970 crisis involves a departure from this, within its own terms, successful Habsburg project and a switch to Bourbon policies of intervention, reform and social engineering. The fact that these policies have been prosecuted by presidents of the left, like Echeverría, and of the right, like de la Madrid and Salinas, is no paradox given that Bourbonism defines not a position on a conventional left–right axis, but rather a style of state–civil society relationships. There is a broad consensus that the stable era of the Peace of the PRI and the economic miracle came to an end during the early 1970s. On the one hand, the political challenge of 1968 went against Habsburg principles; it was a statement of democratic principle by a group (students) which was less easily bought off by traditional concessions. The state responded, in part, by offering democracy *a gotitas*, via the political reform. But whereas carefully calibrated material concessions formed an integral part of Habsburg politicking – these were lampedusan changes, changes undertaken so that things would not have to change – the expansion of the political arena was a potentially risky innovation. Over time, it allowed the electoral challenge of both the PAN and the FDN/PRD to grow, threatening the historic monopoly of the PRI.

At the same time, the i.s.i (import-substitution industrialization) model's loss of dynamism encouraged a quest for economic reform. Echeverría looked to an enhanced state sector to rejuvenate a flagging economy; López Portillo looked to petroleum. Both placed considerable faith in technocrats; both hiked state spending to South American levels (Looney, 1985:10–11). When they failed, leaving a legacy of debt and disillusionment, the administrations of the 1980s began a more systematic political and economic restructuring which involved not only extensive economic liberalization but also calculated attacks on powerful vested interests, and a commitment, part rhetorical, part unavoidable, to greater political pluralism.

So far, economic liberalization has outrun political liberalization. But both represent important new commitments and both have proceeded more rapidly than many expert observers predicted. What is relevant to this analysis is that both also represent commitments to Bourbon-style policies: first, in the general sense of emphasizing the state's responsibility to reform an imperfect and sluggish society; second, and more specifically, by emulating the ancient Bourbon, and Porfirian, project of fostering a modern, rational, capitalism, married to a modern, rational state and bureaucracy (modern and rational are the buzzwords of contemporary Bourbonism). Bourbon economic policy classically involved the dismantling of inefficient corporatist institutions (guild, clerical and mercantile). Bourbon reformers, whether peninsular bureaucrats like Revillagigedo or Porfirian technocrats like Limantour, believed that ultimately the free market would prevail; but, for this to happen, the state had to create the appropriate conditions, it had to intervene, to the advantage of some groups and to the detriment of others. Now, too, state monopolies are cut back or abolished; the traditional unions are spurned; foreign investors are courted; revolutionary heirlooms, like Cananea, are sold off the wall. As in the past, the victims are not only the popular classes, whose living standards suffer, certainly in the short term (Bourbon policy is for the long haul), but also certain élites – the labour élite, for example, and businessmen who now face the stiff wind of international competition.

On the political front, too, Bourbon concerns for efficient, impersonal, responsible, honest government are now fashionable. The police, like the unions, are cleaned up; some prominent grafters are put behind bars. Rational technocracy rules, at least in theory. And with this goes a commitment to political pluralism, real in the case of Baja California, more rhetorical in that of Michoacán. The local caciques of the PRI are understandably worried and committed to the defeat of this reformist programme; unknowingly, they emulate the patrimonial officials of the 1790s, or the entrenched caciques of the 1890s, not to mention an earlier generation of *priísta* bosses. In the face of a vocal opposition, 'the national government time after time warns that the opposition speakers are to be treated with respect, which is all well and good for the people sitting in Mexico City. But the local dignitaries (sic), hearing themselves lambasted unmercifully, cannot muster the same detachment' (Kennedy, 1971:56). The quotation dates from the late 1950s, but it fits the early 1980s, too, when local *priísta* bosses obliged President de la Madrid to renege on his guarantee of free elections in the north. Again, in 1990, they strove for the defeat of the opposition in Michoacán. And the outcome, now as two centuries before, is a heightened resort to repression. As Lorenzo Meyer has commented, the current policies of top-down reform require an enhancement of presidential power and a deployment of armed force: against *La Quina*, against the *cardenista* dissidents of Michoacán. A strong executive, ready to use force, is an essential attribute of Bourbon government since, unlike its Habsburg counterpart, Bourbon government seeks to change society, to bully recalcitrant interests, to dominate rather than to mediate.

In short, the post-1970 crisis, a long, slowly unfolding crisis, has involved a shift in styles of government, a movement from left to right along the Habsburg–Bourbon continuum described above. Like previous shifts, notably that of the 1940s, this has resulted from a combination of internal and external pressures: the decline of the i.s.i. model, the progressive changes in Mexican society which have weakened the PRI's legitimacy, and the development of a new international economic order. Facing these pressures, the Mexican state had several options: one, continued Habsburg governance, threatened stagnation leading to ungovernability; another, the chosen Bourbon response, involves a more aggressive reform of Mexican society and politics, albeit a reform undertaken in the name of liberty and *laissez-faire*. But the latter carries risks too, the risks of popular resistance from below and élite obstruction ('the weapons of the strong') from above. Previous Bourbon experiments succeeded only partially and to the extent that the state could harness powerful social forces, as Díaz did with foreign investment or Cárdenas with syndicalism and agrarianism. If the state could not, if it sought reform by fiat, official blueprints tended to remain as empty statements of intent, like the socialist education programme.

In the current conjuncture, we may hypothesize, economic liberalization does evoke powerful support, both politically and ideologically. Influential interests favour liberalization and, no less important, the refrain 'there is no alternative' is readily sung even by those who may dislike aspects of current policy. Just as the *dirigisme* of the 1930s enjoyed widespread endorsement, encouraging the Bourbon interventions of the *cardenista* state, for example the railway and petroleum nationalizations, so the economic liberalism of the 1980s seems to command, if not consensus, at least majority opinion. Certainly the leftist opposition seems hard put to produce a coherent economic alternative, economic liberalization proceeds *faute de mieux*. In other words, the state's commitment to Bourbon-style economic restructuring possesses, at least for the moment, the necessary ideological clout. Political liberalization is another matter, however. True, there are numerous and vocal demands for it, as there have been for decades in Mexico. But the democratic lobby in Mexico is extremely diverse, and democracy means different things to its different members: to the *panista* entrepreneur, the *panista* Catholic activist, the *cardenista campesino*, the Juchiteco radical, the sindical insurgent, the liberal intellectual, the alternately *panista* and *cardenista* middle-class dissident in Baja California or the federal district. On the face of it, this is a formidable array and, especially in the north, it can put severe pressure on the regime. But the regime's commitment to democratization is questionable and might be cynically summed up as follows: democratization with continued PRI hegemony is highly desirable, but given a choice between the two, democratization is the lesser good. Even if national leaders genuinely favour democratic concessions, there is every reason to suppose that local PRI bosses will follow the ancient tradition of cacical obstructionism. In the political realm, the key players are at best lukewarm reformers, notwithstanding their gung-ho enthusiasm for economic restructuring. A diffuse demand for democratization confronts a political élite which is not only familiar with that ancient demand, but also perennially alert to the danger of losing the revolution, of abdicating power and inviting ungovernability. As the recent history of Chihuahua suggests, the PRI knows how to come off the ropes fighting.

In short, the vigour of economic reform is not matched by that of political reforms. Like previous Bourbon administrations, the current administration looks likely to press ahead with economic changes while sacrificing political reform on the altar of vested interests. If it does, the incumbent bosses may hang tough and survive, as the Bourbon *alcaldes mayores* did in the 1790s, or the Porfirian *caciques* did in the 1890s. In those cases, the resulting imbalance between aggressive economic rationalization on the one hand and abortive political rationalization on the other paved the way to social upheaval: the insurgency of 1810, the revolution of 1910.

Notes

1. After 1940 communists and *cardenistas* were purged from public offices and important trade union posts. In 1948–50 the government intervened to impose loyal bosses in the unions of railway workers, miners, teachers and oil workers. These actions became known as *charrazos* after the first of its kind in the railway workers' union where the imposed leader was known for dressing like a cowboy, *charro* in Spanish.
2. By chance rather than design, these categories roughly correspond to those adopted by Bennett and Sharpe (1985:38), where the authors isolate (a) the independent role of the state as an *actor* (b) the *interests* of the state and (c) the *power* which the state commands.
3. 'La actitud de los estados en el problema de la educación indígena (anexo al proyecto de organización del Departamento de Asuntos Indígenas', 31 Dec. 1935, in Archivo General de la Nación, Presidentes, Lázaro Cárdenas, 533.4/12.
4. However, Alemán's cabinet included a number of businessmen and, more recently, the PRI has sought to recuperate its position in the north (Chihuahua especially) by recruiting *empresarios*.
5. *Evolución del Estado Mexicano. Reestructuración, 1910–1940*. Mexico: Ediciones El Caballito, p.11. The same (anonymous) introduction appears in all three volumes of this work. Perhaps it should be mentioned, in mitigation, that this work originated in a series of radio programmes.
6. By populist I simply mean a regime which seeks actively to mobilize and to recruit support, not least on the basis of state patronage, that is, perks, public works and other material benefits.
7. Roughly, 1760–1810. The Bourbon dynasty, of course, came to power at

the beginning of the eighteenth century, but its reforms, initially implemented in Spain, did not begin to affect Mexico until the accession of Charles III (1759).

8. It would be interesting, but beyond the scope of this chapter, to compare the quantifiable indices of state-building in the countries of Latin America during the first half of the twentieth century. How unusual was Mexico's expansion of public employment and expenditure? Perhaps not very.
9. As most historians now recognize, the retreat from radicalism began under Cárdenas himself, in 1938–40; however, what for Cárdenas and the *cardenistas* was a temporary retrenchment became, under Avila Camacho and Alemán, an irrevocable trend.
10. Jalapa, of course, is hardly a typical community. As a state capital and administrative city, it possesses a distinct political character.

2· ELECTORAL REFORM AND THE PARTY SYSTEM, 1977–90

Silvia Gómez Tagle

During the past decade elections in Mexico have gone from being a more or less secondary aspect of political life to occupying a central place in the struggle for power. The changes in what can be called the *operación electoral* have been related both to the political system as defined by electoral legislation and to an increasingly urban-based, de-corporativized electorate.

The *operación electoral* has been defined by Cotteret and Emeri (1973:15–16) as 'a set of procedures, juridical and material acts which lead mainly to the designation of governors by the governed'. These authors add that electoral law is constituted by a set of rules which aim to classify citizens, differentiate between types of elections and regulate ballot counting:

> These rules vary over space and time, since they are a reflection of the nature of the political regimes which apply them, so it is very difficult to make a synthesis and it would be naive to think that every law works towards the perfection of the election of representatives. On the contrary, they appear to be the result of a series of accords between opposing forces and ideologies which, for short-term reasons or for principle, try to establish a particular meaning and reach. Electoral law simply registers the modified terms without breaking these accords.

From this perspective electoral legislation does not reflect the democratic ideal but the concrete conditions in which political struggle is carried out. It is the expression of a system of domination because it defines the rules in the struggle for political power, but it is also a space of negotiation which is constantly modified by the shifting balance of forces. The possibility of reaching agreements over the electoral rules and the capacity to change them over the years, without recourse to violence, is in my opinion the distinctive quality of democratic regimes.

Up until 1985, that is, even after the 1977 electoral reform, federal elections were more a space for political bargaining than a well-defined terrain of struggle for political power. Negotiations took place over the distribution of seats, and the votes which each candidate actually received was only one factor in determining the outcome. The results of elections have been dubious for a long time. However, since 1988 this fact has given rise to increasingly serious conflicts, sometimes accompanied by violence, which have undermined the legitimacy of the system.

When the 1977 reforms were introduced the left and right opposition forces were extremely fragmented, whereas the official party was strong. Today three important political parties represent currents which can be more or less differentiated by their programmes and ideologies. These are the Partido Acción Nacional (PAN), the Partido Revolucionario Institucional (PRI) and the Partido de la Revolución Democrática (PRD).

This chapter attempts to analyse the transformation of Mexican elections in the light of the party system and broader social change: to what extent has the system acquired the flexibility of a democratic system? or does the very rigidity of a political system based on a predominant single party continue to impede the changes in the electoral legislation which are called for by the social changes of the past 30 years?

The political reform of 1977

The 1977 reform marked the beginning of a period of change which went beyond the party system to affect the form of the state, culminating in the recomposition of the governing bloc which had ruled since 1930. This process clearly responded to multiple pressures which can be traced to the social movements of the 1970s. Some of the changes which may have motivated the interior minister, Jesús Reyes Heroles, to propose the political reform in 1977 include the following:

- the exhaustion of the development model which had allowed for growth and stability between 1954 and 1970
- the political crisis of 1968
- the conflicts between Echeverría and the business sector, which led to the formation of a new right that was independent of the PRI
- the support of businessmen for PAN
- the tensions created with the US government by Echeverría's populist and nationalist discourse
- the recurrent appearance of armed leftwing groups in rural and urban areas
- the erosion of the ties between the mass organizations and the official party.[1]

The political reform was offered as a safety valve for a series of social tensions which had been building up and had not found channels of expression. The explicit aim was to allow the participation of minority opposition groups in a legally recognized institutional space, thereby avoiding the reawakening of *México bronco*, while simultaneously assuring that the strength of the state and the dominance of the PRI would not be affected through free and fair elections and alternation in power.[2]

The political reform introduced changes in three main areas:

(i) an amnesty which allowed many ex-guerrillas and political prisoners to participate in political life;
(ii) the electoral reform; and
(iii) the incorporation of the 'right to information' in the constitution.

For the *operación electoral*, the constitutional reform of 1977 was the most serious and extensive in recent decades. Seventeen articles of the constitution were changed and a new regulatory law was passed, the Ley Federal de Organizaciones Políticas y Procesos Electorales (Federal Law of Political Organizations and Electoral Processes, LFOPPE). The most important of these changes can be categorized as follows: the electorate and voter registration; political organizations; electoral bodies; the electoral process; and electoral disputes.

The progress of political democracy has historically been based on universal suffrage and secret voting. In Mexico, theoretically, these two principles have long been recognized and the vote was formally given to women in 1952, while in 1970 the voting age was reduced to

18 years. From this perspective the national electorate is defined in very broad terms.[3] The problem, however, has not been the formal definition of voters but the ways in which voter registration is carried out, since in order to vote each citizen requires a credential and to have her or his name included in the polling station's register.

Until 1982 it appeared that official policy consisted of registering all those citizens who requested it. As many do not even possess a birth certificate, proof of identity or residence was not demanded. Sometimes the size of the electoral register was increased by the inclusion of fictitious names in order to create the false impression of a high voter turnout. But from 1982 onwards registration began to be limited to areas where the opposition was believed to be strongest. Government officers in charge often erased the names of people included in the electoral rolls for districts where it was likely that another candidate besides that of the PRI would win. Credentials were often deliberately withheld from opposition supporters, and there were frequent cases of official voter credentials being used by PRI supporters to vote several times in the same election. As one PAN militant noted, 'in Mexico the voter credentials used in elections are always authentic because all the credentials have been issued by the Federal Voter Registry; what are inexistent and "false" are the citizens who receive them.' A citizen's right which is clearly stipulated by the law is in practice insufficient to guarantee a free vote.

Something similar occurs with the other principles of political democracy, that is, the secret character of the vote and the vote count. The law establishes norms which are not met in practice. The root of the problem lies in the dominance for over 70 years of a political party which began life as the project of the revolutionary group which came to power following the armed struggle of 1910–17. It has been this symbiosis of the PRI and the government which has allowed for the manipulation of electoral results. LFOPPE opened up new possibilities for the development of political organizations, contributing to a very different panorama in 1991 which questioned the relevance of the official party.

Political parties were recognized as public interest groups and were therefore given some benefits: government funding to carry out electoral campaigns; access to the mass media; guarantees concerning their functions; and a new option for civil organizations known as 'political association'.

The Federal Electoral Commission (CFE) was created and

entrusted with the running of the whole electoral system, with equal participation from the parties, two representatives from the national congress (elected by the PRI's majority vote); a notary elected by the Colegio de Notarios (also controlled by the PRI); and the minister of the interior, elected by the president. The local and district electoral commissions were to be chosen by a free draw. Until 1985 this structure of the CFE allowed the government and the PRI to retain power because they had the support of the Partido Popular Socialista (PPS) and the Partido Auténtico de la Revolución Mexicana (PARM) and frequently that of the Partido Socialista de los Trabajadores (PST). However, it is noteworthy that this balance of forces changed so dramatically that by 1986 the PRI's need for assurances gave rise to new changes in the legislation.

These changes turned out to be so important that, without them, in 1988 the PRI would have lost control of the CFE and with it the elections themselves. The free draw to select polling station and district officers allowed for a minimum level of impartiality if only because it introduced an element of chance.

Likewise, the LFOPPE defined (see Articles 235–41) for the first time norms to guide many aspects of the electoral process and the resolution of disputed ballots, in an attempt to avoid irregularities. It included the principle of jurisprudence in the assessment of elections and made it possible for the Supreme Court to obtain information concerning elections and to revise the resolutions of the electoral colleges, although how obligatory their recommendations should be was not made clear.

Changes in the *operación electoral* have responded to pressures from emerging social forces, but it should be remembered that, independently, the political reform also set in motion a series of changes which encouraged the emergence of new political actors. We should therefore see the interaction between society, the state and the party system, passing through the electoral system, as a dialectical process of mutual determination.

The most important change in this respect was that the LFOPPE stipulated in Articles 31–4 that a party's registration was conditional on the proportion of votes it received, unlike before when the decision rested with the electoral authorities. Parties had to poll 1.5 per cent of the total valid national vote in order to continue participating in future elections and to have a right to the distribution of seats by proportional representation (PR).

For the first time the right to participate in elections was opened up to political forces which had been excluded since the 1940s, such as the parties of the radical left (the Partido Comunista Mexicano, PCM) and the radical right (Partido Demócrata Mexicano, PDM, formerly Partido Fuerza Popular de los Sinarquistas), and to the new socialist parties which emerged after 1968.[4]

The Partido Social Demócrata (PSD) took part only in the 1982 elections because its share of the vote was just 0.20 per cent. PARM also lost its registration in 1982 because it only gained 1.34 per cent in the elections for deputies by majority vote. This is a unique case since, despite the low vote it received in 1982 and its highly irregular distribution (concentrated in the federal district, Tamaulipas, state of Mexico and Veracruz), the CFE granted PARM definitive registration, allowing it to participate in the 1985 federal elections. It is possible that in this period PARM had the backing of the president, which would explain the decision of the CFE. Similarly, the PDM and the Partido Revolucionario de los Trabajadores (PRT) were granted registration in 1990 despite receiving less than the required vote in 1988.

Whereas in single-member districts the only winner is the party which receives most votes and the rest are eliminated, in a system of PR almost all parties, even those receiving a relatively low share of the vote, gain some representation in parliament. In Mexico PR allowed almost all parties to participate in the Chamber of Deputies. After 1977 100 out of a total of 400 deputies were elected in this way, increasing to 200 in 1986. Between 1961 and 1979 only PAN had won 15 per cent of the vote (in the 1973 federal elections) and it was the opposition party which won most single-member districts and party seats, a forerunner of PR (see Table 2.1).[5]

In 1977 the principle of PR was introduced for the first time, although it applied to only 100 of the 400 deputyships. It was not until 1983, with the constitutional reform of Article 115, that it was extended to the state congresses and most municipal governments. But its implementation has been subject to constitutional norms and the electoral laws of state governments and has sometimes suffered serious set-backs (see Madrazo, 1985). PR has never been extended to the senate, although this has been a constant demand of the opposition.

Initially there were three multi-state territorial divisions for the election of deputies by PR. They were increased to four in 1982 and

Table 2.1: Federal elections prior to the political reform of 1977 (percentage vote)[1]

Year	Election	PAN	PRI	PARM	PPS	Others[2]	Turnout[3]
1961	Deputies	8	90	–	1	1	68
1964	Deputies	12	86	1	1	–	67
	Senators	11	88	–	1	–	66
	President	11	88	–	1	–	69
1967	Deputies	12	83	1	3	–	62
1970	Deputies	14	80	1	1	4	64
	Senators	14	80	–	1	5	64
	President	12	85	1	1	2	65
1973	Deputies	15	70	2	4	10	60
1976	Deputies	8	80	3	3	6	62
	Senators	7	80	1	5	6	65
	President	–	88	2	4	7	69

Source: Silvia Gómez Tagle, 1990a.
1. Proportion of votes received by each party; 2. Includes votes for unregistered candidates; 3. Proportion of electorate which voted.

five for the elections of 1985 and 1988. The demarcation of both the 300 simple majority districts and of these multi-state divisions allowed for the manipulation of the electoral results since it combined areas of high PRI support with those favourable to the opposition. For example, in 1985 it was clear that PAN strongholds in the north were distributed between three different multi-state divisions, while the federal district was divided into two. In spite of everything, the possibility of winning elections through the PR system stimulated competition and the development of opposition parties, especially when the system began to be extended to state congressional and municipal elections. This appears to have benefited mainly the development of the opposition in some specific regions; for example, in 1983 PAN received 65 per cent of votes in Chihuahua, winning in the major cities and towns: the capital, Ciudad Juárez, Ciudad Camargo, Casas Grandes, Delicias, Parral de Hidalgo, Meoqui and Saucillo. Also in Chihuahua, the Partido Socialista Unificado de Mexico (PSUM) won in Ignacio Zaragoza and the PST in Cuauhtémoc (see Gomez Tagle, 1987: Table 8). Between 1980 and 1983 PAN won in the capital of Durango, Monclova (Coahuila) and

Hermosillo (Sonora). PSUM won in Juchitán and Tlacolulita (Oaxaca) and in Alcozauca (Guerrero) (see Orlando Espíritu, 1984).

The political parties

The PPS and PARM have participated in elections since the 1950s but their position has almost always been subordinated to that of the PRI. In 1974, on the left, the PST emerged with a new electoral project which was initially quite independent of the government. In the same period the PCM also tried to engage in electoral struggle and in 1976 put forward Valentín Campa as its presidential candidate and succeeded in organizing a national campaign. Sinarquismo, an extreme rightwing popular movement, decided to return to political activity with the PDM.[6] But in 1976 neither the PST, PCM nor PDM was able to participate in the elections and PAN chose to abstain, which meant that the only official presidential candidate belonged to the PRI. Since 1977 the situation has been totally different due to the increasingly important presence of parties of all ideological positions in electoral contests. In the period 1977–88 the right has only had PAN and PDM to turn to in elections, unlike the left which has participated through a variety of parties.

The development of PAN in the past decade has been closely linked to the politicization of businessmen and the urban middle classes. This process accelerated following the nationalization of the banks which, on the one hand, sharpened conflicts between the PRI government and the private sector, while, on the other, provoking a sharp fall in income for a large part of the urban middle classes (see Loaeza, 1987).

There are many conservative groups which have organized around a specific set of issues. Some very radical and openly anti-communist ones emerged in 1979 when the PCM was granted registration. Others directly represent economic interests, such as the Consejo Coordinador Empresarial (CCE), which emerged in the 1970s during the clashes with the Echeverría government. However, none has tried to establish political parties, preferring instead to support PAN.

The PDM was able to participate in elections thanks to the 1977 reforms, since it had previously been unsuccessful in its petitions for registration. It is a rightwing party with support of popular sectors and, apart from occasional conjunctures, has never identified itself with PAN. It has remained faithful to its original *sinarquista* traditions with all their contradictions: in favour of private property but against the large estates; democratic in name but militaristic and authoritarian in practice (see Aguilar Valenzuela and Zermeño Padilla, 1989). Following its registration, the PDM grew rapidly and increased its electoral support from 284,000 votes in 1979 to 485,000 in 1985. But in 1988 its tally fell to 235,000 votes and it failed to win 1.5 per cent of the ballot in any of the elections, causing it to lose its registration (tables 2.1 and 2.2). This situation can be attributed, on the one hand, to internal conflicts which have damaged the party's image and alienated its active members and, on the other, to the fact that it has always been geographically limited to the Altos de Jalisco, San Luis Potosí, el Bajío and Michoacán. Nevertheless, the moderate position held by its leaders during the disputed 1988 elections was rewarded by the government in 1990 when the PDM regained its registration.[7]

From 1979 onwards the possibility of 'conditional registration' allowed into the electoral arena almost all the leftwing currents and groups which wished to form political parties. Registration was given to the PCM and PST in 1979, to the PSD and PRT in 1982, and to the Partido Mexicano de los Trabajadores (PMT) in 1985 (the last time a party received 'conditional registration').

In response to the fragmented nature of the electoral left the PCM promoted its unification. In 1982 the PSUM was created as the result of a fusion between the PCM and various political groups without electoral registration, such as the Movimiento de Acción Popular (MAP) (see Ibarra, 1985). There followed a series of new attempts to unite with other groups (even the PPS was an enthusiastic promotor of left unity), but in practice there were problems, despite programmatic and tactical points of convergence, because of the essentially incompatible interests of different leaders. Nevertheless, in 1987 a further step towards unity was achieved with the creation of the PMS, which included the two registered parties PSUM and PMT, together with unregistered groups and organizations. The convergence of the PSUM and PMT was especially important since every party with electoral registration has what we might call 'greater political capital', making unity between them more difficult. The creation of the PMS has been the only experience of its kind in contemporary Mexico. On other occasions, the 'unity of the left' has implied only conjunctural alliances of two or more parties for electoral ends, such as the Frente Democrático Nacional (FDN) in 1988, or the incorporation of unregistered parties and groups into parties which did possess registration.

Table 2.2: Federal elections after political reform (percentage vote)[1]

	1979	1982			1985	1988		
	Deputies	Deputies	Senators	President	Deputies	Deputies	Senators	President
PAN	11	18	16	16	16	18	18	17
PDM	2	2	2	2	3	1	1	1
PRI	70	69	65	67	65	51	51	50
PARM	2	1	1	1	2	6	7	6
PPS	3	2	2	2	2	9	9	11
PST/PFCRN	2	2	1	1	2	9	9	11
PCM/PSUM/PMS	5	4	4	3	3	4	4	4
PRT	–	1	1	2	1	1	–	–
PMT[2]		–			2			
Others[3]	6	–	8	5	–	–	–	–
Turnout[4]	49	67	71	75	51	48	48	50

Source: Silvia Gómez Tagle, 1990a.

1. Proportion of votes received by each party; 2. 1985 was the only year in which PMT participated in federal elections. PSD participated in the 1982 elections only but did not gain any seats; 3. Includes annulled votes and votes for unregistered candidates; 4. Proportion of electorate which voted.

The PPS and PST define themselves as leftwing, but in reality they have sought alliances with the PRI and only in some local elections have they managed to mount real opposition. In general they have acted more as sources of legitimation for the government-controlled electoral system.

It is difficult to distinguish the programme and principles of the PARM from those of the PRI, although changes within the ruling party have distanced it from the 'postulates of the Mexican Revolution', which PARM defends without really being a leftwing party. In elections during the 1980s PARM remained subordinated to the PRI, appearing as an opposition party only in very localized situations, such as in the municipal elections in northern Tamaulipas. As a result, it lost its registration in 1982 when it failed to win 1.5 per cent of the national vote.

In spite of the fact that until 1988 the 'revolutionary bloc', represented by the PRI and its allies, (PPS, PARM and PST), remained united, the signs of its decomposition began to be seen in increasingly adverse results in the federal elections of 1982 and 1985, the presidential election of 1982 and in multiple state and municipal elections. We can therefore say that since the beginning of the 1980s the elements of the 1988 crisis were already present. The electoral losses for the PRI can be attributed to a series of factors which relates both to the party's internal problems and to changes in society as a whole.

The changes which have occurred within the PRI since 1980 have been initiated mainly by the president of the republic, since he is also the party's principal leader. Since the presidency of López Portillo important changes have been taking place in the criteria used by the executive to recruit PRI candidates and government officers, which have eroded the ties between the mass organizations and the party. Corruption, economic crisis and declining incomes have added to the problems and accelerated the weakening of the PRI while favouring the development of independent social forces (see Gamboa Villafranca, 1988).

From 1982 onwards this process acquired new dimensions. Structural change and economic reconversion deprived PRI leaders of necessary negotiating resources to maintain clientelism. In terms of clientelistic relations we can say that the austerity policies dried up the spoils which could have been distributed through the system of local bosses or corporate leaders. For this reason administrative modernization and privatization of state companies have shown themselves to be incompatible with a political system based on a single party which is closely tied to the government.[8]

The weakness of the PRI's mass organizations (especially the labour and popular sectors, but also the peasant sector) has been revealed by their inability to oppose the executive's austerity policies and particularly those aspects which undermine the party's negotiating capacity *vis-à-vis* the members. Some PRI union bosses, such as Arturo Romo, who in 1980–82 sought less socially damaging solutions to the crisis, failed in their attempt to influence the leadership because the absence of union democracy stopped them from mobilizing the workers in support of their economic projects. Since 1980 there have been innumerable occasions when labour leaders have protested about the negative impact of austerity policies on their members' wages, only to back down and end up contradicting themselves by supporting the government's economic policy.[9]

The IMF-imposed austerity measures also led to the emergence of opposition from some leaders and intellectuals linked to the PRI, whose search for alternative solutions culminated in the formation of the Corriente Democrática (CD). Many members of the PRI exhausted all institutional channels to achieve democratization of the party in order to recuperate the legacy of the revolution. These dissidents included Cuauhtémoc Cárdenas, Porfirio Múñoz Ledo, Ifigenia Martínez, Leonel Durán, Castillo Mena and Leonel Godoy.

This recuperation did not mean a return to the programmes and practices of 70 years earlier, but the exact opposite: the democratization of the party implied the real possibility to renew leaders at all levels in order to make room for the emergent Mexico of the 1980s.

In 1987 the issue of the presidential succession created a confrontation between those wishing to continue with the traditional method of electing the official candidate, that is, selection by the out-going president, and those who wanted democratic elections. When the attempt of the latter failed the CD put forward Cuauhtémoc Cárdenas as its nominee. PARM was the first to give its support, while the PPS and PST followed soon after. In late 1987 the latter changed its name to that of Partido Frente Cardenista de Reconstrucción Nacional (PFCRN), to take advantage of the name of Cárdenas. Together, these groups formed the Frente Democrático Nacional (FDN) and were later joined by the Movimiento de Acción Socialista (MAS), dissidents from the PRT and other leftwing organizations. Finally, just prior to the July 1988 elections the PMS presidential candidate Heberto Castillo withdrew from the contest to support the single candidacy of Cárdenas.

The 1988 election results

Before analysing Mexican electoral data we must remember that they are generally unreliable. The manipulation of results in accordance with the PRI's wishes has been a common practice for many years. This has been possible because of the PRI's close relationship with the government (allowing it to control the electoral process) and the sporadic nature of electoral competition prior to 1988.

A first conclusion which can be drawn from Tables 2.1 and 2.2 is that both electoral participation and the PRI vote fell between 1961 and 1988. The highest turnout and the greatest PRI support have been recorded in isolated regions where opposition parties have little presence. We can thus talk of an important difference between elections in urban areas (for example, Mexico City, Monterrey, Guadalajara, Tijuana, Cuidad Juárez) and predominantly rural areas like Chiapas, Oaxaca and Campeche. In the first category there has been a lower turnout and lower PRI support since the 1970s, while in the second category the PRI continued to gain much support until 1982 (see Gómez Tagle, 1990a: Vol. 1, Table 7).

At national level, too, voting in federal elections reveals some erratic figures. In 1976 the turnout for the presidential election registered a massive increase to 69 per cent of the electorate. By contrast, in 1979, in the first elections for deputies after the political reform, participation fell to 49 per cent. In 1982 it again jumped incredibly to 67 per cent for deputies, 71 per cent for senators and 75 per cent for president. These are the highest figures for voter turnout since 1961 (Tables 2.1 and 2.2). It appears that despite the absence of electoral competition the government wanted to give an image of great electoral legitimacy through a very high level of participation.

It is strange that Mexicans should have been such enthusiastic voters precisely when there were no options to choose from, that is, when their votes counted for nothing, while in 1988, with three strong candidates, participation should have fallen to 50 per cent, the lowest ever registered in a presidential election (Table 2.2). In that year a study was made of the returns of 29,999 polling stations, out of a total of 54,000, whose results were made known. It was found that the candidate of the PRI, Carlos Salinas de Gortari, received a large proportion of his votes in rural areas, in polling stations which claimed to have registered a 100 per cent turnout, of which the PRI won between 90 and 100 per cent support. On the other hand, there were many stations where Salinas did not win more than 27 per cent of the vote (Barberán *et al.*, 1988:37).

If the vote count in 1988 had excluded the results of those districts in which fraud was most denounced by the opposition then the outcome of the presidential election would have been very different: around 38 per cent for Cárdenas and 35 per cent for Salinas or vice versa. In any case these are only approximate figures since the CFE did not provide disaggregated data for each polling station. In spite of the impossibility of knowing the exact result, it is less clear that Salinas won 51 per cent of the vote; it appears that the votes he needed to make up this figure were assigned to him by electoral officers.

Although the figures are inexact, a comparison of Tables 2.1 and 2.2 gives some idea of the differences between federal elections before and after the political reform of 1977. In the latter period there has been a marked fall in voter participation and a decline in support for the PRI. The leftwing vote was fragmented among the various parties which had gained conditional registration. In 1985 six parties of the broad left, the PPS, PARM, PCM, PST, PMT and PRT won the same proportion of the vote (12 per cent) as the first four had won in 1979. In sum, this broad left vote did not benefit from the general increase in voting between 1979 and 1985. By contrast, the FDN alliance of 1988 helped its candidate win 30 per cent of the poll, even according to official figures. If we consider the votes for each party in 1988, the PPS and PFCRN quadrupled their 1985 tallies, PARM tripled its share and the PMS won more than in 1985, returning to its figure for 1982. This implies that the candidacy of Cárdenas introduced a new dynamic to the elections.

PAN had participated in elections since the 1940s but responded with renewed enthusiasm to the 1977 reforms. Between 1977 and 1987 it benefited more than any other party from the changes, growing as an organization and winning several elections at local and federal levels. In elections for federal deputies in 1982 it received 17.52 per cent of the vote, around the same as it would in 1988 (17.97 per cent), but it won only one deputyship from single-member districts, with 50 by proportional representation. The increase in support for PAN in Chihuahua raised the possibility that it might win the governorship in the 1986 elections. As noted above, in 1983 it won the most important municipalities in the state. The gubernatorial election was perhaps the first election since the political reform where the PRI saw its control of a state being seriously threatened. Likewise, it was the first time that the government had tried to justify electoral fraud on the grounds of national security.

In 1988 PAN won 38 single-member districts and 63 PR seats (Table 2.3). The different outcome, despite a similar proportion of the vote, can be explained partly by the decline of the PRI vote, which allowed the PAN to win more seats from single-member districts. Additionally, PAN benefited in the distribution of PR seats from the elimination of two small rivals, the PDM and the PRT. The biggest change, however, in the 1988 elections was produced by the presidential candidacy of Cárdenas. The FDN, comprising PARM, PPS, PFCRN and PMS pulled many votes away from the PRI and won in many districts and several states. Nevertheless, due to each party presenting its own candidates, thereby fragmenting the vote, there were many cases where the FDN did not win.

The FDN or one of its constituent parties won deputyships in only 29 single-member districts and the election of senators for the federal district and Michoacán. Yet it won 110 PR deputyships because its total vote was much higher than that of PAN (Table 2.3).

The PRI won only 234 single-member seats and lost one other which went over to the FDN, ending up with 233 deputies. As a result the PRI had to rely on Article 54 of the constitution, which had been modified in 1986, in order to keep its majority in the Chamber of Deputies by gaining another 27 seats through PR, making up the 260 needed for an absolute majority. Only in this way could it retain control of the electoral college, without which it could not have ratified Carlos Salinas de Gortari as president-elect.

Changes in the *operación electoral*, 1986–90

In 1986 the civic movement of Chihuahua 'in defence of the vote' led to a convergence between right and left parties around the demand for guarantees concerning free elections. However, in the same year, following a series of public meetings to address the issue of 'political renewal', the president imposed a new electoral law, the Federal Electoral Code, whose characteristics pointed in the opposite direction. In some ways it was a better-organized law than the LFOPPE but it reinforced executive control over the electoral process. With hindsight it appears a prophetic law, as though de la Madrid knew

Table 2.3: Federal elections after political reform. Deputies elected by party

	1979			1982			1985			1988		
	SM[1]	PR[2]	Total	SM[1]	PR[2]	Total	SM[1]	PR[2]	Total	SM[1]	PR[2]	Total
PAN	4	39	43	1	50	51	9	50	59	38	63	101
PDM	–	10	–	–	12	12	–	12	12	–	*	–
PRI	291	–	291	298	–	298	289	–	289	233	27	260
PARM	–	12	12	–	*	–	2	9	11	–	–	–
PPS	–	11	11	–	10	10	–	11	11	–	–	–
PST/PFCRN	–	10	10	–	11	11	–	12	12	–	–	–
PCM/PSUM/PMS	–	18	18	–	17	17	–	12	12	–	–	–
FDN (1988 alliance of PARM, PPS, PFCRN, PMS)										29	110	139
PRT	–	–	–	–	*	–	–	6	6	–	*	–
PMT	–	–	–	–	–	–	–	6	6	–	–	–
Annulled	–	–	–	1	–	–	–	–	–	–	–	–
Total	300	100	400	300	100	400	300	100	400	300	200	500

Source: Silvia Gómez Tagle, 1990a

Abbreviations:

1. SM = deputies from single-member districts; 2. PR = deputies by proportional representation.

* Party receiving less than 1.5 per cent of the vote, the minimum required to receive share of seats by PR.

what was about to happen in 1988; with the old legislation Salinas would not have become president. The constitutional reform of 1986 and the Código Federal Electoral (Federal Electoral Code) made the following provisions:

- The authority of the federal executive was strengthened through the designation of presidents of every electoral body from the CFE to the polling station.[10]
- The PRI's participation in the CFE and all electoral bodies was increased by a ruling which linked representation to share of the vote in the previous election. As a result in 1988 the PRI had 16 representatives in the CFE.[11]
- The concept of governability was given constitutional status for the first time. This guaranteed that a party would have an absolute majority in the Chamber of Deputies although it received less than 51 per cent of the votes, or less than 51 per cent of deputies from single-member districts.[12]
- As a complement to the governability clause the number of deputies' votes by PR was increased to two hundred. However, whereas these seats had been previously reserved for parties with less than 20 simple-majority deputies, now the PRI was included in the distribution of PR seats.[13]
- Prior to 1986 the process of checking the voting figures could only be done at the polling stations. Results were annulled if it was shown that ballot papers had been tampered with or if the *actas* (the official record of the vote) had been altered. From 1986 onwards the law stipulated that 'when the results of the *actas* do not correspond to the votes, or when the *actas* are missing, the vote count will be carried out again by the district committee'.[14] This apparently harmless provision meant that it was sufficient to control the 300 district committee presidents, named by the minister of the interior, in order to carry out the vote count in accordance with the needs of the PRI.
- 'Conditional registration' was abolished with the aim of stopping new parties from competing in elections.

In spite of these measures there were two important positive changes in 1986. These were the establishment of the Tribunal of Electoral Disputes (TRICOEL) and the Assembly of Representatives for the federal district. The former was meant to be an autonomous body whose function was to ratify election results from a 'jurisdictional' rather than a 'political' perspective.[15] Yet in 1988 it was shown that the TRICOEL was totally incapable of conferring legitimacy on a corrupt electoral process. There are several reasons why the tribunal was unable to act: first, the results in about 80 per cent of the 300 electoral districts were contested by one party or another, obliging the TRICOEL to try and get hold of around 240 electoral packages from the same number of district committees; second, since parties and citizens lacked the necessary legal instruments to prove the fraud, it was impossible to ratify properly the electoral results. Among other lacunae, the law does not state under what conditions parties can call for an annulment of elections for president, senators or deputies elected by PR. Only in the case of deputies for single-member districts are there rules to assess the vote, but even these are inadequate; third, the decisions taken by the TRICOEL were not binding for the electoral colleges, making any 'jurisdictional' assessment useless (see Gómez Tagle, 1990b).

The inhabitants of the federal district have been deprived of their right to elect their local government by the president of the republic since it is he who appoints the capital's mayor, or *regente*. Due to increasing popular pressure for participation, the Assembly of Representatives was created in 1986. However, it held no legislative power and was instead limited to the role of a consultative body of the mayor. As a result, its functions have been severely restricted and the population of the federal district is still without full citizens' rights.[16]

In sum, a series of factors helped the PRI win a majority in the Chamber of Deputies on 1 September 1988 and, seven days later, allow the chamber, in its role as electoral college, to ratify the triumph of Salinas, namely: the vertical structure of electoral authorities from the minister of interior to the polling station; the possibility for district committees to 'legally' alter electoral results; the power which the electoral colleges held over the TRICOEL and the CFE in the ratification of results; the governability clause introduced into Article 54 of the constitution; and other extra-legal forms of ensuring PRI victories.

The conflicts generated by the ratification of the results of the 1988 presidential elections cast doubt on the results' legitimacy. For this reason Salinas immediately offered a new political reform. For the third time since 1977, parties, organizations and citizens were called upon to give their opinion on what this reform should consist of.

But in the first nine months of 1989 no agreement was reached between the PRI and the other parties. For the first time in its history the PRI lacked the two-thirds majority needed to make constitutional reforms, obliging it to enter into negotiations. However, there was a limit to the president's and the PRI's willingness to negotiate, that is, the objective of maintaining control over the electoral bodies and guaranteeing the PRI a majority in the Chamber of Deputies after the federal elections of August 1991. Salinas was apparently trying to recuperate electoral legitimacy without running the risk of the PRI losing its majority in Congress.[17]

Finally, the PAN decided to vote in support of the constitutional reform in exchange for a commitment from Salinas that elections would be free and fair. The PAN wanted the president to sign a letter of intent to formalize this agreement but Salinas, the minister of the interior and the PRI's parliamentary group refused to sign and in practice have not respected the commitment. In the new law there are no guarantees that the vote will be respected in the future. This will continue to depend on the will of the president.[18]

The constitutional reform was passed by the PRI, PPS, PARM, PFCRN and PAN in October 1989. During the first six months of 1990 the parliamentary groups of each party negotiated how the new regulatory electoral law should look. Some points of agreement had been reached by the PAN, PRD and other parties but not with the PRI. However, on 14 July 1990 the PRI put forward its proposal for a Federal Code of Electoral Institutions and Procedures (COFIPE). With only minor changes, the COFIPE was approved the next day by important sections of the PAN, PPS, PARM and PFCRN. The only groups to vote against it were the PRD, a dissident faction of the PAN, the independent deputies and about ten members of the PFCRN.[19]

The following changes were the most significant ones introduced by the COFIPE:

- The governability clause of Article 54 was modified, creating two options if no party were to win an absolute majority:

  (a) the party which wins 35 per cent or more of the vote will be given as many seats as necessary to make up an absolute majority and if it wins over 35 per cent it will be awarded two seats for every additional percentage point. In this way, with just 40 per cent of the vote the PRI could end up with 260 seats in 1991.

(b) if no party wins 35 per cent of the vote or of majority-elected deputies, seats are to be distributed in proportion to the votes for each party. This provision was introduced by the PAN to defend proportional representation in an extreme case. Over-representation of a party which wins 35 per cent persists, however, which means a serious regression for democratization.

- A supposedly autonomous Federal Electoral Institute was set up. It was to be presided over by the minister of the interior, six magistrates (proposed by the president), two representatives from each chamber (one from the majority party and one from the opposition minority), and representatives of the parties in proportion to their share of the vote (with a maximum of four). Thus, in 1991 the president could control the institute through the minister of the interior, the six magistrates, the two majority representatives from the Chamber of Deputies and the Chamber of Senators and the four PRI representatives.[20]
- There was much discussion over how the magistrates of the COFIPE and the new Federal Electoral Tribunal were to be elected. The PRI finally won sufficient approval for the following mechanisms. The president puts forward a list of twice the number of magistrates to be elected. The Chamber of Deputies elects them on the basis of a two-thirds majority, which means the PRI must negotiate with other parties. But if no agreement is reached the magistrates will be chosen by a free draw from the list of names given by the president.[21]
- Similar mechanisms for the selection of polling-station officers caused much controversy and constituted one of the objections raised by the PRD. A sample population would be drawn from the electoral register and, after a long period of training, the district committee presidents would choose the 'ideal candidates'. These functionaries are at the same time part of a bureaucratic structure dependent on the federal executive, which means that polling-station officers would ultimately remain under the control of the president.[22]
- The district committees were allowed to keep their power to carry out a second vote count and modify the results, as they did in 1988.
- The district committees were given greater power to issue *constancias de mayoría* ('certificates of majority vote') to the deputies-elect. In 1988 this function belonged to the Federal Electoral Commis-

sion, which permitted public opinion to know about voting irregularities in many districts and to criticize the official results.

- Limits were imposed on the possibility of establishing electoral coalitions by a series of requirements in order to gain registration. In an attempt to avoid a repetition of what happened with Cuauhtémoc Cárdenas in 1988, the new law prohibited parties from supporting a candidate who had already been registered by another party.[23]
- One positive aspect is that the new Federal Electoral Tribunal will have more important functions than those of TRICOEL. Four regional bodies were to be established with more resources. The type of proof required for annulling elections was more clearly defined and the electoral colleges are now obliged to obey the decisions of the tribunal or, if they wish to change them, they must win a two-thirds majority in the Federal Electoral College. Yet, at the same time, the autonomy of the tribunal is dependent on the president, since he selects the magistrates.[24]
- COFIPE consolidates and regulates the bureaucratic structure of the Federal Electoral Institute, establishing channels for top-down control from the president to the polling-station officers. With no supervision from political parties, a professional bureaucracy is being created to serve the state by administering electoral processes. Until now the National Agency for Voter Registration was the only electoral body with its own patrimony and full-time staff. It has been efficient in managing the electoral register but the experiences of the past decade suggest that this efficiency has been at the service of the PRI. There is, therefore, no reason to expect that this new bureaucracy, provided with wider powers, will be the defender of democracy, since the staff will be selected by the same *priísta* functionaries.[25]

The constitutional reform and the COFIPE also have some positive aspects, such as access to information, increased funding for parties and more clearly defined functions for electoral bodies. The principle of 'conditional registration' was re-established for new parties wishing to participate in elections. This provision has the advantage of not restricting the party system to the most important options, that is PRI, PAN and PRD. New parties will participate, possibly factions which leave the main three. There are different opinions regarding this measure. Some believe that it is a government strategy to divide the opposition; others argue that it is preferable that opposition unity be achieved through political will rather than as a result of legal restrictions.[26]

At the end of this process of negotiations Abel Vicencio Tovar, parliamentary leader of the PAN, justified his party's position, saying that the new law was the best that could be won because 'it is not possible to achieve democracy from one day to the next' (*La Jornada*, 25 July 1990:9).

The experience of the PAN in Baja California was a positive development. The triumph of its candidate for the state governorship was recognized without difficulty. The experience of the PRD has been very different because its victories have not always been recognized, as in the elections for local deputies and mayors in Michoacán, for mayors in Guerrero, and in many other states since 1988.

In Guerrero and Michoacán violence continued for several months, culminating in the intervention of the army in the first week of April 1990 in order to impose, via repression, the official election results. In the first two years of the Salinas government there was a serious contradiction between the authorities' violent response to PRD victories in various states and the recognition of the PAN victory in Baja California.

Difficulties of the transition

The complex process of restructuring in the PRI and the recomposition of the left since 1982 still continue to pose problems. Since 1988 the PRI has been trying to recover its social bases of support and political allies and has had some success with the PFCRN, PPS and PARM. However, serious conflicts continue to be seen within the party, as manifested at the 14th National Assembly in September 1990. On 3 March 1990 Salinas invited all *priístas* to work for true democratization of the party. Yet when the difficult moment arrived, rather than accept the proposal to select the presidential candidate democratically, Salinas refused to give up the right to name his successor, a right which his predecessors enjoyed. In this way one, among several, limits to democratizing the PRI was revealed.[27]

Looking at the electoral prospects of the largest political groups in the past decade, the right has found in the PAN a party which could represent its interests and turned it into an effective option at the local level. Chihuahua in 1986 and Baja California in 1989 are just two examples of this process.

The left, through its multiple internal realignments, could not consolidate its unity, nor on its own increase its electoral appeal even when it did create interesting cases of socialist government as in Alcozauca, Guerrero and Juchitán, Oaxaca. Only after the Democratic Current split from the PRI did the left see a qualitative transformation of its electoral fortunes.

There are two elements which show more clearly the changes in Mexican elections between 1979 and 1987. First, a constant and generalized increase in electoral contests of all types throughout the country endangered the PRI which appeared threatened by another party with a similar share of the vote; second, the changes in electoral law introduced by Miguel de la Madrid in 1986 and Salinas de Gortari in 1989–90 have tended to strengthen the security mechanisms of the system in order to maintain control of electoral results and guarantee the PRI the presidency of the republic and a majority in the Chamber of Deputies. The tension between these two processes has been growing because the PRI-government cannot dispense with the image of a democratic system either. Between 1979 and 1991 there has been a constant redefinition of alliances and contradictions between the PRI and the opposition. From 1979 to 1985 that opposition was made up of the PAN, PDM, PCM, PSUM, PSD, PRT and PMT. The PST was an opposition party which gradually lost its autonomy and preferred to negotiate a place in the electoral arena with the PRI. The PARM and PPS generally appeared as allies of the PRI. In 1988 all parties were in opposition: the PPS, PARM, PMS and PFCRN supported Cárdenas; the PAN was with Clouthier; the PRT remained on the ultra-left; finally, the least critical of the electoral process was the PDM.

Since 1988 the closeness between the PAN leadership and Salinas may explain the recognition of the electoral victory in Baja California, but it has also created serious internal conflicts for the PAN. The willingness of PAN leaders to negotiate allowed Salinas to push forward a constitutional reform which modified the *operación electoral* in order to provide the PRI with as many legal guarantees as there were in 1986–8, so that it would maintain its congressional majority after the 1991 elections and possibly the presidency in 1994.[28] At the same time the PRI won back its old allies, the PPS, PARM and PFCRN. The PFCRN leadership refused to join in the formation of the PRD in May 1989, arguing that it was dominated by the figure of Cárdenas. At the same time, it accepted talks with Salinas and has tended to support the government's policies while maintaining formal political independence. When the PDM was granted its registration again in 1990 the PRI won back another ally, at least in the electoral bodies. Since 1988 the PRD has been isolated in the electoral struggle, as it has not entered into negotiations with Salinas, whom it has continued to consider as an illegitimate president.

Recalling the definition of Cotteret and Emeri (see p. 64), it is worth considering the question of the *operación electoral*. In Mexico the *operación electoral* had been built on the balance of forces existing prior to the political reform of 1977. The dynamic unleashed by parties and elections after 1977 led to an increasing discrepancy between an *operación electoral* dominated by the PRI-government and a society of emerging political forces. The legislative changes from 1986 onwards have been insufficient and in many aspects represent a regression in the democratization of elections and the political system. It would appear that the PRI began to see that if there were clean elections it would lose them; at the same time the conviction grew throughout Mexican society that political democracy was indispensable to break the vicious circle which has corrupted the country's post-revolutionary regimes. This conviction has spread to social groups, expressing contradictory demands: for example, the removal of trade union bureaucracies; the displacement of caciques in rural areas; the revival of purchasing power; the privatization of state companies; the punishment of government corruption; the reduction of tax burdens on large companies; and free trade. In some way the demands both of the right and of the left have converged in the call for political democracy. It is for this reason that the tensions between government control, democratic demands and electoral struggle have grown since 1979 to the point of putting at risk the legitimacy of the political system as a whole, thereby undermining the credibility of the presidency.

Finally, let us take up again the question of what changed in 1988. It seems that the most important developments were the break-up of the PRI's popular alliances and the configuration of a new political force on the left led by Cárdenas. To try and explain this as the result of a personal decision of the CD leaders to propose the candidacy of Cárdenas would be to fall into an excessively voluntaristic interpretation of history. But it would be wrong to deny the importance of that decision in the crystallization of a new alliance of social forces very different to that which the FDN parties represented prior to 1988. The candidacy of Cárdenas helped unite groups which were previously dispersed and citizens who were unhappy about the national situation but who had not found a satisfactory response from existing parties. The elections of July 1988 expressed, on the one hand, the culmination of a serious rupture within the PRI which began with the de la Madrid government's attempts to reduce state intervention in the economy; on the other hand, the popular vote revealed that the people were determined to struggle for political change via electoral means. The struggle was expressed not solely through the specific demands of social movements, which of course have never been abandoned, but also in the demand for a new political system in which access to power would really be determined by the results of an electoral contest.

Another element of electoral mobilization in 1988 was its ideological content; the people voted for the left. Those citizens dissatisfied with the PRI, who had felt frustration with the government's policies, had suffered a dramatic fall in income – the most serious decline since the revolution – and were fed up with the bureaucracy and government corruption, turned out to vote not just against the PRI or for the PDM, PRT or PAN. The majority voted for Cárdenas and the diffuse leftwing option he represented. This vote reflected more than left unity, but we should not dismiss the role played by the FDN parties in putting forward candidates, organizing campaigns and defending, whenever possible, the results of the poll.

Others voted for the PAN and its candidate Manuel J. Clouthier, who was also a charismatic leader of great appeal beyond his own party. However, the PAN vote in 1988 did not represent a qualitative change since it followed the same trends observed between 1979 and 1985.

Since 1979 the social significance of elections has changed, allowing us to talk of a change in political culture. Political democracy took on an importance which previously it lacked. Frequently it became a banner for popular struggle, mobilizing the masses in election campaigns (both Clouthier and Cárdenas attracted surprisingly large crowds), on the day of the election itself and in the protests against fraud which followed. Yet the control exercised by the government over the election results has allowed the PRI to retain power, often against the will of the people as expressed by the vote.

These mechanisms of control over the *operación electoral* have been reinforced by the new electoral reform, revealing the problems faced by the people in the struggle for democracy as a result of the rigidity of the existing power structure. The transition to political democracy will require a deep transformation of the predominant party system which has characterized the country since Calles invented the official party of the Mexican Revolution.

Notes (*Translation by Neil Harvey*)

1. For reasons of space the changes in the electoral operation and party system will be analysed here only from the perspective of elections. There are, of course, many other aspects of social conflict which have an impact on the political system.
2. These concepts are taken from the speech made by Minister of Interior Jesús Reyes Heroles at the annual message of the governor of Guerrero on 1 April 1977 (see *Gaceta de la Reforma Política*, 1, 1977:ix).
3. In France there was a long discussion over whether or not the voting age should be lowered to eighteen (Cotteret and Emeri:25).
4. After 1946 the Interior Ministry, which was directly dependent on the president, was given the power to decide which parties could participate in elections and which could not. Likewise, it established very difficult requirements for a party wishing to apply for registration, such that no new parties entered the electoral arena between 1957 and 1977. 'Conditional registration' was abolished in 1986 but re-introduced in 1990.
5. After 1961 the system of party deputies was, in a way, a precursor of PR: these seats were given as a sort of consolation prize to the opposition. Initially party deputyships were awarded to parties which received 2.5 per cent of the national vote. This was lowered to 1.5 per cent in 1973 but, even so, neither the PPS nor the PARM managed to win this amount in federal elections. Nevertheless, in 'the spirit of the law', the authorities granted them some seats in the Chamber of Deputies.
6. *Sinarquismo* emerged in Mexico in the 1930s among extreme right-wing groups opposed to communist and anarchist groups whom they felt were being protected and promoted by the socialist tendencies of the Lázaro Cárdenas government. The Spanish *sin*, *anarquismo*, to literally denote 'without anarchism'.
7. During a session of the Federal Electoral Commission on 14 May 1990 it was decided to grant the PDM electoral registration (see *La Jornada*, 15 May 1990:1).
8. The concept of spoils is used by Sartori when speaking of 'parties of the system' to describe the illicit use of resources in the maintenance of clientelistic relations (Sartori, 1976:77).
9. There was a notable weakening of the traditional sectors at the 14th National Assembly of the PRI in September 1990, reflected by a reduction in its representation to under 50 per cent. However, the leaders did not dare express their anger openly (Bailey *et al.*, 1990).
10. CFE, Article 171: Functions of the president of the CFE.
11. CFE, Article 165.
12. Reforms to Article 54 of the Constitution.
13. CFE, Articles 310 and 208–13.
14. CFE, Article 299, paragraph II.

15. CFE, Book 8: TRICOEL. CFE, Book 9: Assembly of Representatives of the Federal District.
16. Book 9: Assembly of Representatives of the Federal District.
17. Declarations made by the PAN deputy, Miguel Alcántara Soria, in relation to the 1989 constitutional reform of electoral procedures. According to Alcántara Soria this reform was designed to assure maximum government control over the Chamber of Deputies in the coming years 'giving the PRI time to prepare itself for the alternation of power in Congress'. He added that 'the PRI is willing to respect the vote if it is guaranteed control of the Chamber of Deputies during a period of transition. The position of Salinas and his advisors was unshakeable, they had to assure a PRI majority' (*La Jornada*, 21 October 1989:1 and 13).
18. Supporters of the PAN who voted against the new law argued that 'to coincide with the PRI on so many issues places us in a vulnerable position . . . we are leaving things up to the good will of the president' (Bernardo Batiz, *La Jornada*, 1 August 1990:9). 'In the future the PAN will be seen as an accomplice to fraud and it is now upholding presidentialism' (Pablo Retes, ibid.). For Miguel Angel Conchello the new law represented a small advance 'at the cost of the prestige of the PAN' (*La Jornada*, 15 July 1990:6).
19. The COFIPE was passed on 14 July 1990 with 369 votes in its favour from deputies of the PRI, PAN, PPS, PARM and PFCRN (*La Jornada*, 15 July 1990:10).
20. COFIPE, Book III: Instituto Federal Electoral. El consejo General, Chapter 1.
21. COFIPE, Designación de magistrados del Consejo General y del Tribunal Electoral, articles 74 and 268.
22. COFIPE, De las mesas directivas de casilla, articles 119 and 193–7.
23. COFIPE, Coaliciones, articles 58–64.
24. COFIPE, Tribunal Federal Electoral.
25. COFIPE, Servicio Profesional Electoral, articles 168–70.
26. COFIPE, Registro Condicionado, articles 33–5.
27. 'Rodolfo González Guevara, dirigente de la Corriente Crítica renuncia al PRI, porque es antidemocrático y nunca podrá independizarse del gobierno', *Excelsior*, 14 September 1990:1 and 30.
28. According to official figures, the PRI polled 61 per cent of the vote, winning 320 of the 500 Congressional seats and 31 of the 32 Senate seats in the August 1991 mid-term elections.

3· MICHOACÁN IS DIFFERENT?
Neoliberalism, *neocardenismo* and the hegemonic process

John Gledhill

As a result of the municipal elections of December 1989, the PRI governor of Michoacán, Genovevo Figueroa Zamudio, enjoys the dubious distinction of looking out from his office over a state capital governed by the Partido de la Revolución Democrática (PRD). His embarrassment is compounded by his failure to secure a result which left the PRI with effective control over a majority of the state's *alcaldías*,[1] and it is perpetuated by the fact that some of the victories assigned to the PRI by the Electoral Commission have continued to be contested by the PRD occupation of town halls or the formation of parallel civic governments ('organs of popular power') in disputed *municipios*. Although three of the opposition triumphs fell to the PAN, there was ample evidence that a significant proportion of former PAN voters from the urban *colonias populares* had defected to the PRD. Scandal surrounded the electoral proceedings even in cases where a genuine PRI majority in the ballot box was virtually certain. One of the more colourful examples was Cotija, a small town in the Sierra Blanco noted for its cheese and drug-trafficking; here the PRI candidate for municipal president was the brother of the previous incumbent, recently convicted of leading a gang of highway robbers. But the usual catalogue of fraud, such as manipulation of electoral lists and irregularities in the distribution of electoral credentials, was accompanied by what looked more like tactis of desperation in areas where the PRD was evidently dominant. As in Guerrero, *perredista* candidates were being offered respectable sums to withdraw from the campaign and on election day itself minors trooped to the *casillas* to register votes for the PRI, not with a view to engineering a majority for the ruling party but simply to force the annulment of that secured by the PRD. Despite all this and much more, it was not a good day for the Party of the Institutional Revolution.

In this chapter I address the question of what this signifies and whether it matters. Whether it matters is not, I think, an idle question. Although it is important to bear in mind that a significant number of PRD voters were disenfranchised by the non-delivery of their electoral credentials, abstentionism was certainly higher than in the gubernatorial and presidential elections of July 1989 and 1988 respectively. One thing that Mexico has in common with the USA is that a majority of the electorate does not participate in elections, and much of *neocardenismo*'s electoral performance has been based on mobilizing the lower-class abstainers. A majority of Michoacanos believes that the result of the two previous electoral processes was defeat for the PRI, but the fact that the official outcomes stand and allot real power to the victors has had some demobilizing effect. Although less demobilization has occurred in Michoacán than many anticipated, serious questions must be raised about where the PRD can go in the future from the base it has established electorally. Nor are the Michoacán local election results necessarily totally disastrous from the point of view of the national regime. Michoacán does not represent a microcosm of modern Mexico as a whole in social or economic terms. Although the state is not so marginal as to make ungovernability tolerable, the local elections can at least be cited as proof of the central government's commitment to democracy, and both the defeats and the seamier side of the process have been blamed on the governor's failure to get to grips with the task of 'modernizing' the party at the local level.[2] In national terms it is, of course, of vital importance that the presidential candidacy of Cuauhtémoc mobilized a huge urban popular vote from segments of the electorate which normally abstain. But Salinas did weather the storm unleashed on 6 July 1988, and the most that can be claimed for *neocardenismo* nationally since the presidential election is that it is not yet self-evidently a spent force. And if Michoacán is not *neocardenismo*'s only bastion, it seems so self-evidently different with respect to the peculiar place of *cardenismo* in its regional political culture as to constitute a special case.

Michoacán may be different, but I think it would be unwise to assume that nothing of more general significance can be learned from the regional case. Michoacán remains a 'predominantly rural state'. But this statement really needs to be qualified in the light of the fact that the nature of the urbanization process in the state[3] reflects massive rates of out-migration across state boundaries, the bulk of it to the metropolitan cities. Continuing social and economic ties between rural Michoacanos and urban relatives not only in Mexico but also in the USA make a rigid division between urban and rural analytically misleading, and this line of argument could be extended in a number of other directions by considering other dimensions of the rural–urban nexus which shapes life within the region. Furthermore, rural Michaoacán is marked by very considerable social and economic heterogeneity (Linck and Santana, 1988). Politically speaking, even today the entire region is far from being Cardenista, and from an historical point of view it would be an error to assume that Michoacán as a whole has a 'natural' and primordial affinity with *cardenismo*. Cuauhtémoc was not strikingly popular as state governor in some areas of the state where the PRD is currently in the ascendant, and the old *cardenismo* faced even more substantial resistance in some of these areas in the past. Exploration of the reasons for what is often a shift of some magnitude not simply in attitudes but in people's willingness to take physical risks in political mobilization in Michoacán may therefore help to clarify the nature and potential of *neocardenismo* elsewhere. Conversely, an examination of its limits and contradictions in the Michoacán context has worthwhile implications for the wider picture. Lastly, major structural transformations at the level of national societies are certainly shaped historically by conjunctures involving processes at regional level as well as the more frequently stressed conjunctures of national development and larger international processes. This argument must, of course, imply that all regional analyses are fundamentally inadequate, but it also implies that they are indispensable. It would, however, be difficult to discuss regional responses to crisis in a way which relates to the question of continuities and change in national societies without at least offering an outline of the particular conceptualization of what is happening at national level which underlies my understanding of what is happening regionally.

What is in crisis in Mexico today?

'Crisis' has become an aspect of Mexican culture. Many families are in a perpetual state of crisis in the sense that their situations only oscillate between bad and worse, but what I mean by this apparently bizarre statement is that the notion that the country is in crisis has become one that ordinary people have interiorized and use in the same matter-of-fact way in which the English talk about the weather. In intellectual and political circles, distinctions are frequently drawn between 'conjunctural' and 'structural' crises, and between 'economic' and 'political' crisis, the issue in the latter context focusing on the implications of the economic situation for the stability of the regime. This kind of discourse has again become quite routinized. As Salinas himself has suggested, the time may be approaching when it becomes necessary to start thinking of the stability of the regime in terms that are distinct from rule by the PRI, and one might regard the defection of the *neocardenistas* from the party as something of an advantage for a president seeking to consummate this kind of transformation. But discussion at this kind of level is still very close to the ideological terrain of the contemporary political process and I think it is desirable to try to define the issues in terms of a broader set of analytical categories and against a much longer time frame.

The crisis to which neoliberalism is a response is clearly not something which is peculiarly Mexican, since neoliberalism in a broad sense is a global phenomenon. It would be tempting to suggest that it is a crisis of a particular kind of statist development paradigm, which is more or less the account of the matter provided by neoliberal ideology itself. But the reorientation of the relationship between state and civil society being carried through by neoliberalism is, I would contend, not equivalent in substance to its ideological representation. The state is not relaxing its regulatory grip on civil society. It is changing the nature of its regulatory function with regard to the economy in a manner which is undeniably favourable to large-scale capital and the increasing centralization and concentration of capital on an international scale. This process is accompanied by a consolidation of state intervention and centralization of power in areas of social life concerned broadly with social control.[4]

Latin American historical experience does, however, lend particular nuances to the local manifestations of these larger tendencies and the realities of social conditions in Latin America may quite rapidly be productive of divergent patterns of development. It is not, however, immediately apparent what the political consequences of economic restructuring are likely to be under modern conditions: the immediate effects of present developments are even higher levels of social polarization and a rather more varied series of effects arising from the growing internationalization of the domestic economy. Some of the latter may have deleterious consequences for middle strata, but increased immiseration of those at the bottom of the social ladder might not be as unmanageable as some fear. This is the point at which historical specifics become more salient.

Those of us who work on rural Mexico are prone to stress that much of the non-economic history of this part of Mexican reality enjoys a subterranean existence. In the decades since the Cárdenas reforms there has been an apparently cyclical ebb and flow of agrarian mobilization, of the right as well as the left. Much of this history has gone largely unanalysed,[5] with the exception of the particularly sharp peak which occurred in the Echeverría years, which seems, in retrospect, to have proved something of a watershed. Echeverría's agrarian concessions represented more or less the maximum consistent with maintaining the terms of the regime's pact with capital, and the other side of the coin to these concessions, the 'statization' of peasant agriculture, is now under attack from more or less all sides of the argument, including organized sections of the peasantry.[6] Furthermore, the years of statization were also years of increasing internationalization of the agro-pastoral sector, adding to the contradictions facing any policies orientated towards dealing with the basic foods issue, rural poverty and rural–urban migration. Beneath the apparent cycle of agrarian mobilizations there was, of course, a profound process of social change in train: the urbanization of society and the simultaneous growth of an urban middle class and an urban underclass. In the case of regions like Michoacán, this process was accompanied by a significant flow of people across the border into the USA: if seasonal international migration tended to reproduce rural households, the creation of *emigrado* communities in the north had a much broader impact on the region's social and economic development. Some of this might be seen as positive in a sense, in so far as links with the north help ameliorate the impact of domestic recessions, though many of the social consequences of the process are negative and the situation today is rather different from what it was in earlier years. International migration became rather less socially selective in the years following the termination of the Bracero Accords, but migration opportunities are now becoming increasingly unequally distributed once again, and not simply in the international sphere. On the one hand, there is an emergent rural underclass which has diminishing prospects of moving anywhere because of its poverty and low educational levels, whilst primary school headmasters are labouring on construction sites in San Francisco.[7] This closing of the exits might, of course, have implications for the rise of *neocardenismo*, though it is worth stressing that relatively successful US migrants may be active *perredistas*, particularly older men from the middle stratum of the peasantry forced to resume a migratory career by the deterioration of their economic possibilities at home. What I want to stress, however, is that both the rural–urban and international migratory processes which have accompanied past patterns of agrarian change have produced a situation in which the rural sector is inextricably linked to the urban sector. Rural households are generally dependent on income remissions from elsewhere, including those households which are still producing marketable surpluses.[8] The transformation of rural society has created an almost impossible series of problems for social policy, since it is necessary to balance the goal of helping poor rural producers effectively decapitalized by the rural credit institution *Banco Nacional de Crédito Rural* (BANRURAL) (or dependent on income remissions) against the market-dependence for foodstuffs of the rural as well as the urban poor. One might argue that neoliberalism is simply recognizing the hopelessly contradictory nature of this situation and hoping that spontaneous social strategies will supply coping mechanisms to sustain the situation whilst the *ejidos* disintegrate through neolatifundist appropriation of land and other kinds of relations with private capital.[9]

With regard to the development of the rural economy in Michoacán, the peasant sector was not, in practice, being sustained by the process of statization in the years before de la Madrid, the impact of state support for *ejidatarios* possessed of better quality land being essentially one of checking private-sector appropriation of that land. In a sense the system was already in crisis. But the reality of crisis has been magnified tremendously by the impact of adverse developments elsewhere in the larger international and urban systems in which rural households are inserted, since these have major impacts on their incomes. Since Michoacán's agrarian structure is so varied, this longer-term pattern of rural malaise manifests itself in a variety of different ways. But most point in the same general direction. Even marginal peasant farmers who might be expected to dedicate exiguous resources to supplementing their incomes by self-provisioning in maize may, for example, turn instead to plundering what forest resources are left to them by the expansion of private capital in this sector (Linck and Santana, 1988). The shape of rural development was already determined by urban and international markets, and every aspect of rural life is now profoundly commoditized (Gledhill, 1991).

Certainly, there have been differentiating effects, and some benefits have been derived from agricultural transformation by persons who are not large-scale entrepreneurs. But what local smaller-scale accumulation has occurred is somewhat fragile, and much of it is directly or indirectly dependent on the state. Among the indirect forms of dependence we should certainly number the licit and illicit ways in which state employees can pursue entrepreneurial activities in their private capacities.

This combined process of statization and spontaneous economic adaptation provides an important part of the background in which we should set the history of rural social movements. To some extent modern agrarian movements, particularly in indigenous areas of the state, represent resistances to forms of capitalist expansion, particularly those related to the appropriation of forest resources and the expansion of commercial animal husbandry.[10] But this is not the only dimension to today's movements, since the strength of the agrarian cause also reflects a reaction to the failure of alternative modes of livelihood. The failure of urban society to deliver social mobility is also a factor in the appearance of other kinds of movements which are rural but more concerned with ethnic questions in their own right than as a basis for agrarian claims. A number of such developments in the Meseta Tarasca is associated with the return of young and now unemployed professionals from the cities. Another type of development, a reaction to the statization process, is the attempt to organize communities of existing *ejidatarios* to defend themselves against the depradations of the agro-bureaucracy and external capitalist interests, and secure modifications in the community's relations with the state. Such developments are often associated with the demand for autonomy from the tutelage of the state bureaucratic apparatus (Gordillo, 1988). Self-management is seen as a condition for realizing a process of accumulation rather than decapitalization. But in the last analysis they inevitably involve negotiation with the state and a demand for resources from it as the condition for survival in a world dominated by private-sector intermediaries and the agro-industrial giants of transnational capitalism. The issue is further complicated by the fact that producer unions in Michoacán are predominantly of the mixed type, with private interests and *ejidal* caciques allied to them playing the dominant role. If we take a longer-term view, it becomes apparent that the kind of scenario envisaged by many analysts in the 1960s, a transformation of the agrarian movement based on leaderships with urban experience and a growing alliance between popular forces in the urban and rural sectors, has not been realized in practice. If anything the tendency is towards greater fragmentation and regionalization of rural movements. The central form of peasant organization adopted by the independent movements of the 1960s proved readily co-optable, whilst the more recent attempts to work through umbrella organizations uniting autonomous regional movements has not yet proved entirely successful for other reasons. Besides divisions relating to the question of making alliances with political parties, good intentions are not sufficient to unite what are socially heterogeneous movements pursuing different kinds of goals and divided to a considerable extent by the factor of ethnic composition. Following the Echeverría concessions, the stakes were raised considerably for groups seeking to pursue a militant agrarian cause. The fundamental balance of social power presents an almost intractable difficulty; the leverage of state power is a necessary condition for a successful resolution of a conflict with a decentralized private power which often wields means of physical coercion as well as the wherewithal to secure favourable juridical decisions. It is also worth noting that the government of Salinas de Gortari has shown some adeptness in manipulating these contradictions to its own advantage by showing a degree of official approval for the principle of the autonomy of peasant organizations. Ideologically speaking, there are evident advantages for a neoliberal regime in emphasizing the evils of statization, but there is also a more substantial advantage in seeking to replace a relationship with peasant organizations mediated through bureaucratic or *cacique* intermediaries with more direct forms of negotiation which serve to further inhibit the formation of horizontal regional and inter-regional linkages between groups, in favour of more verticalized and selective relations with the centre. Although this strategy seems to date to have been a failure in the case of the Meseta Tarasca,[11] it may yet have some potential nationally. Yet even in the absence of any evolution in strategies of political control, one might still conclude that the fragmentation and heterogeneity of the forces of organized popular resistance to current patterns of transformation creates a situation in which a great deal can be achieved simply by a *laissez-faire* approach supplemented by considered acts of repression.

It is in this context that *neocardenismo* becomes potentially significant, as a political force which has shown itself to have some capacity to weld disparate forces of opposition together. As Göran Therborn has argued, all ideologies provide human subjects with three orientations: towards what exists, what is good or just, and what is possible (Therborn, 1980: 15–16). The third orientation is crucial in analysing social action because it is possible for people to harbour profound antagonisms towards the existing order without acting to challenge it simply because of fear of repression or resignation to the practical impossibility of change. The significance of *neocardenismo* may lie precisely in that it makes the possibility of change thinkable to those previously characterized by resignation. At both regional and national level, the social forces expressed by *neocardenismo* are clearly diverse, and it is noticeable that a number of PRD candidates in Michoacán's municipal elections of 1989 were *comerciantes*. The candidate in Jiquilpan, for example, the owner of a substantial hardware business, had achieved a notable, if unrecognized, victory for the PAN in the town on a previous occasion, after being denied the PRI nomination. The participation of elements of the regional bourgeoisie alongside peasants and urban workers in populist movements is scarcely unusual, but *neocardenismo* does not seem to represent the standard kind of populism with which Mexico has long been familiar. The caudillistic dimension of the movement in general is undeniable (Tamayo, nd), and particularly evident in Michoacán, but it does not seem to reflect Cuauhtémoc's personal charisma or capacity as a leader[12] but his peculiar structural position as a symbol and the embodiment of an idea, that is, a *cardenismo* revitalized, recreated and reappropriated by its mass base. The movement seems to depend little on his direction, which remains unclear and ambiguous. Reconstructed in a regretful popular consciousness formed in the years after 1940, *neocardenismo*'s power is not based on what was actually achieved historically during Lázaro Cárdenas' presidency,[13] but on its myth, a myth that is not an illusion or fantasy but the unfulfilled but conceivable possibility of constituting an alternative outcome to the social revolutionary process. Legitimate bearer of the more egalitarian and democratic discourses of the Mexican revolution, and able to appropriate the mantle of a nationalism which neoliberalism is perceived to have abandoned, the new *cardenismo* has succeeded, for a while at least, in lending political unity to fragmented and heterogeneous popular social movements. It is, therefore, also a child of neoliberalism, and in my view it gains its force from the fact that a determined effort is being made to change the nature of the hegemonic process.

Cardenismo and hegemony

It is important to distinguish the question of the post-revolutionary hegemonic process from the narrower question of the political power of the PRI. In the Gramscian sense,[14] hegemony is a dynamic process of 'establishment of unstable equilibria', shaped in a significant manner by the actions and reactions of subaltern classes. Hegemony includes the cultural, moral and ideological leadership of allied and subaltern groups, and is a combination of practices, including symbolic practices, which present the hegemonic group's dominance in a universalizing manner, as the motive force behind the development of the whole society. Gramsci insists that the class exercising hegemony must also exercise a decisive direction over the economy, but that no hegemony can be based purely on the narrow 'economic–corporate' interest of the dominant class, and that all hegemonies have an ideological cultural dimension. In the case of Mexico, the bourgeoisie's hegemony has been expressed through the institutional revolution; a mediating state stands above civil society, maintaining a balance between different sectors, seen as separate corporate interests, and protecting this national arrangement from external forces which would undermine it. Neoliberal ideology posits an open civil society of citizens and associations whose mutual relations are to be regulated through government. But the dynamics of hegemony do not rest entirely on discursive dimensions of power. One dimension of the power of the PRI clearly arises from the non-discursive realm, through control of repressive apparatuses, electoral fraud and the purchase of loyalties. The longevity of the official party's rule through successive crises has depended on its ability to reappropriate the universalizing discourse of the revolution, but this has in its turn been endlessly recreated through processes of social struggle which are determined by non-discursive factors, conjunctures of socio-economic crisis and political balance of force, the ossification of agencies of control such as the CNC, and secular processes of social change.

As rampant inflation and social crisis affected large segments of the Mexican population, the de la Madrid administration sought to cope with the mounting crisis of economic management by conceding the inexorable logic of transnationalization whilst simultaneously beginning the process of privatization of the state sector. This created the space in which an alternative political force could appropriate the broader discourse of the revolution, but the realization of this possibility rested, in the last analysis, on the fact that the post-revolutionary hegemony was not entirely the patrimony of the PRI, and that a particular alternative project had retained its force in mass consciousness, because it corresponded to unsatisfied social needs and aspirations. Although Salinas de Gortari has displayed considerably greater adeptness in terms of political management than his predecessor, his determination to press forward with modernization by continuing further on the same course of sacrificing the national autonomy dimension of the old post-revolutionary hegemony and reducing the direct economic role of the state has so far depended on the use of the same non-discursive methods for retaining power. Large segments of society remain to be convinced that the present course of economic policy will improve their material lot, and attempts by the administration to appeal to anti-statist sentiments are hampered both by the fact that its practices with regard to political democracy remain suspect and by a more general fear that existing social inequalities are likely to be magnified. In distinction from its predecessors, the present crisis can now be seen as one which is irrevocably concerned with the question of re-establishing and redefining the broader hegemonic process in a fundamental sense.[15]

The movement in Michoacán

I will attempt to defend this line of argument by giving some more details on the movement's development in rural Michoacán. The region where I have done my own ethnographic research, the terrain of the ex-*hacienda* of Guaracha in the Ciénega de Chapala, was notoriously antagonistic to the original Cardenista reform, and subsequently became a zone of *neolatifundismo* and extensive international migration, until there was a significant return to the land under the aegis of BANRURAL in the 1970s, now radically reversed. There was some intimation that the Ciénega's long history of political quiescence was already ending prior to Cuauhtémoc's defection from the PRI, in the sense that some attempts were made at mobilizing peasant communities against *caciques* and the agro-bureaucracy and later against de la Madrid's crisis measures, such as the effective termination of CONASUPO operations in the area, but the limitations of these developments were perhaps more striking than their achievements. Once Cuauhtémoc declared himself, mobilization took a quantum leap forward. A majority of the inhabitants of local communities refused to recognize PRI municipal authorities or pay their taxes, and the Cardenistas began to seize *presidencias* after the PRI declared itself triumphant in the gubernatorial elections, with widespread popular support.

One of the most significant dimensions of *neocardenismo* from the point of view of this segment of the population is that it implies a change of government and a change of style of government. That such a result seems possible is a consequence of the fact that *cardenismo* has a natural association with power. Ironically, it was Lázaro Cárdenas' role as president of the republic which has made it possible for *cardenismo* to become what it was not in the days when it first emerged as a regional movement, that is, an organic movement which can be presented as the common patrimony of all Michoacanos. One dimension of the movement's power in Michoacán lies precisely in the fact that it can be appropriated as a regional movement, lending it a unificatory quality other forms of political opposition would lack. But there is also considerable emphasis, in the spontaneous comments of rank-and-file affiliates of the PRD, on the fact that their struggles form part of an alliance of forces at national level. Certain solidarities, in particular with Guerrero, receive particular emphasis, but there can be no doubt that *cardenismo* has enhanced confidence in the viability of collective action.

Since *neocardenismo* derives much of its force from its ability to confront neoliberalism on the ideological terrain of the foundations of post-revolutionary hegemony, it thereby embodies a multi-class project. Its strength in rural areas like the Ciénega lies in the fact that the natural leaders of agrarian communities drawn from the upper ranks of the land reform peasantry have committed themselves to a course of opposition to the regime, along with elements of the regional urban petty, and in some cases, not so petty, bourgeiosie and intellectuals.[16] By upper ranks of the land reform peasantry I mean people who may rent additional land and possess some capital but who are not major agricultural entrepreneurs whose orientations are focused on the private sector. If they have tractors they will generally be purchased with BANRURAL credit, and many of this stratum owe their relative prosperity to the employment of close kin within the state sector. There seems little doubt that much of the leadership conceives of *neocardenismo* as a vehicle for defending or improving the terms of their insertion into national society at the expense of the upper echelons of the national élite and the interests of foreign capital. Their commitment to social and political transformation, though in many cases sincere, is therefore premised on the assumption that any radicalism will be at someone else's expense, and that such policies will be implemented through a reformed national state machine dominated by a political movement led by their strata.

Neoliberalism has brought such elements into an antagonistic relationship with the PRI, and the success of the *cardenista* alternative in July 1988 suggests the possibility of achieving a reorientation of the national regime, but this is only part of the process which sustains the PRD as a mass movement, and there may be limits to the kind of confrontation with the regime which parts of the movement are willing to undertake in the event of a peaceful conquest of power proving impossible. It is also important to stress that the PRD's strength is not uniform throughout the state in this context. It is noteworthy that the PRI seems to be retaining stronger support in cases where less antagonistic relations obtain between *ejidatarios* and the state apparatus, as is the case, for example, in the sugar-growing area of Los Reyes where most *ejidatarios* rent their land and work in the mills, and landless mill workers still enjoy the benefits of a past epoch of corporatism, although recent policy towards the cane price and the threat of privatization complicate the issue. In other zones, there is a more absolute gulf between prospering commercial farmers and marginal farmers and agricultural labourers without the existence of an intermediate stratum based on the *ejidos*. In general terms, middle strata seem to be significant both as a component of PRD support and a source of leaders to the local movement. Nevertheless, one should not entirely discount the prospect of an alliance of forces such as is represented in *neocardenismo* providing the vehicle for radical social change, since the prospects of such change may depend rather more on whether the existing apparatuses of power can continue to function coherently than on the animus or intentions of any of the individual groups of actors involved in social and political conflict.

In practice, even the PRD's alternative social and economic programme remains extremely vaguely defined, partly, one assumes, as an attempt by the leadership to avoid alienating the elements from higher social strata included in its popular base. The following extracts from the PRD's mainfesto for the local elections of 1989 provide an indication of the kind of balances which are currently being struck:

> . . . we *cardenistas* have a clear *compromiso* with the citizens of Michoacán: to achieve the changes which our State requires, to

> achieve development with democracy and improve the standard of living of Michoacán's families.
>
> We do not promise to do everything, we undertake to do that which the community considers indispensable, giving preference at all times to the zones with greater needs.
>
> We will be rigorous guardians of respect for the labour rights of all the workers and in defence of the peasants.
>
> We propose an economic development which generates employment and just earnings for our population. Private enterprise will be fully respected and we will create investment programmes in the cities and the countryside.

Other aspects of the manifesto, which stressed the desirability of municipal autonomy in terms of decision making regarding the use of resources allocated to local government by the state government, emphasized the style of administration to be expected from the PRD: open meetings, permanent consultation of public opinion and vigorous action against corruption. These pretensions to democratize municipal life should not be undervalued as an aspect of the PRD's message, and it is worth stressing that the PRD has made serious attempts to ensure that members of the municipal government would be drawn from different communities rather than simply the *cabecera*. There was therefore a potential radical democratic project embedded in the manifesto; it is also important to emphasize that the oral propaganda of the PRD on social questions tends to be considerably more radical than the written version, particularly when it is entrusted to some of the intellectuals who participate in the movement.

Nor should one understate the step represented by the occupation of *presidencias* and the sense of their potential power that people acquire through collective action. It is dubious whether the election results would have been as they were in the absence of the direct action undertaken by the *perredistas*, but the action has an additional value in itself. It must be stressed, however, that no serious attempts were made prior to the elections to use repressive power against the *perredistas* in most of the lowland communities.[17] The ambiguities of the PRD's official social programme may not at the present time constitute much of an impediment to its securing the active support of poorer elements of the population, in so far as the symbolic force of *cardenismo* lies in its promise of empowerment and dignity, and to some extent action itself provides that. Yet if a dream of freedom and dignity is the basis for the movement's appeal to the poor, and such dreams are not irrelevant even to the less poor in a society in which power is as unequally distributed as it is in Mexico, one must question the extent to which its impetus can be sustained as Salinas' sexennial proceeds. The PRI has, after all, retained control of the state apparatus at national level, and denied the PRD control of the state government of Michoacán, in July 1989. Neither the government nor national policies can therefore be changed directly by democratic means, which implies not only deepening crisis for poorer families, but a space for the PRI to rebuild its own power after the disaster of July 1988, if only by default and the negative process of securing a consensus of resignation.

The dilemmas facing the *perredistas* are substantial. As municipal authorities under a state government still controlled by the PRI both their powers and resources are limited, threatening a further process of disillusion, particularly if decisions have to be made with regard to the use of available resources which entail addressing the social questions. Although discipline has so far been remarkable, the PRI has orientated its attack on the PRD around the question of violence, and frustration alone may lead the movement into a situation of greater confrontation, which might result in some defections. Yet at least some elements of the PRD's base are likely to demand greater radicalism in the movement's stance on social questions, and expect its backing for direct action on, for example, agrarian issues.

In essence, the PRD has so far failed to formulate a completely coherent hegemonic project of its own, defining the exact terms of which an alliance of diverse social forces is to be based and interests and aspirations reconciled. It centres its strategy on the objective of taking political power through a sustained struggle to win electoral victories rather than the strengthening of its bases through the direct organization and initiation of social struggles. To adopt the latter strategy would, of course, imply a more specific project on fundamental questions of social policy, including redistribution of resources, which would not be without political risk. But to fail to respond adequately to the possibility of mass mobilization created by the triumph of 6 July would be to risk instead a slow fragmentation of the movement, converting the PRD into another political party. The situation is already complicated by the break-up of the political coalition which supported Cuauhtémoc's candidacy in 1988, and the appearance of other political rivals to the mantle of *cardenismo*, in particular the PFCRN (Partido del Frente Cardenista de Reconstrucción Nacional). If the PRD is to sustain, let alone strengthen, its mobilization of a mass base in Michoacán, it will have to keep the alternative it offers, the image of the possible, alive in concrete forms which transcend caudillistic loyalties. One positive possibility offered by the capture of municipal government does lie in the prospect of changing the style of the latter towards more participatory and democratic practices. A genuinely popular and imaginative form of local government might be able to mobilize resources from the community which could compensate for the reduction in funding to be expected from the levels of government still controlled by the PRI. Since so many *perredista* activists have a past history in the PRI,[18] one might imagine that even this would require some changes to old habits, although it must be said that it is not terribly difficult to improve on Michoacán's traditional standards of civic responsibility.

But it remains necessary to be realistic about the magnitude of the barriers in the way of the realization of an alternative hegemony in Mexico in the sense of a fundamental shift in the relations of forces which have shaped post-revolutionary national development. Even in the comparatively heady political atmosphere of Michoacán, the contradictions of the situation are apparent enough as one surveys the panorama of social inequality which characterizes the state and ponders on what needs to be done and what could conceivably be done to change the situation. Even at its lowest ebb, the present regime continues to command not only the macro-mechanisms of power, but a considerable number of effective micro-mechanisms,[19] and the questions of social power which the political process has yet to address in a decisive manner are formidable. All these propositions seem even more valid at the national level.

Hegemony and the social question

In Mexico, as elsewhere, it seems hard to countenance what neoliberalism seems to countenance, that is, the abandonment of the social question to resolution by free market forces, and international free market forces at that. Since Mexico is no longer an agrarian society, and in reality the *campesinos* are no longer what they once were in either cultural or socio-economic terms, attention tends to focus on the crisis of the urban underclasses and its possible political implications. In so far as the consequences of neoliberalism for rural areas are judged important, this is most often in the context of envisaging increases in rates of rural–urban migration. I have suggested some reasons for seeking to avoid making a sharp separation between urban and rural dimensions of crisis, and it would be possible to expand on this theme in other directions by considering the broader environmental and nutritional issues raised by Mexico's present pattern of economic development. But if solving the problems of urbanization requires some attention to the countryside, the latter continues to demand some attention in its own right.

Given the institutionalization of *agrarismo* in the structure of the state apparatus and in legislation which sets limits on private landholding, it is no easy task to end the agrarian side of the Mexican revolution, however many times presidents declare that there is no more land to distribute. Furthermore, whilst the urbanization process has shaped the problems of the countryside, the limitations of the urban alternative to rural existence must, to an extent at least, encourage agrarian resistance. Difficult and often bloody though such struggles have proved, independent[20] agrarian organizations like the *Unión de Comuneros Emiliano Zapata* in Michoacán have continued to exploit the contradictions of the post-revolutionary hegemony by focusing direct action on cases where the legal situation was favourable, with some success in the early 1980s. But the pattern of action became increasingly defensive after 1983 (Zepeda, 1986: 366–7), the phenomenon of internal factionalism which dogged the movements in the Meseta Tarasca in the 1920s has reappeared in a violent form in some of the communities affiliated to the UCEZ in the last few years, and the situation is complicated by a variety of other forms of mobilization focused exclusively on ethnic politics. Furthermore, even if we take an optimistic view about the potential for solidarity between the different types of social actors found in the countryside and the levels of commitment to fundamental change on the part of peasant leaders and footsoldiers in the mid-1980s, the age of agrarian revolution as such has now passed. This is not to say that urbanized, industrialized Mexico has no further need of agrarian reform, but simply to recognize the real implications of the fact that Mexico is no longer a peasant country. Tackling the social question in the context of a vastly more complex modern class structure represents an infinitely harder task conceptually than the one which confronted Lázaro Cárdenas in 1934, and it is certainly much harder to see what configuration of existing social forces might succeed in establishing an alternative hegemony and pattern of development in the country.

Keeping the discussion at an abstract level, it might be possible to conceive of a hegemonic project which would unite the urban working classes, peasantry and elements of the domestic bourgeoisie in an economic nationalist reaction to the existing thrust of neoliberal policy, given a conjuncture of circumstances unfavourable to maintenance of economic stability. Yet it remains uncertain how much economic nationalism would be possible under modern conditions, and what the consequences of an extreme version of economic nationalism, such as the 'war economy' advocated on a number of occasions by David Barkin,[21] would actually be. Quite lowly segments of the economy of Michaocán, for example, are highly integrated into the US–Mexico economic network, not simply in terms of labour migration, but in terms of various spheres of commerce and domestic production involving both rural communities and small towns. To some extent, at least, one could argue that these networks have acted to moderate the impact of crisis in the national economy (Zepeda, 1987). Admittedly, the increasing internationalization of the economy has some highly problematic implications for industry as well as agriculture. The spectre of Mexico becoming a country of *maquiladoras* is worrying not simply because of questions of foreign control but because this type of industrial development is so mobile internationally. But it is by no means certain that this model of development is incapable of producing at least a kind of economic dynamism benefiting a significant minority of the population, nor, more significantly, is it entirely clear what kind of alternatives are open.

Let us suppose that a determined effort were to be made tomorrow to eliminate Mexico's problems of poverty. How much redistribution of income and resources would be required? What kinds of social and economic reorganization would be required to meet that objective? How much of a sacrifice would such a programme involve for the middle strata of society, particularly if there was an aggressive reaction on the part of the USA? These are not questions I am equipped to answer, but they are not questions which many people, including the Neocardenistas, seem anxious to pose. There are some impressive environmental as well as social and economic arguments for transforming the nature of Third World development processes via a transformation of the relation between town and country. In the framework of a radical redistribution of rural resources and major changes in lifestyles, it is possible to conceive of a process of deurbanization which could have a major impact on the quality of life as well as constituting a more sustainable pattern of development (Redclift, 1987). But this kind of transformation would involve levels of coercive, and presumably centralized, intervention not only in the market but in terms of property relations without precedent in Mexican history, and it might not simply be the dominant class who would need to be coerced. Indeed, one of the major contradictions of Mexico's development process is the fact that 'urban bias' is partly associated with the problem of ameliorating the problems of the urban working classes, whose real incomes are also relevant to the welfare of their rural kin. It is one thing to revolutionize an agrarian society, quite another to dismantle the complex social legacy of an advanced process of industrialization and urbanization.

It has become fashionable in the West to declare socialism an established historical failure on the grounds that East European countries are now abandoning planning in favour of the market and are convulsed by demands for political democracy. Such arguments choose to ignore the fact that the existing socialist societies, whilst certainly not egalitarian, liberated from alienation in the workplace nor free from bureaucratic domination, are not actually societies whose basic structure is determined by economic class relations (Giddens, 1980). Mexico *is* a class-based society, and one in which a very small economic élite has exercised a substantial influence over government policies. This is not to say that mass reactions to the effects of those policies have not influenced the course of post-revolutionary history in a significant way. Nevertheless, the hegemonic apparatus established in post-revolutionary Mexico has chanelled the process of class struggle in a way which has promoted capital accumulation by the few at the expense of the many and at the same time made the state a necessary intermediary in the subordinated classes' attempts to negotiate the terms of their exploitation. There is no denying the extent to which the particular rhetoric of the national revolution has been interiorized by those subordinated classes, even in their radical moments, and one line of interpretation of *neocardenismo* would be to highlight the third-way quality of the *cardenista* paradigm, in a sense a socialism, but a Mexican socialism that leaves the extent to which private property is to be eliminated open, a programme in which the social question is paramount – poverty and misery must be eliminated – but in which the root causes of poverty and misery are left without the kind of definitive definition offered by Marxist versions of socialism.

It has also now become fashionable, if not very original, to argue that class-based politics are increasingly irrelevant to the advanced capitalist societies, and to see the so-called new social movements as the agents of a global struggle against bureaucratization, massification and commodification in search of more decentralized, participatory forms of democratic political order (Gledhill, 1988). The anti-statism and lack of a totalizing social project characteristic of the new social movements is seen as a symptom of their newness and liberating potential, although it is conceded that the processes underlying the production of the antagonisms expressed in the individual movements can lead them, through the contingent 'articulation' of social and political discourses, in what are, in traditional terms, rightist as well as leftist directions (Laclau, 1985: 33). But the experience of *neocardenismo* seems to suggest that the long-term potential of a plurality of heterogeneous social movements to transform the structures of social power depends entirely on their subsumption within a broader, universalizing, hegemonic project, and the enormous weakness of this whole line of analysis is its refusal to recognize that the social question can only ultimately be resolved by addressing the issue of state power. Neoliberalism proposes to strengthen civil society *vis-à-vis* the state, and it is undeniable that this discourse can have some appeal to weaker groups which are struggling to emancipate themselves from bureaucratic domination, including peasant organizations striving to achieve autonomous management of their own process of production. Yet even the most aggressive protagonists in this kind of struggle, such as the Sonoran Coalition of Collective Ejidos, have made demands on the state which relate to the non-discursive conditions of the hegemonic process and the unequal distribution of economic power in particular. Leaving aside the fact that the implementation of the neoliberal project has thus far been dependent on a denial of respect for the political votes of a majority of the citizenry, the market does not even correspond in principle to a democracy in which every voice is of equal value.

Up to a point, perhaps, the creation of democratic institutions from below can be a vehicle in a struggle to transform the larger political system, though as the case of the UCEZ again demonstrates, fostering participatory democratic organization in communities in which vertical caudillistic relations have previously predominated is no easy task (Zepeda, 1986: 359–60). But the state apparatus remains the lever by which mobilization is translated into a shift in the balance of social power, the appropriation of real resources claimed by other elements of civil society and changes in the broader economic conditions which govern the value of those resources as a basis for livelihood. Advances by independent movements are related to the fact that the responses of higher agencies of power are determined by the balance of all the diverse forces which impact on those agencies' behaviour. What appears as the work of a faction conjuncturally dominant in the state apparatus or the result of internal struggles within the apparatus is, in fact, conditioned by relations of force at the level of the whole social formation. Whilst the new social movements may play a significant role in a Gramscian war of position against the existing order, to the extent that they can actually install democratic practices at the base, they also reflect the way the mechanisms of the existing hegemony tend to fragment popular struggles. If negotiation with the state apparatus remains the ultimate focus of social action, then rearticulating those struggles, and creating the social conditions for the realization of their goals, must entail the conquest of the state itself.[22]

Even if this is not the sole factor involved in present changes, neoliberalism reflects the extent to which the model of accumulation established from the 1940s onwards has proved increasingly deficient from the point of view of the private sector. If we assume that resolving the social question in Mexico requires a new, and radically different, model of development, one possible way in which such a change might come about might be through a radical failure of the neoliberal project, which is heavily dependent on the future health of the US and world economy. Should the economic situation of the country deteriorate significantly, exacerbating what remains a substantial social and political crisis, the capacity of the existing political apparatus to control the situation might well prove inadequate, since the strain to which it is already subject is evident enough. This is the risk inherent in any attempt to introduce any fundamental change in the hegemonic process from above.

The classical social revolutionary scenarios were all premised on the radical disorganization of existing state apparatuses, and whilst the content of any modern cataclysm in a developed society like Mexico would certainly be different, it is not impossible to envisage such a scenario, notwithstanding the greater efficiency of modern technologies of repressive power. As Therborn has suggested, following the lead of Barrington-Moore and Skocpol, just as feudalism was not destroyed by its fundamental form of class conflict, that between lord and peasant, there is no real theoretical reason to imagine that the normal form of transformation of capitalist societies would be through its fundamental form of class-struggle (Therborn, 1980: 89). Class relations and their associated ideologies are important in the sense that they are the principal vehicle through which alternative possible social forms are defined, but there is no reason to think that new social worlds will not continue to be created by complex coalitions of social forces, just as they were in the past. Classical forms of working-class organization, that is, trade unions and political representation through social democratic parties, may be judged the normal mode of class struggle under capitalism in the sense that they entail forms of conflict (from the perspective of the bourgeoisie), but forms which secure the reproduction rather than the transformation of the fundamental relations of the system (Therborn, 1980: 54; Gledhill, 1988: 263–4). But the ideologies of the possible which achieve an organized form under a capitalist regime remain vital, since the collapse of an existing hegemonic apparatus cannot lead to social transformation unless there exists an organized alternative, even if the actual shape of the future society is negotiated over a long period through the readjustment of the social forces involved in the initial destruction of the old order and may be different from that originally propounded at the ideological level. Some of these considerations are perhaps equally pertinent to a less catastrophic scenario for Mexico's future.

If the forces congealed in the PRD continue to define the PRI's surrender of power as the only acceptable form of victory – and it is by no means certain that the political leadership of the party will not prove willing to compromise that objective[23] – there is a continuing possibility that a significant shift will eventually occur on the terrain of those pacts with capital that maintain large sections of the population in a permanent condition of crisis and poverty. But it is also possible that the unexpected vigour of the neocardenista movement will moderate the full implementation of the neoliberal agenda in the longer term; radical changes are, of course, scarcely novel in Mexican post-revolutionary history. But there must be some prospect that measures to demobilize the PRD's base will prove sufficient to provide the setting for the completion of a major transformation of the hegemonic process. *Neocardenismo* has formulated some elements of a universalizing discourse, but, like its prototype, leaves the extent of its commitment to redistributing resources and a radical transformation of the bases of social power vaguely defined. Tendencies towards the fragmentation of popular power linked to socio-economic heterogeneity and the continuing functionality of many of the existing mechanisms of domination constitute grave barriers to the achievement of revolutions from below, and even if the hegemonic apparatuses commanded by the PRI were to decay catastrophically, the kind of society which would ultimately emerge from such a breakdown might be radically different from that currently envisaged by the *neocardenistas* in Michoacán.

Notes

1. In addition to Morelia, from the outset the PRI conceded defeat to the PRD in 7 of the other 17 major population centres, including the industrial city of Lázaro Cárdenas, and over 40 smaller *municipios*. With three *municipios* falling to the PAN, and one to the PARM, the PRI was left in control of under half the town halls in the state even according to the official version of the results, but these included a claimed PRI victory in Apatzingán (the Michoacán home of the Cárdenas family since 1940!) based on the annulment of a *casilla* with a PRD majority of 79 and problems in the major city of Uruapan on a scale which eventually forced a re-run of the entire election. I would myself agree that the PRD had cause to question the narrow victory claimed by the PRI in the electoral process I witnessed most closely at first hand, in the *municipio* of Villamar.
2. In a number of cases, such as the town of Sahuayo, eventually won by PAN, fraud occurred in the course of the internal selection process from the PRI's own candidates, although in other cases, such as Cojumatlán, genuinely popular candidates were chosen in the face of resistance from established *caciques*. In the Cojumatlán case the response of Morelia was the traditional one of seeking to resolve the conflict by advocating an accommodation which would leave the *cacique* with a share of power in the new administration, lending some justification to the charge that the governor's hand was insufficiently firm to maximize the image of a cleaned-up party in the minds of the electorate. Several local PRI campaigns sought explicitly to dissociate current candidates from the style and sins of their predecessors, an approach which also makes sense given the past political history of many *perredista* candidates who are defectors from the PRI.
3. Excluding Lázaro Cárdenas, which has received migrants from urban centres elsewhere in the country as well as migrants from rural areas, of Michoacán's urban *municipios* only Morelia displayed significant rates of net in-migration during the 1970s, although the situation changed a little during the 1980s, largely as a result of rural impoverishment. Neither Uruapan nor Apatzingán sustained the high rates of in-migration they achieved during the 1960s in the following decade (see Arroyo Alejandre, 1986).
4. There are, of course, significant differences between countries and regions in the content of the transformations associated with neoliberal-

ism. Given the legacy of their pasts, it is by no means clear what balance will finally be struck in the various countries of Eastern Europe, for example, between a materialist consumer culture, social individualism, technical rather than social rationality in the management of the economy and representative forms of politics. The respective futures of Eastern Europe and Latin America are likely to be interlinked through the question of the distribution of US and other foreign investment between the two areas, given the problematic nature of the global accumulation process as a whole. These are issues which it is scarcely possible to begin to discuss adequately here, and so I will simply assert that what is happening in Mexico today is part of a larger process which rests on global structures, namely the process of capital accumulation on a world scale located within an international political framework of nation states. It is important to stress the significance of the national states system as much as the existence of a global capital accumulation process, since it is increasingly apparent that the former cannot be seen as simply an epiphenomenon of the latter, but is as fundamental to understanding the historical process of modernity as the development of modern capitalism. I would, however, wish, however unfashionably, to defend the idea that present developments are related to the dynamics of the global capital accumulation process in a fundamental way. For one analysis, see, for example, O'Connor (1988).

5. One valuable attempt to rectify this dearth of synthesis is offered by Bartra (1985).
6. See, for example, Rello (1986) and Gordillo (1988).
7. For further discussion and evidence on these points, see Gledhill (1991).
8. In the case of the USA we are often talking of urban employment today, as was also the case in the period prior to the Great Depression and the deportations. One of the reasons for the relative reluctance of many Michoacanos to participate in the 'neo-bracero' programme based on the H2A work permit is that it is oriented towards agricultural labour.
9. This process is certainly occurring in the Ciénega de Chapala region of Michoacán, where rental of prime-quality irrigated *ejidal* land has now returned to levels comparable with the previous point of maximum decay of the system in the 1960s.
10. In the case of the *ejidos* in the irrigated part of the temperate zone of Michoacán, neolatifundist cultivation of fruit and vegetables has had in the past to compete for resources with peasant cultivation of the sorghum and safflower demanded by the animal-feedstuffs and urban cooking-oil industries respectively, a balance which is shifting as peasants withdraw from cultivation.
11. Just before the elections, Salinas made his first (eight-hour) visit to Michoacán since assuming the presidency, targeted on the Meseta. The pretext was the opening of a new section of paved road which scarcely represented a popular demand on the part of the communities, though it was no doubt welcomed by the timber companies and tour operators. The visit, by helicopter, was not judged a success. Assurances were given that Plan Michoacán, a major programme of state investment in the state

introduced as a gambit in the presidential campaign, was not the fiction it thus far had seemed, though little evidence to the contrary has yet materialized, and a more punitive approach to allocation of federal resources seems an inevitable consequence of the local election results.

12. As PRI governor of Michoacán, Cuauhtémoc Cárdenas was not, as far as I could discern, particularly well-liked by the peasantry of the Ciénega, though it must be admitted that the abysmal record of his successor, Martínez Villacaña, forced to resign before completing his period in consequence of scandalous personal conduct and his marked lack of affinity with political modernization, would have retrospectively enhanced the reputation of almost any predecessor.
13. In his later years the old *caudillo* did, of course, adopt a more explicitly favourable posture towards socialism, sought to protect the left from persecution and expressed his support for the formation of new independent mass organizations, in particular the CCI. Whether one should interpret any of his actions as a commitment to the idea of a fundamental transformation of Mexican society must be open to question; see, for example, Armando Bartra's commentary on the significance of Cárdenas' patronage of the CCI (Bartra, 1985: 92). It does, however, seem plausible to argue that Cárdenas' actions reflected his frustration with the turn taken by social policy under Alemán and his successors, and his increasing recognition that the hegemonic apparatus of the institutional revolution was ossifying. As Enrique Krauze has remarked, once out of power, Cárdenas began to understand the problems of concentration of power, to which he had himself made a signal contribution (Krauze, 1987: 181).
14. In his earlier writings, Gramsci's discussion of hegemony concerns the conditions for the proletariat's establishing its leadership of a revolutionary class alliance. In the prison writings, it is broadened into a theory of bourgeois power which transcends utilitarian and instrumental conceptions of the state and, indeed, extends the concept of the state and its hegemonic apparatuses well beyond the domain of political institutions and agencies of government (Buci-Glucksmann, 1978).
15. To some extent, Salinas could be said to have appropriated the programme of PAN, and co-operation between PAN and the PRI could be mutually beneficial in the sense that the former is unlikely ever to win national power in its own right whilst the latter would benefit from moderated opposition from this quarter. Nevertheless, the concession of the state governorship of Baja California to PAN and subsequent promises of greater access to power was followed by a refusal to recognize some PAN victories in Sinaloa in municipal elections in 1989, suggesting that it may not be so easy for the centre to impose its will on the local forces controlling the party apparatus.
16. It must be stressed that some elements of the regional professional classes remain activists of the PRI, including teachers, seeking either to preserve their existing place in the patronage structure or simply to hold on to a federal job they are afraid of losing. But the rise of a dissident and militant teachers' movement in Michoacán has played an important part

in the mobilization of other elements of the population, and militant teachers played an important role in the PRD campaign in the Ciénega.

17. I can attest personally to the presence of a threat of armed confrontation on the part of *priístas* in the *municipio* of Villamar on the Sunday when the municipal election committee met to deliver a final result, which failed to become concrete in part because of the numerical inferiority of the PRI supporters and in part because of the discipline displayed by their opponents. In the Meseta, at least one PRD candidate was assassinated and the general level of confrontation was higher on both sides. In the weeks before the elections a large group of armed PRD militants from the indigenous town of Cherán had blockaded all exit roads from neighbouring Nahuatzen with a view to apprehending, and presumably assassinating, the PRI local deputy imposed on them in the state elections (Salud Maldonado, personal communication). Violence of some severity occurred in cities like Morelia and Apatzingán, in circumstances which suggested systematic provocation, but the PRD generally managed to combat the PRI's attempt to associate it with an image of disorder.
18. Electorally, a past history of activism in the PRI does not seem to be a total disadvantage, although those who take a jaundiced view of Cuauhtémoc invariably begin by arguing that his claims to have been a great reforming governor bear some discussion. Indeed, in some cases one could argue that the personal popularity of PRI defectors was an advantage to the PRD in the context of local elections. Some sections of the population do, however, distrust *políticos* irrespective of their current colour, perhaps not unreasonably in a state where the original *cardenismo* was so strongly associated with *caciquismo* (Gledhill, 1991).
19. These embrace both traditional procedures based on structures of intermediation and patronage, and evolving techniques for the selective manipulation of the remaining economic resources being offered by the state. To these means of control must be added the new possibilities offered by privatization and economic liberalization.
20. Despite some internal disagreements on this question, the UCEZ has maintained its distance from political movements, including the PRD, although its members generally vote for the party, and the movement enjoyed a degree of support from Cuauhtémoc as governor, within the limits of the rules of the game determined by his position in the PRI.
21. See, for example, Barkin, 1987.
22. The Leninist conception of revolution was flawed by its focus on the question of capturing the state at the expense of consideration of the post-revolutionary hegemonic process required to transform society socially and democratically. Gramsci's mature concept of hegemony improves substantially on the Leninist vision of the *praxis* of the revolutionary process, but also entails abandoning faith in the inevitability of human emancipation through the direct effects of class conflict between proletariat and bourgeoisie. For this reason, he can be appropriated as the Marxist precursor of the new post-Marxist theory of social movements. It is possible to read Gramsci in either a voluntarist or structuralist

manner, and this no doubt reflects real ambiguities and contradictions in his thought. But in my reading, Gramsci did not relinquish a commitment to a totalizing view of the social question; he simply accepted its growing complexity under more developed capitalist conditions. Nor did he abandon the idea that the social development of capitalist societies is shaped in a fundamental way by the class and capital accumulation process.

23. There is some evidence to suggest that the upper echelons of the PRD were willing to come to an accommodation with the PRI with regard to the fate of some *municipios* where the results were disputed in the December 1989 elections, but abandoned this position once it was clear that it was unacceptable to their base.

Part II

US–MEXICAN RELATIONS AND ECONOMIC REFORM

4· SHIFTS IN MEXICAN FOREIGN POLICY IN THE 1980s

Mónica Serrano

Over the past three decades Mexican foreign policy has alternated between passivity and activism. Over different periods, it has been possible to identify a correlation between passivity and higher concentration in bilateral relations with the United States, whereas activism has often been associated with diversification efforts aimed at diluting such concentration. The centrality of this bilateral relation, with its concomitant vicinity, dependency and power asymmetry, to Mexican foreign policy has been accepted almost as an axiom from which its two main alternatives have been derived, namely diversification or concentration. At different moments the centrality of the US element has led Mexican foreign policy to emphasize extreme versions of these alternatives – the idea of a special relationship with the US and that of Latin American integration – and to see them as mutually exclusive.

What seems clear is that both the search for an understanding with the northern neighbour as well as efforts to open up new options represent the two faces of the same problem: the proximity to a superpower. The choice and feasibility of either strategy has resulted from the combination of three factors: the rigidity or flexibility of the international environment, Mexico's relative power and the domestic political situation. The perception of significant threats to Mexico's security, stemming from the unbalanced power structure underlying relations with the northern neighbour, has been an important reference for the country's foreign policy. The value of legality as embodied in the principles followed by that foreign policy, that is, self-determination, non-intervention, the legal equality of nations and peaceful solution of controversies, expressed a defensive attitude which was a response to Mexico's historical experience and geopolitical location. This policy gradually evolved as a 'legalistic' foreign policy, by which political postures were normally adopted in procedural terms. This approach enabled the country to pursue certain political aims simply by defending the observance of its fundamental principles. It has therefore been defined as a defensive, reactive and relatively independent foreign policy characterized by continuity and predictability from which both its strength and consistency were derived. Its underlying rationale identified the legal pursuit of independent postures with a potential brake on foreign destabilization and intervention not only in Latin America, but above all in Mexico (Ojeda, 1976: 45). Nevertheless, for a long time concern with preserving such consistency fulfilled the role that planning for long-term goals has normally played in foreign policy formulation.

By the mid-1970s several factors paved the way for a new pattern of activism opened up by the Echeverría administration. Underlying the more recent debate concerning the continuity or discontinuity of foreign policy with this pattern of activism lay the fact of domestic and external factors foreclosing the options that the new policy had attempted to open. This chapter analyses the major foreign policy initiatives of the López Portillo and de la Madrid administrations. It identifies the motives and objectives shaping Mexican diplomacy during these years. On this basis, it attempts to explore the various standpoints from which these policies could be properly assessed: 1) the underlying context to their formulation; 2) the actual content of activism during the two periods; 3) the relationship between activism and diplomatic diversification; and 4) their success in achieving their objectives, namely, in enabling the country to attain a more autonomous and independent position.

The new foreign policy

Foreign policy has been defined as 'that area of politics which bridges the all-important boundary between the nation state and its international environment' and that therefore opposes rigid separations of the diplomatic and political world, on the one hand, from the economic on the other (Wallace, 1977: 7). This is particularly important in the case of Mexico where geographical and economic factors have posed a threat to territorial integrity, and subsequently, have pulled the country towards increasing integration with the USA. There is little doubt that Mexico's place in the international political system has been a constant in the country's position between autonomy and dependence. The USA is one of the main, if not the most important, referent objects for its autonomy, understood as its ability independently and coherently to determine national policies, to resist attempts at outside control, and to control and maximize favourable and unfavourable international trends. Until the 1970s search for automony was confined to the assertion of its regulating principles. This policy set the basis for a tacit understanding with the USA by which Mexico's right to dissent within certain limits was acknowledged (Ojeda, 1976: 92–4). However, if it is true that this strategy had enabled the country to preserve some scope for independent action, it did not provide the necessary mechanisms successfully to exploit new international opportunitities. As the complex dynamic of economic integration continued to reduce the margin of autonomy and to sharpen Mexico's vulnerability to US actions, the need for a new direction in foreign policy became clear.

During the 1970s the perception of limits in the model of import substitution tilted the balance in favour of export promotion. This shift took place alongside emerging signs of tension in the bilateral relations with the northern neighbour.[1] This situation raised doubts about the idea of a special US–Mexican relationship and forced the Echeverría administration to recognize the need for a new and more dynamic foreign policy.

Clearly US policies conflicted with domestic interests. Yet, the tendency to attribute to US policy making considerable cohesion and a deliberate concern to control important factors in society led the Echeverría government to claim that the 'special relationship' had come to an end. Not only did the new foreign policy stress the need to incorporate a new economic dimension, but its activism was defined in opposition to 'bilateral negotiations with the US'. These statements suggested a failure in identifying the features of a hypothetical special relationship and consequently those potential forces leading to both co-operation and competition that could enable the Mexican government to assess the realities of a special relationship.[2]

Prevailing international conditions characterized by detente between the two superpowers and the emergence of alternative poles of power favoured the change of direction in Mexican foreign policy towards greater assertiveness and activism. Throughout the 1970s the country increasingly diversified its international links and acquired a more assertive and autonomous presence in international fora. Yet, a potential friction between the new economic pragmatic dimension and the traditional political function fulfilled by foreign policy soon became clear. Signs of this were evident first in the inherent tension between the observance of traditional principles and the implementation of a more active foreign policy. Although the original content of the new Third World activism that accompanied Mexican foreign policy during the 1970s was intended to be primarily economic, it occasionally forced the government to assume political commitments at relatively high costs. These costs were both economic and political in nature.

A simplistic equation established between passivity and a foreign policy based on principles, together with the improvisation which characterized foreign policy formulation during the Echeverría administration, led to inconsistencies in the application of those principles. This shift carried serious implications for the defensive strength of the traditional foreign policy, whereas the effects of a tourist boycott on the balance of payments revealed the economic limits of the new activism and the high costs that improvised or unnecessary actions could involve.[3]

The tension between the political and economic dimensions of foreign policy was also reflected in the gap that lay between the rhetoric and actual achievements of Echeverría's administration. As commentators were forced to lay greater stress on the problems facing the country, serious doubts arose about the compatibility between increasing dependence and an assertive foreign policy, and to whether structural factors and critical economic conditions made a *rapprochement* with the northern neighbour the only rational alternative. What seems beyond doubt is that this tension embodied a more complex dilemma between the political costs of higher integration with the USA and the economic and political risks of diversification. The failure of Echeverría's activism and the rhetorical nature of his foreign policy have normally been explained as the result of a basic incompatability between dependence and activism, of a lack of willingness or an incapacity to give actual content to the diplomacy of diversification, and of the legitimating role that foreign policy was intended to serve.[4]

It seems more likely that the serious difficulties experienced at the time in the model of import substitution not only set clear limits to the short-term prospects of diversification but, most importantly, made clear the extent to which careful pragmatic evaluation and long-term planning were the *sine qua non* of successful diversification. The Brazilian experience is particularly interesting in this respect. Although economic international relations only gained foreign policy importance in the 1970s, Brazil's decision to formulate foreign policy with an economic dimension can be traced back to the 1950s. This decision provided foreign policy formulation with a basis both to assess relations with the USA and to create reliable mechanisms for export promotion. Although the idea of a special relationship with the USA also permeated Brazilian foreign policy, the limits to Brazilian pro-Americanism were soon evident. On the one hand the bilateral relationship with the hegemonic power was not seen as an end in itself but rather as a means of furthering the country's wider aims of economic development and greater independence. On the other, Brazil developed a complex system of export incentives and subsidies, for example, trade promotion missions normally included fixed quotas of manufactured or semi-manufactured goods, which became an important instrument of the successful diversification of markets and exports, which provided a solid economic foundation to foreign policy in the 1970s.[5] Indeed, it seems that the decisive factor in the Mexican case was the absence of clear direction and internal weakness rather than a total lack of alternatives. Closing the gap between diplomatic and economic diversification could only be the result of a gradual process. Notwithstanding all this, Echeverría's main legacy to foreign policy was an 'internationalist consciousness concerning the close links between major national problems and international factors and about the need to take the country out of its isolationism and passivity.'[6]

López Portillo, the foreign policy of pragmatism

López Portillo's first move in foreign policy indicated a willingness to return to what prevalent conditions suggested advisable, that is, to recover domestic confidence and a friendly relationship with the northern neighbour. The 1976 economic and financial crisis had not only, and significantly, undermined negotiating capacity, but had made domestic problems the main concern of the new administration. The decision to abandon rhetoric and the active presence in multilateral fora coincided with the apparent willingness of the incoming Carter administration to give special attention to relations with Mexico. Signs of this convergence were the creation of new mechanisms to negotiate the solution of bilateral problems and the Mexican decision to expand its oil exports to the northern neighbour.

Nevertheless, problems soon re-emerged. Although interpreted at the time as sign of US pressures placed directly on the Mexican government, the presentation of a new immigration law to Congress and the decision of the Carter administration to suspend the negotiations on the sale of Mexican gas had also a clear domestic dimension. Undoubtedly, the emergence of Mexico as a significant oil exporter in the late 1970s increased national sensitivity with respect to sovereignty by placing the country within the orbit of US national security interests. Even though both US decisions were of a domestic character, and with respect to gas negotiations Mexico's performance was not particularly outstanding, the proximity and asymmetry of the bilateral relationship magnified their effects on Mexico. As links between the two countries and societies expanded so did the scope for potential conflict. It would be wrong to underestimate the interest and eventual pressure of some sectors in the US on the Mexican government's decisions with regard to oil, but Mexican expectations in relation to the price of gas were clearly unrealistic.[7]

Suspension of negotiations on the sale of gas only marked a turning point towards increasing deterioration in US–Mexican relations and again brought to the fore the dichotomy of Mexican foreign policy. The country's new status as an oil exporter together with the underlying strain to the bilateral relation led López Portillo to recover the legacy of Echeverría's activism. The new foreign policy would attempt to correct previous mistakes by avoiding rhetoric for its own sake and by gradually closing the gap between objectives and outcomes. It was an attempt to grant foreign policy with a new pragmatism in the Brazilian style. The crucial role of planning was recognized in the pursuit of clear objectives:

- to foster diversification in order to achieve greater autonomy;
- to pursue a new balance between the bilateral and multilateral dimensions of diplomacy;
- in the light of increasing instability in Central America, to achieve stability in the southern frontier; and
- to perform a mediating role in the recovery of the North–South dialogue.

The basic challenge was the reformulation of a multilateral strategy which could simultaneously reconcile the defence of traditional national interests and the more concrete objectives that would shape the new foreign policy agenda. Diversification proceeded during the late 1970s and early 1980s but followed a new pattern. Most efforts were in terms of markets, but export composition became increasingly dominated by oil, accounting for 75 per cent of total exports for the period 1979–81. The discovery of oil reserves transformed the position of Mexico within the international scene. It significantly increased its economic presence as the fourth world oil producer and highlighted its strategic value in geopolitical terms. These factors indicated that in the long term the discovery and exploitation of oil reserves would involve positive and negative risks in the international arena. On the one hand, by contributing to overcoming the 1976 financial crisis, oil not only offered new prospects for diversification, but most importantly for the consolidation of a more independent foreign policy. The new resources would enable the country to achieve significant rates of economic growth and to have access to new markets and technology transfers. Among the negative risks, one could mention the increasing uncompetitiveness of other exports, the petrolization of the economy, the displacement of domestic agriculture by food imports, an increasing integration with the US economy and an overall higher external vulnerability.

During the López Portillo administration the rhetoric of pragmatism did not lead to a convergence between objectives and outcomes. The initial aim of restoring the balance between the bilateral and multilateral dimensions of diplomacy turned into a determination to abandon the illusion of a special relationship with the USA. Although it is true that a constant source of friction in US–Mexican relations has been the failure of successive US governments to give actual content to the hypothetical pre-eminence granted to Mexico, in the case of the Carter administration, López Portillo's personality became an additional obstacle. If we compare the Mexican case with that of Brazil, both had in common the decision to abandon the idea of a special relationship. Nevertheless in the latter case relations with the hegemonic power were conducted on the basis of clear national objectives, regardless of whether they conflicted with US policies, and of a clear determintion to avoid unnecessary divergences. Two factors help to explain this difference. On the one hand, it is possible that Brazil unlike Mexico, was sufficiently distant from the US for their policies not to collide and, on the other, Brazil's distinctive and non-personalized foreign policy provided it with clear, long-term national objectives (Hurrell, 1986: 93–4).

López Portillo's diplomacy preserved its identification with Third World causes particularly with respect to world trade. In a joint effort with Austria the Mexican government attempted to reactivate the debate over a new international economic order by persuading Washington to hold the last North–South summit in Cancún. Even though foreign policy under López Portillo had replaced previous aspirations for Third World leadership with a more mediating role, as the international political climate shifted towards the right and Third World activism faded in the early 1980s Mexico found itself as a leader of Third World aspirations.

Its strategy to achieve stability in the southern border faced a number of difficulties. First, the decision of the López Portillo administration to break diplomatic relations with the Somoza regime in May 1979 followed by the French–Mexican declaration of August 1981 recognizing the Salvadorean rebel forces contradicted one of the fundamental principles of Mexican foreign policy. It is undeniable that political considerations accompanied both decisions. In the first case, the prospect of an imminent Sandinista victory encouraged the Mexican government to pursue an influential and moderating role within the emerging regime, while the second move was aimed at opening the prospects for a negotiated settlement that could incorporate the left opposition. The ultimate goal of both diplomatic decisions was the avoidance of further internationalization of the Central American crisis and, consequently, the preservation of stability in the southern border. The 1980 San José agreement on energy co-operation with all Central American and Caribbean states contributed to this end by signalling to the Reagan administration that the ultimate solution of the crisis was dependent upon the improvement of socio-economic conditions and not on military confrontation. Nevertheless, gradually it would become clear that the difficulties that Mexican policies faced in Central America not only resulted from regional alignments and polarization induced by the East–West approach of the Reagan administration but, equally important, from the legitimate and concrete national interests of surrounding states including Costa Rica, Panama, Colombia and Venezuela (Herrera Zúñiga and Chavarría, 1984: 473–4).

Mexican foreign policy under López Portillo followed a relatively more consistent path than had been the case under Echeverría. This time, however, it was the oil factor which accounted for a continuing gulf between rhetoric and reality. The discovery and exploitation of oil postponed urgent structural economic reforms while allowing Mexico to indulge in dreams of achieving a middle-power status. In the resulting confusion foreign policy continued defending abstractions such as 'solidarity', 'co-operation' and 'international equality'. Ironically it was the ambitious character of these objectives that endowed the country's foreign policy with a historical dimension as well as with profound weaknesses, (Garza, 1984: 446). The absence of clear and precise definitions of national interests and of foreign policy objectives contributes to explaining both the lack of content of such abstractions as well as the divorce between rhetoric and reality.

If in the previous administration the gap between the economic and political dimensions of diversification could be attributed partly to the absence of structural conditions enabling the economy to provide its foreign policy with a more solid foundation, in the context of the late 1970s the enduring gap seemed to be more the result of incoherence, lack of consistency and internal weakness. Although international options would again narrow during the first half of the 1980s, the López Portillo administration missed the exceptional opportunity offered by the oil resources to consolidate national independence and foreign policy diversification.

Brazil, facing a similarly unfavourable international environment in the 1980s but without oil and without the many-stranded involvement with the US, offers a better example of autonomy and self-assertion. Throughout the 1970s economic factors gradually pushed back ideological constraints on that country's foreign policy, including its close alliance with the US, and led it effectively to diversify its international links. The main policy guidelines of the *Pragmatismo Responsable* were: freedom of action for diplomacy and pragmatic assessment of converging and conflicting interests within a new ecumenical perspective; in other words, the optimization of the country's freedom of manoeuvre and the range of available foreign policy options (Ministerio das Relações Exteriores, 1975). Behind increasing Brazilian assertiveness was a more fragile international economic posture resulting from the combination of the oil crisis, a mounting foreign debt and the increasing protectionism of industrialized countries.[8] Oil needs and the craving for new export markets and sources of foreign investment had led the country first to recognize the Cuban-backed government of Angola in 1975, steadily to expand its economic ties with Arab countries, to identify itself with Third World demands and to increase its economic exchanges with COMECON. Although it was determined not to revive the special relation with the US it also sought to avoid unnecessary divergences. Yet, it was through effective diversification that it sought a counterweight to US power and influence and laid the basis for a broader international role. This quest for maximum diplomatic flexibility explains both the country's moderate and pragmatic approach to various international issues, as well as its avoidance of confrontation: 'rigid polarisation, whether between North and South, or between East and West, would almost certainly limit the country's freedom of manoeuvre by forcing it to opt for one side or another' (Hurrell, 1986: 352–3).

In contrast, the negative risks attached to the discovery and exploitation of oil in Mexico soon became clear. If oil enabled the country to play a more influential role in the international scene it also accelerated the pace of economic integration with the US, reinforcing its vulnerability and dependence. The 1982 crisis placed debt negotiations at the top of the agenda, relegating the political goal of diversification. Foreign trade not only remained geographically concentrated in the US market – in 1981 79 per cent of Mexican exports and 67 per cent of total imports were traded in the US market – but also dominated by oil. By 1982 50 per cent of oil exports were concentrated in the northern market.

Even before the attempt towards diversification had been abruptly interrupted in 1982 there were already signs of new conditions under which the pragmatic foreign policy would be tested.[9] These included the exhaustion of the post-Second World War expansion of world trade, the unhealthy conditions under which credit had been contracted increasing the amount of the external debt from $US40 billion to 90 billion between December 1979 and December 1982, the inherent risks of petrolization of the economy as well as the prospects of renewed bipolarity resulting from the election of Reagan as president of the USA.

The crisis made clear the extent to which the trends of the 1970s failed to materialize in real diversification. The gap between rhetoric and reality was also manifested in the realization that the trend towards increasing bilateral dependence with the USA was not a short but a long-term and non-reversible one. The significant reduction of liquidity suggested that high interest rates would prevail for a long period; this in turn increased the need of export surpluses to service the debt.

If such dependency had it origins in deep-seated geographical and structural factors, the debt crisis further foreclosed the options. Most of the conditions that in the past had favoured an active foreign policy as well as almost all alternatives to increasing dependence on the USA withered away. With a structural dependence upon imports of capital goods the new scarcity of foreign exchange created a direct form of dependence on potential suppliers. Economic autonomy was significantly constrained since the crisis gave international monetary institutions a voice in the formulation and implementation of policy, and successive rescheduling became conditional on the achievements of economic performance. An imminent reconsideration of the bilateral relation with the USA that could check what many viewed as the unrealistic excesses of Mexico's foreign policy was expected. Mexico's capacity to influence events remained limited, and the foundations of the new activism proved to be fragile. The oil card could only be played within confined and special circumstances. As the international situation changed, the foundations of US hegemony remained in place. The weight of the US presence within the institutions that Mexico was forced to turn to for assistance enabled the USA to lay down the rules of the game, to set the agenda, to manipulate choices and to close off new options.

It would be wrong to underestimate the impact of the debt crisis and the adverse conditions of the 1980s upon Brazil's freedom of action. As in Mexico, Brazil saw its position affected significantly by a renewed Cold War rhetoric and the unfavourable international economic environment characterized by a second oil shock, higher interest rates and the increasing protectionism of the industrialized countries. If it is true that these conditions increased its awareness of new limits to its foreign policy, 'Brazil's emergence suffered some serious but not as yet as fatal reverses' (Whitehead, 1986: 89–90). The country's level of autonomy had increased significantly although at the cost of new and real problems, among which a massive external debt and external vulnerability were the most important. Despite this, 'the internationalisation of Brazil's economy did not translate in a uniformly negative impact, while it had opened new possibilities for increased independent action and had strengthened the Brazilian capacity to bargain effectively in the international arena'. (Hurrell,

1986: 353–6). Although the debt crisis increased both Brazil and Mexico's financial and trade dependence on the USA, and revealed their fragile position, Brazil's achievements in the 1970s might prove to be a more solid foundation for future alternatives. Perhaps the most significant difference between Mexican and Brazilian foreign policies in the 1980s was the gradual shift of the first towards its northern neighbour and the 'Latinamericanisation' of the latter.[10]

The idea of a US–Mexican special relationship. A sounder pragmatism?

As the need for a more cautious foreign policy and closer relations with the northern neighbour was being acknowledged by the previous foreign minister, Jorge Castañeda, the difficult external position inherited by the incoming administration became clear. Once de la Madrid entered office he made clear the limits to external action. In his view, 'pressing domestic and external conditions seemed to suggest the convenience of a *rapprochement* with the US, both to achieve greater co-operation and to avoid political and economic pressures' (Garza, 1984: 446).

The management of the external debt since 1982 remained as the overriding external concern. De la Madrid followed a strategy of negotiation and co-operation. Relatively successful negotiations in 1982, 1983–4 and 1986–7, favouring Mexico in terms of access to liquidity, enabled the government to continue servicing its debt at the cost of economic growth and a significant increase in the total amount of external debt.[11]

Between 1983 and 1988 servicing the external debt implied an annual transfer of an estimated 6.1 per cent of the GNP and a high proportion of export incomes (39 per cent in 1987, the best year). An export surplus became possible after the contraction of the domestic market and the success of export promotion policies, which included an undervalued peso. Real exchange rates and real wages were the principal mechanisms through which the government achieved external competitiveness (Dornbusch, 1988: 247).

Economic considerations as well as domestic and external criticisms led de la Madrid to impose new limits upon Mexico's commitments in Central America. Earlier unilateral policies were replaced with a multilateral approach by which the identification of common interests would gradually set the basis for negotiations. In this way the previous emphasis on bilateral relations with Nicaragua was followed by a new regional consensus. To a certain extent this move reflected a return to the traditional limits of Mexican dissidence. The collective effort enabled Mexico to play a more impartial role, closer to that of mediator, and to downplay the potential interventionist character of the former foreign policy.

The reformulation of policy towards Central America opened the debate about the continuity or discontinuity of foreign policy formulation. Perhaps the main sign of continuity was expressed in the determination of de la Madrid to maintain a presence in Central America but above all in the decision to keep the emphasis on the socio-economic dimension of the regional crisis, notwithstanding potential disagreement with the ideological stress of Reagan's policies in the area. The main differences were the decision to pursue a new strategy of collective diplomacy, which materialized in the creation of the Contadora group in 1983.[12] This was aimed at reducing tensions by proposing general policy lines and concrete negotiations to the five Central American states. In that same year a Mexican initiative led to the setting up of a support committtee for economic and social development in the region.

By 1985 a concrete proposal, 'The Act of Contadora to Promote Peace and Cooperation in Central America', was finally achieved. Nevertheless, the combination of domestic opposition to negotiations involving guerrilla movements in El Salvador, the reluctance of the Nicaraguan government to negotiate with the opposition, Costa Rican diagreements, but above all US dislike for the initiative played against any concrete achievements.[13] If it is true that the scheme offered by the Contadora not only threatened the US position within the negotiating process but entailed clear competition with US regional initiatives, it could also be argued that, in principle, it represented an acceptable option as it contributed to containing the conflict. Moreover, internal differences within the Reagan administration help to explain both the pressures exerted on Mexico as well as the possibility of a continued Mexican role throughout the crisis. Among certain sectors of the US government, Mexican foreign policy was seen as a major obstacle to the success of US policies in the region. Covert and economic pressure to force a change of direction in Mexico's position in the region was even considered.[14] Yet, internal division also contributed to the room of manoeuvre enjoyed by Mexican foreign policy towards Central America. Although the weight of external pressure against US military intervention should not be underestimated, it seems fairly clear that it was the Congress that foreclosed such an option.[15] Despite this, US opposition should not be underrated. By 1986 the Contadora made a final attempt to break the long impasse generated by the persistent US demand for a 'pluralist Nicaraguan democracy' and the Nicaraguan requirement of an immediate halt to US backing of the Contras. The impasse was finally broken by the Arias plan of August 1987 which continued to fulfil the Contadora's goal of pacification and moderation.[16]

While it is true that the Contadora set the basis for renewed attention to Mexican foreign policy in Latin America and provided the framework for increasing diplomatic contact among Latin American countries, the concertation of a Latin American front of debtors could not be interpreted as another sign of continuity. Not only did the previous foreign policy lack a clear strategy towards Latin America but the new efforts could barely grant a solid basis for renewed activism. The Cartagena consensus represented more an act of solidarity in defence of the thesis of shared responsibility between creditors and debtors than an alliance for common action. Similarly, the subsequent 1987 Acapulco declaration embodied a Latin American consensus about the need for some debt reduction both to stop negative transfers and to limit the size of the debt. Although since 1988 the Brady Plan has helped to reduce Mexico's debt, and those of Costa Rica and Venezuela, this has been carried under the lines set by the US, namely, on a voluntary and case-by-case basis. After eight years, Latin America's overall debt problem remains far from being solved. The outflow of interest payments and profit remittances shrank slightly, but the region's net export of capital remains at around $20–25bn. The debt crisis has had a centrifugal effect; each country, almost always preceded by Mexico, has remained engaged in essentially bilateral negotiations with its creditors. Despite increasing protectionism of industrialized countries, Latin American states are still competing against each other for access to markets. This situation has been further complicated by an increasing US deficit politicizing access to its market. And what now seems clear is that 'just as the growth of Latin American debt in the late 1970s proceeded at a pace that was clearly unsustainable, so the post-1982 growth in US imports from Latin America proceeded at a pace too fast to continue' (Whitehead, 1986: 121). The debt and the new protectionism gave rise to two new dimensions of dependency and competition: that of trade access to industrialized countries on favourable terms and access to liquidity on comparable terms.

Under the de la Madrid administration the activism of foreign policy was preserved but in a more moderate and discrete version, in most cases shielded by the concertation of multilateral channels. It is perhaps this transit towards multilateralism that is the most singular feature of foreign policy in the 1980s. If the new circumstances demanded a change that enabled Mexico to share responsibilities, commitments, risks and achievements with other governments, they also set the limits to a new collective activism. The new diplomacy departed from the assumption that at the inter-American level Mexico could no longer afford the price of being the traditional and 'lonely provocateur' (Ojeda, 1986: 121).

The implementation of a 'sober' foreign policy in the 1980s, by placing pragmatism high on the agenda and significantly reducing the range of realistic promises, in itself closed the gap between objectives and outcomes. In the Latin American area the distance between rhetoric and achievements can be explained in terms of external constraints reducing the number of options available. Nevertheless, it is not yet clear whether Latin American renewed dependence on the USA has been the result of a global recession and international changes leading other international partners to withdraw or of a long-term re-establishment of the conditions on which US preponderance has been previously based (Whitehead, 1986: 102). Following this line of analysis a global economic recovery could again open new prospects. The extent to which this hypothetical situation could also be applied to the Mexican case remains as one of the most complex questions underlying foreign policy formulation.

In the case of the bilateral relationship with the US, the pragmatism was embodied in de la Madrid's determination to pursue a *rapprochement* that made room for co-operation while avoiding potential sources of conflict. Ironically, it is at this level that the success of his efforts met more obstacles. Just as there were mixed results for the government in its 'political obsession to regain private-sector confidence' following the nationalization of the banks, the more co-operative attitude shown by the de la Madrid administration did not bring immediate results (Maxfield, 1989: 224). As the bilateral relation continued to deteriorate there was mounting dissatisfaction among Mexican circles and serious doubts about the prospects of a policy of concessions.[17]

The legacy of the debt crisis was the implementation of an economic programme that further accelerated the pace of economic integration and dependence on the US market. This in turns set the basis for the need for closer co-operation. The paradoxical situation between the will to co-operate and a prevailing political climate of high tension induced, on the one hand, a lack of consensus in relation to policy towards the northern neighbour and, on the other, an awareness that the sources of conflict are very deep indeed. As the characteristic asymmetry of the bilateral relation permeates every detail and aspect of the same relation so do the sources of conflict. Consequently potential friction is in-built in the same relation, as well as in the economic and political realities of both countries.

As mentioned earlier, Mexico's differing views about the nature and means of dealing with the Central American crisis provided the first area of friction. In addition, the 1982 crisis opened a new period of uncertainty about the risks to the US economy stemming from the huge border shared with Mexico. A negative vision dominated the Reagan administration concerning most aspects of the relationship with the southern neighbour. Mexico's insolvency threated the US banking system, and it was feared that a stagnated economy would soon lead to massive migration. Moreover, Mexico's continued activism in Central America was seen as challenging US 'policies in the area and further increasing the risk of migration. Finally, corruption and governmental inefficiency raised serious doubts about the solidity of Mexican stability' (Aguilar Camín, 1988: 190–91).

By 1987 this perception appeared to be no longer restricted to US élites or official circles but seemed to have permeated US public opinion. Since the Second World War, until 1965, the US government had officially encouraged Mexican immigration. It continued to do so, though tacitly, until 1971 when it became an issue of the bilateral agenda. Even though most studies have shown that both countries overall gain more than they lose from migration, under the conditions of the 1980s a consensus emerged within the US Congress about the need to protect the national borders. In 1970 there were 4.2 million people in the US of Mexican origin, by 1987 this figure had increased to 11.8 million, while from 1980 onwards the birth rate among Mexican–Americans has been three times that of the rest of the population. In October 1986 the Simpson–Rodino immigration reform was finally adopted.[18] It is true that the new legislation granted amnesty to those Mexicans who had entered the USA before 1985, but their illegal status has complicated its implementation. Ironically, Simpson–Rodino introduced what was thought to be a more effective approach of sanctioning employers, which was first proposed by Mexico in the 1950s.[19]

The second source of concern was drug-trafficking. Although the traffic of marijuana and heroin had been intense during the 1960s, since the 'interception operation' the two countries continued co-operating effectively on narcotics control. Nevertheless, the 1980s saw an expansion of the drug flow, stemming from the fact that economic policy remained the overriding concern of the Mexican government, the spread of corruption in the Mexican police and a burgeoning demand for drugs in the USA. Drug production increased during the 1980s and Mexico became the natural path for Colombian cocaine. This situation caused alarm amongst US public opinion about the safety of its society and reinforced negative views of Mexico as one of the main factors underlying US social decomposition.

Tensions between the USA and Mexico on drugs reached a climax in 1985 with the murder in Mexico of a US drug enforcement officer under apparent local police complicity. The USA responded by slowing normal traffic across the US border, provoking strong Mexican reactions. A year later representatives from a US customs commission and the State Department presented allegations of Mexican corruption in the US Congress, while reports claimed the involvement of a relative of de la Madrid in drug-trafficking. Bilateral relations finally met their lowest point when the US Congress passed an anti-drug bill that included provisions for punitive measures against Mexico unless its record on drug control showed substantial progress (Lowenthal, 1987: 88).

These events have made evident the limited room for action on both sides in relation to many of the economic and social links. Even in cases where US administrations have granted special attention to relations with Mexico, the results have barely met expectations. Intergovernmental relations are likely to remain hostage to pressures emerging from socio-economic relations. The dynamic of relations between the two governments has been characterized, on the one hand, by an increasing tendency towards conflict associated with limited diplomatic contact and state collaboration and, on the other, by the degree of mutual interest in managing bilateral problems. Unilateral responses of either government to domestic crisis entailing conflicting agendas have normally made matters worse. Nevertheless, it seems clear that the sources of conflict could be either checked or aggravated depending on the global context of the bilateral relation, and prevailing economic and political conditions on both sides of the border (Rico, 1989: 387). The tensions that accompanied the de la Madrid *sexenio* indicated a structural change and not solely an apparently deliberate policy of mounting pressure exercised by a conservative US government. The implications of immigration for US cultural integrity and social cohesion, of Mexico's external debt for its financial system, as well as Mexican stability for US security have paved the way for a structural change that has placed Mexico high on the agenda of its northern neighbour (Cornelius, 1988).

Both the lack of negotiating power and the apparent failure of a policy of concessions made it more difficult for the government to negotiate improved relations with the USA. As tensions mounted a debate developed over the extent to which such an unprecedented level of conflict resulted either from deliberate US pressure intended to bring about a change of direction in Mexican foreign policy, from a simple lack of willingness on the part of the Reagan administration to co-operate, or from the in-built sources of tension within the bilateral relation.[20] Although the answer to this question seems to lie in the complex interplay of all these factors, it could be said with some certainty that de la Madrid's strategy of concessions tested the limits of the special relationship. And what seems ironic is that Mexican political stability, normally identified as the cornerstone of such a special relationship, became the clear target of either negligence or deliberate pressure.

The huge border with the US has accentuated some of Mexico's problems but it has also offered some advantages: emigration north has clearly alleviated the demand for jobs; in terms of trade Mexico has also occasionally benefited from special treatment, as recent trade agreements have made clear. The coincidence of incoming administrations in both countries offered hopes for improved relations, as long as both shared an interest in granting increasing links some measure of control. Yet the history, asymmetry and complexity underlying all these links make prospects for overall improvement uncertain. As one problem is solved, many more emerge. The improvement of relations during the last years of the de la Madrid administration, the framework of agreements inherited from those years, as well as the positive outcome of more recent contacts through debt negotiations and legislative commissions, have suggested a change of direction.[21] Although it is difficult to assess the extent to which such change responded to the legacy of de la Madrid's willingness to co-operate, or to a change of personalities in the US presidency as Bush succeeded Reagan, undoubtedly the experience of the 1988 elections in Mexico played a part. This has proved again that successive US governments have acknowledged that economic development and political stability in Mexico represent compatible interests, even if they have not always succeeded in agreeing on the best way to achieve such goals.

The results of the 1988 elections again forced the US to turn its attention to the question of political stability. But equally important was the perception of a clear basis for a new understanding between the two countries. As Kissinger stated in the *Washington Post* early in 1989, 'No other Latin American leader shares to the same degree the preference for market economics, private capital and cooperative solutions' as does Salinas. Mexico's 1989 debt package was the first renegotiation under the Brady Plan and a major indicator of the new attitude of the US towards the Salinas administration. An asymmetric and *ad hoc* integration has taken place between the two economies where problems and dislocations have abounded. If Mexico has traditionally concentrated around 65 per cent of its trade with its northern neighbour, it has recently emerged as the third trading partner for the US.[22]

The ideas of economic integration with the northern neighbour and liberalization were traditionally opposed by most circles in Mexico. Given the asymmetry between the two countries in size, power and wealth, it has been believed that integration would not automatically translate into economic modernization and that it could even foreclose future possibilities for development. Similarly, a number of doubts concerning prospects for Mexican industry remain. It has been feared that as the country is forced to maximize its comparative advantages in a restricted number of goods the development of a national capital goods industry will be limited. In addition, and given the limited size of qualified labour in Mexico, there is deep concern with industries tending to concentrate in basic assembly activities. Furthermore, a particularly fast liberalization preceding more recent efforts towards achieving a free-trade agreement has had uneven effects upon regions, enterprises and productive sectors.[23] There has been strong criticism of the lack of provisions and sufficient time for an orderly adaptation of enterprises. In addition, the timing of such liberalization has been questioned coinciding as it clearly did with a period of structural adjustment in the US aimed at reducing that country's huge trade deficit.[24]

For the past decade the underlying question of US–Mexican relations has been whether these countries will continue towards unpredictable and random integration, or whether they will attempt to pursue a mutually advantageous economic relationship (Pastor and Castañeda, 1988: 265–7; Lowenthal, 1987: 94–102). It is increasingly acknowledged that the relevant question no longer refers to the desirability of integration but to its successful administration. In the context of emerging trade blocs the question and prospects of providing economic integration with some measure of control has not only come to the fore but has dominated the bilateral relation. Salinas' decisions have made clear the extent of his commitment to restructuring the bilateral relation and to institutionalizing a special relationship through a free-trade agreement. Underlying the significant change in US attitudes towards Mexico, from rumours of border militarization before 1988 to a new consensus favouring co-operation, was an increasing realization of the American dimension of many bilateral problems. In relation to immigration, as in many other areas, the apparent failure of unilateral solutions has made clear the need for co-operation. As Saskia Sassen states, the globalization of production and the growth of services in the US economy raise serious doubts as to the effectiveness of a policy based both on unilateral measures, such as the 1986 immigration law, and strict control of US borders (Sassen, 1990: 372, 380–82). Moreover, high co-operation has increasingly been considered as potentially beneficial for the USA, particularly in the light of the market opportunities which Mexico could offer. As Dornbusch has stated, 'beyond the interest in Mexico's stability, the US also has good ecnomic reasons to want a major trade deal'.[25] Despite this, it is not yet clear whether US–Mexican co-operation will take place within a wider framework or through specific approaches to bilateral problems.

Informal negotiations for a free-trade agreement between the two countries started in March 1990 with the creation of a Joint Committee on Trade and Investment and were followed in June by Salinas' request for formal negotiations during a visit to Washington.[26] Not only did that request represent a reversal of the previous Mexican reluctance to any formal negotiation of this kind, it is not yet clear whether Bush shares the same enthusiasm.[27] Given the present conditions a free-trade agreement would particularly benefit Mexico not only because its trade with the US already accounts for more than 85 per cent of its total trade but most importantly because most of its trade restrictions have already been dismantled while Mexican products continue facing protectionist barriers in the US market. Given the tariff structure of the US market, such an agreement could reduce the uncertainty regarding access for Mexican exports and, equally important, it could significantly constrain the capacity of the USA to use trade as a form of pressure for political purposes. Notwithstanding this, a link between democratization and trade liberalization is likely to remain. It is true that Salinas' policies have been warmly received in the USA and that his role in transforming Mexico and US–Mexican relations has been increasingly acknowledged. Yet Kaufman's view that his actions have contributed to 'improving the image of the Mexican political system in the minds of the US public' could be questioned by his apparent half-hearted commitment to democratization. Salinas' hesitation in opening the political system could offer a useful weapon to those sectors in the USA opposed to the conclusion of a free-trade agreement (Purcell, 1990: 425).

At the time of writing the prospects for such an agreement remain unclear. The initiative confronts several obstacles: the pace of US economic cycles, domestic opposition, and US commitments in other countries and regions, amongst others. Evidence of this was provided by the gradiose scheme envisaged in Bush's 'Initiative for the Americas' for a regional free-trade area. Yet, even if a free-trade agreement does not materialize, another alternative could be a less conflictive managed agreement, similar to trade regimes established under national security considerations with countries like Taiwan and Israel. What is clear is that the development of a vigorous export capacity, as Mexico has expanded new product lines and shifted the composition of its exports towards non-traditional items, has created the conditions for new tensions.[28] Bilateral trade conflicts are likely to intensify particularly in the light of the huge US commercial deficit, leading to renewed protectionism.

Although it is true that a significant change has taken place in Mexican opinion, suggesting relatively wide support for Salinas' policies, profound political sensitivities remain attached to the question of political autonomy. Over the past decades, increasing integration with the USA has led the Mexican political élite to identify a number of critical issues. In this light, there is little doubt that a free-trade agreement could significantly strengthen the impact of this process upon areas such as cultural identity, the structure of property rights and the risk of foreign intervention in domestic political affairs.[29] This partly explains the government's concern with making a distinction between a common market and a free-trade agreement, the apparent redefinition of sovereignty in its foreign policy, as well as its efforts to strengthen economic links with other Latin American countries, Canada, the European Community and Japan.[30] Despite this the quest for the free-trade agreement has overshadowed other aspects of Mexico's foreign policy. Not only does Mexico remain economically detached from Latin America but the economic prospects with other regions seem dependent on the country's access to the increasingly protected US market. Although its economic performance has improved significantly, the solidity of economic expectations is still to be seen. Debt restructuring under the Brady Plan, and policies aimed at recovering confidence, like the bank privatization and the more recent prospects for a free-trade agreement, have temporarily reduced financial instability. Yet today as some years ago, the ultimate success must be measured by the reversal of capital flight and the initiation of substantial investment in the Mexican economy.[31] Among the weak angles of the economic policies, apart from the negative effects of a prolonged lack of investment leading to a permanent loss of wealth one could mention fiscal adjustment through cutbacks in essential investment rather than through tax collection, the increasing trade deficit of the past two years, the accumulated internal debt, and the vulnerability of a strategy significantly dependent upon external demand at the cost of more diversified forms of economic growth oriented to the internal market.

Conclusion

If it is true that foreign policy continuity and consistency do not represent in themselves a valuable policy, their potential utility depends upon their flexibile and intelligent application as well as on the awareness that fundamentally they serve long-term defensive goals *vis-à-vis* the USA. Despite their failures, diversification efforts revealed the need to provide foreign policy with some measure of planning so that it could also respond to the needs of economic development. The conciliation between these two dimensions, that is the economic and political, remains one of the fundamental challenges of Mexican foreign policy.

The option of economic development at the political cost of autonomy poses a dilemma; again the need for a balance between the two traditional alternatives inevitably reappears. All *rapprochement* towards the northern neighbour raises the question of political autonomy and it is exactly at this level that the independent character of the country's foreign policy could still represent a valuable asset. Yet, as some of the past experiences have demonstrated, under certain circumstances a narrow interpretation of what constitutes an independent posture entails the risk of lack of perspective and unnecessary confrontation. The pace of integration has further complicated this task and could lead again to extreme positions. Although the Salinas administration recognized the challenge of conciliating self-determination and increasing globalization, and sovereignty with interdependence, the equation of a defensive vocation with isolationism suggests the difficulties of defining foreign policy in relation to both crucial and controversial issues. (Salinas de Gortari, 1990b). If sovereignty means that a state decides for itself how it will cope with its internal and external problems, including whether or not to seek assistance from others and in doing so to limit its freedom by making a commitment to them, the implications of recent decisions such as the free-trade initiative are fairly clear (Waltz, 1979: 96). If the hasty character of this decision indicates a renewed belief in the possibilities of a special relation, the new apparent commitments towards Latin American integration suggest either an awareness of the attached political costs or further doubts regarding its desirability. One could argue reasonably that a hypothetical special relationship has acquired a new meaning as the result of Mexico's current significance for its northern neighbour, but the present convergence could also be significantly influenced by the ideological similarities and the more subjective element of personalities. The precipitated nature of economic decisions and the underlying policy ambiguity portend a longer period of schizophrenia about the US and Latin America. Whether Mexico finally decides that its future lies increasingly in the north, testing the realities of a special relationship will prove a very difficult task. Although it is true that concrete steps are now being taken towards Latin America these have focused mainly on trade liberalization, and limited attention has been paid to those areas where shared interests result from their status as developing nations. No Latin American collective action has been seriously considered on issues such as improved access to capital, markets and technology, foreign investment more conducive to national development, the increasing economic rigidity leading to a deepening North–South divide and greater participation in international organizations. Latin American concerted action in these areas, by forcing US attention to their pressing demands, could test the realities of a much publicized special relation towards the region. What is clear is that under present conditions, the USA would not be able to afford a bilateral special relation with all Latin American states, and the simultaneity of export promotion efforts throughout the region raises doubts as to absorption capacity of the US market. As Laurence Whitehead has said in a reference to the economies of South Korea, Taiwan, Hong Kong and Singapore, 'not all Latin American countries can be "tigers" at the same time'. In the light of the limited achievements of the Brady Plan a case could be made for voluntary preferential treatment for all Latin American states. New conditions seem to offer better prospects for US–Latin American co-operation. Until the debt crisis Latin America remained the major growth market for US exports of capital goods. Between 1976 and 1981 exports to the region accounted for 25 per cent of exports growth and the potential of the region's contribution to reviving US exports has been estimated in as much as 20 per cent of the current US trade deficit (Lowenthal, 1987: 57).

In its efforts to make of Mexico 'part of the First World and not of the Third World', the Salinas administration should probably bear in mind that in decades only one country, Japan, has successfully joined the group of rich countries and that the lessons of the economic success of East Asian states could not be easily reproduced in the Latin American context without grave social costs.[32] It would be wrong to suggest that the adjustments of the 1980s, including liberalization and export promotion, were unnecessary but it would be equally erroneous to underestimate the implications and costs of extreme versions of such policies for national sovereignty, the economic and sociopolitical demands of internal development and over-specialization. It is true that modernization involves both risks and costs but its receptiveness among all social groups and ultimate viability depends on a minimum consensus. An apparent uncritical faith in this strategy has led to overstating the applicability of East Asian models and even to claiming that 'we have left behind the most pressing issues of the crisis like the external debt'. In the absence of a productive boom or an export miracle Mexico will remain trapped in the dilemma of managing the external debt (Salinas de Gortari, 1990b; Whitehead, 1987: 179).

Whatever the direction that foreign policy might take in the 1990s vicinity with the US will remain the main referent object of autonomy. A minimum balance between traditional principles and medium- and long-term objectives could offer better prospects for the preservation of autonomy. By enabling both parties to identify and to negotiate a number of critical issues such balance could set the basis for a reformulation of the previous agreement to disagree. It would be unrealistic to expect complete harmony in US–Mexican relations, despite a political willingness to co-operate on both sides of the border; the two parties are likely to continue disagreeing on the main factors underlying bilateral problems as well as on wider international issues. [33] What seems particularly important is to develop the capacity to identify potential issues leading to conflict, to assess how serious a disagreement could be and consequently to evaluate the potential costs of different alternatives for both Mexico's autonomy and for the state of US–Mexican relations.

Notes

1. The US decision to impose a 10 per cent tax upon all imports and the 'interception operation' demonstrated Mexico's vulnerability to US unilateral actions.
2. Ojeda, 1976: 175–9. For more recent views concerning the prospects for US–Mexican co-operation see Pastor and Castañeda, 1988.
3. Although increasing levels of imports had already revealed the limits of the model of import substitution, foreign indebtedness and tourism had enabled the country to compensate constant deficits in Mexico's trade balance. By 1970 the need of a change in domestic and external policy was clear. The increasing sympathy showed by Mexico to the Arab cause and its vote supporting the UN resolution equating zionism with racism had serious consequences. In 1975 a letter published in the *New York Times* requesting American Jews to implement a tourist and investment boycott against Mexico uncovered the latter's vulnerability and raised serious doubts about the national or personal motivations underlying Echeverría's foreign policy (see Ojeda, 1976: 196–7).
4. Some authors have argued that both the maintenance of diplomatic relations with Cuba in the 1960s as well as the new activism were intended to appease the left, particularly in the aftermath of profound crisis experienced by the political system in the late 1960s. Although greater autonomy and independence could, by drawing support across the political spectrum, enable the government to generate a new national consensus, it could also be argued that Echeverría's notion of indepen-

dence foreclosed that option. Concerning this debate see Pellicer de Brody, 1972, and Ojeda, 1976: 168 and 179.

5. Mexico's difficulties in export promotion is in part related to those factors obstructing industrialization policies. Capital organization characterized by industrial-financial fusion has weakened the state's capacity both to stimulate private investment and to incorporate it into its wider development strategy. The relatively high mobility of capital has provided investors with a powerful weapon. Their veto power was first clear at the time of oil nationalization when Central Bank reserves dropped by 38 per cent. Since then the task of providing investment confidence has proved both costly and difficult. In contrast, the absence of a similar industrial-financial fusion together with the decision since the 1970s to shift funding priorities from state-owned companies to private business granted industrial planning authorities more leverage over investment and industrial decision. For a historical and comparative study on bankers' alliances and macro-economic policies in Mexico and Brazil, see Maxfield, (nd). On the foundations of Brazil's foreign policy achievements see Hurrell, 1986: 88–107.
6. In contrast with Brazil, where export promotion was the main factor underlying its diversification of international ties, in the Mexican case diplomatic diversification preceded substantial export promotion. Between 1970 and 1976 diplomatic links had expanded from 67 to 129 but export diversification had clearly failed. Although between 1970 and 1975 export concentration in the US market had been reduced from 68.4 per cent to 59.9 per cent this was not the result of diversification but of a contraction in US demand (Ojeda, 1976: 184–9; and Gil Villegas, 1988: 263).
7. Energy Secretary James Schlesinger vetoed an agreement between six US corporations and PEMEX on the grounds that the agreed price would adversely affect the lower rate of Canadian exporters and would force up the domestic US price (Lowenthal, 1987: 84).
8. These conditions put Brazil in a delicate position from which the only escape was to increase export capacity to avoid external imbalance and to service the external debt. The 1968 decision to introduce a policy of frequent mini-devaluations favoured export promotion, which increasingly shifted towards manufactured goods. Apparent similarities between Brazil and various Asian cases indicate that the alliances between private financiers, industry and the state's monetary and planning authorities might account for what is considered as the Asian states' capacity for rapid industrialization (Maxfield, nd: 48).
9. The main factors responsible for the 1982 crisis were: 1) the instability which had lately accompanied presidential succession, 2) an expansionary fiscal policy leading to a budget deficit of 8 per cent of GDP; 3) the appreciation of the exchange rate by almost 25 per cent; 4) negative interest rates on domestic savings encouraging dollarization and capital flight; 5) an increase in the external debt which financed the public deficit and compensated capital flight from $US40 billion to 90 billion between December 1979 and December 1982; and 6) a sharp increase in interest

rates from 8.8 per cent in 1978 to 16.8 per cent in 1981, as the US shifted to tight monetary policy (Dornbusch, 1988: 243–4).

10. Between 1974 and 1979 Brazil's exports to the region had increased by 12 per cent and by 1981 had already surpassed exports to the USA. More recently Brazil has emerged as the driving force behind economic integration in the region.
11. By the end of 1988 Mexico owed slightly over $US100 billion. Between 1983 and 1988 the economy grew only 0.1 per cent. As the economy stagnated the external debt grew, as a percentage of GNP, from 54.2 per cent in 1982 to 75.4 per cent in 1987. The reduction of this proportion in 1988 to 56.8 per cent was not the result of economic growth but of the effects of a 7 per cent debt reduction, mostly via the sharp decline in Libor rates from 13.3 per cent in 1982 to 6.9 per cent in 1986 and the success of anti-inflationary policies where a stable peso meant a higher GNP in dollar terms.
12. In the context of asymmetric relations it was reasonably argued that a multilateral strategy would provide Mexico with wider room for manoeuvre (see Heller, Claude, 1990).
13. Although the change of US policy is normally attributed to the new hard-line policies of the Reagan administration, after the Sandinista victory the prospects of similar trends in El Salvador led Carter to adopt a military solution. Once order had been re-established US policies would try and strengthen the political centre. But while his classification of the 'centre' was extended to cover almost all forces on the right, Carter's classification of 'extreme left' was stretched to embrace many of the forces without whose participation there could never have been an authentic democratic centre (di Palma and Whitehead, 1986: 231).
14. In 1984 a CIA analyst resigned after objecting to a request from the director of the agency to modify a report on Mexico to help persuade the White House to pass a programme of economic and covert pressures aimed at achieving Mexico's support for US policies in Central America (Ojeda, 1986: 211).
15. Since May 1983, when it expressed second thoughts about Reagan's intention to overthrow the Sandinista regime, Congress demanded from the executive a clearer definition of its policy objectives towards Nicaragua. Other legislative constraints to Reagan policies were the numerous bills and amendments linking economic and military aid to progress in the human rights record of Central American states and the Contras' acceptance of the Sandinistas' concessions. Yet US linkage between security issues and internal change not only determined a systematic suspicion and underestimation of the Sandinistas' conciliatory gestures but a dubious distinction between military and 'humanitarian' aid which enabled the US administration to continue supporting its allies in the region (Best, 1987: 73).
16. Although initially the proposal was received with suspicion in Nicaragua, the prospects of a change in the US Congress position regarding a halt in Contra funding led the Sandinistas to seriously consider the initiative. In addition, the German and French decision to recognize and reward the

'positive steps' taken in Honduras and El Salvador threatened to isolate Nicaragua. But most importantly, while the plan kept the Contadora's main features it reintroduced the crucial concept of symmetry by giving equal treatment to Nicaragua and El Salvador. Finally, for the five Central American states the prospects for finding a solution to the ten-year crisis were particularly appealing (*Latin American Weekly Report*, 26 February 1987, and Robinson, 1988: 591–613).

17. Such a policy has also been questioned in the context of a special relation between the US and Britain. As early as 1927 Sir Maurice Hankey, cabinet secretary, questioned its effectiveness: 'Time after time we have been told that if we made this concession or that concession we should secure good will in America. We gave up the Anglo-Japanese alliance, we agreed to pay our war debts, and we have again and again made concessions on this ground. I have never seen any permanent result follow from a policy of concessions. I believe we are less popular and more abused in America than ever because they think us weak' (Reynolds, 1989: 96).
18. The 1986 law has had mixed results. About 1.8 million undocumented immigrants applied to legalize their status, fewer than expected but still a significant number. Its success has been questioned by evidence of continued illegal immigration. Moreover, the globalization of production in the US and the resulting transformation of its occupational and income structure towards greater casualization of the labour market further facilitates the absorption of immigrants (Sassen 1990: 372).
19. The revision of the *Congressional Record* carried out by González Gutiérrez led him to conclude that the reform of immigration laws was not conceived as an instrument to exert pressure on Mexico. Underlying its consideration lay a number of issues of a more immediate and electoral character: to recover the control of US borders, to guarantee a sufficient supply of labour and to avoid discriminatory practices against the Hispanic community. Those concerned with the negative effects on Mexico were a minority in Congress, mostly of Hispanic origin, representing border districts and particularly aware of the dependency of the zone on Mexico's economy (González Gutiérrez, 1988: 257–62).
20. A new element of Mexico's foreign policy towards the USA was the use of lobbying. Since 1983 ministries and state-owned companies employed lobbying with uncertain results. In 1985 the de la Madrid government contracted with similar results the services of Michael Deaver, advisor to the White House. These attempts did not lead to any clear conclusions as the high economic cost of such strategy and its implications for foreign policy became clear (see Chabat, 1990).
21. An indication of such change was the 1985 bilateral accord which extended 'injury test' protection to Mexico and reduced the incidence of countervailing duties, following by a joint statement of November 1986 concerning the prospects for a common framework to regulate trade and investment (see Castro Martínez, 1990).
22. Trade between the US and Mexico tripled (mainly because of oil) between 1976 and 1981, reaching $US31bn in 1981. Although bilateral

trade had fallen drastically by 1983 it was back to over $US30bn by 1985. US sources still acount for around 65 per cent of Mexican foreign investment (Lowenthal, 1987: 74–5).

23. Both liberalization policies as well as the prospects for a free-trade agreement seem to benefit particularly the *maquiladora* sector, tourism and export-oriented industries. Not only have economic policies relied on low wages but, as Alain Touraine has stated, 'the reinsertion of part of the national economy in the world economy has come at the cost of the growing marginalization of a large sector of the population' (quoted in Castañeda, 1990: 420).
24. This situation has left previously protected sectors of the Mexican economy in strong competition with those US sectors with the strongest comparative advantage. Although there are some agricultural and industrial sectors where the US is not yet competitive, many sectors, including agriculture, could be severely affected. Even if Mexican products achieve a free entry to the US market, they will be constantly forced to keep a competitive edge (Whitehead, 1989: 208).
25. Robert Pastor seems to share this view when he affirms that 'President Bush has a momentous chance to reshape our most important difficult relationship; he should not dawdle' (Pastor, 1990: 32).
26. On 21 September 1990 Salinas sent a letter to Bush formally requesting the start of negotiations for a free-trade agreement. Bush asked Congress for permission to begin these negotiations on 26 September 1990 but it is not yet clear whether the US administration will opt for the 'fast track'. This decision, by reducing the period of negotiations and limiting the scope for lobbying against the agreement, could significantly influence the final outcome (*Latin America Weekly Report*, 8 November 1990, WR-90-43).
27. Salinas' request was met with continuation of informal talks and promises of actual negotiations only after the December GATT round. It remains unclear if Bush will recognize such an agreement as 'one of the nation's highest foreign policy priorities, requiring a long-term vision and a genuine bipartisan approach' (Pastor, 1990: 32).
28. A 1990 US embargo was imposed on imports of Mexican tuna and shrimp. Steel exports remain subject to import quotas which have only benefited product lines where the Mexican steel industry cannot easily compete (*Latin American Weekly Report* 8 November 1990, WR-90-43).
29. Roberta Lajous has focused attention over the future of *fideicomisos* granted to foreigners during the 1970s and due to expire in 30 years, as well as on the increasing acquisition of coastal property by foreigners. In these circumstances the resurgence of potential conflict regarding the protection of the lives and economic interests of US citizens cannot be ruled out. Similarly, and given the potential impact of a free-trade agreement on the *ejido*, it is not yet clear whether such an agreement could be undertaken without major social reorganization (Meyer, 1990: 266–7 and Lajous, 1987: 399).
30. A more dynamic definition of sovereignty was first made explicit during the independence celebrations in September 1990. Independence was

then defined as an 'unfinished fact' and the state's sovereignty mainly in relation to other states. Although conceptually difficult, the meaning of sovereignty as a political idea comes into being when exercised; it is usually easy to recognize it in practice, and particularly evident is the failure to exercise it (Buzan, 1983: 41).

31. The government's achievements in recovering public confidence have been acknowledged but, as in 1988, sustainable economic growth remains as the main challenge. The government could help in co-ordinating anti-inflationary measures, and through fiscal authority provide the financial framework for growth, but it could not make the growth. Today, as before, the private sector has to take over and move ahead with investment, production and employment. Capital has come back but mostly on a temporary basis, and it is 'certainly not investing for the long term, in real assets, but merely holding government debt' (Dornbusch, 1990: 317–22 and 1988: 261).
32. It is interesting to note that the four East Asian countries are currently reconsidering the external orientation of their economies. Beyond the crucial role of geopolitical factors, their trading conquests were the result of decisive, single-minded and innovative policies including a rationalized exchange regime, selective import liberalization, directed credit and finely tuned export-promoting instruments. In addition, liberalization is seen increasingly as a useful instrument as long as it improves external competitiveness or serves to appease trade partners (Whitehead, 1986b: 146–7).
33. For an historical perspective of the underlying causes of contradiction and conflict between the national interest of the two countries see Meyer, 1990.

5· MEXICAN TRADE AND MEXICO–US ECONOMIC RELATIONS

Nigel Harris

For much of the history of capitalism, capital accumulation has taken place, or so people have thought, on a reasonably clearcut national basis. A national state provided a protective and guiding framework, supporting services to, and sometimes active participation in, an identifiable national capital embodied in a set of companies, employing a distinct national labour force to supply, in the main, a domestic market. The picture in reality was never so simple, but in the post-war period, it has become, although to different degrees, increasingly remote from reality. It now seems that accumulation has become dominantly a global process, and states seek to attract or hold a share of global capital (whose relationship to the national state is contingent upon the quality of state provision and taxes, and the quality of the labour force, not some overriding loyalty); subsidiaries of international companies or their subcontracted suppliers import parts of a world output to process and supply to world markets. Of course, this is vastly oversimplified and in many sectors and countries there remain national companies in the old sense, but the trends seem not to be in this direction. One aspect of this is the unanticipated but radical and continuing change in the comparative advantage of parts of manufacturing industry as between more and less developed countries (MDCs/LDCs).

The governmental and business leaders in LDCs who, during the great phase of growth in the world economy between 1947 and 1974, detected the results of this trend and were able and equipped to exploit it, even if they were unaware of its full implications, experienced extraordinarily swiftly growing economies. Those that unequivocally opposed the trend, seeking rather to create an independent national economy, either had a more mixed record, were seriously afflicted by the economic difficulties of the 1980s or, in some cases, experienced absolute decline. Countries with real capacity to exploit the trend but which nonetheless were governed by administrations opposed to doing so are among the more interesting cases, for the changed world demand continued to work upon such economies even though governments sought to frustrate its effects. Mexico is perhaps one of these cases.

The first part of this chapter examines some of the trends in world trade in the 1980s and the medium-term experience of selected developing countries to demonstrate some of these points. Mexico's trade performance is examined to see how far it conformed to the general trend and how this related to the broader question of the country's relationships to the USA.

World trade

One of the well-known features of the remarkable growth of the world economy in the post-war period has been the disproportionate expansion in international trade. A steadily larger share of national production has been produced for foreign markets. There has been a much faster rate of growth in trade in manufactured goods, led by the two sectors, chemicals and engineering products. While the pace slackened after 1974, despite the well-known difficulties in sub-Saharan Africa and Latin America, in the 1980s growth still remained relatively high. Between 1980 and 1988, trade expanded on average by 4 per cent annually, compared to production at 2.5 per cent a year; manufacturing exports grew annually by 10 per cent in volume and 16 per cent in value, while the value of manufacturing output grew by 6.5 per cent a year. Within manufacturing exports, capital goods grew annually by a fifth, on average, to reach nearly 30 per cent of world trade (GATT, 1989, I).

Between a quarter and half of world manufacturing exports in the 1980s was in the group of products Machinery and Transport Equipment. However, the highest rates of growth by commodity groups were spread across the field, as shown in Table 5.1. Thus, world demand included a range of goods affecting potential output in a variety of M and LDCs, a continuation in breadth, if not in relative shares, of the trends that have persisted since the 1950s.

Table 5.1: Sectors with the highest rates of growth in world trade, 1973–87 (percentage annual rate of increase)

Sectors	1973–87	1979–87	1987
Office machinery, data processing equipment/parts	19	18	27
Transistors, valves	18	15	30
Telecommunications equipment and parts	11	13	18
Engines and motors	7	13	13
Toys, sporting goods	15	12	32
Clothing	15	11	28
Measuring, controlling instruments	20	11	17
Passenger motor vehicles	14	11	17

Source: GATT, 1989, II: 38.

Newly industrializing countries (NICs)

Depending upon initial capacities, the continued expansion of world demand sustained relatively high rates of growth in many of the older NICs, brought accelerated growth to a number of new proto-NICs (for example, Malaysia, Thailand, Indonesia) and began high growth in a number of newcomers to rapid industrial growth (People's Republic of China, Mauritius, Jamaica and, in garments, even Bangladesh). Thus the geographical shift in comparative advantage in selected sectors of manufacturing away from the MDCs which underlay the emergence of the famous four Little Tigers (South Korea, Taiwan, Hong Kong, Singapore) has continued in the 1980s. But now the process is redistributing some sectors of manufacturing away from the four themselves and creating increasingly complex patterns of interdependence.

This growth in manufacturing exports and production is in painful contrast to the experience of trade in primary commodities. By 1986, the value of this trade was at a lower level than at any time since the Great Depression, and, in lead and copper, at a lower level than that of 1932. In the four years to 1988, oil prices for the OPEC group were more than halved (Banco de México, 1989; Colmenares Páramo, 1990). Countries of sub-Saharan Africa, some of which were heavily dependent upon the export of one primary commodity, were the most disastrously affected; as is well known, heavy indebtedness considerably complicated the trade picture for a number of Latin American countries.

Nonetheless, despite the known cases of severe difficulty and

Table 5.2: Value of manufactured exports (Mf.exps) and exports of machinery and transport equipment (M/Tpt) and their share in total exports of the leading NICs ($USm), with a relative index

Country	Mf.exps	(% exps)	Index	Exps.M/Tpt.	(% exps)	Index
Hong Kong	57,477	(91)	100	15,790	(25)	68
South Korea	56,447	(93)	98	23,671	(39)	100
Taiwan	56,155	(93)	98	20,530	(34)	87
China	34,639	(73)	60	1,898	(4)	8
Singapore	29,404	(75)	51	18,426	(47)	78
Brazil	16,171	(48)	28	6,064	(18)	26
South Africa	15,771	(80)	27	591	(3)	3
India	14,600	(73)	25	1,606	(11)	7
Mexico	11,366	(55)	20	6,317	(33)	29
Malaysia	9,382	(45)	16	417	(1)	2
Thailand	8,219	(52)	14	1,739	(11)	7
Israel	8,164	(85)	14	1,728	(18)	7
Portugal	6,232	(61)	11	1,737	(17)	7
Totals	324,023	(78)		101,014	(31)	

Source: calculated, World Bank, 1990: 204–7.

decline, a majority of LDCs, including those containing the bulk of the population, were by no means in crisis. Of the 77 countries in the World Bank's annual listings, 12 experienced on average negative annual rates of growth (1980–88), but 22 achieved rates of 4 per cent or more, for example, China at 10.3 per cent, Pakistan 6.5 per cent, Thailand 6.0 per cent and India 5.2 per cent. In export terms, the outturn was both better and worse than the growth of gross domestic products. Twenty-two countries faced an average annual decline and 34 countries a rate of growth of 4 per cent or more. (There were some extraordinary rates here: Paraguay at 15.7 per cent a year, Turkey 15.3 per cent, South Korea 14.7 per cent, Taiwan 13.9 per cent, China 11.9 per cent, Portugal 11.6 per cent, and Thailand 11.3 per cent.) These rates of growth are dominated by the exports of manufactured goods; by now nearly 60 per cent of the value of the exports of the LDCs as a whole are manufactured goods, but this figure is dominated by the 21 leading exporters.

Table 5.2 sets out the relative ranking (Hong Kong: 100) of the 13 leading NIC exporters of manufactured goods in 1988, with a following ranking in terms of the key group of products, machinery and transport equipment (South Korea:100). The figures for one year

Table 5.3: Changing composition of NIC exports to the OECD group manufacturers by level of technology (percentage share)

Technological level	1964	1980	1985
High	2.2	21.5	25.0
Medium	15.9	18.5	21.6
Low	81.6	59.8	53.2
	100	100	100

Source: OECD, 1988: 24.

are not a secure basis for generalization, but some rough observations are in order. In 1988, Mexico, with the fourteenth largest GDP in the world (the fourth largest among LDCs), was twenty-fifth in the total value of exports (the ninth largest among the LDCs). Of the 13 largest exporters on manufactured goods, it was ninth with one-fifth of the value of the largest exporter, Hong Kong; indeed, the total manufactured exports of two of the leading countries, Korea and Taiwan, were nearly one-fifth larger than the total for Latin America as a whole. However, if we separate out the value of the export of machinery and transport equipment, bearing in mind its crucial importance in world trade, Mexico becomes fifth largest, with one-third of the value of the leading exporter, South Korea. While the value of exports of machinery and transport equipment is far from being an unequivocal measure of technical advance, although the contrast between the two sets of figures for Singapore and China is suggestive, Table 5.2 indicates something of Mexico's strengths in an international division of labour. Furthermore, it is this sector which has experienced sustained growth, from 1 per cent of total exports in 1965 to 33 per cent in 1988 (compared to South Korea's growth, at a far higher absolute level, from 3 to 39 per cent).

The 1980s have brought to fruition a longer drawn-out process of upgrading the capital and skill intensity of the exports of the NICs while stimulating the redistribution of industrial capacity in labour and lower-skill activities away from them, a process, as we shall see, clearly apparent in the case of Mexico. An OECD estimate of the effects of this process for the leading NICs is contained in Table 5.3. Growth in the 1980s has intensified this shift, particularly given the character of one of the leading sources of that growth, the USA.

The United States market

Much of the growth in NIC manufactured exports has been in response to the prodigious increase in US demand (the USA is simultaneously the world's largest exporter). Related to this growth and on a far smaller scale has been the increase in intra-regional trade in East and South-east Asia. In the second half of the 1980s, US manufactured imports from all sources were roughly equal to nearly one-third of its domestic manufactured output. The leading NICs increased their share of US imports by between 20 and 28 per cent a year, and by the middle of the decade, the US market was absorbing nearly 60 per cent of the manufactured exports of the NICs. This growth did not simply reflect the relative contraction of US manufactured output, but also changes in patterns of specialization; nor was it a mark of economic failure, for while the USA lost some 5 million manufacturing jobs over the same period, it added 28 million non-manufacturing jobs, increasing the total employed labour force by a third (Drucker, 1986).

An element of growing importance in the growth of US manufactured imports has been trade under what used to be tariff schedules 806.30 and 807.00 (they are now tariffs 9802.00.60 and 80). These tariffs, as is well known, permit US manufacturers to part process goods abroad; where the manufacture of commodities starts and finishes in the USA, the tariff on the reimport is levied solely on the value added abroad. Trade under these tariffs is thus an important index of the technical integration of the US manufacturing economy with trading partners abroad, that is, the emergence of a single manufacturing economy located in several countries. US imports in the 1980s increased annually by about a quarter, but imports under these two tariffs grew by 140 per cent a year – this growth rate was exaggerated by a change in the regulations in 1986 which brought in a new category of goods – from under 10 per cent of the total in 1980 to 17 per cent by 1987. Seventy-five per cent of the goods imported under these schedules were vehicle engines and other parts (14 per cent were semi-conductors, 8 per cent 'other machinery') (1988 US International Trade Commission). Two-thirds of these imports came from three countries, Mexico, Canada and Japan. On average, Mexico supplied 45 per cent of the imports (1984–7), Canada 17 and Japan 6.2 per cent. Smaller shares came from West Germany and other parts of Europe, South-east Asia and the Dominican Republic.

Mexico's position in this trade rested initially on the singular geographical advantage of its northern regions. The transport costs of heavy goods, of which vehicle engines are an example, limited long-distance imports for mass production industries, creating the locational strength for the border zone. Furthermore, northern Mexico is adjacent to California and Texas, states in the north with among the highest rates of growth in the USA since the Second World War. California's growth continued strongly in the 1980s, reflected in the increase in its population by six million, quarter of the national population growth. California is now economically the largest state in the union, with leading positions in manufacturing, foreign trade, agriculture, construction and tourism; its economy has grown at twice the national rate. On an index of 1978=100, the gross state product reached 210 in 1989, compared to that of the US at 170.

Much of this growth has been in the south, immediately adjacent to Mexico's Baja California Norte and the city of Tijuana. The Los Angeles basin has been a particular focus for high growth, in part based upon Mexican supplies and, even more, Mexican immigrant labour (McCarthy and Burciaga Váldez, 1986). The character of the labour supply may perhaps be part of the explanation for the combination of activities in the region, from the most technically sophisticated, particularly in the defence, electronic and aerospace sectors, to some of the least, namely garments and footwear. While nationally the garment industry contracted by one-fifth in the 15 years to 1989, in Los Angeles it increased by nearly 60 per cent. Furthermore, as costs of domestic production increase relative to prices of competing imports, firms can relocate further south in Mexico while retaining their sales position in Los Angeles, as is predicted for small furniture factories to be affected by the new Californian air pollution regulations.

Southern California has attained a dynamism which is now no longer so heavily dependent upon the defence budget – defence spending was equal to 14 per cent of gross state product in 1970, but is now only 8 per cent – so it is not expected to be radically affected by current cuts in federal military expenditure. Furthermore, the character of the growth, increasingly linked to trans-Pacific trade, gives grounds for believing that the current US recession will not affect the state in the long term as deeply as many others, so that those Mexican activities linked to California also need not be threatened.

Table 5.4: Mexico. Direction of trade, 1982–3 and 1987–8 (percentage shares)

Mexican trade with:	1982–3 exports	1982–3 imports	1987–8 exports	1987–8 imports
Industrial countries	85	88	91	95
USA	56	60	72	75

Source: calculated from IMF, 1989, pp. 279–80.

Mexico–US trade

Mexico, with its close proximity to the USA, a country both with the largest national market in the world and where the decline in comparative advantage in some sectors of manufacturing has been most marked, would have had to struggle hard to escape the powerful market demand that stimulated manufacturing exports in many of the NICs. Resistance would have been particularly difficult, both because the country's industrial structure and potential fits the external demand well, and because the long border with its northern neighbour could only be policed at high cost. The border, in the post-war period, has always limited the possibilities for import substitution strategies. In the 1980s, the trend observed in the NICs towards an increasing concentration on the US market has no less affected Mexico as can be seen in Table 5.4. The export figures are, of course, strongly affected by their changing composition, and particularly the declining share of oil which supplied many more markets than did manufactured goods and other raw materials.

In 1965, 16.5 per cent of Mexico's total exports were manufactured goods, the major items of which were: sugar (5 per cent), textiles, garments and footwear (2.6 per cent), chemicals (3.9 per cent), and iron and steel (2.2 per cent) (World Bank, 1979, 1981; Mertens, 1986: 2). By 1970, as Table 5.5 shows, the share of manufactured goods in total exports to the USA had risen to 31 per cent, and over 50 per cent by 1975. The shift took place almost by default and without substantial government stimulation. Successive administrations emphasized issues of economic independence, rather than interdependence, and industrialization to supply the domestic market rather than external demand.

What checked Mexico's becoming an exporter of predominantly manufactured goods, and indeed reversed it, was the discovery of

Table 5.5: Sectoral shares in Mexico's exports to the USA (percentage)

	Selected years				
	1970	1975	1980	1985	1987
Foodstuffs	47.8	21.2	11.3	9.1	11.7
Raw materials	10.7	10.0	5.0	4.2	3.9
Fuels	5.0	12.1	52.9	41.5	19.4
Manufactures	30.7	50.7	28.4	42.3	61.2
Other	5.8	6.0	2.4	2.9	3.8
	100.0	100.0	100.0	100.0	100.0

Source: calculated from CIA, Jan. 1989, pp. 53–6.

significant oil reserves. Oil exports, and borrowing on the basis of potential oil exports at continuing high prices, provided the basis for a renewed dash for diversified national industrialization. In this sense, President López Portillo was the last of the *cardenistas*. The meaning of this version of economic nationalism had, however, become transformed in modern conditions. It was possible only with increased imports, particularly from the USA, and increased reliance on the export of primary commodities, pre-eminently oil. In exporting terms, the country regressed while considerably increasing the vulnerability of its economy to the concatenation of events that closed the boom in 1982, namely declining oil prices, rising interest rates on the now large cumulative debt, and substantial budgetary and manufacturing trade deficits.

After 1982, as is well known, the need to service the debt – taking up to 6 per cent of GDP in the 1980s – and the fortunate long boom in the USA, pulled the economy violently in the opposite direction, resuming the trend that had existed before 1975, but now with active government encouragement. Up to 1987, the country's export of manufactured goods expanded in volume terms by a heroic 79 per cent. While non-oil exports grew annually in the four years to 1986 by 12.6 per cent, manufacturing exports increased by 28.6 per cent, and exports of metal products and machinery by 34.5 per cent a year. The performance lowered the cost of servicing the external debt from 44.5 per cent of export revenue to 38.4 per cent in 1987.

Table 5.6 illustrates the switchback of the late 1970s. Manufactured goods constituted 51 per cent of total exports in 1975, 28 per cent in 1980, then returning to 61 per cent in 1987. Part of this, but only part, reflected changing price relationships, for buoyant raw material

Table 5.6: Indices of value of non-oil earning items, Mexico's external account, 1882 and 1986 (1980 = 100)

	1982	1986
Agriculture, livestock, fisheries	83	119
Manufacturing:	99	270
Metal products and machinery	95	310
Food, drink, tobacco	92	124
Chemicals	112	205
Basic non-ferrous metals	312	350
Non-factor services	89	111
In-bond industries	110	220

prices, particularly that of oil, gave way to stagnant or declining ones in the 1980s. By contrast, the index for oil and natural gas exports fell from 159 to 61, while their share of total exports declined from 63 to 29 per cent.

Table 5.7 shows the performance of selected elements in the country's manufactured exports to the USA as well as the growing technical sophistication and specialization of this sector. The downturn of 1980, the check to Mexico's following the trend of other middle-income countries, is also apparent in many key items. On the other hand, if we take garment manufacture as a surrogate for labour-intensive production, perhaps its steady decline in share, from 122 per cent in 1975 to 4 per cent in 1987, suggests the same processes that affected the Asian NICs, a loss in comparative advantage where labour costs are an important item in determining prices. The growing diversification of exports in the more technically advanced fields is shown in some of the faster-growing sectors. Scientific instruments increased its share from under 1 to nearly 3 per cent between 1970 and 1987, computers grew from 0.6 to 1.2 per cent, and aircraft engines from 0 to 7.7 per cent (INEGI, 1988).

This trend is confirmed by a more detailed examination of US imports from the country by sector and subsector. Between 1970 and 1987, the branch of manufacturing which grew fastest, at 41 per cent, above the rate of growth of manufactured exports, was machinery. Within this sector, engines (especially car engines) and heavy industrial machinery (especially, mining construction equipment) and within the subsector, business machines, computers and scientific instruments (especially electrical medical apparatus, optical instruments and

Table 5.7: Changing shares of selected items in Mexico's manufactured exports to the US, selected years (percentages)

Item	1970	1975	1980	1985	1987
1. Chemicals	6.6	4.7	5.6	6.1	3.3
2. Semi-finished goods	25.9	14.4	12.1	11.5	13.0
a) metal manufactures	9.9	4.4	3.2	3.3	3.9
i) steel	6.7	1.6	0.9	1.3	1.6
3. Machinery	33.9	48.4	52.8	51.8	46.9
a) engines	2.6	2.9	1.8	11.1	8.1
b) electrical machinery	23.5	35.0	14.7	31.8	28.5
(i) electrical and switchgear	4.2	6.5	9.3	9.0	8.4
(ii) telecommunications equipment	6.9	15.0	19.3	9.1	6.4
(iii) transistors	9.3	8.5	3.9	2.8	2.5
c) heavy industrial machinery	0.3	1.9	2.2	0.8	1.0
d) business machinery	5.3	5.2	2.5	3.7	3.8
e) scientific instruments	0.9	1.6	2.7	2.3	2.6
4. Transport	3.5	7.1	5.5	10.4	16.4
a) road vehicles	2.5	5.3	5.4	10.2	16.2
5. Consumer goods	30.7	25.5	24.0	20.2	20.1
a) consumer electronics	4.6	1.3	1.4	6.9	7.4
b) apparel	9.8	11.7	8.3	4.5	4.3

(These are only a minority of subsectors and commodities; they do not therefore sum to 100)

Source: calculated from CIA, 1989: 53–6.

medical instruments) grew 200 per cent faster than manufacturing as a whole. Transport grew nearly 400 per cent more, and, within this, road vehicles expanded five and half times more than the average (by 1987, nearly 60 per cent of this subsector was made up of cars, which had increased, from a low base point, by 8,690 per cent). Sectors which grew less than average in exports included chemicals in general (but not 'other chemicals', including cosmetics and plastics), semi-finished non-ferrous metal manufactures (but not including copper and aluminium manufactures), metal manufacture (especially steel) and consumer goods. Within consumer goods, it was garments which accounted for much of the decline, while consumer electronic goods grew nearly 60 per cent above the average for manufacturing as a whole. Leisure goods declined, but cameras, from a low base point, expanded substantially.

The core of the great expansion of the country's manufactured exports has not at all been in goods based upon cheap labour; such exports are in continuous decline. It is the export of road vehicles and car components, especially engines, which has provided the largest items of growth. In 1970–73, imports of vehicles and vehicle engines were, in value, nearly six times the country's exports; in 1980–82, they were still nearly five times the value of exports. But by 1986–7, the value of exports was 41 per cent higher than that of imports. A process seen so dramatically in South Korea, and Yugoslavia and a number of other countries, was also occurring in Mexico.

Maquiladoras

One of the more remarkable areas of growth in manufacturing has been in in-bond, or *maquiladora*, plants. These are offshore activities, permitted to import raw materials or parts without restriction or duties for processing in Mexico, provided all or part (the regulations have changed during the years of operation of the scheme) of the output is exported. Such activity has been in the past closely related to US imports under tariffs 806 and 7. The output of the *maquiladora* sector, like that of Hong Kong, is important not by reason of its size but because changes accurately reflect external demand without the intermediation of government, except, of course, in such things as the management of the currency and provision of infrastructure.

The *maquiladora* sector began in the 1960s, as the East and South-East Asian tiger economies had done, by exporting traditional manufactures, produced by a cheap labour force. Unlike the Asian case, with the exception of Singapore, the companies concerned were foreign-owned, most of them being registered in the USA. Initially, operations were concentrated in the border region, which was made into a free-trade zone. From 1965 growth fluctuated on a rising trend, most strongly affected by the level of the peso–dollar exchange rate; there were sharp contractions in 1974 and 1980–2 when the peso was strong. From 1982, with a radical depreciation of the peso (the currency remained undervalued up to 1987, with the exception of a short period in 1985), employment in *maquiladoras* expanded with remarkable speed from 123,000 in 1982 to virtually half a million in October 1991 (INEGI, 1992: 10; Banco de México, 1990). One projection, by Hilker (in González-Arechiga and Barajas, 1989: 287), suggests employment could reach three million by early in the next century (a Free Trade Agreement with the USA would of course, supersede this). By the late 1980s, the *maquiladora* sector was said to produce about a quarter of the value of the country's manufactured exports, although providing only about one-fifth of its manufactured output.

Simultaneously, the growth of employment and output went with a rapid change in the composition of the *maquiladora* sector. Beginning with small poorly organized plants, belonging to relatively small US-registered companies, often from states in the North American border area, employing a high proportion of unskilled or semi-skilled workers, especially women, on, in dollar terms, very low wages, these were the much deplored 'hit and run' sweatshops of early reports (NACLA, 1975). In fact, the employment and income profiles of the workforce did not seem to be significantly different to sectorally comparable plants operating within the USA (Stoddard, 1987). Since the 1970s, the average size of plant has increased, many of them owned now by major international companies (including a growing number of firms registered in Japan, West Germany, and even South Korea), and capital and skill intensities have risen considerably, with a decline in the proportion of women employed, although in 1989, this was still 50 per cent. The transformation has developed even though the crisis of 1982 caused a radical fall in the dollar value of *maquiladora* pay and one might assume this would encourage increases in labour intensity. The ratio between *maquiladora* pay and comparable levels is said to have fallen from 1:5 in 1975 to 1:15 in 1987; in 1989, it was officially claimed that *maquiladora* labour costs were 38 per cent below 'overseas' levels, but 17 per cent above non-*maquiladora* levels on the border (INEGI, 1990). As it is, it appears that there is now much greater stress on quality in a technically more sopisticated output, and on '0' error delivery systems (Palomares and Mertens, 1987). Perhaps, while the majority of plants remains close to the USA, the process noted in South-east Asia (Henderson, 1989), whereby research and testing facilities in the major companies have followed the location of plants as output has been technically upgraded, will not occur in Mexico. However, plants are now increasingly being sited in the central areas of the country, so that this may also affect decisions on the location of research units.

Border locations as well as the bias in tariff schedules 806 and 807 encouraged *maquiladora* plants to import most of their inputs from the USA. On average, in the mid-1980s, the use of Mexican inputs constituted no more than 1.5 per cent of the final value of the product. However, this is decreasingly true, the closer the plant is to indigenous sources of inputs: 17 per cent of final value derives from Mexican inputs in Nuevo León state with its strong manufacturing base in Monterrey (González-Arechiga and Barajas, 1989: 287–8). Sklair (1989: 202) also reports that indigenous inputs constitute 17 per cent of final values for plants sited in the interior, closer to the concentration of manufacturing activity in the Central Valley of Mexico. Import substitution policies in the past perhaps encouraged the location of plants to supply the domestic market in the Central Valley; liberalization in the 1980s is still too new to affect significantly territorial distributions, but we can presume that, in the future, just as *maquiladora* activity moves further south towards the Central Valley so increasingly Mexican companies will move to supply them both there and in the border region.

The *maquiladora* sector has been the source of much controversy on both sides of the border. Fears are frequently expressed in Mexico that such activities are particularly subject to economic fluctuations in the North American economy. This is undoubtedly true although it requires much qualification, depending upon the sector of production concerned and the location of its markets (thus, California has experienced persistently high growth the past half century even during recessions in the USA). There is also evidence to suggest that the larger the market, the less the aggregate instability (Blackhurst et al., 1977). Stoddard (1987) cites work which suggests that in the 1974 US downturn, *maquiladora* plants were significantly more stable than control groups of plants in both Mexico and the USA. However, protectionism in the north could pose particular problems for Mexico as it already has done (steel, cement etc.). Leaving aside any likely results of a free-trade agreement between the two countries, Mexico has an important advantage over South Korea and Taiwan: much *maquiladora* production is in the hands of important US-registered companies which are likely to exercise considerable influence to prevent the restriction of their intracompany flows across the border. Furthermore, the US administration is not unaware that *maquiladora* output plays a role in maintaining the competitiveness of US-based production relative to imports. Thus what has hitherto been seen as a disadvantage by Mexicans, that is, the ownership of part of Mexican industrial assets by US-registered companies, restricting the stimulation of Mexican component suppliers, might be a strength in combating US protectionism.

The *maquiladora* sector is closely linked with the manufacturing processes of the economy to the north, where there has been much discussion as to which country gains from the arrangement. In particular, the trade unions and some of the localities which have suffered from plant relocation have maintained that Mexico has 'stolen American jobs'. In the mid-1980s, the AFL–CIO estimated that US companies had transferred directly 300,000, and indirectly, one million, jobs to Mexico. On the other side, the federal government estimated at the same time that the, then, over 1,000 *maquiladora* plants drew raw materials, manufactured inputs and services from 5,000 suppliers in 44 states of the USA (cited in Thorup *et al.*, 1987: 14). A congressional study argued that for each job transferred to Mexico, seven more were directly or indirectly created in the USA; if the same ratio holds today, this would suggest that three and a half million jobs were sustained in part or whole by *maquiladora* activities. In fact, the argument is not really about *maquiladoras* but about imports; do imports in general decrease domestic output and employment, or, through providing cheaper inputs, for example, increase both? As always, the fact that the second option appears to be more generally true than the first can be of no consolation to those suffering unemployment as the result of relocation; job losers rarely coincide with job gainers.

The *maquiladora* phenomenon is likely to be of declining significance as import restrictions become fewer and Mexican external trading conditions conform to GATT norms. The proportion of Mexican import value covered by licences declined from 84 to 22 per cent between 1985 and 1988, and the average tariff level from 24 to 11 per cent (Kate and de Mateo, 1989). If this trend continues, the effects of a free-trade agreement with the USA on trade flows would be relatively slight, although more important results might result from the continued resiting of parts of US manufacturing capacity, and plants from other countries supplying the American market, south of the border.

Is it possible, as some commentators argue (Womack, and Walsh Sanderson, in Thorup, 1987, and on vehicles, Altshuler *et al.* Ch. 8) that changes in technology, in particular, automation or roboticization, computer-aided industrial design, flexible production methods, could reverse the trend in the redistribution of manufacturing capacity from the USA to Mexico? There will undoubtedly be reverse shifts in comparative advantage, as US-based garment companies have been able to regain a larger share of value added in manufacture through automating fabric cutting, while sewing continues to be undertaken abroad. But it seems unlikely that this could form a general trend. The continued liberalization of national economies, despite increased temporary and product-specific protectionism, is likely to continue to change the price relationship between capital and labour, to the advantage of world labour. It is likely to refashion technology to take advantage of the vast, relatively low-paid labour force that now becomes available rather than substituting relatively expensive capital. The ageing of the labour forces of the MDC can only exaggerate this change. Thus it is likely that increased technical ingenuity will be directed at combining the skills of the MDCs with the young labour forces of the LDCs, the advantages of highly specialized and rapidly changing models in the markets of OECD group with the cheap mass production of standardized components by the LDCs. Indeed, the trends of the last 40 years are confirmed now by the relocation of parts of Japanese manufacturing, particularly in vehicles and consumer durables, to South-east Asia.

The growth, diversification and increasing sophistication of Mexico's manufactured exports in the 1980s has been impressive, but it should not conceal the damage suffered in terms of international competitiveness in the years of the oil-fuelled boom between 1978 and 1982, and the slump which followed. The official course of real wages in the eight years to 1990 is evidence of that, although this does not include an element for the buoyant black economy. The disasters deflected the country from following the same sort of trajectory as the East Asians; in 1973, Mexico held 1 per cent of world manufactured exports; in 1988, 0.9 per cent. In the vehicle industry, a crucial element in the country's emerging comparative advantage, output reached 505 in 1980 and 529 in 1988 on an index of 1965=100. By comparison, Brazil's industry, measured on the same index, was 191 in that year, and 1,201 and 1,102 in the two later years. For South Korea, the figures for the three years are: 0.1; 127 and 1,118 (and for Taiwan, 3; 137; 258). The great expansion in the US market in the 1980s provided enormous opportunities for the NICs, but the Latin Americans, burdened with debt and with relatively introverted economies, could not exploit them.

The dramatic decline in the level of imports after 1982 was sustained by a 20 per cent devaluation in the peso with an additional daily devaluation amounting to 14 per cent a year. This turned round the country's trade balance with surprising speed, and, in particular, up to 1987 produced a modest surplus in manufacturing. If we break

Table 5.8: Percentage distribution of surpluses (+) and deficits (–) in Mexico's trade balance, selected periods

		1970–73	1980–81	1986–87
Overall trade deficit/surplus		–100	–100	+100
Components:	Foodstuffs	+86	–32	+25
	Raw materials	+5	–4	+5
	Fuels	–10	+222	+64
	Manufactures	–181	–286	+5

Source: calculated from CIA, 1989: 49–56.

down that balance by surplus/deficit elements, as a proportionate share, the picture from the early 1970s is as set out in Table 5.8.

In essence, Mexico has traditionally paid for its deficit in manufacturing by the exports of raw materials, foodstuffs and non-fuels in the early 1970s and early 1980s (when the deficit reached prodigious proportions) or by running a deficit trade balance. Indeed, the country has something of the appearance more characteristic of pure primary-producing countries, with a manufacturing sector designed to service the domestic market while the external balance is sustained by raw material exports, characteristic in the past of, for example, Australia. By the mid-1980s, however, for the first time, all major sectors were in surplus, although manufacturing, overwhelmingly the largest item in the trade balance, still contributed only a small amount to the total. This change occurred when the share of manufacturing in both exports and imports increased rapidly. In the case of imports from the USA, manufacturing accounted for 74 per cent of the total in the early 1970s, 76 per cent in the early 1980s and over 80 per cent in 1986–7. There was particularly more rapid growth in machinery imports, 43 per cent of manufactured imports in the early 1970s, nearly 50 per cent in 1986–7, with marked growth in electrical machinery but declines in heavy industrial machinery and transport. This picture was in striking contrast to the East Asians where there was little export of primary commodities, and a massive surplus in manufacturing trade.

However, the pace of growth of manufactured exports was increasingly threatened by high domestic inflation and a slower rate of depreciation in the peso. Of course, many of the sectors of manufactured exports that are emerging as important are ones where labour costs are not a high proportion of total costs, and where they have low price-sensitivity, particularly those which are the internal transactions of international companies. But price competitiveness is still important for other parts of manufacturing and is very important in fuels, which still play an important role in generating export revenue. Furthermore, the progressive liberalization of imports noted earlier, along with the fixing of the exchange rate as an anti-inflationary element in the *Pacto de Solidaridad Económica* (from December 1987), have threatened the trade balance. In 1988, the balance was in surplus to the tune of $US1.8 bn, but the balance in manufacturing trade was negative again ($US2.6bn). The trade balance was again negative in 1989, 1990 and 1991; high oil prices resulting from the Gulf crisis may, of course, offer some relief here (oil exports were 70 per cent above targeted levels two months after the Gulf crisis broke), depending upon how long Iraqi and Kuwaiti oil supplies remain suspended. A strong peso has sustained cheap imports and thus domestic supply while more general restructuring takes place, but it occurs when, unlike in Brazil, the trade surplus does not cover debt servicing, obliging the government to increase its external debt. A recession in the USA, affecting demand for Mexican exports and tourist receipts, could make for severe problems in the early 1990s, even if the medium-term prospects are promising.

Other elements

Trade in commodities is only part of the important advantages that Mexico, in the emerging pattern of comparative advantages, now derives from its geographical proximity to the USA. There is also illegal trade which is, for obvious reasons, difficult to quantify. The range of estimates for the country's unrecorded economic activities ranges from 26 per cent of GDP (by the Centre for the Economic Study of the Private Sector, CEESP; the estimate excludes unrecorded remittances from the USA, tax evasion and earnings in the narcotic traffic) to 50 per cent (by the Confederation of Industrial Chambers).

Trade in services is of increasing importance. The tourist surplus, about one and a half billion dollars in 1982 and two and half in 1988 (tourist numbers rose from just over 4 million in 1985 to 6.3 million in 1989), is an important revenue earner; about 90 per cent of tourist arrivals are from the north. Some of the earliest *maquiladoras* in Ciudad Juárez were in the service sector, and there seems to be an enhanced potential here in, for example, processing US bank and airline data. From casual observation on the border, Mexican medical services are of increasing importance to meet a growing demand from aged Americans who winter on the northern side of the frontier or in Mexico itself, perhaps partly to gain access to cheaper medical care than is available in the USA. The ageing of the American population is likely to increase Mexico's role in this field. Since the services required generally by the aged are labour intensive, the demand for Mexico's relatively youthful labour force is likely to increase, whether this demand is met in the country itself or requires migration north, to fill those immovable jobs such as personal and public services, restaurants and hotels, as well as agriculture and mining.

Trade is the more manifest element integrating the production system of different territories, even though the creation of a single, or at least, closely inter-related labour market is much better known. In fact, a partially integrated labour market has operated for a much longer period of time than the now-emerging integrated manufacturing and service system between north and south. Capital flows between the two are similarly of significance in the process of integration and closely related to the other two items – capital exports as trade displacing and labour employing are well known. While two-thirds of foreign direct investment in Mexico is of US origin, totally some $US23bn, Mexicans are estimated to hold $US40bn in the USA excluding the increasing operation of leading Mexican companies, for example Cemex and Vitro, in the US economy.

A free-trade area

By the criterion of a greater degree of interaction between two territories, in terms of the flows of commodities, capital and labour, than with third parties, Mexico and the USA already constitute a single economic region. Restrictions exist, and are especially cruel in the case of labour, but flows are already so derestricted, or take place clandestinely, that one can begin to visualize a single unified economy. This implies ultimately the emergence of parity of pricing, including wages.

This reality is, in terms of production, relatively recent. It is, however, not the immediate source of a proposed free-trade agreement between the governments of the two countries. That, like the moves to economic union of the Americas, 'from Anchorage to Tierra del Fuego', and the other negotiations within the Southern Cone group, between the USA and the Andean Pact group, between Mexico and Chile, seems rather to be a political pre-emptive strike against the possible failure of the Uruguay Round of trade talks (at the time of writing), the creation of a unified European market and, possibly of, an Asian Pacific Rim region which might exclude US participation. The last US Trade Act, with its notorious 'super 301' clause, can similarly be seen as part of Washington's bargaining position in the increasingly acrimonious discussion of trade issues. However, the fears that the world will divide into a triad of economic regions, namely, dollar, yen and deutschmark zones, seem exaggerated since, short of generalized catastrophe, the dominant powers are too heavily dependent upon the other two to risk separation. With luck, free-trade agreements may therefore turn out to be no more than half-way houses to the general internationalization of economic relations. Mexico now has much to gain from free trade. In important areas, comparative advantages are shifting in its direction. But, ultimately, the full exploitation of these opportunities will require not merely the free movement of commodities and capital – as we have seen, these are already relatively derestricted – but also of labour. Without this, the market case becomes nonsense. Then it might be feasible for the country's relationship to its northern neighbour to emulate what occurred between Italy and West Germany in the 1950s, when the German labour market gained immeasurably from Italian immigration up to the point where the Italian economy began to grow swiftly and its workers returned to meet a stronger labour demand.

The relative weakness which will emerge in the labour markets in the MDCs is only slowly becoming apparent. As mentioned earlier, the US population is ageing and the numbers of people in the active age groups are set to fall when services in general, now the predominant sector in the US economy, and services specifically for an ageing population, require increased labour inputs. Nearly 80 per cent of the Mexican population, by contrast, is below the age of forty. Manufacturing, many services and many of the retired may indeed be relocated to developing countries, but ultimately a core of services cannot be moved; the dustbins of New York cannot be emptied in Michoacán, nor the restaurants of Washington be supplied from Oaxaca.

The USA is already partly dependent upon Mexico in a number of ways, and this dependence is likely to grow. In the past, this was not so. However, the emerging world order offers great possibilities to the middle-income countries like Mexico to renew the process of rapid economic growth. The obstacles are well known and much attention has been devoted to them, sometimes at the cost of failing to see the growing strengths of the Mexican economy. Many of the problems facing the country are not solved by economic growth (indeed, some may become worse) but in the long struggle to employ all who want to work at levels of productivity capable of sustaining acceptable incomes, Mexico becoming a major manufacturing supplier to the USA is an important step forward.

6· HIJACKING THE 'PUBLIC INTEREST'

The Politics of Telecommunications Policy in Mexico

Mike Heller

The analogies sometimes drawn between recent political changes in Mexico and Eastern Europe apply equally well to the often disastrous consequences of 'state leadership'[1] in large areas of production and services. Public ownership and pervasive state intervention are now under the spotlight of policy reform. By most economic and social standards of performance, state-producer monopolies have proved poor substitutes for competition, enterprise autonomy and private ownership. In addition, there comes a point beyond which traditional bureaucratic modes of patronage and cronyism become incompatible with the modernization and rational administration of public services. This is especially evident in the absence of a real structural separation between the 'regulators' and the 'producers' in markets for state-sector goods and services. It can be argued that public ownership usually has the effect of conflating these functions in a network of relatively autonomous state-centred interest groups which may be fluid and in conflict with one another. Consequently, there are no intermediary, that is, state levels between consumer and producer needs.

Similar criticisms of the existing model of state leadership in Mexico were quietly expressed by many of the more radical young technocrats of the ruling Partido Revolucionario Institucional (PRI) during the course of the 1982–8 *sexenio*. By 1988 it seemed they would safely secure a new mandate to attempt sweeping reforms from within, with a modernizing Mexican Gorbachev at the helm. But, even before the presidential elections of that year, which may yet turn out to have failed to provide a sufficiently strong mandate, aspects of the restructuring of the state sector met with considerable opposition from old-guard *políticos*, and from the *técnicos* and *especialistas*, sections of the bureaucracy which dominate public service and utility agencies.

Ultimately, as in Eastern Europe, state power brokers have proved Janus-faced players in the retreat of the state. They themselves have been responsible for interpreting and implementing reform initiatives intended to undermine the institutions where they hold vested interests. It is that much less surprising, therefore, that they have sought to bend emerging rules of the game to their own advantage. In this context, various so-called nationalist and neoliberal projects have been employed alternately, and sometimes simultaneously, by public- and private-sector players whose underlying primary motives are individualist and parochial.[2] Factional highjacking of the declared ideal ends of policy before and during the transition to a new regulatory regime can be achieved informally within the formal legal-bureaucratic structures of the state.

This chapter aims to explain some of the failures of the Mexican model of state leadership in the telecoms sectors, and early pressure towards liberalization.[3] Two arguments underlie the analysis. The first is that state telecoms became severely overloaded by the tasks of service provision at a time of rapid growth in demand, technological change and forced cut-backs in public spending. In frustration, a growing number of large corporate users and fledgling private-sector suppliers have tried to leave the official market for telecoms-based services, and (often illegal and/or cross-border) 'bypass' networks have multiplied. Second, the objectives of revolutionary nationalism enshrined in the constitution and the legislative framework encouraged rent-seeking by government, which took an increasing proportion of the economic surplus generated by state monopolies. The same nationalist decrees served well as a smokescreen, or even the vehicle in some cases, behind which state officials monopolized opportunities for self-advancement, frequently in collusion with 'concessionary capitalists'. While on the one hand some state officials sought to extend the state's monopoly, others have found it expedient to collaborate with private firms in usurping the position of public-sector players. In some cases, examples are given below, the same official plays on both sides, as liberalizer and nationalist. This combination of factors has persistently distorted the overall policy process.

These distortions are illustrative of the sort of phenomena which from a neo-Weberian political theory perspective can be termed 'closure-seeking'. 'Closure' defines a dynamic process of conflict between individuals and interest associations powerful enough to exclude competitors and monopolize segments of political and economic markets, and opposing interests that seek to usurp power from below by employing similarly monopolistic strategies. In its macro version the theory deals with the principal faultlines in society, such as class or ethnic relations of exploitation. It is also well suited to being adapted, as here, to unpacking the dynamics of power (dual exclusion and usurpation) in micro-empirical settings such as government–business and intra-bureaucracy relations.[4] In this view, the policy process is seen as a predictably multi-causal and multi-layered conflict resulting from the pursuit of self-interest by policy players, on both sides of the formal government–business divide, with unpredictable outcomes. The mode of market regulation can come to play a central role in dealing with this basic closure tendency in human action.

It may be useful for short-hand purposes to say that the closure approach, as employed here, shares some assumptions with the better-known economic rent-seeking theory. It is, in the last analysis, economistic, in that economic goals are seen to have a direct and dominant bearing on the action of state players in political markets, in much the same way that profit motives are the principal driving force in private-business sectors. Rent-seeking has been defined as the maximization of self-interest by actors in institutional settings where it generates 'social waste rather than social surplus'. (Buchanan *et al.*, 1980: 4). Realistically, a great deal of public involvement in the economy can be seen to be motivated by the search for illegitimate rents, that is, incomes gained by the exercise of monopoly power. One of the several dimensions which closure theory can add to this insight is its account of non (directly)-economic factors, such as maximization of status objectives on the basis of power resources other than property and money; compelling ideologies may be one such resource.[5]

Telecoms in Mexico

Economic crisis, manifested in the rapidly diminishing reinvestment of monopoly rents by public-planning and budget managers, aggravated the shortcomings of telecommunications and intensified the intra-state struggles over scarce resources. Acknowledgement of the failure to reconcile the twin goals of public-revenue maximization and adequate levels of service provision commensurate with the demands of users, as well as the continuing profitability of suppliers has been the key factor behind the recent moves by the political leadership to liberalize, or privatize, segments of telecoms.

However, in the climate of tentative toe-dipping economic modernization of the late 1980s the reform process was itself hijacked. Unofficial liberalization, in the absence of a coherent macro framework to re-regulate telecoms, which would include, at a minimum, formalized competitive bidding for contracts for liberalized services, entrenched a network of patronage between a few unaccountable state regulators and an élite of well-connected but not necessarily well-qualified business interests (both suppliers and users of telecoms services). In addition, efforts to instil a new dynamism within the public sector by means of the decentralization of state agencies, while appearing innovative in an advanced technological guise, were implemented on the ground in such a way as to generate new sources of privilege.

Before looking at the case studies it would be useful to first discard some ideological baggage. It is easy to be misled by the ideological overtones of deregulation which so often dominate popular debates about telecoms policy, and economic policy in general. Since liberalization normally requires new regulations and a transition from pervasive to parametric forms of state intervention, such as the formation of powerful regulatory bodies to control privatized firms and structure new markets, as in the UK, it is more accurate to talk of varieties of *re*-regulation. The nature of the transition is shaped by political struggles and economic factors specific to the sectors and country in question, so that the forms and pace of liberalization vary enormously. The idea of liberalization remains valid as a description of the response of governments to demand and supply pressures set up by resource constraints in the public sector, growth in the range and quantity of TNS[7] actors, technologies, market segments and global organizational innovations in 'best business practice' applications in key economic activities. Liberalization is not automatically an ideological shift to market modes of a kind implying rejection of public-interest goals.

Telecoms in Mexico has, with few exceptions, been a state monopoly. However, the monopoly is by no means monolithic. At the time of research in 1988 there was a complicated division and overlap of labour, as well as conflict between and within agencies. It is worth noting that pressures towards liberalization can take different forms. They have included administrative reform ('decentralization' or enterprise autonomy, ostensibly with the purpose of building cost accounting or even competition into the public sector), liberalization of private-user and of commercial supplier networks, and proposals for wholesale privatization of the principal service providers.

The following are the main telecoms agencies dealt with in the chapter. TELMEX is, at the time of writing, that is prior to imminent privatization, a majority-owned non-controlled parastatal holding a renewable exclusive concession to operate public voice telephony. The Directorate General of Telecommunications (DGT) began the 1982–8 *sexenio* with an almost complete circle of closure, as chief regulator of telecoms services, including responsibility for overseeing TELMEX, and as sole supplier of the major non-telephony services, that is, telex, telegraph, audio-visual and computer data and transmission, satellite infrastructure, teleinformatic services. Without much risk of simplification it can be said that, by comparison, TELMEX was a relatively dynamic and modern profit-motivated company, while the DGT was an unresponsive and inefficient bureaucracy shackled to central government.

As stated, until 1983 the DGT both regulated and supplied telecoms services. That year a new Directorate General of Normativity and control (DGNC) was formed to take charge of regulation, that is, awarding licences to use, supply and commercialize services. In practice, many key decisions were still taken by the Under-Ministry of Communications and Technological Development, henceforth called *subsecretaría*. It oversees all the telecoms agencies of the Ministry of Communications and Transport (SCT). The other major restructuring of the *sexenio* involved the Directorate General of National Telegraphy which in 1986 became a relatively autonomous ('controlled') parastatal. TELENALES, as it was later called, was closely linked to the *subsecretaría* and attempted to take over from the DGT as the state's vanguard high-technology telecoms agency with plans for a so-called Integrated Telegraphic Services Digital Network (ITSDN).[8]

The central intra-state struggle towards the end of the 1982–8 period involved the previously hegemonic DGT and the dominant *subsecretaría faction which included TELENALES and the Directorate General of Technological Development (DGDT).*[9] *The subsecretaría*'s gradual dismemberment of the DGT comes as less of a surprise if seen in the context of the *en masse* movement of clientelist groups within the state at sexennial interludes.[10] The new, more liberal-minded administration of President de la Madrid appointed a telecoms team headed by *universitarios* linked to engineering and law faculties of the National Autonomous University (UNAM). This was a significant departure from the past when the SCT, and particularly the DGT empire, had been a stronghold of engineers trained in the National Polytechnic (IPN), considered to be on the left of the political spectrum. An apparently weak and politically isolated IPN engineer was chosen to head the DGT for the 1982–8 *sexenio*; in the long term he failed to assert his more genuinely statist and nationalist objectives.[11]

The real strongman in Mexico's telecoms in the period examined was the *subsecretario* (under-minister) who headed the new clique (*camarilla*). His power base appeared to lie in the linked worlds of academia and public-sector industrial enterprises, where he and some senior colleagues had worked previously, without any clear ties to particular national business groups. His policy actions throughout the *sexenio* indicated that he was committed in principle to the dominant role of the state, albeit in a restructured decentralized form under different management, though significantly, he proved also to be susceptible to approaches by multinational firms seeking special concessions. During his time as *subsecretario* he followed traditional practice by multiplying the number of institutions and departments to throw at problems and friends. As was the case in the past, official policy statements during this period were invariably laden with nationalist rhetoric, supreme confidence about the state's ability to push through and manage technical change, and barely hidden disdain of business solutions. Frequent platitudes about the dramatic impact of high-tech telecoms on mankind exemplified a deeply rooted technological determinism, and gave a strong sense of political status-maximizing based on the monopolization of false expertise. The opinions of senior state officials on the subjects of technical change and international regulatory trends were frequently sharply at odds with the more informed but less publicized perspective of TELMEX managers and telecoms players in the private sector, who claimed their own capacity for self-reliance in telecoms innovation.

TELMEX: 'milking cow' for the treasury

By the end of the last *sexenio*, government and TELMEX were engaged in crisis management to contain the public outcry against deteriorating service, 3–9 year waiting lists for phone installation, and the petty corruption of many TELMEX employees. The private consumer watchdog AMEDEC found in 1987 that at any one time over 20 per cent of the country's 8 million phones may be out of order; it came as no surprise to hear also that TELMEX received more complaints from the public than any other public service agency (*Uno Más Uno*, 2 October 1987). And, as anyone who has lived in Mexico knows, the quickest way to have your phone repaired is to flag down a TELMEX van and negotiate a bribe. Even line installation was governed by informal rules laid down by the powerful telephone workers who have also operated elaborate informal maintenance contracts with large users outside the jurisdiction of the phone company. Privately, one TELMEX manager claimed that the allocation of lines was virtually a black market over which senior management had little control (Interviews with TELMEX managers and large telecoms users).

Following high growth rates in the 1960s, indicators show a dramatic decline in line installation and productivity since the company was nationalized in 1972 (TELMEX, 1987b). The nature of the relationship between government and the parastatal lies at the heart of the crisis, which cannot be explained simply by the effects of the 1985 earthquake, the population boom, external economic schocks or labour–management problems, though each of these has contributed to the current malaise.[12] The bottom line is that government has used TELMEX as a milking cow for treasury coffers. TELMEX is the fourth largest firm in Mexico and contributes almost 1 per cent of federal government revenue. Telephone consumer taxes have been amongst the highest in the world, averaging 80–90 per cent on local services, yet government has repeatedly failed to reinvest, at the levels promised, in network modernization and expansion. Company reports have claimed that even deducting the amount reinvested by government in TELMEX from the total tax collected and paid by the company, it still surrendered the equivalent of 206 per cent of net profits in 1986 (TELMEX, 1987a:14).

A related problem was that cross-subsidies between international and domestic charges, by which users of the former subsidize the latter, were extreme if compared with the situation of most countries. In 1983, local calls accounted for 60 per cent of operational costs yet provided only 15 per cent of total revenue (TELMEX, 1983: 120). To cover these costs international and long-distance prices were set far above the international average while basic local rates remained the cheapest in the world. TELMEX saw the excessive cross-subsidy as a severe constraint on growth and called publicly for price reforms (*El Financiero*, 3 May 1988). Powerful users, supported by the ministries committed to liberalizing foreign trade, lobbied successfully for a series of substantial cuts in international tariffs in 1988.

At first cross-subsidies were intended to raise political support for the government, and to help domestic business interests. However, the benefits have been systematically cancelled out by the heavy tax burden in most categories of calls. The evidence leads us to conclude that government's primary motivation was rent-seeking, that is, to secure maximum revenue from TELMEX in the short term at the inevitable cost of decreasing investment in plant growth. Lip-service was paid to 'social telephony' under the cover of the cross-subsidy but, in effect, high prices on international calls, priced in US dollars, functioned only to keep TELMEX afloat. Over 1.5 million pending applications for phone installation suggest that plant growth could instead have been demand-driven at domestic prices guaranteeing adequate returns to be used for corporate investment. The political controls over the company also left TELMEX unable to raise credit in international markets. All in all, the phone company seems to have been at the mercy of government's cyclical fumbling and often mutually incompatible policies.[13] The principal closure dynamic in TELMEX–government relations has been a relatively one-sided affair in which finance and treasury ministries have monopolized rents from the basic phone service. Ultimately, the effect has been the exlusion of telephone consumer interests, which suffered from deteriorating service and lost opportunities for expansion and modernization.

There is another important factor in the TELMEX saga which sheds light on the company's dilemma. Relations between TELMEX and its head of sector, the SCT, have been characterized by conflict. The traditional SCT view is that telecoms should be a social, not a commercial service. For this reason they have supported the use of cross-subsidies, and in public statements the *subsecretaría* argued strongly against liberalization and privatization in 1988. But underlying this there was a deeper desire to handicap TELMEX. Many SCT officials, both regulators and suppliers, felt threatened by the relative autonomy of TELMEX, were jealous of the company's privileges and superior working conditions and were unable to relate to the private-enterprise culture of TELMEX managers. The SCT set strict terms on the monpoly concession enjoyed by the telephone company and, more recently, officials began to find ways to undermine the monopoly itself. In principle, introducing competition should be welcomed. However, the choice of competitors, like the policies which restrict TELMEX room for manoeuvre, can be shown in many cases to have corresponded more closely to bureaucratic or state interests than to any detached search for rational market structures. This is true at least for the early transitional stage of liberalization, though the same pattern may well carry through into later stages.

One example of this is the refusal to extend TELMEX's concession to include data transmission which the company claimed it needed in order to enter profitable VANS markets and satisfy the demands of large users for integrated services (TELMEX, 1987d). Officially the DGT leases circuits of the Federal Microwave Network (FMN, the backbone of the telecoms infrastructure) to TELMEX. In fact, TELMEX has long owned, operated and maintained about 85 per cent of the FMN. Even so, users still had to contract data transmission facilities through the DGT, a cause of excessive red-tapery. Charges for data transmission were kept extremely low, despite the fact that the main users were large corporations and multinationals, and the DGT syphoned off a large proportion of the profits, so that, on balance, TELMEX received a very poor return on the circuits it made available.

The phone company's own monopolistic strategy has, not suprisingly, focused on extending its concession to include a range of new services from which it is currently excluded. TELMEX has also sought actively to usurp the state's position by pushing the privatization issue onto the negotiating agenda by every opportunity. There is, however, no evidence to suggest that TELMEX is prepared willingly to surrender its market shares to future competitors unless the losses to its control of the rents from basic infrastructure are more than offset by opportunities to profit from its dominant position in a future liberalized market for value-added services.

DGT: failure of a bureaucratic empire

The DGT and other SCT agencies, having lost much of their operational leverage in the control of the basic infrastructure to TELMEX, were keen to retain any remaining budgetary and regulatory powers. But, besides the general objective of limiting the phone company's monopoly, the DGT's most obvious interest in preventing

TELMEX from commercializing data services was to protect its own high-speed data transmission service TELEPAC from competititon. TELEPAC has been floundering ever since it began operations in 1980. Budget allocations and productivity levels have never been high enough to enable utilization of more than 60 per cent of capacity, and expansion plans have been revised downwards by 80 per cent since 1982 (DGT, 1988b: 20–22). Around 700 applicants were still awaiting connection in 1988, and existing users complain of problems of inefficiency and saturation.[14] DGT officials claim that the situation is made worse by the fact that, in retaliation for being excluded from data service markets, TELMEX does not provide sufficient feeder-lines needed for users to access TELEPAC. Data services are a clear case of supply lagging behind demand because of intra-state conflicts over monopoly rights in potentially highly profitable and dynamic markets.

An example of the duplicity of some senior SCT officials with regard to TELMEX can be seen in secret contracts signed with multinational telecoms carriers to provide services via satellite in Mexico. In August 1987, at a government conference on Mexico's service industries attended by UN and GATT officials, the *subsecretaría* announced publicly that it was opposed to the idea of allowing foreign companies to provide telecoms services because, it claimed, this would threaten TELMEX.[15] It failed to mention that over the previous 2–3 years it had already agreed in principle to allow at least five North American carriers to enter the market for national and international data, and even for voice transmission.[16] This would effectively have undermined TELMEX's long-distance monopoly, which accounts for 60 per cent of the company's revenue (the foreign carriers were especially keen to target TELMEX's largest customers). The initiative came from the carriers and, as usual, no effort had been made by SCT officials to plan rational structures of competition, which might have included national firms. In any case, the agreements should have raised difficult constitutional questions since satellite transmission is one of the strategic sectors reserved exclusively for the state. The secrecy surrounding the deals, and the evident policy contradictions which they embodied have fuelled speculation among senior DGT officials that personal-interest factors played a part in the *subsecretaría*'s collusion with US carriers.

The DGT itself had reason to be concerned. The entry of foreign satellite carriers would threaten its own monopoly, the national

Morelos Satellite System. Launched in 1985 at huge cost[17] with nationalist fanfare, Morelos has remained underused, often serving as a mere toy of government propaganda agencies; for example, it was widely used in 1988 to enable real-time coverage of the PRI's presidential campaign trail. However, there is ample evidence, from official studies as well as telecoms industry sources, of high demand for satellite circuits amongst different categories of users. There seems little doubt from a practical point of view that the decision to purchase the satellite system was sound in conventional public-interest terms, even if powerful private political and media business interests did play a major part in the early policy initiatives. For example, the Federal Microwave Network, underdeveloped since its establishment in 1968, was clearly overloaded and in need of extensive, and expensive, repair or replacement. The conclusion of numerous cost-benefit studies was for the need to employ a satellite network for credible economic, political and geo-strategic reasons.[18] Yet critics of the satellite programme have failed to give sufficient attention to questions of regulation and intra-state conflicts over domains of responsibility and financial resources which have slowed up utilization; nor have they tackled the question of mismanagement, inefficiency and corruption which may also have had a significant impact on the relative efficiency of the programme. For purely ideological reasons most critics are opposed to private-enterprise solutions to the under-use of Morelos, a view which also carries considerable weight in the policy-making establishment.[19]

Commercialization of the domestic satellite system has been virtually non-existent, largely because of competition among different sub-directorates of the DGT–SCT and the regulators in the DGNC over rights to deal directly with users, and thus appropriate the benefits attached to this prestige project. Prospective users must find their way through several bureaucratic labyrinths to get authorization, and often receive conflicting instructions and technical specifications. A bias against commercial practices and industrial or private-sector users – state-owned corporations such as BANAMEX and PEMEX have received favoured treatment – and a general resistance to new demands on telecom services, combined with the simple lack of adequate incentives and management within the DGT, have meant that many opportunities for innovation were lost in the first few years. In addition, the SCT has indulged in prolonged internal discussion over regulations designed to perpetuate state-property and maintenance rights which have no obvious social or economic justification. Until recently, for example, users were compelled to cede ground-segment satellite stations to the state. This was a considerable disincentive to the use of Morelos except for those enterprises that were state-owned! The DGT actively defended strict nationalist–statist regulations in the forlorn hope that it may eventually receive funds to install a network of earth stations large enough to service all users. Other factors, such as the unwillingness of TELMEX and the DGT to work together on co-ordinating the use of satellite phone circuits with the company's central exchanges, have contributed to the inability to meet targets on the utilization of Morelos.[20]

Morelos has been affected by another characteristic feature of state telecoms policy. The musical chairs of *sexenio* politics encourages top state officials to initiate irrational money-spinning prestige projects and to divert funds away from those started by previous administrations. The Morelos programme belonged to the López Portillo administration. The rush to secure multi-million US dollar contracts in the final big budget year of the 1976–82 *sexenio* provided the now classic scenario for 'illicit rents' and political manoeuvring prior to intra-state job rotation and the entry of some officials into the private sector. The new *subsecretario* who took over in 1982 is said to have expressed his disapproval of the Morelos project during pre-election policy discussion forums organized by the PRI in 1981, at more or less the time that contracts were signed with equipment suppliers, and there is much to suggest that the satellite system was subsequently neglected in terms of investment and regulatory initiatives.

Not only did Morelos not promise future political gains, but its operation was in the hands of the DGT. As we saw earlier, since taking over the overall administration of telecoms, the new *subsecretaría* faction has directed its efforts to undermining the socialist engineers who, over the years, had built up the DGT's hegemonic hold over the sector, though it is obvious that the conflicts over ideology are far less important than the material dynamics of power maximization. From the outset they attempted to take control of Morelos by creating a new Sub-faction Directorate for the Exploitation of National Satellites within the DGT, and the ensuing conflict between departments contributed to the failures of the satellite programme. It was only as the end of the *sexenio* drew near that the DGT was forced to rush through authorizations for the establishment of private networks via Morelos in order to be able to submit a relatively acceptable figure on use (DGT, 1988a). There have, in addition, been allegations that some corrupt officials were selling off private satellite circuits at a discount to users in the financial services sector, the implication being that Morelos may not, in fact, have been quite as underused as officially claimed.[21]

TELENALES: competition and closure within the monopoly

The 1982–8 *sexenio*'s biggest white elephant turned out to be TELENALES, the agency responsible for telegraphic services. TELENALES provided the perfect vehicle for the *subsecretaría* to establish its own high technology empire, though this was far from apparent to outsiders when it first became a parastatal in 1986. In early 1988 it emerged that TELENALES was investing heavily in sophisticated networks to expand telegraphy and introduce a range of value-added services, including electronic mail, financial management and high-speed data transmission via satellite. This came as a great surprise to most experienced telecoms observers, not least because telegraphy is regarded worldwide as a stone-age telecoms service, now easily substituted by cheaper, more efficient technology. The addition of a telegraphic 'T' to the usual ISDN definition has a sad poignancy which was not commented on by the Mexican press. Instead they greeted TELENALES's announcement with great enthusiasm (for example, *Computerworld* (Mexico), 28 March 1988; also, *El Financiero*, 30 May 1988).

Mexico already had two state agencies with facilities for advanced data transmission, TELMEX and the DGT, which, under the constraints of political controls, had proved unable to satisfy market demand. To add another to the list seemed nonsensical, in view of the duplication of efforts that it would cause. At first sight, the choice of TELENALES appeared particularly inappropriate. For many years it has been a bankrupt enterprise beset by serious problems of overmanning, union militancy, astonishingly low productivity rates, rapidly falling demand for its services, technical and administrative obsolescence, and an average of 300 per cent government subsidy per telegram (DGT, 1985; also, TELENALES, 1987).

The *subsecretaría*'s decision to divert scarce resources into a massive revamping of a decentralized TELENALES only makes sense in the familiar context of patronage and cronyism. A high-technology project of the kind envisaged would not have provided opportunities for extracting and channelling surplus rents had it been attempted within existing agencies with long-established interest configurations, namely the DGT and TELMEX. Further explanation can be found in the fact that since the promulgation of the constitution in 1917 telegraphy has been a strategic sector reserved exclusively for the state. The *subsecretaría*'s quiet and audacious redefinition of the term to include *all* forms of data transmission was clearly an attempt to ensure that most of the key VANS delivered over the electronic highway of the future would remain in state hands.

The gradual emasculation of the DGT was part of the overall plan. From December 1987, by statute, TELENALES began to receive directly all the income from the DGT's telex and international telegraph services – the latter had remained a DGT service since 1960 and as such was highly profitable and economically strategic, used mainly by Mexican migrants to transfer their income from the US by giro – as well as the revenue gained by renting microwave circuits to TELMEX. Together these accounted for 65 per cent of the DGT's income. This accounting ploy enabled TELENALES to appear to be balancing the books in time for the change of administration, as well as making available some of the massive investment funds required for modernization. The ultimate objective was to transfer the services themselves to TELENALES. Seeing the writing on the wall, the DGT has itself submitted plans to become a parastatal. In view of the increasing reality of competition with TELMEX and TELENALES, it seemed the only chance of survival.[22] The TELENALES story is a wonderful example of bureaucrats restructuring the state sector for private-interest ends, to entrench a new power base in state telecoms, under the cover of nationalism and modernization.

DGNC: guerrilla deregulation[22]

The bid by the *subsecretaría* to perpetuate the state's hold over data services put it at odds with a parallel, though nominally dependent, regulatory agency, the Directorate General of Normativity and Control (DGNC). It is the DGNC which was responsible for most unofficial liberalization in the mid to late 1980s, including the granting of licences to private-sector suppliers of data and voice services (only data services are dealt with here). As well as TELENALES, the DGT and TELMEX also saw their monopolies threatened by different aspects of DGNC reforms. In order to begin to understand the DGNC's relative autonomy during this period it helps to take note that the director general is said to have enjoyed an independent power base resting on close personal connections with other ministries – his job put him in direct contact with the ministries of home affairs and foreign relations as they are involved in regulating broadcasting and international networks – with at least one large industrial group said to be on close terms with his family – which turns out to have significant telecoms and electronic media business interests – and with the then president of the senate, the country's highest legislative body – his father, who is also former minister of communications and transport. From a modest beginning in the DGT in 1982, he moved rapidly to build up his own bureaucratic-regulatory empire, forming alliances with key departments in the SCT, such as the Directorate of Juridical Affairs whose signature was required on every authorization. He quickly proved particularly adept in the creative task of liberally re-interpreting existing strict legislation.

Unofficial liberalization, my own term, owes little to any formally rational attempt at re-regulation. It is best understood as an *ad hoc* process involving two interlinked pressures to usurp the state's monopoly on services. On the one hand, regulators have been forced to make concessions in order to legalize rampant blackmarket activities, or simply to soak up some of the excess demand resulting from bottlenecks in public-sector supply of telecoms network-based services (TNS); on the other, regulators have colluded with leading business, often multinational, interests to issue licences of dubious legality. In both cases policy has usually been decided by closure around private interests rather than a firm's competitive, public or national merits. Some examples will help explain the background and nature of these reforms.

There has been increasing bypass of the official telecoms infrastructure, justified by the poor quality and distribution of public networks. This is especially evident in border regions where many in-bond assembly plants (*maquiladoras*) have installed advanced point-to-point international links. In Mexico City some of the country's largest telecoms users have directed an increasing amount of data traffic via private high-velocity digital radio. These authorizations, issued by the DGNC, were difficult to justify within the legal framework, but it is obvious that the scarcity value of telecoms opened up many opportunities for collusion with large users, especially since the radio spectrum was a finite resource. TELMEX was also increasingly worried by what appeared to be an impending boom in the use of private satellite circuits which bypass its own network. In addition, in a potentially dramatic development, one company, SOS de México, obtained a concession in 1988 from the DGNC to provide rural data, telex and voice telephony services by radio.[24]

Another area is teleinformatics. Services such as remote data processing, have, until ambiguous partial liberalization in 1981, been included in those telecoms-based commercial services reserved exclusively for the state. The DGT has attempted, at great cost and with little success, to operate a large-scale computer processing service centre called INFONET. (Some details can be found in DGT, 1988b, and in Heller, Michael, 1990.) In theory, any applications by other prospective non-state suppliers are judged by whether they compete with the value-added services which INFONET claims to provide, and on condition that processing facilities are located in Mexico. The relevant passages of legislation form part of the well-known package of laws which are said to encourage the development of national capabilities while protecting the consumer public from the cold winds of global capitalism.[25] Ironically, the inability of state agencies to supply these services in sufficient quantity and quality has driven users to import contraband services from the US on a massive scale. In effect, during the 1970s and 1980s transborder data flows have substituted for urgently needed liberalization.

In 1987 a confidential DGNC document noted that approximately 100 companies were acting illegally as intermediaries between domestic users and service industries in the US, accessed via TELEPAC (Departamento de Servicios de Teleinformática, 1987). Since equivalent services were not on offer in Mexico, blackmarket operators had stepped in to fill the gap. As a consequence, the authorities lost control over a crucial area of telecoms-based services regulation, and the drain of foreign exchange is compounded by the impossibility of retrieving taxes on contraband. Obviously without regulation consumers are also much more likely to be victims of unscrupulous business operators. Even in the case of basic DGT monopoly services such as telex, users have found that clandestine arrangements with overseas suppliers, involving a complicated triangulation of messages across frontiers, sometimes including those transmissions which begin and end in Mexico, can prove to be cheaper and more efficient![26]

In addition, about 400 companies have legitimate international private circuits directly to parent companies (multinationals) and service suppliers in the USA. Again, some of these services could have been provided locally in Mexico if telecoms authorities had allowed it. In fact, many of the registered 900-odd users of national private data circuits are already members of so-called closed user groups, in which one firm supplies services to the others; the commercialization of these services is prohibited, but the DGNC makes little effort to verify the true nature of the relationship between the firms. Because of the loose nature of relevant legislation, and the complicated requirements of high-technology users who are sometimes trying to integrate several overlapping bypass networks, obtaining these concessions depends on personal contacts between applicants and a few key officials in the DGNC. The illegal activities, once detected, can only continue because regulators have turned a blind eye.

In response to market pressures the DGNC began, as of 1986, to authorize a limited number of suppliers of Professional Data Services. Decisions about which firms qualify for licences have been suspiciously arbitrary, and the definition of the term has remained open to interpretation. It is perhaps revealing that the DGNC seemed especially eager to authorize the more glamorous expensive projects, even though they appear to have broken every rule in the book. For example, in 1987 a company called DIGICOM received the go-ahead to commercialize the data services of a computer centre located in the USA. It was to use the Morelos satellite system to reach nearly 200 clients in Mexico with a network of transmission–reception earth stations under the independent control of the company. This set several precedents, notably the use of Morelos for international traffic, and the franchise of Morelos commercialization to a private firm. Not surprisingly, DGT officials did their best to hold up the operational stage of the project. In retaliation, the director general of the DGNC threatened to find a way of allowing DIGICOM to retain ownership of the earth stations, rather than forcing them to cede ownership to the state, as the law requires.[27]

Another of the early concessions was awarded to the US financial group CITIBANK to offer a range of public data-processing and information services. CITIBANK thus became one of only a handful of foreign companies which, during the 1982–8 *sexenio*, were granted the right to retain 100 per cent ownership in major investment undertaking in Mexico; REUTERS already operated a huge network of telecoms-based information services in Mexico but, interestingly, had not been required to obtain the necessary authorization. There have been a number of other cases of similar significance. Yet, smaller

Mexican firms, sometimes offering the prospect of joint-ventures with US firms, complain that their own applications receive no reply from the SCT.[28]

Among the advanced VANS which Mexican firms claimed in 1988 that they were ready and keen to develop were teletext, electronic mail, videotext, telex switching, and data-bank access. According to officials in the Ministry of Commerce and Industry (SECOFI) there may also be a large market for specialist services with export potential, such as off-shore data processing. Such services would require a change in the law in order to operate legitimately.[29] Yet, nascent usurpers of state privileges have, as mentioned above, already sprung up. The DGNC is aware that some firms operate public electronic mail in Mexico City using a combination of private circuits and TELMEX's public switched network. However, the SCT's official interpretation is that mail of any kind is a state monopoly. This particular regulatory bottleneck is unlikely to be cleared while the various state agencies are immersed in their own conflict over which will receive the rights to monopolize electronic mail and exclude prospective competitors. Judging by past experience, the consumer is unlikely to benefit from the choice of yet another inefficient, underfunded and clientelist public service.[30]

The attitude of officials in the DGT is that the DGNC has conspired with powerful industrial groups and foreign interests to undermine its monopoly on various fronts. For example, the parent company of DIGICOM entered into a joint venture, through another subsidiary, TEVESCOM, with the multi-media conglomerate TELEVISA to provide teletext data transmission services via TV terminals. The same group is also thought to be behind a small company which has somehow managed to continue providing electronic mail in Mexico City. The parent company of these firms appears to have been a particular favourite of the director general. There is also evidence that the DGNC has been in close contact with US communications consultants about the possibility of offering bundles of Morelos satellite circuits to US firms to set up communication networks between the US and Caribbean locations.[31]

In sum, the DGNC has made attempts to push forward the process of liberalization, but it has done so in an *ad hoc* and informal fashion, responding on a case-by-case basis to initiatives from users and suppliers, and to opportunities for collusion. The regulatory empire built up by the director general of the DGNC has proved to be highly personalized and secretive in its negotiation with prospective telecoms users and suppliers.

Finally, on the supply side the DGT and the *subsecretaría* have been guilty of official collusion with public-sector clients. It is hardly surprising, for example, that the DGT's monopoly teleinformatics agency INFONET had little incentive to supply the national market when it turns out that, since 1982, 70–98 per cent of its capacity has been taken by the petroleum parastatal PEMEX. Until recently PEMEX has also soaked up a large part of TELEPAC's data transmission network. The company has been given favoured treatment in the allocation of satellite circuits, as have banks, notably BANAMEX, and other nationalized corporations. Ferrocarriles Nacionales recently undertook a prestigous technological fix progamme to install satellite telecommunications, making it possible that one of the world's slowest rail systems will be served by one of the world's most sophisticated high-speed signalling networks. El Nacional, a government-owned newspaper, was one of the earliest users of the Morelos satellite with a network to distribute photoprinting images and text to any part of the country. There are many other examples of the DGT expending much effort on installing networks or one-off teleconferencing facilities for government offices. Yet according to DGT officials few of the services supplied to state users are ever paid for. Even TELMEX must give government and parastatals a 50 per cent discount on all bills.

Given the very slow progress made in catering for all but the largest private-sector users, it is difficult to escape the conclusion that state telecoms monopolies are regarded, first and foremost, as at the service of the state sector as a a whole, though even within this limited market there is considerable competition based on the ability to lobby successfully for special favours. Such forms of intra-state collusion and market rigging are unlikely to contribute to the development of a more dynamic and modern telecoms sector. It is more probable that they constitute a deliberate strategy on the part of state groups to channel rents, and artificially bolster up state agencies which would otherwise find it difficult to survive the discipline of markets geared competitively towards the maximization of consumer interests.

Conclusions

I have argued that Mexico's model of state leadership in telecoms, and recent unofficial liberalization, has been shaped by power and self-interest among rival state regulators, major national and multinational users, and private and parastatal TNS suppliers. This is a fairly unexplosive conclusion. Nevertheless, it gives some indication that grand plans such as those for laying down natural monopoly electronic highways of Integrated Digital Service Networks as the basis of the future information society in Mexico – favourite slogans of telecoms bureaucrats who see their role as one of directing the process of technical change – will in practice be tempered by considerable clashes of interest.

This does not mean, however, that the goals of universal integrated service provision are not worth pursuing at government level. Regulations affecting the availability, cost and quality of telecoms network-based services can have a significant impact on overall competitiveness and performance in other economic sectors. Key activities rely increasingly on a range of services requiring high speeds and volume, dependable and well-distributed voice and computer data communication within and across national frontiers. One of the more important telecoms debates centres on how regulators can reconcile the socio-economic benefits of competition among suppliers with the need for rational means of technical integration between systems. Fortunately, the ever-reliable technological fix allows room for optimism. The remaining challenges lie in the realm of politics.

I began this chapter by comparing political changes in Mexico with those of Eastern Europe. It is not surprising that as popular demands for political pluralism swell to the surface in conditions of economic crisis they focus on changing the visible face of the power structure, that is the PRI in Mexico, or the Communist Party in the socialist countries. Ironically, the political project of leading PRI technocrats, including Salinas, may already be far more radical, in economic terms, than the platform of the main opposition.[32] There is a sense in which the state has begun, under force of circumstances, to turn in on itself. Political democracy improves accountability, even in telecoms. Yet it can also unleash strong social forces against any substantive economic reform or the use of markets that appear to threaten the benefactor state. The danger is, however, that the old-style vehicles of pervasive intervention bring a repeat of the abuses and inefficiency of monopoly power, and a continuing downward spiral of fragmentation among competing state empires. Until recently, political and consumer groups have been slow to take the initiative in negotiating the future structure of competitive markets and the transition to new state-regulatory regimes embodying rules, obligations and incentives. For as long as this reluctance persists, the political debate around the provision of telecoms network-based services will continue to be dominated by a simple opposition between public or private ownership of the means of production.

It is still unclear at the time of writing how the changed political situation will affect the nature and prospect of regulatory reform in Mexico's telecoms. This chapter has offered an analysis of a few of the micro-level determinants of past state failure in the telecoms sector; I have also suggested that the reform process holds many dangers. Solutions will not lie simply with the privatization of state monopolies. Government rent-seeking and the cyclical fumbling of TELMEX could conceivably continue to play havoc after a change of ownership; conversely, a private monopoly is more likely to end up colluding with its regulator. Telecoms markets can instead be negotiated in a less closed fashion among a wide spectrum of users and prospective suppliers to decide national, developmental and social priorities for the sector. One of the difficult practical tasks which lie ahead for regulators is how best to prevent TELMEX from stifling future competitors through its control of basic infrastructure.

There is, at least, widespread recognition that liberalization is both a complex and urgent task. Beyond the domestic political and economic pressures for reform lie external factors which government is equally unable to ignore. The simultaneous push of global co-operation and competition between countries and firms, technological change and related socio-technical developments in the organization of production and consumption continue to force the pace of regulatory change in telecoms. The factors most likely to slow down the further development of national capabilities are internal, notably the rearguard closure action of state players unwilling to abandon the privileges of monopoly.

Notes

1. The term *rectoría*, introduced in the constitution to define the 'strategic and priority' activities of the state and the primacy of government in the economy, is translated here to mean 'leadership'. The term implies a certain flexibility with regard to the form of state intervention but, at least during the period in question, served to justify a continuation of traditional modes.
2. If this conclusion applies equally in other sectors of the economy, as I suspect it does, it puts into some doubt the argument that a dispute

between nationalism and neoliberalism constitutes the principal divide in Mexican policy making. A well-known example of the latter view can be found in Cordera and Tello, 1981.

3. By 'failures' I mean the avoidable shortfall or gap between government's stated socio-economic goals and the final outcome of policy.
4. As yet, there have been few attempts to undertake empirical work from the closure perspective. A useful contribution to the theoretical debate can be found in Murphy, 1988. The application of closure theory in the analysis of government–industry relations has been developed by Cawson *et al.*, 1990. My own approach has emphasized individualistic closure-seeking behaviour, and closure within the state (Heller, Michael, 1990). It explicitly rejects interpretations of Weber which view the state mainly as an actor and that stress the ideal of a formally rational bureaucracy. Instead it draws on Weber's more instructive and realistic analysis of the dynamics of power in economic markets, and employs this framework to look at the operation of political markets.
5. However, it is important to note that closure theory and neoclassical rent-seeking theory differ sharply in their analysis of the nature of monopolization, or what constitutes the 'natural' functioning of political and economic markets.
6. The research was undertaken during a one-year stay in Mexico City between 1987 and 1988. The data are based on discussions with government officials, public- and private-sector managers and consultants, as well as written source material of various kinds. The arguments presented are an evaluation of circumstances up to and including the time of fieldwork. Essentially, it is a study of policy making during a formative period of rapid transition from one regulatory regime to another. As expected, there have been considerable changes in the framework of telecoms supply and regulation following the changes of government in late 1988.
7. Telecommunications Network-Based Services (TNS) is a term denoting the trend towards the technical and economic convergence of basic and value-added network (VANS) services. 'Basic' usually means voice and ordinary computer data transmission. VANS are specialized services, such as data bank access, electronic mail and remote data processing, which are delivered via telecoms networks. In Mexico, the latter are often called teleinformatics. Some of the main obstacles to breaking down market barriers separating the two forms of services are political. Many national telecoms authorities have tried to keep a tight grip on basic infrastructure and services, slowing down the pace of innovation in VANS. At the heart of the concept of convergence is the idea of a future so-called Integrated Services Digital Network (ISDN) which will enable the simultaneous handling of digitized voice and data, (and possibly visual) traffic via the same digital links and exchanges. Mexico's plans for ISDN are already well advanced and, as in other countries, have given rise to some interesting political debates about the control of network infrastructure (see TELMEX, 1987c).
8. All the agencies mentioned, with the exception of TELMEX, are part of

the overall structure of the Ministry of Communications and Transport (SCT). TELMEX itself is closely tied in by the fact that the minister is chairman of its board of directors; half of the remaining board members are also senior SCT officials.

9. For present purposes I have simply included the DGDT in the *subsecretaría* faction. It is widely suspected among telecoms observers that the DGDT was a costly and chronically ineffective institution, and a convenient source of jobs for the boys. In practice, its principal functions were to liaise with foreign technology sources and plan the *subsecretaría*'s secretive regulatory policy. Despite a great deal of rhetoric and agency building, including the creation of a Mexican Institute of Communications, only piecemeal attempts were made to integrate national equipment components in a few marginal projects. In practice, almost no effort was made to act on the guidelines laid down in the National Development Plan (PND) for promoting domestic R&D and technology transfer, which, by contrast, TELMEX was forced to adhere to.
10. This pattern is well analysed by Purcell, 1980.
11. The information outlined here was supplied by people who have a close working knowledge of these institutions.
12. Among the important issues which it has been necessary to leave out of the present discussion are those concerning the telephone workers union (STRM). From being a traditionally militant union subject to the controlling influence of the government-allied Confederation of Mexican Workers (CTM), STRM has recently shown signs of being both more independent from the old-style unionism and more willing to co-operate with management to improve productivity and introduce new working arrangements and technology, which it had previous resisted. It is clear from discussions with union leaders and TELMEX managers in 1988 that the threat of privatization and massive lay-offs has been a significant factor in this change of attitude.
13. Further details can be found in my own works referred to earlier, as well as in Pérez-Escamilla, 1987.
14. Interviews with DGT officials in charge of TELEPAC, and with large users of the service.
15. Most newspapers gave prominence to these reports, which included an exposure of the fact that TELMEX's prices for international calls were among the highest in the world.
16. Copies of original documentation, including the official authorization for these companies to provide services.
17. The official cost of the space and control segments was US$150m, but interviews at the DGT revealed that end-of-*sexenio* accounting in 1988 had showed up bulk expenditures of over US$320m with no satisfactory explanation offered for the massive discrepancy.
18. See, for example, SCT, 1981. This brought together the conclusions of several studies, both internal and independent.
19. There is a fairly large body of literature written mainly by academics in the field of media studies which, almost without exception, is overwhelmingly critical of the satellite programme, questioning both the rationale

for its original inception as well as its subsequent use. For example, Esteinou, 1988; however, evidence collected during my research on the background to the purchase of Morelos and current use patterns puts many of the previous findings in doubt.

20. Interviews with TELMEX managers and officials of the DGT.
21. Interviews with large business users, especially in the financial sector where there is a high demand for satellite links in order to bypass the public network.
22. The information comes from officials of TELENALES, the DGT, and the Ministry of Planning and Budgets (SPP).
23. Unless otherwise stated the description of liberalized services is based on several months of research in the offices of the DGNC, where I had access to files and personnel.
24. For many years SOS, a wholly Mexican-owned company, has provided radio communication services for taxi operators and airlines. Now, besides the new services recently authorized, it is also planning to expand into cellular telephony, and may eventually use the Morelos satellite system.
25. This is a reference to the Mexican Constitution as well as to the Laws of the General Means of Communication.
26. Interviews with DGT officials.
27. Interviews with DGNC and DGT officials. Copies of the documents of authorization were obtained.
28. Interviews with several Mexican firms interested in supplying value-added network services.
29. Interview with officials in SECOFI.
30. By clientelist I mean a form of distributing a service under conditions of scarcity which depends on the patronage of state officials or on the willingness and ability of consumers to resort to bribery.
31. Copies of correspondence between firms and telecoms authorities, and interviews with DGT officials.
32. In talking of the political opposition in Mexico I am referring to the *cardenista* PRD which came a close second in the presidential elections of 1988, yet which appeared in many respects to put forward similar policies to those of the traditional PRI barons, including strong opposition to privatization and economic liberalization.

Part III

SOCIAL CONCERTATION IN STATE–SOCIETY RELATIONS

7· THE LIMITS OF CONCERTATION IN RURAL MEXICO

Neil Harvey

The question of democratization in Mexico has resurfaced in recent years with renewed intensity. Authoritarian practices have been discredited and new possibilities have opened up. Yet the extent to which democratic politics is embraced is an open question. The historical weight and structural underpinnings of authoritarianism are not to be underestimated. Behind a democratic facade there lay perhaps the most effective authoritarian regime in Latin America, 'effective' in the sense that it traditionally revealed a capacity to postpone political crises through a combination of co-optation and repression. The governments of the ruling Partido Revolutionario Institucional (PRI) reproduced a form of authoritarianism whose flexibility distinguished them from their counterparts in Latin America. This system had depended on a simple formula which, in 1988, entered into crisis, that is, the denial of electoral democracy in exchange for occasional concessions from the state. The vote given to Cuauhtémoc Cárdenas, the presidential candidate of the opposing Frente Democrático Nacional (FDN) broke with this tradition and expressed the hope for a democratic transformation of the system.[1]

Events since July 1988, however, suggest a more limited process of change and the persistence of authoritarian practices. My aim here is to show how electoral democracy is being resisted by the PRI and the government, while new, more direct relationships are being established between the state and popular organizations. These relationships may be more democratic than before, in the sense that they are not conditional on affiliation to the PRI, but at the same time they reproduce the familiar pattern of political bargaining between state and sectors within civil society.

Why has the Salinas government placed such an emphasis on concertation and why has it been so important in rural areas? Concertation involves the co-ordination of actions between federal and state government and the organized interests of sectors within civil society, for example, peasant organizations, neighbourhood groups and labour unions. This is nothing new, although the targeting of opposition grassroots organizations has become increasingly important.

Several observers have commented that this new-found respect for grassroots autonomy is really a new co-optive strategy of a government which had to respond quickly and effectively to its highly questionable victory in the July 1988 elections. While there is much truth in that assertion, concertation with non-PRI groups was being actively promoted by Salinas and other important functionaries during the presidency of Miguel de la Madrid (1982–8).

At first sight, concertation appeared to be a victory for the Salinas team of technocrats which is openly hostile to the oppressive networks of bureaucratic and corrupt practices which have so damaged the credibility of the PRI throughout the country. It represented a convergence of interests, an anti-*cacique* pact between some peasant organizations and the technocratic, modernizing sectors within the PRI and the government. At the same time, it was a selective alliance which targeted those groups with greatest production potential, while offering little to the majority of poor peasants, the landless and the seasonal workers. However, a shift occurred in 1990, suggesting that concertation was even more limited than it appeared in 1989, due to the intromission of local élites.

Concertation is also a means to avoid the most challenging transformation required for democratization in Mexico, that is, respect for the vote. It was precisely the rural vote that gave Salinas his majority and it was the rural vote which appears to have been the most concocted. In subsequent elections fraud has been denounced in all states and, significantly, the most vehement protests have been registered in predominantly rural areas. Is it the case, then, that concertation is simply a second-best alternative to the full respect of democratic aspirations in the countryside? Is it not just a strategy of containment, giving the PRI time to reform itself while squeezing out the *cardenista* alternatives?

State–peasant relations, 1970–88: the search for a new alliance

State–peasant relations in post-revolutionary Mexico have been a cornerstone of the political system. The incorporation of agrarian reform movements into the CNC and the official party in 1938 effectively secured social peace in the countryside, except for localized expressions of discontent. It was not until the 1970s that new movements emerged throughout the republic, often promoted by participants in the 1968 student movement, reform-minded functionaries in state agencies and progressive priests and lay-preachers. The main cause of the discontent, expressed in a wave of land invasions during the Echeverría presidency (1970–76), was the failure of agrarian reform to achieve an equitable distribution of land. The CNC became increasingly ineffective and submissive to a government whose policies since 1940 had been more favourable to large-scale private agriculture than the reform sector of *ejidos* and indigenous communities.

Hardy (1984:83) argued that by 1970 the CNC had ceased to function as a representative of the peasantry and had become a simple intermediary, or 'transmission belt', for the implementation of government policies devised by state agencies. The possibility of changing agrarian policies was effectively closed while concessions were negotiated between the national leaders, themselves selected by the president, and the bureaucracy. Furthermore, all land petitioners were obliged by the agrarian authorities to form committees which were automatically affiliated to the CNC, and, by extension to the PRI. The strength of the CNC thus depended not on its capacity to represent its members' interests at the level of the state, but rather on its privileged position in the hand-out of concessions.[2]

It was in response to this lack of representation, and the accompanying corruption, inefficiency and opportunism of many CNC leaders, that the new independent organizations emerged. The Echeverría government responded by calling for democratization of the CNC and by forming a bloc of officialist organizations, known as the Congreso Permanente Agrario (CONPA), fearful that radical movements would escape official control. He promoted the formation of *uniones de ejidos* (UEs), designed to unite neighbouring plots in single, productive units which could benefit from increased state spending and technical support. Although the results of the project were not significant, they did provide a new institutional framework for the development of new UEs in subsequent years.

In fact, after 1976 the federal government promoted efficient and productive UEs as part of the programme Alliance for Production, while simultaneously restricting further land redistribution. A selective alliance was thus established between state agencies and producer organizations, undermining the earlier alliance with the CNC based on the promise of land reform. Those independent groups which still fought for land rights now came up against repression, while the CNC underwent an internal crisis. The system of alliances had shifted towards the comparatively few organizations which could increase their productivity and thus take advantage of new subsidies and assistance.

This selective opening thus favoured some independent organizations which had split from the CNC and which would attract the attention of Salinas in the period 1982–8. Such were the cases of the Coalición de Ejidos Colectivos de los Valles Yaqui y Mayo (CECVYM) in Sonora and the Unión de Uniones (UU) of Chiapas. The CECVYM grew out of the successful struggle for 75,000 hectares of land in 1976, half of which was prime, irrigated land with high production potential. The CECVYM began to struggle against the Rural Credit Bank (BANRURAL) to gain control over production decisions, credit and marketing.

Its success in establishing its own credit union attracted attention from other producer organizations, including small-scale coffee growers in Chiapas. In 1980, three UEs came together to form the UU and immediately looked to the experience of the CECVYM as a model for autonomous control of production and marketing. Taking advantage of the relative opening towards producer groups, both the CECVYM and UU established links with federal government agencies which helped them overcome the opposition of local municipal and state authorities, including the CNC (see Harvey, 1990b: chs 4–6).

The case of the UU illustrates the tendency towards concertation with some non-PRI organizations during the period 1982–8. Although the main struggle of the UU concerned matters of production, one of its member groups, located in the Lacandon forest area, had also been pressing for solution of land petitions for 26 *ejidos* since 1975. Despite winning an agreement in 1981 that the titles would be given, the local delegation of the Secretariat of Agrarian Reform (SRA), under pressure from the state governor, delayed implementation. By 1986 no progress had been made, and the 26 faced eviction. At the same time these communities were being blamed for causing ecological damage by bringing more land into cultivation. The UU argued that they were forced to clear more land since they lacked security of tenure and needed technical and financial assistance to make more intensive use of the land they already held.

The UU proposed that, to protect the environment, the SRA should first recognize the existing tenure and took this argument to the secretaries of Planning and Budget (SPP) and of Urban Development and Ecology (SEDUE), Carlos Salinas de Gortari and Manuel Camacho Solís, respectively.[3] Camacho promised to put pressure on the SRA so that the titles would be handed over. In this way both Camacho and the UU could overcome the opposition of state governor Absalón Castellanos Domínguez, who had a personal interest in exploiting the timber resources of the affected region and who had been repressive with independent organizations such as the UU. Such close levels of concertation help explain why the UU was generally pleased that the PRI unveiled Salinas as its presidential candidate in October 1987.[4] The titles were finally handed over by Salinas in his first agrarian act as president in January 1989.

This new relationship, based on concertation with federal government, may also be characteristic of most of the 50 groups which came together in the Unión Nacional de Organizaciones Regionales Campesionas Autónomas (UNORCA) in 1985. UNORCA has led struggles in defence of small producers of maize, beans, rice and other basic grains in the face of increasing production costs and the declining real value of guaranteed prices.[5] By August 1988 it had grown to include 75 organizations from 25 states. Although some of these already participated in the CNC, the majority were independent, like the UU of Chiapas.

One of its principal promoters was Gustavo Gordillo, an agronomist who had helped set up autonomous movements in Sonora, Zacatecas and Chihuahua. Gordillo's proposals for new state–peasant relationship based on respect for grassroots autonomy attracted Salinas who, in the aftermath of the July 1988 elections, recognized the inevitability of having to negotiate with popular movements, hence the decision, in December 1988, to name Gustavo Gordillo head of the newly created sub-secretariat of social concertation with the SARH. Furthermore, the decision was illustrative of the government's interest in promoting a new set of peasant leaders to take the place of the often corrupt and inefficient regional bosses of the CNC. By recognizing these new intermediaries, the administration also raised a challenge to the CNC that it modernize and democratize itself.[6]

Concertation under Salinas and Gordillo in 1989–90

The highly contested presidential election of July 1988 resulted in the highest-ever vote for an opposition candidate, the lowest ever for a PRI candidate and widespread allegations of fraud. Although Salinas was ratified as president, he knew he would have to implement political reform and win new supporters. His official vote was 9.6 million, lower than the 16 million recorded for Miguel de la Madrid in 1982 and the 20 million which he had been promised by the various sectors of the party. The CNC leader Hugo Olivares Ventura had promised 10 million, but delivered barely 40 per cent of that.[7]

In response to the advances made by Cárdenas in rural areas, including the mass desertions from the CNC to the new Cardenista Peasant Confederation (CCC), the Salinas government has deployed two strategies: the signing of new *convenios de concertación* with producer organizations; and the promotion of a new umbrella group of peasant movements, known as the Congreso Agrario Permanente (CAP).[8] Within the first three months of 1989 SARH officials rushed to the countryside to sign ten *convenios* with 66 organizations in 18 states. The targeted groups included many of those affiliated to UNORCA. At the same time, Salinas made several speeches in which he emphasized the need to respect the autonomy of peasant organizations and to leave behind the traditional paternalism of the state.

On 6 January, during the ceremony to commemorate Carranza's 1915 agrarian reform law, he said that the time had come to recognize the maturity of the peasant organizations, to let them control the use of credit, fertilizers and inputs. Functions and resources would be transferred to the producer groups, reflecting a demand of UNORCA, while the state maintained its commitment to promoting rural development. These ideas, which appear to have come from Gordillo, were incorporated into official policy documents, including the National Development Plan (PND), 1989–94.

Under sub-heading 5.3.1, 'Modernization of the countryside', the government affirms its emphasis on concertation. It says that there will be a decentralization of resources and functions to the states; a strengthening of the autonomy of action of producers and their organizations; concertation with state governments and producer groups to formulate and carry out rural development programmes in order to make more rational use of local and federal resources; and, a firm policy to promote efficiency in production. The policy would require a democratization of the relations between state and peasants: 'to modernize the countryside implies that the peasants be the ones who determine their production programmes and their commitments and work systems, without the authorities exercising any form of anachronistic and corrupt tutelage'.

The PND also speaks of 'associations' between peasants and businessmen, in an attempt to attract new investment to a heavily undercapitalized sector, and a thorough decentralization of resources to the state governments and the producers.

At the same time, pressure was being applied on the CNC to reform and modernize its structures. At an Extraordinary General Congress of the CNC in May 1989, the chairperson of the PRI, Luis Donaldo Colosio, recognized that old practices no longer worked and were rejected by the rank-and-file and called on the state leaders for proposals to hold democratic elections of agrarian committees, the base-level organizations of the CNC. Colosio added that 'democratization will allow us to transform old *cacicazgos* and imposition into forms of honest, honourable and legitimate co-ordination at the service of interests of the rural population of Mexico (*La Jornada*, 19 May 1989: 10 and 40). The members demanded a greater participation in all electoral processes through a direct vote, while the CNC leader in Chiapas, Mario Albero Manzano, warned that 'we have lost contact with the peasant base' (*La Jornada*, 19 May 1989: 10 and 40). It is significant that one of the impacts of the independent movements has been to force the CNC to appreciate the need for its own democratization.

The second strand to Salinas' strategy is the creation of the CAP. Previous governments had attempted without success to unify peasant movements in a common front but had failed, largely because the decision was not taken by the base and the independent organizations were left out. In December 1988 ten organizations signed a joint Agreement for United Action (CAU), bringing together a wide range of rural social movements and demands.[9] The government responded by calling for the formation of a broader front, which would include the CNC, as a plural and open forum for discussion and formulation of proposals regarding rural issues.

In January a committee to organize the founding congress of the CAP was set up with two representatives each of the ten organizations which decided to participate. These included five groups which had signed the CAU agreement (CIOAC, CCC, UNTA, CODUC, and UNORCA) and five officialist organizations: the CNC, the Independent Peasant Confederation (CCI), Mexican Agrarian Council (CAM), 400 Communities-National Movement (MN400P) and the General Union of Workers and Peasants of Mexico (UGOCM).

The five organizations which had signed the CAU but did not support the CAP warned that it was a co-optive strategy of the Salinas government and decided to observe how it developed and allow time for internal discussion with their members before committing themselves to the CAP. For example, the UGOCP waited until its first national congress in March 1989, when it was decided to participate, while insisting that it would immediately withdraw if it felt that the CAP was not promoting the interests of the agrarian reform sector. The CNPA preferred observer status only, arguing for an end to repression of its leaders before participating in such a forum. During the first three months of the Salinas administration, over 30 peasants belonging to independent organizations were murdered, reflecting a darker side to concertation and a continuation of previous harassment of autonomous political movements. According to human rights monitors in Mexico, 14 leaders of regional peasant organizations were killed between December 1988 and November 1990.[10]

However, most groups saw the CAP as an opportunity to present their demands and proposals and influence the course of agrarian policy, which had increasingly favoured private export agriculture at the expense of the reform sector. In April Salinas responded by inviting the CAP to make proposals to the National Plan of Agrarian Concertation. At the end of May the constituent assembly of the CAP was held at which the following agreements were made:

- to support land invasions where presidential resolutions had not been implemented;
- to call for a reduction in the size of private holdings and demand the abolition of the *amparo* law by which landowners could protect themselves against expropriation;
- to press for the creation of a special state agency to defend peasants' democratic rights; and,
- to call for the break-up of the government's cabinet on agricultural affairs, which was accused of promoting privatization of the reform sector.

The CAP also demanded full peasant representation in decision-making bodies and its manifesto included demands which had been agreed by the independent groups which signed the CAU in December 1988. In sum, it appears to have been a radical and independent document which did not sacrifice political allegiances for concessions, but insisted on respect for the autonomy of each member organization. The participation of independent movements such as the UGOCP and CIOAC was therefore important in securing this recognition. In practice, however, there are several problems with the CAP which must be mentioned.

The first concerns its position on the broader economic policies of the government. Although the CAP may provide an important counterbalance to the private sector's National Agricultural and Livestock Council (CNA), on issues such as debt repayments and stabilization there are profound differences between the member organizations. An early source of tension for the CAP was the decision of the CNC to sign the extension of the Pact for Stability and Economic Growth (PECE) in June 1989. Other members of the CAP were highly critical of the effects which the PECE had had on their members, since prices for agricultural products have deteriorated as wages and prices were frozen. The independent movements claimed that the signing was done without consent of the majority of peasants, reflecting the continued subservience of the CNC to the government. In July further doubts over the possibilities of the CAP were raised by government plans to abolish guaranteed prices and the continued use of repression in the countryside.

This discontent coincided with widespread protests over electoral fraud by the PRI in Michoacán, a mainly rural state with strong support for the PRD. In response, in August 1989, a new body was formed, the Unified Peasant Coalition, which is receiving support from the PRD and pro-Cárdenas currents in the CCC, UNORCA, UGOCP, CIOAC, CNPI and some smaller, regional groups. This new group marks a return to a purer, independent front without the ambiguities of the CAP.

The results of these two attempts to achieve peasant unity remain to be seen. Several observers have raised doubts concerning the extent to which the government is committed to putting its words of concertation into practice by responding effectively to the demands of the CAP. At the same time the administration faces calls from the private sector for privatization in the reform sector and is committed to conditions established by agreements without the World Bank. In

February 1988 the SARH signed an agreement with the bank for a US$300m. The conditions tied to the loan included the privatization of state-owned companies, an increase in the cost of credit and withdrawal of subsidies for irrigation and fertilizers. Rendón and Escalante (1989: 140) remark that the government's formulation of agrarian policy has in effect been conditioned by what is a relatively small amount of money. Neither this agreement, nor a subsequent World Bank loan of US$500m in 1989, contained any incentives for most small producers in the under-capitalized rain-fed regions. In fact, the groups most likely to benefit are private agro-exporters in the more developed regions. As Robles and Moguel (1990: 11) argue, such a policy is likely to deepen social and regional inequalities.

In this sense, Sarmiento (1989) argues that the effectiveness of the CAP will depend on its ability to develop a new agrarian policy. Moreover, it is dependent on the government's commitment to end repression, release imprisoned peasant leaders, control local *caciques* and their gunmen, provide economic support to *ejidos* and indigenous communities, restrain privatization and, above all, respect democratic rights. This last issue appears to be the most difficult for the government to accept and is another limit to concertation. Similarly, Emilio García (1989), a member of the CNPA argues that

> neither concertation nor pluralism defines the relations between the state and peasantry to-day. Alongside the speeches in favour of concertation is the constant presence of repression, the refusal to solve years-old demands for land, and the corporatist goals of the state.

Gordillo also recognizes the difficulties of reforming the state's relations with the peasantry on the basis of greater respect for grassroots autonomy. He emphasizes the unwillingness of local and regional functionaries to accept the participation of peasant organizations in decision making. The reason is clear enough. Functionaries often form an important part of alliances with local élites, including landowners and traders.[11]

The implementation of the policy of concertation has provided new problems for peasant groups. In December 1988 the government announced its decision to help the poorest sectors through the National Solidarity Programme (PRONASOL). However, a shift occurred after its first year, when Salinas was attempting to regain credibility. In 1989 peasant movements which were independent of the PRI could use the new direct channels of negotiation with the president and his advisors in charge of PRONASOL in order to develop solutions to concrete demands. This changed in 1990 as a result of local-level animosity to the programme from traditional PRI bosses, municipal presidents and state governors who saw themselves being bypassed in the distribution of new resources. Some governors, as in Hidalgo and Oaxaca, began to block the flow of money to agreed projects where independent groups were involved. Furthermore, most areas targeted for assistance through PRONASOL have been precisely those where the PRI lost in the July 1988 elections: La Laguna, Michoacán and Chalco (state of Mexico) (see Moguel, 1990).

This shift in the political role of PRONASOL and concertation has been institutionalized at local level by the formation of municipal solidarity councils. These decide how funds will be distributed and, given their partisan composition, constitute a serious obstacle for groups organized independently of the PRI. They are made up of the municipal president, a representative of the state governor and a representative of the municipal authorities. The council then sets up a municipal solidarity committee which is responsible for administering the resources and approving projects. Needless to say, these arrangements tend to reproduce the control of the PRI in municipalities contested by opposition parties, rather than fostering productive use of public resources. Federal government officials recognize that groups affiliated to UNORCA, for example, have a far greater capacity to organize successful productive rural co-operatives than the CNC and other PRI-affiliated bodies. Yet the political logic of a predominant party and the entrenched interests of local *caciques* restrains such democratic concertation (Moguel, 1990).

These obstacles have led Bartra (1989: 30) to underline the limits of concertation in Mexico's new political environment since July 1988. He criticizes Gordillo for focusing solely on state–peasant relations at the expense of a broader analysis of the links between peasant organizations and other social movements, including opposition parties. He sees a danger in the reproduction of political negotiating between state agencies and peasant movements since this excludes not only the less well-off peasants but also the PRD. He warns that:

> In times of crisis and political transition, to *depoliticize* negotiations with the state and promote deep reforms outside the

> arena of the new opposition, tends to legitimize the existing political system and can end up as neoclientelism; a technocratic and 'modern' corporatism but as oppressive as the previous system.[12]

Electoral fraud in rural areas, 1988–9

I now turn to the question of electoral fraud in rural Mexico in order to highlight the limits of concertation as a democratizing strategy. It is well known that the rural vote had been traditionally controlled by the PRI. High rates of abstentionism, combined with the transporting of voters to polling stations (*acarreo*) and the hand-out of presents to CNC-loyalists, for example, machetes, tools and money, have been common practices. Where opposition candidates have stood, the PRI has not hesitated to use fraud to secure its victories. Furthermore, independent peasant movements usually abstained from electoral politics, suspicious of the motives of opposition parties and fearful of reprisals from local bosses.

The elections of July 1988 marked a significant challenge to the PRI in several rural areas, although the official candidate would eventually claim victory on the basis of the rural vote. Victories for the FDN and the conservative PAN were concentrated mainly in the most modern, urban sectors, suggesting a desertion of middle-class voters from the PRI and the support of some important social organizations such as the student and urban popular movements. Nevertheless, the elections were highly contested in several rural states, suggesting a significant shift in political behaviour.

In fact, support for Cárdenas' candidacy took off following his visit in February 1988 to the Laguna region which straddles Durango and Coahuila. Here, due to their discontent with government policies, official corruption and falling incomes, *ejido* peasants gave a hero's welcome to Cárdenas, in contrast to the protests seen when Salinas visited the region. These *ejidatarios* had benefited from the massive land redistribution carried out by the father of Cuauhtémoc, General Lázaro Cárdenas, in the 1930s. More importantly, thousands of CNC members deserted to the rival CCC and pledged their support to Cárdenas in the July elections.[13]

Cárdenas was also well received in areas with a long tradition of agrarian struggle, such as parts of Michoacán, the mixteca region of Oaxaca and southern Veracruz. Peasants were responding not simply to the mythical figure of Lázaro Cárdenas but to what they perceived

Table 7.1: Voting by polling station, July 1988

	Returns made public	Returns not made public
Cárdenas (FDN)	4,022,282 (39%)	1,757,123 (20%)
Salinas (PRI)	3,506,605 (34%)	5,886,361 (67%)
Clouthier (PAN)	2,268,980 (22%)	1,054,274 (12%)
Others + null	515,677 (5%)	87,856 (1%)
Totals	10,313,544	8,785,614

Source: *La Otra Cara de México*, 6, July–September 1988: 2.

as a radical alternative to the damaging policies of the out-going administration.

Nevertheless, fraud was easier to carry out in the countryside than in the cities where opposition parties had a greater capacity for vigilance. One week after the polls and the infamous break-down of the federal electoral commission's computer system, the government announced that the PRI candidate had won 50.36 per cent of the vote, defeating Cárdenas' vote of 31.12 per cent and the PAN's 17.07 per cent. However, the opposition cried fraud and demanded that the government make public all ballots and polling station returns. In fact, only 55 per cent of the 55,000 returns were made public. Of these, it was shown that Cárdenas was leading Salinas by 39 per cent to 34 per cent and, as Table 7.1 reveals, Salinas' victory was therefore calculated on the basis of a 67 per cent majority in the 25,000 polling stations where returns were kept secret (see Fox, 1989a; Velázquez Zárate, 1988).

Significantly, most of the missing returns were from rural districts and it was here that, according to calculations made by the Mexican Socialist Party (PMS, one of the parties supporting Cárdenas), most fraud was committed.[14] The PMS–FDN argued that it was in predominantly rural states that the subtraction of votes from Cárdenas and the inflation of the Salinas vote were highest (see Table 7.2). This correspondence also explains why it was in these states that there was most protest against fraud (Michoacán, Guerrero, Veracruz, Jalisco, Puebla, Chiapas). Official results also showed some electoral districts in rural areas with unbelievably high turn-outs, yet the national figure of 50 per cent was the lowest recorded for a presidential election.[15]

According to the PMS calculation, the number of Cárdenas votes

Table 7.2: Official and PMS data on presidential votes

	Official		PMS	
	Salinas	Cárdenas	Cárdenas	Salinas
Veracruz	948,971	470,748	725,585	589,012
Guerrero	309,202	182,874	416,487	105,685
Michoacán	142,700	394,534	553,314	166,930
Chiapas	591,786	42,482	177,733	337,799
Coahuila	178,147	98,320	232,544	155,964
Durango	226,822	67,081	181,098	137,110
Puebla	781,085	193,142	305,799	287,966
Oaxaca	400,833	190,029	282,516	224,989

Source: Velázquez Zárate, 1988.

which was not recognized in the seven most rural states was 1,123,000. The breakdown is given in Table 7.3.

We should remember that the official margin of victory for Salinas over Cárdenas of 3.7 million votes was, according to the PMS calculation, concocted out of the 1.5 million votes allegedly subtracted from Cárdenas and the 2.2 million which were added to Salinas' tally. It is significant that 1.1 million of Cárdenas' lost vote occurred in the seven rural states listed in Table 7.3. Furthermore, according to PMS calculations, Cárdenas would have won in six other, mainly rural states and would have had a greater win in Michoacán and a narrower defeat in Chiapas. As it happened, his only majorities were in Michoacán, Morelos, Federal District, Baja California and the state of Mexico.

In the protests which followed, the major opposition candidates

Table 7.3: PMS calculation of votes which were subtracted by CFE from Cárdenas

Veracruz	255,000
Guerrero	234,000
Michoacán	159,000
Chiapas	135,000
Coahuila	134,000
Puebla	113,000
Oaxaca	93,000
Total	1,123,000

Source: Velázquez Zárate, 1988.

called for an annulment of the elections and were supported by large demonstrations in major cities. However, Salinas succeeded in gaining ratification in September and was inaugurated as president on 1 December. He had won, but without convincing the public of the legitimacy of his victory. However, the Cárdenas camp decided to take up their seats in the Chamber of Deputies rather than insist on a mass campaign of civil disobedience. Nevertheless, protests continued in the countryside as local groups of *cardenistas* did engage in civil disobedience in order to demand respect for the democratic vote. Rural discontent was fuelled by the continued reliance on fraud in elections for state legislatures and municipal presidents after July 1988. In several cases, particularly Tabasco (November 1988), Michoacán (July and December 1989), Sinaloa (October 1989) and Guerrero (December 1989) the opposition parties complained of electoral rolls which excluded thousands of non-PRI voters. Electoral credentials were often not issued in time and official results of PRI votes were alleged to have been inflated.

Furthermore, official recognition of opposition victories was rarely won without protests and direct action, including the occupation of municipal palaces and blockades of important roads. In short, respect for the vote continued to be something which could be achieved only through long and bitter struggles. For this reason, 1989 saw an increase in political violence as local supporters of PRI, PRD and PAN clashed. The PRD claims that since July 1988 over 60 of its members have been killed in what it alleges to be a government campaign of intimidation; most of the violent conflicts and killings have occurred in mainly rural states. We should remember that one of the demands of the organizations which signed the CAU and joined in the CAP was precisely respect for democratic rights.[16]

For example, the Regional Union of *Ejidos* of the Costa Chica of Guerrero, which supported Cárdenas in July 1988, has participated in the protests against electoral fraud in its region. One of the most important demands is for the dismissal of municipal presidents on charges of inexplicable enrichment, a common complaint in rural municipalities. By demanding accountable authorities, peasant movements seek to extend democratization to the very foundations of the political system.[17] A survey of the national press between December 1988 and June 1989 shows that pro-Cárdenas peasant groups continued to denounce electoral fraud and participated in direct action in at least 12 states: Tabasco, Veracruz, Chiapas, Morelos, Oaxaca,

Veracruz, San Luis Potosí, Hidalgo, Guerrero, Michoacán, Durango and Puebla.[18] Moreover, despite the continued use of fraud against its candidates, the PRD has made significant gains in Oaxaca, Guerrero and Michoacán. Yet the most common form of protest continues to be abstentionism, which has averaged almost 70 per cent in municipal and state elections since July 1988.

Conclusions

Concertation should be seen as an achievement of independent peasant movements but one that has limitations for the deeper process of democratization in rural Mexico. After many years of struggle official recognition of autonomously organized alternatives has been won for some groups, but it should be remembered that concertation is limited in that it tends to target the better-endowed and better-organized, while excluding the majority of poorer peasants and the landless. The gains, however, are not unimportant, as some groups have successfully taken control of key aspects of production, marketing and credit provision while simultaneously eroding traditional paternalistic and clientelistic practices. Attempts at peasant unification have therefore been marked by a concern for political autonomy from the state and the consolidation of democratic forms of internal organization. The impact on the CNC has been noted, placing it in the ambiguous position of being both government supporter and peasant ally.

Concertation is also limited by its sole focus on relations between the state and social organizations. However much these relations are democratized the state remains the central actor in the allocation of resources, formulation of policy and the site of struggle. This neocorporatism may actually be strengthening the state *vis-à-vis* civil society rather than allowing the latter to take control of its own programmes for economic and social change. This paradox is seen clearly in the partisan use of PRONASOL funds and the continued practice of electoral fraud in rural areas. In this way the possibility of a fully democratic transition is again being postponed, and concertation is offered as a second-best solution.

The political role of concertation corresponds to the needs of the ruling party to maintain a separation between the PRD and social movements. In some regions it has had success by marginalizing the efforts of the PRD to win support for its basically electoral strategy. The recuperation of Chalco, the state of Mexico and Morelos by the

PRI was due in some measure to the selective use of PRONASOL funds. Such a strategy tends once more to sacrifice accountability and the efficient use of public money to the political needs of the ruling party.

Notes

1. Of course, this popular expression of democratic demands was not an overnight phenomenon but has complex social and historical roots which go beyond the scope of this chapter. However, at least three main developments can be identified: the split within the PRI in response to pressure for the democratization of internal selection procedures; the electoral mobilization and successes of the conservative Partido de Acción Nacional (PAN) in the 1980s; and, the gradual consolidation of new social movements and independent unions in the 1970s and 1980s, many with their origins among the generation of 1968.
2. As Hardy noted: 'Mexican agrarian reform has institutionalized the peasants' desire for a piece of land. They soon learn that obtaining a plot is legally conditioned and regulated. They also know that they need the CNC to "represent" them in their demands and to facilitate all the necessary institutional procedures. There are other peasant confederations which carry out this function but none can open doors, jump interminable queues, gain access to private offices or consult documents and archives with the same ease as the CNC does' (1984: 177–8).
3. The president of this group told me: 'In June 1986 we went for talks with Salinas and Camacho. Salinas told us that the government was very worried that the Lacandon issue had still not been resolved and was thankful that we had informed him of our position and that we were prepared to resolve the matter. Then, in a breakfast meeting with Camacho we gave him our proposal and he responded favourably. He named Salvador Garcilita as "executive spokesperson" to the Commission of the Lacandon Forest, and organized a meeting in Palenque in October 1986 with the governor, the SRA, the Secretariat of Agriculture and Water Resources (SARH) and us in which an official document was signed, recognizing the rights of the twenty-six' (interview, Ocosingo, Chiapas, October 1987).
4. Interview, advisor to UU, San Cristóbal de las Casas, October 1987.
5. The economic crisis has severely affected the production of basic grains in Mexico, exacerbating a longer-term trend towards dependency on foods imports. The SARH budget as a share of public spending declined from 5.1 per cent in 1983 to 4.7 per cent in 1984, remaining the same in 1985, falling to 4.2 per cent in 1986, 3.7 per cent in 1987 and 2.7 per cent in 1988. Guaranteed prices for staple crops such as maize fell in real terms by 41 per cent between 1981 and 1988, forcing many poorer peasants to abandon cultivation. The shortfall has meant a steady increase in grain imports from 4.5 million (m) tons in 1985 to 5.2m in 1986, 6.6m in 1987, 8m in 1988 and a record 9m in 1989; see *Uno Más Uno*, 26 December 1988: 2; *La Jornada*, 24 May 1989: 27.

6. The recognition of new forms of representation constitutes an important change in the political system and provides a concrete example of the impact of popular movements on institutional change in Mexico (Harvey, 1990b).
7. 'Los líderes de la CNC de fiesta por los 50 años; la central se desgrana' *Proceso*, 617, 29 August 1988: 31.
8. As opposed to Echeverría's Congreso Permanente Agrario (CONPA).
9. These included groups which can be broadly categorized as left-wing or pro-Cárdenas and those which are more moderate. The first category is made up of the following:

   National Plan of Ayala Network (CNPA),
   Popular General Union of Workers and Peasants (UGOCP),
   Independent Confederation of Agricultural Workers and Peasants (CIOAC),
   Cardenista Peasant Confederation (CCC),
   National Union of Agricultural Workers (UNTA);

   The second category includes the following:

   National Network of Indigenous Peoples (CNPI),
   Peasant Unity Coordinator (CODUC),
   Peasant Democratic Front of Chihuahua (FDCCH),
   National Union of Autonomous Regional Peasant Organizations (UNORCA) and
   National Plan of Ayala Movement (MNPA).

   The signing of the CAU was based on the following demands:

   - an increase in the federal budget to agriculture;
   - the fixing of fair guaranteed prices;
   - the participation of peasant organizations in the different government agencies in the countryside;
   - the reduction in the size of private holdings and the abolition of certificates protecting landowners from expropriation;
   - an end to repression, and respect for human rights;
   - respect for democratic rights; and,
   - respect of the rights of indigenous peoples and seasonal workers.

10. See the following reports: Centro de Derechos Humanos 'Miguel A. Pro' (1990) 45–57; Comisión Mexicana de Defensa y Promoción de Derechos Humanos AC (1990); and Centro de Derechos Humanos 'Fraya Francisco de Vitoria' (1990).

    Repression continued to be highest in areas of protracted land disputes. In December 1988, Sebastián Pérez Núñez, a former local deputy for the PMS and CIOAC leader in Simojovel, Chiapas, was killed by gunmen at the service of a local landowner. His death was followed by those of Elpidio Domínguez and three other members of the Emiliano Zapata

Union of Comuneros (UCEZ) in Michoacán and Arturo Albores, a CNPA Leader who had been a founder member of the Emiliano Zapata Peasant Organization (OCEZ) in Chiapas.

11. Interview, Mexico City, 10 July 1990.
12. It is worth noting that the policy of concertation has not been limited to peasant organizations but has also included urban popular movements. See Haber, Ch.8, this volume.
13. 'Los campesinos esperaron cincuenta años y Cárdenas volvió, reencarnado en su hijo', *Proceso*, 589, 15 February 1988: 6–11.
14. The PMS calculation was made by taking the results of 60 per cent of polling stations as a base for projecting the remaining results. Due to the government's refusal to make all ballots available for scrutiny, it is impossible to know the true vote and the true extent of the fraud and, obviously, the opposition's figures should be treated with due care. Nevertheless, the PMS calculations give some approximation as to what happened and are useful for showing the regional distribution of alleged fraud.
15. It is probably the case that the 50 per cent turn-out was an accurate figure, although it was lower than official figures for previous presidential elections. It is more likely that those earlier figures were inflated rather than that the 1988 figure was deflated.
16. Three PRD members were killed in Puebla in August 1989; four militants of the Coalition of Workers and Peasants of the Isthmus (COCEI) were assassinated in December 1989 in an attack by local PRI supporters. In January 1990 the PRD claimed that another 14 members had been killed in clashes with local *priístas* and security police in the state of Michoacán, following alllegations of government fraud in local elections (see: 'PRD says killings are part of plan', *Latin American Weekly Report*, WR-90-05, 8 February, 1990: 11). In Guerrero, one PRD member died and another 50 were seriously injured when police broke up a march in Acapulco on 27 February, 1990, prompting the PRD leadership to take the matter of government repression to the United Nations Commission on Human Rights (see: 'State police turn on PRD demonstrators', *Latin American Weekly Report*, WR-90-10, 15 March 1990: 8).
17. See: 'Una experiencia de participación electoral en el Guerrero cardenista', *Pueblo*, 139, October 1988: 20–21.
18. Information taken from *Cronologías*, a monthly summary of events covered by national newspapers which is published by SIPRO (Servicios Informativos Procesados), Mexico City.

8· CÁRDENAS, SALINAS AND THE URBAN POPULAR MOVEMENT[1]

Paul Haber

Popular movements have been forced to make key strategic decisions regarding electoral participation and their relations with Cárdenas and Salinas.[2] The potential costs and benefits of these decisions may mean the difference between organizational prosperity and decline, or perhaps even extinction. Salinas has offered a number of popular movements the opportunity to enter into the highly publicized process of *concertación social* (social co-operation).[3] If a movement chooses to enter the process, and Cárdenas makes significant strides over the next five years, that movement could find itself severely isolated. Critics of the *concertación* process have stressed repeatedly that entry into such a relationship with Salinas splits the left, weakens Cárdenas and the PRD and thereby hinders Mexico's democratization.

On the other hand, the Cárdenas phenomenon may prove ephemeral, and co-operating with the administration promises significant increases in political and material resources.

Most popular movements have rather abruptly become preoccupied by the question of electoral participation. The vast majority, which trace their origins to the events of 1968, have historically shunned elections and parties as both bureaucratic and bourgeois. This no longer characterizes the national reality, suddenly extremely fluid and heterogeneous on the question of electoral participation. The electoral reforms which began in the late 1970s have offered the left opportunities to gain official offices promising to enhance access to political, economic, social and cultural power resources. But the decision to participate directly in electoral politics risks bureaucratization of the movement and a moderation of political behaviour as the movements replace mobilization with negotiation as their primary tactic. Popular movements shied away from active alliances with leftist parties for fear of being subjected to the ambitions of distrusted party élites. They are characteristically extremely protective of their independence and the potential benefits must be substantial for most of them to negotiate autonomy. The dramatic rise of Cárdenas provoked movements across the country to become active in electoral politics.

In sharp contrast to the de la Madrid administration, Salinas has concerned himself actively with popular movements and has moved, aggressively in some key cases, to build working relationships with them. At least in political terms, the most important of Salinas' *concertación* programmes directed at the very poor is the Programa Nacional de Solidaridad (PRONASOL). After the political costs associated with de la Madrid's austerity programme and technocratic leadership style, Salinas had little choice but to address the erosion of popular support. PRONASOL represents a central effort on the part of the adminstration to demonstrate that modernization[4] does not ignore the poorest of the poor. The majority of PRONASOL funds have been channelled through organizations loyal to the party/state.[5] However, a number of agreements have been signed with popular movements which have been, and continue to be, highly critical of the political system and the current administration. By entering into these arrangements with opposition movements Salinas hopes to demonstrate a pluralistic commitment to a civil society increasingly dissatisfied with a transparent authoritarianism. PRONASOL is consistent with other efforts by the administration to develop new relationships with important social actors who have fallen outside the historic boundaries of the inclusionary system. By promoting important popular movements willing to work with the administration, Salinas creates competition for moribund state and party bureaucracies as well as dividing the opposition. For a relatively small commitment of resources, the strategy appears to be paying substantial dividends.

Under the auspices of PRONASOL, a large number of *convenios de concertación* have been signed. These 'co-operation agreements' are contracts between federal and local governments with political and social groups to undertake various types of projects designed to mitigate conditions of poverty. The 1989 PRONASOL budget was 2.3 billion pesos (*Proceso*, 718, 6 August 1990). Under the auspices of this programme, Salinas claimed to have implemented 'more than 44 thousand works and actions in the areas of health, education, nutrition, food supply, services, infrastructure and productive projects' (Primer Informe de Gobierno, 1 November 1989).

Salinas has demonstrated a willingness to negotiate and intervene on the side of particular movements in local disputes. To enter into *concertación* can mean that a movement receives not only material but also political resources. His administration contains a number of people in positions of influence who have long ties to popular movements. This has enhanced communication and created political space for the movements to augment their limited political power. His approach contains strong incentives for popular movements to negotiate such agreements.

In contrast to the opportunities and dangers contained in the Salinas offerings, popular movements are also attracted to the Cárdenas camp. The emergence of Cuauhtémoc Cárdenas as an independent political force and the subsequent formation of the Partido de la Revolución Democrática (PRD) has created an opportunity for a nationalist/populist centre – left coalition capable of gaining political office and thereby introducing significant shifts in policy favourable to popular movements. The Cárdenas position has been that Salinas is an illegitimate president and as such should be dealt with as little as possible. Under no circumstances should deals be made that would compromise a movement's autonomy and ability to criticize the president and his policies. The signing of *convenios* has not been warmly received by the Cárdenas camp and has created important divisions between them and those movements which have moved publicly into this type of agreement with the administration.

Relations between popular movements and the Cárdenas camp have become problematic since the electoral shock of July 1988. While it may have been true for a short period before and after the July election that 'all left and social movement forces of any importance are part of the [Cárdenas] coalition', this is clearly and importantly no longer the case (Fox, 1989b: 60). While some movements remain ardent Cárdenas allies, many others are neutral or actively hostile. Many have agonized over this decision, and many continue to grapple with its consequences. A number of movements have experienced important internal divisions over the question.

This chapter evaluates how one of the most important urban popular movements (MUPs) in Mexico, the Comité de Defensa Popular, General Francisco Villa de Durango (CDP), has managed these decisions.[6] This case suggests the problems which Cárdenas has encountered in competing with Salinas for movement alliance. Not only is Salinas in a position to offer rewards which can be delivered in the short term but, as the following discussion will illustrate, the structure of the PRD has hampered the making of party–movement alliances.

Strategy and organization of the CDP de Durango, 1968–88[7]

The early years

The 1968 repression of the student movement in Mexico City forced student activists to rethink strategy. Some chose armed revolution, a movement which was quite quickly annihilated. A larger number decided that armed revolution was not a viable alternative but that the creation of rural and urban popular movements with a revolutionary orientation was possible and worth pursuing. Durango was selected as a provincial area ripe for radical organizing because it had recently spawned social movements in opposition to the way in which a major iron mine was being operated.

Although this movement failed, as did the student's efforts between 1970 and 1972 to create *campesino* organizations, the students persisted. While never abandoning their links to the countryside, they moved their centre of operations to the capital city of Durango, where it remains today. In June 1972 the student leadership divided the city into zones and those areas thought to be most auspicious for mobilization and organization were identified. The students then began the long and difficult task of attempting to persuade poor renters in PRI-controlled or unorganized neighbourhoods to organize for the creation of *colonias populares*.

The strategy of developing *colonias populares* (working-class neighbourhoods) in urban peripheries was central to almost all MUPs of this period, and continues to be so for a large number today. This strategy was consistent with the revolutionary Maoist ideology which inspired the students. From this perspective, the revolution was a long-term struggle and it was necessary to create liberated zones in which the struggle could fashion models of revolutionary living. These areas would attract new converts and could also be used as bases from which the revolutionaries could expand through the creation of new *colonias* and other activities. The *colonias* attracted Durango's poor because they offered an opportunity to own a home and to develop a new sense of identity by contributing to a just revolution.

Some form of land invasion is a vital element in the establishment of most *colonias populares*. Early attempts were met by violent resistance from government officials and landowners. The crucial lesson of these experiences remains central to the current political strategy of the CDP: the importance of building working relations with federal agencies and negotiating agreements in concert with mass mobilizations. In almost any direct confrontation with private landlords, and/or state and federal firepower, the popular organization will lose. But by exploiting intra-governmental élite splits, and working with reform-minded bureaucrats and political office holders, it has proved possible to develop an organization capable of extracting concessions from the state and providing some basic services to movement members. In subsequent years, the CDP has proved itself capable also of shaping the way in which policy is designed, implemented and evaluated. Along with efforts to influence policy outcomes, the CDP has long dedicated itself to building a new identity for the urban poor, distinct from that promoted by the party/state.

The CDP: 1980–86

Up until 1980, the CDP was only able to establish and maintain three *colonias*; between 1980 and 1986, ten new CDPista *colonias* were founded through invasions of private, *ejido* and public land. Over the course of this period, the CDP became increasingly skilful in its negotiations with federal and state authorities. Very often discussions would be held prior to or simultaneous with mass mobilizations. Extensions of pre-existing *colonias* were achieved and advances were made in the extension of low-interest housing credits and services, principally water, electricity and drainage. The CDP developed working relationships, which were often conflictual, with federal, state and local governmental agencies.

By 1986, a number of fundamental CDP characteristics were clear and remain so today. A formal decision-making procedure had been formulated, which included a six-member permanent commission, with roughly the same members being elected every year at the annual CDP congress, a 35-member political commission (also elected, and made up mostly of the CDP's most important organization and neighbourhood activists), functional working groups centred around tasks such as supply (*abasto*), women, culture and propaganda, as well as a detailed structure and set of formal procedures down to the neighbourhood level. Although the CDP's organizational structure gives the appearance of widespread participation in decision-making processes, in reality power is narrowly concentrated in a very small number of people.

Like most other popular movements in Mexico, the CDP does not foster collaborative decision-making processes as much as it counts on rank-and-file support for leadership decisions it sends down through the organization for consultation and ratification. The party, as presently constituted, does not require a highly participatory decision-making process but rather the persistent ability to form broad-based consensus within the organization. On those rare occasions that consensus cannot be built around leadership decisions, changes are made. The CDP has so far avoided a scenario all too common in the history of popular movements of forging ahead without a rank-and-file consensus which can lead to serious internal problems or even to extinction. The lack of participation is most noticeable around key strategic decisions, such as political alliances. Rank-and-file participation is more evident in decisions which pertain to particular CDP *colonias*.

1986–8

1986 represents a significant turning point for CDP political strategy. Until 1986, the CDP had, in common with Mexican popular movements in general, shunned electoral participation as élitist bourgeois activity which could never produce the type of revolutionary structural change deemed necessary. To participate in such activity was considered to run the high risk of diverting attention away from the 'real' areas of social struggle and, perhaps, in the process being co-opted by reformist thinking. In 1983, the CDP had formally remained neutral regarding electoral participation, although some activists did suggest to rank-and-file members that they vote for the Partido Socialista Unificado de México (PSUM) if they were going to vote. But when the Partido Acción Nacional (PAN) received the majority of votes in many CDP strongholds in the 1983 election, a process began which, by 1986, resulted in the CDP's participating in its first formal electoral alliance with the Partido Revolucionario de los Trabajadores (PRT). In all respects, the CDP was the senior partner in the alliance; it set policy position and controlled candidate selection.

Prior to 1986, many of the CDP *colonias* had not permitted the entrance of police and had in fact instituted their own system of law and order, complete with local police forces and judicial systems. This had been a sore spot in relations with the police, military and government, and the local press had strongly and consistently criticized this practice. This, combined with the frequent painting of public and private spaces with CDP art and propaganda, had resulted in the press characterizing the CDP as lawless and dangerous to public order and decency. With its entry into electoral politics, the CDP leadership saw that it would need to change its image.

In the 1986 election, the CDP won two *regidores* in Durango, one in Suchil and one in Coneto de Cononfort as well as one seat in the state legislature. Offices won by CDP candidates in this election were beneficial to the organization in a number of ways: they were instrumental in the CDP's effort to change its image in the eyes of public opinion and political society from that of a radicalized and somewhat dangerous organization focused primarily on defending itself against state policy and begging for services, to that of a political organization capable of presenting alternatives, negotiating publicly recognized successes, and implementing increasingly large-scale and sophisticated public-works projects.

The CDP has become increasingly concerned to convey itself as an organization that, while maintaining its primary focus on the low-income urban population, also works in the interest of rural communities and on issues which are of interest to all Durangueños, such as ecological issues, legislative reform and 'ridding public offices of official corruption'. As on the federal level, when the opposition gains access to legislative office it also gains the legislative floor as a stage from which to put forth its policy positions. Not least important about this space is that it receives coverage in the print, radio and television media. Even a cursory review of local newspapers makes clear the marked changed in CDP coverage over the course of the last several years.

As a direct result of the offices held for the 1986–9 term the CDP has gained invaluable legislative experience which has helped it as a social movement to present projects in technically and politically effective fashion. It also gained new insights into the workings of local and state government. This helped it in its self-appointed role as government watchdog and to develop stronger campaign positions in the 1988 and 1989 elections.

The election of *cedepista* Gabino Martínez to the state legislature was of particular importance. As in the federal legislature, the overwhelming majority of state legislators are not accustomed to initiating legislation. They have acted historically as approval stations, and more recently debating forums, in response to executive initiatives. Gabino Martínez presented a large number of legislative initiatives which went to the core of what the CDP deems to be the corrupt and unjust execution of public office. Although far from being always successful in a body controlled overwhelmingly by the PRI, he nonetheless proposed a series of proposals for constitutional changes on a number of occasions. His most important initiatives centred around Article 27, pertaining to the *ejido* laws, and Article 130, which structures church/state relations. Martínez participated in important changes in the state electoral code and introduced legislation designed to expose and limit improprieties between public officials and companies awarded public-works contracts. He argued fiercely against proposed rate hikes for basic services, defeating some and making implementation of others more difficult. A trained lawyer, a historian and an intellectual, his aggressive oratorical style went far to enhance the aura of professionalism surrounding the CDP.

Many political actors and observers comment, oftentimes privately, that Governor José Ramírez Gamero has, through his own political behaviour, inadvertently helped the CDP politically. Two events are most often cited. The first came soon after the 1986 election when the governor met publicly with the CDP and agreed to work with it on a number of needed public-works projects. As time went on, and the projects remained undone, the CDP was able to gain media attention by questioning the governor on his commitment. The second incident was when the governor took out full-page advertisements to proclaim that the CDP was controlled by criminal elements dedicated to the breakup of Durango society.[8] Although he was supported publicly by official party elements, including a barrage of paid ads throughout the media, many if not most informed observers view the governor's accusations as factually wrong or exaggerated and his actions as politically counterproductive.

Although it may be true that the actions of Ramírez Gamero in some ways helped the CDP, it is important to note that his dedication to closing doors to the organization also made life difficult for it. In particular, the governor's perseverance in limiting state funding to projects which would benefit the CDP and its constituents made raising the standard of living within CDP *colonias* much more difficult. It may well be that the governor's ability to dry up funds contributed to the CDP's willingness to sign a *convenio* with Salinas.

In 1988, the CDP entered a political alliance with the Partido

Mexicano Socialista (PMS), running a number of candidates and supporting first Heberto Castillo for president and then Cárdenas. Its key electoral victory was the gaining of a federal deputeeship for CDP founder and leader Marcos Cruz. The advantages to the CDP have not come primarily through Cruz's legislative behaviour, but rather through the recognition gained by and the opportunities afforded a federal deputy. It has also enhanced the CDP's ability to keep up to date on national developments, thereby working to decrease its somewhat isolated and provincial image.

In sum, the CDP has evolved from a small group of students organizing in a semi-clandestine manner in urban poor neighbourhoods to an institutionalized popular movement capable of mobilizing thousands of people at short notice, as well as negotiating with public officials on the international, national, state and local levels. While as late as 1976, the movement was still based in only one *colonia*, today it has 20 in which it is the major institutional and political force, and committees are present in 25 more in the capital city itself. In addition, it is now active in a half-dozen other municipalities, principally Nombre de Dios, Gómez Palacio, Lerdo and Suchil. Although the active rank-and-file and more loosely affiliated following, willing to show up for an occasional rally or vote for the CDP, is still the urban poor, the CDP has managed to diversify its membership base and subsequently has also modified its organizational structure. In 1986, the Unión de los Pueblos de Emiliano Zapata (UPEZ) was formed as an organization of rural communities within the CDP. Since 1983, the Unión de Comerciantes has become very active in defending the rights of street vendors and small businesses. During 1989 the CDP took bold steps in the creation of its own political party and in its relations with the Salinas administration. While both moves were risky, they were ripe with possibilities. They had the potential radically to augment the CDP's organizational power, and thus its political significance, as well as markedly improve its ability to deliver services to the poor communities which represent a significant portion of Durango's political geography.

Politics of *concertación*

The twin decisions to enter into a formal and highly public agreement with the president (February 1989) coupled with the decision to form a state-level political party (spring 1989) in lieu of entering into a political alliance with the PRD are certainly the two most important steps the CDP has taken in recent years. These crucial decisions have produced a storm of commentary and debate, some of it published, most of it not.

Why did the CDP make these decisions and what have been the implications? Immediately following the July 1988 election, an agreement was reached between the CDP and the Cárdenas leadership not to negotiate with Salinas. It was, and still remains, the position of the Cárdenas leadership that relations with the president are to be kept to a minimum. Under no circumstances should any individual, group or movement do anything which compromises its ability to make polemical attacks on the president nor should it compromise its ability to criticize his administration's policies. Certainly from the point of view of the CDP, this initial agreement was to last only until a more realistic position could be worked out regarding relations with Salinas.

The needs of a strong opposition party are different from that of a popular movement. Political parties are in the business of winning elections, and the priority of the PRD is quite clearly electoral, with attention being given to state elections, the upcoming federal elections in 1991 and particularly the presidential election in 1994 when Cárdenas is expected to make another bid. Cárdenas has stated publicly that his reasons for taking a 'non-negotiation' position are founded on moral grounds; he will not, nor should anyone else, make deals with someone who steals an election from the people.[9]

The CDP sees its priorities in a different light. It is in direct competition with other political organizations, not least of all the PRI, to deliver material benefits to its constituents. Its prosperity, and ultimately its very survival, is dependent on this. Because the party/state, and more particularly the Salinas administration, now controls the resources needed to deliver these services, the CDP must deal directly with the administration. It is important to note that there do not exist alternative sources of funding, governmental or non-governmental, domestic or international, which could begin to duplicate the type of federal spending contemplated in the *convenios*.[10]

The *Convenio de Concertación*

For a number of reasons, including power struggles and difficulty over developing a coherent policy position on popular movements, the Cárdenas leadership did not produce a clear position acceptable to the CDP. Although both public and closed-door meetings were held, an acceptable and unambiguous agreement was never reached. As the situation dragged on and the policy remained vague, the CDP became increasingly restless. It was also becoming increasingly dissatisfied with the lack of popular movement voices in the upper echelons of the decision-making structures of the Cárdenas coalition; in particular it was frustrated by the lack of CDP influence in the evolving direction of the Cárdenas movement.[11]

Meanwhile, political opportunities were being presented by Salinas, and even before his inauguration signals were being sent which indicated that the new president was planning a new and aggressive popular movement policy. Feelers were sent out regarding the concept of a *convenio* as part of PRONASOL designed to increase the President's popular image and to reinforce the regime's faltering legitimacy. The CDP's leadership found the package increasingly attractive and, in the face of internal divisions and unclear policy alternatives from the Cárdenas organization, decided in early 1989 to enter independently into an agreement with the administration.

Seen from the perspective of the CDP, the benefit-to-cost ratio was clearly in favour of signing the *convenio*.

Actual and potential benefits

1. The *convenio* does not merely mean that the CDP will be able to deliver more basic services, but also that it will be politically supported and funded to begin small businesses.[12] The development of an independent economic base from self-generated profits has been a goal of many popular movements, which so often suffer from financial shortages and uncertainty.
2. The development of a strong political relationship with the administration augments the political resources at the disposal of the CDP in its dealings with the state government and private capital. Federal connections can help prevent repression and undermine the state government's ability to otherwise stymie CDP projects, political demands and organizational empowerment.
3. As the CDP builds a working relationship with key players within the administrations it may, over time, be able to influence policy in a way that benefits not only the CDP directly but other popular movements as well. The whole issue of the relationship between the Mexican state and the PRI is under question. The development of improved relations between the state and non-*priísta* social movements, through the *convenio* process, may encourage reforms which open new political spaces for popular movements. These spaces may become important in the popular effort to compete

with the PRI in the formation of public policy. Assuming that this influence will be used by *convenio* signers such as the CDP to affect policy outcomes in ways favourable to popular movements in general suggests that movement benefits may transcend the individual signer. That is, this influence may be used to encourage the realization of the social, political and economic reforms supported by all popular movements. These include respect for movement autonomy, redistribution of state resources in the direction of the Mexican poor and a role for popular movements in the design and use of public resources.[13]

Actual and potential costs

1. Potential isolation from the Cárdenas camp. The cost of this could increase markedly in the future if the CDP eventually is seen to have been co-opted by Salinas and as having sold out on the PRD. Should the PRD gain important victories in Durango or at the national level the CDP could find itself isolated from a very important political force.[14]
2. There has been some moderation by the CDP in its criticism of the president and his policies although this has not been as obvious as some analysts first imagined it might become.[15] This is part of the bargain for receiving *convenio* benefits and conditions, particularly the type and amounts of benefits received. This runs the risk not only of attracting criticism from the left but may lead to disillusionment by the CDP rank-and-file who may see it as a decision to sell out. This is clearly not a problem to date, since the leadership was clearly successful in developing a consensus around the decision to sign and since services are being delivered which are directly tied to the *convenio*.
3. The Mexican political system has been accurately defined as an inclusionary authoritarian regime (Purcell, 1975), and its co-optive abilities are well known. By pursuing a *convenio* strategy the CDP runs the risk of being co-opted and losing its status as an independent popular movement.

The *Convenio de Concertación* was signed on 13 February 1989. The response to the signing was mixed. Many of those who disagreed argue that if the CDP has not yet been co-opted then it is dangerously close to being so. Much of the strongest criticism of the signing comes from Mexico City-based popular movements which support Cárdenas, such as the Asamblea de Barrios and the Unión de Colonías Populares. They argue that now is the time for popular movements to join forces in strict opposition to the party/state system in general and to the Salinas administration in particular. The usual way of doing business and cutting deals must be avoided, even at a cost. This is not just another president. These groups argue that it has now become possible for the left to make significant strides in effecting structural change and that continuing to bargain with the Salinas administration undermines such possibilities.

The CDP used a number of arguments in response. One of the more interesting and persuasive has been that popular movements located a substantial distance from the capital, particularly those which operate in areas such as Durango in which the state government is fastidiously determined to stymie popular efforts, have special problems which the *convenios* can help to allay. The CDP argues that it may not be necessary for movements based in or around Mexico City to sign *convenios* with the president because they are able to deal directly with central federal agencies and can make use of the vast opposition resources available only in the capital. The CDP does not have this luxury and must deal with regional branches of federal agencies, which are often controlled by the governor who is dedicated to blocking CDP advances. The only way to force these agencies to comply is through presidential order, which the *convenio* represents.

Convenio specifics

The *convenio* is an agreement whereby federal, state, municipal and CDP resources are to be combined in the implementation of public-works projects and the creation of CDP-owned and/or -operated businesses. The total investment of the 1989 agreement was valued at 3.2 thousand million pesos. The overwhelming majority of the funding was federal, with 1.95 thousand million being channelled through the SPP and 112.5 million pesos through DICONSA. The Durango state government committed 150.3 million pesos and the CDP almost a thousand million. It is important to note that CDP communities are able to contribute their matching funds in one of three ways: cash, materials or labour. The overwhelming majority of the CDP commitment was met through providing unskilled labour.

The problems of implementation have been varied. The CDP is undergoing a tremendous learning process as it develops the organizational and technical abilities to run so many projects simultaneously, particularly the small businesses. Paperwork demands have overwhelmed many activists unaccustomed to meeting these kind of technical requirements while those who do have experience have been stretched teaching others. Rank-and-file members must have the projects explained to them and in some cases they must produce records difficult or impossible to locate.

There is a political dimension to the implementation. Many within the CDP accuse the director of the Durango branch of the Secretaría de Programación y Presupuesto (SPP) to be dragging his feet, in response to pressure from the governor who is in no way interested in seeing the CDP succeed. The outgoing municipal president in Durango declined to sign off on the agreements, a requirement for many of the *convenio* projects, because he could not be responsible for their successful implementation by the time he left office on 31 August 1989. This delayed significantly the start-up dates for many schemes.

When the president visited Durango on 13 February 1989, he not only signed a *convenio* with the CDP but he also signed one with the CNOP, the so-called popular branch of the PRI. This committed funds far in excess of the CDP agreement, approximately 17 thousand million pesos. As late as mid-August, the local press was reporting that the CNOP had yet to implement a single project outlined in its *convenio*. The problems apparently stemmed from the organization's lack of ability to carry out the projects. The governor, obviously concerned that the PRI ran the risk of losing these funds should they not be spent by the end of the year, held a public meeting on 9 August with leaders representing 34 *colonias* which are targeted in the CNOP *convenio*, urging them to mobilize their communities so that the funds could be spent (*El Sol de Durango*, 10 August 1989).

It is important to note that the signing of the *convenio* was not a one-time decision done for benefits accrued in the February 1989 agreement; the first agreement was premised on a political strategy which, despite its risks, holds the potential to augment significantly the CDP's power, influence and ability to deliver services over the years ahead. It is clearly the CDP's intention to agree a number of annual *convenios* with the Salinas administration for progressively larger amounts of money. In addition to the highly publicized fiscal-year *convenios*, which include a large number of diverse projects, the organization has entered into other types of agreements and has plans to sign more.

For example, on 7 September 1989, the Unión de Pueblos Emiliano

Zapata, the organization of rural communities within the CDP, signed a *convenio* pledging over a thousand million pesos, divided roughly into thirds between the Secretaría de Agricultura y Recursos Hidráulicos (SARH), the rural credit bank (BANRURAL) and community resources. It has also signed and begun implementing an ecological project which focuses on the pollution of the Tunal River caused over a 15-year period by the large, wood-products plant, Celulosico Centauro. This begins what is billed as a long-term commitment on the part of the CDP to reverse the damages incurred as a result of past development plans and governmental behaviour which have ignored ecological concerns. The CDP not only wants to clean up existing problems, such as the Tunal River disaster, but also work to ensure that Durango's future development plans are both economically just and ecologically sustainable into the twenty-first century. An interesting aspect of the ecological project is that the CDP has received government funds, in addition to funds from the owners of Celulosico Centauro as well as from the Inter-American Foundation.

This strategy has forced the CDP to make some significant changes in its internal organization, and it promises to bring in more in the near future. Most importantly, it has become clear that the organization must develop a technical and administrative expertise capable of managing the new projects. It has begun to do this by importing highly trained engineers and economists from Mexico City. Members of MUPs, and those who analyse them, have long discussed the importance of devloping such capabilities. The CDP is making major strides in this direction and its ability to institutionalize this capability and accrue substantial benefits will likely affect the decisions of other MUPs in the near future; likewise, other movements will probably be persuaded against the *convenio* strategy should the CDP prove unable to sustain the promised benefits, and/or should the costs become intolerably high.

The Salinas logic

> *The modernization and internal democratization of our party depends necessarily on the dismantling of the [corporatist] sectors. The party must be perceptive of the new attitudes, groups and initiatives of the society and within this terrain construct its new scheme of alliances.*
>
> Luis Donaldo Colosio Murrieta, PRI National Director, 10 August 1989

Modernization obliges us to adopt new attitudes, a new political culture based on dialogue, tolerance and cooperation.

Carlos Salinas de Gortari, Primer Informe de Gobierno, 1 November 1989

Salinas stands to gain politically from the signing of *convenios* although he also risks further straining relations with important party/state actors who are staunchly opposed to political reform. In the case of the CDP, the *convenio* both neutralizes criticism from one of Mexico's most influential popular movements and divides the Left. Many inside observers are willing to state, off the record, that relations between Governor José Ramírez Gamero and Salinas are strained, making Salinas' relations with the CDP even more desirable. It is said that these strained relations are a product of the governor's political bossism and lack of creativity in designing and implementing an effective economic development plan for Durango, combined with his inability to neutralize effectively the opposition. It has also been suggested that Ramírez Gamero, who is CTM affiliated, is a victim of Salinas' anti-labour policy. In addition, Ramírez Gamero came out early and strong in favour of labour candidate del Mazo in the PRI's 1988 candidate selection process for president.

By signing *convenios* with the CDP, Salinas may also be able to put effective pressure on the PRI, particularly the CNOP, to 'modernize', and thereby become more politically and economically effecitve. It would become politically more effective by being forced to improve its relation to its constituency through the process of signing and implementing the *convenios* while economic effectiveness would depend on the extent to which the *convenios* contain elements of economic development and job creation in addition to services. This could potentially have the additional benefit of improving the electoral appeal of the PRI, thereby making the visible and costly forms of voter fraud less necessary, and generally legitimizing the party/state system.

CDP, PRD and electoral strategy

El Partido del CDP (PCDP) and the election of July 1989

Although the signing of the *convenio* did not lead to a formal rupture between the CDP and Cárdenas, as occurred with the Frente Popular Tierra y Libertad de Monterrey (FPTyL), it certainly has changed their relationship and put its long-term health in jeopardy. On the state level, the PRD leadership responded publicly with harsh and open criticism. It is probable that once the *convenio* was signed the possibilities for electoral alliance were over. But the alliance was already in trouble.

Interviews with the PRD and CDP leadership yielded different versions of why the alliance faltered. The PRD position is that the *convenio* is a significant political error. The fact that the CDP's intention to sign the first agreement was made public without first consulting the PRD angered the party leadership.[16] The CDP claims that it is not a political error and that the harsh reaction of the PRD to its decision was infantile and demonstrates the PRD's lack of political vision; in the CDP view, it was this which initiated the alliance breakdown.

In my judgement, it is quite clear that it is the CDP which decided to call off the alliance, deeming it in its best interest to do so. The negative reaction by the PRD to the signing merely reinforced a decision-making process, which was already quite advanced, to form an independent party. The most convincing explanation for why the CDP decided to form its own party is that it proved impossible to come to a power-sharing agreement within the alliance. The specific issue which tore them apart was that of candidate selection. Although the July 1989 elections were for municipalities and state deputies, the most thorny issue was who would receive the legislative seats awarded on the basis of proportional voting.[17] The CDP has long been disgruntled by the fact that in their view the PRD, and before that the PMS, received undeserved influence in the alliance simply because it possessed the party registration. (In addition to political rewards, the PMS received 100 per cent of the federal matching funds associated with the 1988 election.) In the view of the CDP leadership, it was the CDP which had the popular support; if the party leadership would not accept the CDP's position as the junior partner in the alliance, then the alliance was over. The fact that the PCDP received more than twice the number of votes that the PRD received (7.62 per cent and 3.16 respectively) supports that claim.

The state legislature approved a temporary party registration for the CDP by making additions to the state electoral code. This stimulated some political observers and opponents, including the PAN, to suggest that the Salinas administration, if not the president himself, had played a role in the affair. Soon after the CDP had gained its temporary registration it moved to develop an inter-party electoral alliance with the PRD.[18] The PRD formally refused to enter into such alliances, insisting that the condition for doing so was that the CDP rescind its independent registration. This was clearly unacceptable to the CDP. At a formal meeting between the CDP and local PRD leadership, Cárdenas repeated his much-publicized position that state-level organizations make alliance decisions independent of national leadership. The PRD state-level leadership decided against it. It stated publicly that it was refusing to do so on moral grounds, that the CDP had been 'captured' by the party/state and that it would form no alliances with such parties.[19] It was in the context of strained relations between the PRD and the CDP that the CDP made a series of agreements with the PFCRN, PPS and PARM to support common candidates.

The State Electoral Commission, controlled by the PRI, is legally responsible for first determining official results. These results are then debated, changed or ratified and eventually approved in the electoral college, also controlled by the PRI. During July and August the commission released a number of different results, suggesting, but not proving, the highly politicized nature of vote counting in Durango. The official numbers sent by the commission to the electoral college on 15 August, 1989 were the following: PRI = 63.30 per cent; PAN = 21.62 per cent; PCDP = 7.62 per cent; PRD = 3.16 per cent; PPS = 2.02 per cent; PARM = 1.49 per cent; PFCRN = 0.76 per cent.

The CDP received more votes than did the PRD in all regions of the state except for the municipalities of Gómez Palacio, Guadalupe Victoria, Mampini, Rodeo and Tlahaulilo. Of these, Gómez Palacio is clearly the most important. The PRD was aided here by a long history of *cardenismo* and also fielded a particularly strong candidate from the Corriente Democrática (CD), Jorge Torres Castillo.

It is also the electoral commission which decides how to divide the ten legislative seats to be awarded on the basis of proportional voting. Many political voices in Durango, particularly those of the PAN and the CDP which were the most adversely affected, accused the commission of not respecting the spirit if not the letter of the electoral reforms which instituted proportional seats beginning in 1979. Many of these same observers allege that the commission was acting at the behest of the state governor.

As stated by one of Durango's more influential columnists, Mariano Alvarado, if the electoral commission had distributed seats commensurate with the number of votes officially received, ignoring for the moment the question of election fraud, then the PAN would have received six, the CDP three and the PRD one (*El Sol de Durango*, 12 August 1989). But the actual outcome was three for the PAN, two for the CDP, two for the PRD and one for the PRI. The commission was able to do this because of the broad powers of interpretation allowed it by the wording of articles 153 and 154 of the state electoral code.

The political strategy behind the decision to divide the seats more evenly between the opposition parties rather than in accordance with votes received is not difficult to deduce: it reduces further the power of the PAN which has been in steady decline from its zenith during the 1983–6 period when it held the municipal presidency of the state capital. The PAN was also widely believed to have won the 1986 governor's race, only to lose it through official corruption and repression; second, by awarding two seats to the PRD and two to the CDP the commission fuelled the competition between them and made a resolution of the CDP/PRD split more difficult.[20]

An interesting aspect of the CDP vote is where it came from. In the opinion of most observers it came from the PAN and not the PRI, that is, the increased CDP vote count came at the expense of the PAN. This has contributed to growing tensions between the organizations. Until the signing of the *convenio* and the politicized nature of the PCDP's temporary registration, the two had usually managed to maintain cordial relations and had worked jointly on some legislative projects. More recently, this relationship, public and private, has seriously deteriorated. Attacks and counter-attacks in the local media have become common.

The case of Nombre de Dios

Perhaps the most significant outcome of party registration and CDP electoral results was winning the control of two municipal governments, Nombre de Dios and Suchil. In both cases, early official results claimed PRI victories and were only overturned through political negotiation between the CDP, the electoral commission, the governor and Mexico City. Among other things, this complicated process demonstrates, once again, the highly politicized nature of vote counting and deal-making in Mexico.

The most dramatic municipal outcome, and the most significant in terms of political influence and size, is Nombre de Dios. There are 39 municipalities in the state of Durango and Nombre de Dios is certainly in the top ten in terms of population size and economic activity. It is also well known, and widely commented upon, that the most central figure in Durangan politics for over four decades, Antonio Ramírez Martínez, father of the current governor and head of the CTM with long and close ties to Fidel Velásquez, was born in Nombre de Dios and has long considered it a part of his personal political domain.

The CDP's ties to Nombre de Dios go back to the 1970s. However, it was only during CDP founder Marcos Cruz's 1988 electoral campaign for federal deputy of District 5 that these relations became organizationally significant, when it became clear that there was significant opposition to the then-municipal president, Ignacio Gutiérrez. He was alleged to be excessively corrupt and politically inept, judged so even by those who have learned to expect a certain level of corruption from local office holders. The CDP was successful in leading a campaign to oust Gutiérrez from office, using the upcoming visit of Salinas in February 1989 to pressure the governor to force Gutiérrez's early retirement.[21] It is a common occurrence for political parties, particularly opposition parties with scarce resources, to prioritize which elected offices they will pursue. Nombre de Dios was given significance second only to the capital city itself.

The CDP sought unsuccessfully to form a political alliance with the PRD, whose state leadership refused a deal despite the fact that their own candidate in Nombre de Dios stated publicly that he desired such an alliance. Although the CDP did not finally post its own candidate until quite late, that is, in May, as opposed to the more popular March, early official results showed the PRI candidate winning the election by only 50 votes. But on the evening of the official count in Nombre de Dios an unexpected event changed the political balance. A CDP rank-and-file member, Carlos Luna Avila, was killed when a group of *priístas* approached the municipal palace, at the time occupied by the CDP in protest at the preliminary official election results. This group included the former municipal president, Ignacio Gutiérrez, as well as his cousin, Paul Gutiérrez, who had just been officially designated the official winner of the municipal presidency by the local election commission, and Benjamín Avila, PRI candidate for the state assembly from that district. The details of the case are complex, disputed and still in litigation. To date, only Ignacio Gutiérrez has been charged with the killing and is currently in custody; Benjamín Avila has entered the new state legislature. The CDP has initiated what they say will be a long-term battle to bring the other two before the court as well.

At the time of the killing, a number of voting booths had produced official counts which the CDP was in the process of challenging through official channels. It is, of course, possible that they would have obliged the PRI-controlled electoral commission, electoral college and, more importantly, Governor José Ramírez Gamero to decide in favour of the CDP with or without the killing of Luna. What is more likely is that this incident provided the catalyst that federal and state officials needed to accept a CDP victory in Nombre de Dios.

On 31 August 1989, CDP candidate Octavio Martínez Alvarez, became municipal president of Nombre de Dios. The CDP took great care to form a balanced administration. Of the nine *regidores* (aldermen) appointed by Martínez Alvarez, three were PRI, three CDP, one PRD, one PAN and one PRT. The leadership has stressed the importance of demonstrating a clear alternative in Nombre de Dios. National attention is on them and they are determined to avoid the type of problems incurred by the COCEI in Juchitán.[22] The importance of municipal governments for the opposition is an issue throughout Mexico as more and more opposition parties win municipalities. The track records which the CDP is able to establish in Nombre de Dios and Suchil will be important for future elections and for public perception of the CDP in general.

In sum, in the context of strained relations with the PRD, the CDP decided to initiate a political process which culminated with the registration of its own political party. The fact that it achieved temporary registration, coupled with a very expensive and well-funded campaign, led to accusations of intervention by the Salinas administration.[23] The CDP did quite well, receiving almost 8 per cent of the vote from a seven-party field and establishing itself as the third most powerful electoral force in Durango, behind the PRI and the faltering PAN. During the 1989–92 session it will have two state deputies, two municipal presidents and about 20 *regidores*. Although the electoral future of the PCDP is unclear, the party's participation in electoral politics appears firm. It is also clear that much depends on the future of Cárdenas and the PRD, and the relations which form between them and the CDP, as well as the CDP's evolving relations with Salinas.

Conclusion

Popular movements have been an important ingredient in Mexico's rapidly changing political landscape during the 1980s. Well before the left's recent strides in the electoral arena, such movements were emerging in radical opposition to the political system and the national economic development strategy which was promoted by the party/state. Clearly they have not yet achieved, nor, perhaps, will they achieve, revolutionary structural change but they have managed in some cases to influence public policy and the way policy is made.

Popular movements have made significant contributions to the steady advances of the Mexican opposition over the course of the 1980s; they have contributed to and influenced the Cárdenas movement, including the shock of July 1988, just as the Cárdenas movement has radically altered individual movements, umbrella organizations and relationships between grassroots movements throughout the country. Popular movements have contributed, through critique and the promotion of alternative political visions, to the erosion of the ideological hegemony so long a basic characteristic of the regime. Perhaps none of them has grown in terms of size or scope as has the CDP.

In the simplest of terms, what accounts for the CDP's success is its ability to learn from mistakes and to take advantage of opportunities afforded it by the political, social and economic contexts in which it operates. Even the CDP's critics concede that it has developed extremely effective strategies and tactics for influencing political outcomes.

The CDP has been intentionally, and effectively, organized historically to reach consensus around decisions taken by a small core of movement leaders. The fact that it is now entering a dynamic stage in its institutional history through the creation of a political party and the management of expanded development activities, made possible through the *convenio* process, may threaten this structure. Whether it will need to make significant changes in relations between leadership, activists and rank-and-file as a consequence of these developments remains to be seen; whether it makes the needed changes, whatever they may turn out to be, also remains to be seen.

Popular movements, particularly important ones such as the CDP, represent a challenge for both Salinas and Cárdenas. In fact, both are in competition for the movements' support. The case of the CDP is highly suggestive regarding the potential which Salinas' National Solidarity strategy and the *convenios* have for dividing the left by creating divisions between Cárdenas and popular movements and between and even within movements themselves. If Salinas is able to establish a successful track record, and the PRD continues its present policy of excluding key movements such as the CDP from decision-making power within the party, it would appear probable that more movements will develop the kind of working relationships with Salinas which Cárdenas seeks to avoid. Of course, Salinas' track record on coming through with economic and political resources to those movements which enter the *convenio* process will also determine the number of movements willing to negotiate with him.

The prolonged economic crisis, years of austerity programmes and the 1985 earthquake brought the rising tide of opposition to a head in July 1988. But while the economic crisis has certainly contributed to major shifts in party politics and collective actions within civil society, the new opposition has not been able to undermine the ability of the state to act. This has been demonstrated most dramatically by the economic reforms which began during the de la Madrid administration, and which have only accelerated during the Salinas administration. These reforms, such as the selling off of many state-owned enterprises, wage and price controls and the promotion of foreign investment, have been vigorously opposed by the left and the populist centre-left. While the opposition has been able to debate how modernization will take place, and to modify its contours, the policy of modernization itself has not been effectively challenged.[24] Neither the Cárdenas coalition, nor any other opposition, has been able to put forward a coherent alternative. Some analysts see this as a deficit and others see the development of such a plan as unnecessary at this stage.

In July 1988 Cárdenas was in a strong position with popular movements. Although he still commands the allegiance of many important MUPs, such as the Asamblea de Barrios de la Ciudad de México, the Unión de Colonias Populares del Valle de México, the Coordinadora Independiente de Torreón, the Unión de Colonos, Inquilinos y Solicitantes de Vivienda de Veracruz and the Unión Popular Independiente de La Laguna, the numbers have clearly been reduced. There have been, since the beginning, those more radical movements, such as the Unión de Colonos, Inquilinos y Solicitantes de Vivienda 11 de Noviembre and the Movimiento de Izquierda Revolucionaria, which have persistently shunned him as a '*neo-priísta*' and '*neo-capitalista*'. But the number of movements which has split from the PRD has grown, and now includes such key actors as the Frente Popular Tierra y Libertad de Monterrey. An increasing number professes neutrality, such as the CDP, and a number has divided factions over this issue, such as the Frente Popular de Zacatecas and the Unión Popular Revolucionaria Emiliano Zapata.[25]

Cárdenas can do little to match the material resources which Salinas can offer popular movements. But the PRD is in a position to give more political space to the movements within the party, a major complaint of many movements, although doing so would create another set of problems. Should the party decide on this, it may well be possible for Cárdenas to keep within the coalition movements such as the CDP which will go on making *convenio* agreements with the administration while insisting that this has not compromised them politically. The CDP leadership claims that it wants to remain within the Cárdenas fold and build a united democratic front. What it requires is the freedom to make its own internal political decisions and to have a voice in the making of coalition decisions to which all members will be bound.

Julio Moguel makes the interesting observation that the critique of corporatism, a central theme throughout the development of the PRD, has led to the exclusion of popular movements (*El Cotidiano*, July–August 1989: 20–23). He argues that basing membership and the structure of organization on the individual citizen may work well in the electoral arena but the absence of sectoral representation and *corrientes* (political currents) within the PRD results in a lack of effective voice for many popular organizations. This issue was of central concern throughout the formation of the PRD and during its first year of operation.

Popular movements can cut two ways for Cárdenas. They are a potential ally able to bring out the vote within poor sectors of the electorate and often have large numbers of organized activists not only capable of mass mobilizations but also of taking responsibility for some of the many jobs which must be done in any successful political party. Lack of material and human resources which characterizes the opposition in general makes this all the more important. But, grass-roots organizations can also be divisive, wanting a hand in decision making which creates internal cleavages and radicalizes the party beyond where Cárdenas and the current leadership want it to go. A strong argument can be made that the PRD's electoral prospects are enhanced through distancing itself from the more radical movements. The backgrounds of Cárdenas and most of the PRD leadership do not suggest a strong disposition to the creation of a mass-based movement but rather towards a nationalist populist party attempting to win elections with a loyal following. While this strategy may sustain the allegiance of some popular movements, for many others it will prove insufficient.

As of the time of writing, despite serious public discussion regarding more effective mechanisms for the participation of popular movement leadership within the PRD, organizational structures and procedures capable of addressing this issue have not yet been established. The one thing which does seem clear is that the issue of popular movement participation in party decision-making processes will be decisive to the future of popular movement membership in the PRD and perhaps to the future shape of the PRD itself.

Central to the making of the PRD has been the extent to which it and *cardenismo* in general would represent a mass party leading a mass movement or become an electoral machine for disaffected *priístas* and those on the left willing to join forces with them. Many movement leaders have been concerned that the Cárdenas leadership during the post-1988 period has focused too much on contesting the presidential election and subsequent state elections in which the PRD has fared poorly. Many have charged that the electoral focus of the PRD leadership has relegated the making of a mass movement to the periphery. What is more likely is that the leadership is in no way interested in building a radical mass movement. People have been willing to take militant actions in the name of Cárdenas but these actions have been largely restricted to Cárdenas' strongholds, such as Michoacán and Guerrero in this period.

For decades the party/state enjoyed a high degree of immunity from influential criticism in its running of government. Of course there was always criticism, but rarely the type which the party/state was forced to respond to with significant national reforms. Even those cases in which oppositions were able to force local reforms were few. The criticism came from individuals and organizations incapable of seriously challenging party/state rule on a national level. This has changed, and popular movements now represent important actors in this new and highly contested political climate. The Mexican political system no longer enjoys immunity from scrutiny; public policy is closely monitored and debated. In fact, in analysing the systemic political implications of MUPs today, it could be argued that their most important role is as government watchdogs.

A large part of the current political debate is directly concerned with the legitimacy, or lack thereof, of the party/state system itself.

The *convenios* have the potential to contribute to system reform. In the case of Durango, in which the Salinas administration signed two agreements with identical requirements for compliance with both the CNOP and the CDP, the possibilities for significant changes in political structure are obvious. Could it be that, at least in some instances, the state is willing to alter its relationship with the PRI and instead of treating the official party as a state agency make some progress in distancing itself from the party apparatus and forcing the PRI to compete with the opposition? It has been rumoured in Durango that the state government has become involved in 'helping' the CNOP to administer the programme. To the extent that this is true, the party/state continues essentially intact. But the possibilities here are important and will likely be played out over the course of the administration and beyond.

Even if it should end up that the CDP is in a sense 'co-opted', it is not clear what the implications of this will be. In the post-revolutionary past, the incorporation of opposition movements and individuals has strengthened the authoritarian character of the regime. We should not jump to the conclusion that this will be so with the CDP. The word co-optation itself is often used loosely and polemically. In the future analysis of popular movements and the state, it will become increasingly important to be precise in the use of this key term.[26]

Although the notion understandably provokes scepticism, there nevertheless remains the possibility that the signing of *convenios* will provide political openings to movements such as the CDP to effect favourable changes in party/state policy *vis-à-vis* popular movements in general. The CDP is dedicated to its own organizational prosperity, delivering services to Durango's poor, contributing to an ecologically sound and sustainable economic development policy in which the benefits are more widely distributed than has been the case historically. It is concerned about mitigating official corruption because it is bad government and also because it works against the group organizationally. The CDP favours Mexico's democratization because it is good for Mexico and for the CDP itself. It will use a number of means to achieve its goals, including electoral politics and relations with Salinas and Cárdenas.

Clearly not all movements agree with the CDP's decision to enter into the *convenio* process. In a document prepared by the Asamblea de Barrios for the I Convención Nacional Urbano Popular held on 2–3 December 1989 the comment was made that the proposed three billion 1990 PRONASOL budget, although grossly insufficient to meet the needs of Mexico's 40 million poor or even the 17 million severely poor (official figures), was sufficient 'to enact a politics of co-optation, manipulate demands and create a facade of attention to the poor'.

There is also a large body of criticism of the *concertación* process by both foreign and domestic observers. Neil Harvey (Ch. 7, this volume) expresses the views of many when he states that:

> electoral democracy is being resisted by the PRI and the government, while new, more direct relationships are being established between the state and popular organizations. These relationships may be more democratic than before . . . but at the same time they reproduce the familiar pattern of political bargaining between state and sectors within civil society . . . the introduction of new forms of corporatism is constraining the democratization of the system as a whole. . . . Is it not just a strategy of containment, giving the PRI time to reform itself while squeezing out the *cardenista* alternatives?

There is today an advanced process of division of urban popular movements into two camps. The first camp, although insisting on formal autonomy, nonetheless has clearly stated that the PRD is the most important political movement in Mexico today. It has dedicated itself to increasing its influence within the PRD. The Asamblea de Barrios typifies this type of movement.

The second camp, most of which has some formal relationship to the umbrella organization CONAMUP, takes no explicit stand on Cárdenas or on elections. However, it is quite clear that the majority of its leadership is either actively anti-Cárdenas and PRD or struggling to maintain neutrality. Although reconciliation is of course a possibility and favoured by some within both camps, it is very possible that, at least for the short run, we are seeing the emergence of two distinct projects.

This division works to the advantage of Salinas, whose policies are designed to split the left whenever possible. The Cárdenas challenge is to garner substantially more active popular movement support while simultaneously minimizing its divisive qualities. This is certainly a very difficult task, and perhaps an impossible one, particularly as long as Cárdenas is seen by most popular movement leadership as incapable of gaining state power.

Notes

1. This chapter forms part of a much larger project on urban popular movements during the 1980s. My interpretation of the CDP's history is based on six months of fieldwork during which I carried out extensive interviews with the party's leaders, activists, rank-and-file members, and outside observers and critics. Without their generosity of time, and willingness to answer questions and point me in new directions, this project would have been impossible. I am particularly grateful to those who allowed me access to personal archives, which have proved invaluable in constructing the CDP's history, and to Juan and Mayela Salazar who shared their home with me. I would also like to express my appreciation to the Fulbright Foundation and the John D. and Catherine T. MacArthur Foundation for financial support.

   This chapter was written in late 1989. Since that time, certain events have changed some of the author's interpretations and conclusions concerning the implications of CDP activities and political agreements. Most important is the observation that, by 1991, it is now clear that the Salinas policy of concertation, aided by signs of economic recovery, has demonstrated itself to be very effective in splitting the opposition and reducing the likelihood of a united oppositional front. While the reasons for splits between popular movements such as the CDP and the PRD are complex and attributing 'blame' to one side or the other is superficial, it is nonetheless true that such splits have contributed significantly to Salinas' fortunes and the left's decline since 1988. The chances of repeating the kind of alliance embodied by the FDN in 1988 anytime in the near future seem less likely than they did in 1989.
2. Popular movement refers to movements composed primarily of poor or working-class people. The category includes independent labour unions such as the Coordinadora Nacional de Trabajadores de la Educación (CNTE) and independent peasant movements while excluding middle-class social movements. Popular movements form independently from the state and must maintain an autonomous status; popular movements which are co-opted fall out of the category. As will be discussed below, determining whether a movement has been co-opted is difficult, leaving aside problems of definition.
3. *Concertación social* has a number of components ranging from wage and price controls to programmes designed to persuade important social actors to co-operate with the administration's policies and style of government.
4. Modernization is the Salinas theme song. Essentially all actions, policy and reforms are defended and promoted in terms of their contribution to the political, economic and social modernization of Mexico, defined largely in terms of rationalizing and updating those institutions, practices, policies and beliefs deemed to be anachronistic and thus a hindrance to the country's progress.
5. The term party/state refers to the fact that Mexico's dominant political party, the PRI, serves as a political wing of the state. Because the two are

so tightly intertwined, when speaking of relations between social actors and the state, it is often necessary to account for the reinforcing actions between the state and the party. Recent contradictions between the state and the party have not yet altered the basic equation.

6. The CDP's importance stems from its relatively long history, its role in umbrella organizations, particularly the Organización de Izquierda Revolucionaria – Línea de Masas (OIR–LM) and the Coordinadora Nacional del Movimiento Urbano Popular (CONAMUP), membership strength, internal organization, leadership capabilities and the ability to effect governmental policy on the local, state and federal levels. Unlike most existing urban popular movements, which have formed during the 1980s, the CDP has a continuous history dating back to the early 1970s. It is a highly organized and institutionalized sociopolitical organization.
7. Scholarly work on the CDP is almost non-existent. However, two publications by Juan Manuel Ramírez Saiz (1986a and 1986b) were very useful, particularly in orienting me during the early stages of research. Equipo Pueblo (1986) was also helpful.
8. On 30 June 1987 the *Sol de Durango*, a leading daily paper, published a full-page ad which contained among other charges, the following: 'No toleraré actos de desorden'; 'Ejecutaré órdenes de aprehensión pendientes'; 'El CDP trata de chantajear al gobierno'; 'Los lideres de CDP son filibusteros, pues no son duranguenses'.
9. Many observers believe that an added element in Cárdenas/Salinas relations is that the two have taken a strong dislike to each other and that personal animosity plays some role.
10. Although the CDP has recently become a political party itself, its internal logic is still much more that of a popular mass movement. The winning of political office has not yet become its priority. Whether this changes over time remains to be seen.
11. Not surprisingly, the domination of ex-*priístas*, or neo-*priístas* as they are referred to in Mexico, has been a contentious issue in internal PRD debates since its inception.
12. *Cocinas populares*, day-care centres, a building supply centre and *tortilla* factories were all specifically detailed in the *convenio*. These businesses are all to be owned and managed by the CDP itself.
13. The possibility of *convenio* benefits transcending the individual signer has been met with deep cynicism by critics. Many argue that the *convenio* process is bound to back-fire eventually on the individual signer who has been seduced by short-term benefits and thus sacrificed the interests of Mexico's poor in the process.
14. Although the potential isolation from the Cárdenas camp should not be dismissed, it is unlikely. When and if the CDP decides to form another electoral alliance with the Cárdenas camp negotiations will take place and an agreement be sought. What is less likely than undesired alienation is that the CDP pays some price in terms of position and influence in the PRD for not having 'more fully and actively' supported the PRD prior to the new alliance.
15. The CDP denies that it has moderated its political behaviour as a

condition of the *convenio* process. It is able to point to a number of actions and public displays to back up this claim. For instance, Marcos Cruz, a CDP founder who is currently serving a term as federal deputy, in a speech given on the floor of the National Assembly (*Cámara de Diputados*), criticized the Mexican political system for 'maintaining an authoritarian presidential system'. He also criticized harshly the presidential decision to direct the majority of PRONASOL funds to the PRI instead of other political and social organizations and inquired why a government which has identified itself as a modernizer had decided to channel so large a percentage of the scarce PRONASOL budget into ineffective corporatist coffers.

So, while the CDP has refrained from being inflammatory in its public utterances against Salinas and his policies it has not refrained from criticism. Some call this co-optation, others do not. For some this is a cost well worth paying which does not cause harm and to others it is selling out on the revolution, democracy and organizational autonomy.

16. Personal animosity is a secondary but still important factor in the CDP/PRD relationship at both the state and national levels.
17. The state legislature in Durango is one house. In 1989, 25 deputies were elected. Fifteen of these seats came as a result of direct district voting. The PRI won all of these. Ten of them were proportioned out by the state electoral commission to all parties which received at least 2 per cent of the vote.
18. Permanent registration was contingent upon the PCDP receiving 4 per cent of the poll, or 12,000 votes, in the July 1989 election. Although the electoral code contained a provision which prevented the CDP from making formal political alliances with other parties, it remained possible to present common candidates, that is, what was not possible was to go on the ballot with all parties supporting the same candidate in one box; it was, however, possible to have separate boxes on the ballot for each party but with two or more of the parties presenting the same candidate.
19. As it turned out, there were a few instances of common candidates. The most important of these were in Gómez Palacio and in Suchil. In the first case, the CDP submitted the name of PRD candidate, Jorge Torres Castillo, without formally consulting the PRD. In the case of Suchil, the state-level leadership bowed to local pressure by party members to support the CDP candidate.
20. The most likely way a resolution would be reached would be through the PRD accepting junior status with the more powerful CDP.
21. The CDP had, over a period of time, succeeded in making Gutiérrez a political embarrassment and liability to the governor. Had he not 'chosen to resign in order to better prepare himself for an upcoming bid to the state legislature' (the official story as reported widely in the local press) the governor would have faced the likelihood that the CDP would have raised this issue with Salinas in the February meeting.
22. Elias Chávez wrote an article which was published in *Proceso*, 667, 14 August 1989: 14–17, which documents a number of extremely serious allegations against the COCEI. In essence, he paints a picture of a

supposedly popular movement as corrupt as the PRI. Indeed, the COCEI leadership is described as colluding with the PRI and the BANRURAL in service of illegal personal gain. Leadership corruption is spelled out in detail, including malpractice towards COCEI membership.

23. Both the PRD and the PAN repeatedly made harsh allegations to the press regarding CDP funding levels, accusing the organization of accepting money from the Salinas administration and thereby selling out on their opposition status.
24. Many popular movements have in fact embraced the concept of modernization for their own and have used it to criticize the administration's poor performance in restructuring the existing archaic political and economic systems. For instance, CDP founder Marcos Cruz exclaimed that 'it is a disgrace that the social sector continues to be thought of fundamentally in terms of that which is controlled and manipulated at the discretion of corporatist élites and forces. This process is the antidote to modernization and democracy.'
25. The reader should keep in mind that alliances and strategies can change quickly; what is true at the time of writing may not be accurate for long.
26. Jonathan Fox thinks of co-optation 'in terms of external intervention in an organization's internal decision-making process – the key arena of autonomy. This is distinct from a tactical retreat which might mean keeping a discreet silence at times, while retaining the capacity to break into open opposition should the state not keep its part of the bargain' (personal correspondence, 12 December 1989). Under this definition the CDP would not be seen as being co-opted as a result of the *convenio* process.

9· CLIENTELISM OR TECHNOCRACY?

The Politics of Urban Land Regularization*

Ann Varley

In recent decades, the Mexican government has been providing property titles for families living in the illegal housing areas that surround many of the nation's cities.[1] This chapter argues that land tenure legalization has played an important part in maintaining political stability in the urban areas during the last 20 years. The political implications of regularization are overlooked by international agencies promoting legalization as a strategy for improving housing conditions in so-called 'squatter settlements'.[2]

Although illegal housing development affects all types of property, the main concern of this chapter is with the regularization of *ejido* lands, the significance of which has recently been assessed by Antonio Azuela (1989a: 9):

> the urbanization of the *ejido* is a clear example of the current crisis in Mexican corporatism, a crisis characterized by the imbalance between the population which has received benefits from the post-revolutionary state, and the growing population which has not only not received such benefits but has even had to subsidize those who have done so.

In this case, the residents of *ejido* lands subsidize the beneficiaries of the agrarian reform. After buying their plots from the *ejidatarios*, they

* I am grateful for the support received from the British Academy in the form of a Research Grant covering the costs of research in Mexico in April 1989. This research up-dated and extended the results of earlier work, for which fieldwork was carried out in 1981–2, with the support of the Social Science Research Council (now ESRC).

must also, later, pay for a land title, and part of the money paid for legalization is used to compensate *ejidatarios* for the 'loss' of their lands.[3]

With hindsight, it may seem curious that Mexican corporatism has not played more explicit attention to the urban poor. They form a large part of the population, over half of which now lives in cities of over 100,000 people (UNECLA, 1989). This chapter interprets regularization as a strategy employed by the state to bring about what it describes as the 'social integration' of the urban poor, meaning, in practice, their *political* integration; but why was such a strategy necessary? Why were the urban poor not incorporated into the post-revolutionary political system in the same way as the workers or the peasants?[4]

It has recently been argued that in the early 1940s the Avila Camacho government instituted a series of urban policy measures intended to do precisely this, by creating a legal and territorial basis for corporatist organization of the *colonos* (Azuela and Cruz Rodríguez, 1989). These measures involved the city authorities either establishing new settlements or regularizing existing ones. They may, perhaps, be thought of as an attempt to create an 'urban *ejido*' in the *colonias proletarias*.

The attempt to formalize corporatist control of the urban masses did not, however, prosper. The regime failed to win the urban poor over to the ideology and therefore the political project of the post-revolutionary state on the same basis as the worker or the peasant. The urban poor were seen primarily as workers, the term *colonia proletaria* itself defines residents as *workers* rather than a discrete social group in its own right (Azuela and Cruz Rodríguez, 1989: 34). We may add that the urban population was far less significant, in numerical terms, than it is today, and that most of the urban poor were still tenants in the city centre, making the official attempt to create a territorial basis for their corporatist political organization somewhat premature.

Instead of pursuing Avila Camacho's efforts, subsequent governments looked no further than the *ad hoc* incorporation of *colonos* into the catch-all CNOP. The inadequacy of this response has been revealed by the problems accompanying the explosive growth of the urban population, in the context of a style of development leaving many urban residents incapable of housing themselves by conventional means. The thousands of illegal and unserviced housing areas around

Mexico's cities accommodate large populations with specific needs and demands calling for a specific political response. This chapter explores the place of land tenure legalization policies in that response. First, it will review the scale and significance of the problem for those concerned. It will then examine the evidence for the political significance of regularization, as revealed by the timing of its emergence as a national policy, and the selection of particular cities and settlements as targets for legalization programmes. Whereas some interpretations of the relationship between the government and the urban population stress an increasing 'technocratization' of demand-making, this chapter argues that regularization plays a conservative role in Mexican urban politics. This is largely because *ejido* lands' regularization follows the 'agrarian route to legalization' (Varley, 1985c: 209): the process is determined, not by any specifically *urban* legislation, but by the Agrarian Reform Law, and it is the responsibility of agencies belonging to the government's 'agrarian sector'.[5] Consequently, it reproduces, in an urban context, the characteristic forms of Mexico's agrarian policy and politics (Azuela, 1989b: 126).[6] At the same time as 'the city invades the *ejido*' (Durand, 1983), the *ejido* invades the city by lending an agrarian logic to urban politics.

The scale of the problem

There are no reliable estimates of the total number of illegal housing plots in Mexico's cities (Varley, 1985c: 245). As Iracheta (1988: 55–6) concludes, official figures of the number of plots which have been legalized in the capital vary wildly, to the extent that no government agency probably knows the real scale of the problem.

The unreliability of official pronouncements on the issue is illustrated in the following statements about Mexico City. During a presidential visit in 1988, it was announced that 392,714 properties had been legalized in the federal district since 1982, an 'unprecedented' achievement (Mexico, Presidencia de la República, 1988b: 827). And yet, when the new *reguente* promised in 1989 that 27,000 plots would be legalized in just three months, he claimed that 'I need three months to do more than has been done for years' (*La Jornada*, 29 March 1989).[7] Not to be outdone, President Salinas de Gortari later announced that, nationally, 300,000 plots would be legalized by the end of 1989 (*La Jornada*, 22 April 1989).

It is clear, however, that there are millions of urban Mexicans living on illegal plots of land. Iracheta (1988: 56, 62) suggests that in the mid-1980s there were approximately three-quarters of a million illegal plots in Mexico City, housing over four million people and accounting for about one-third of the city's residential areas.[8] The figures quoted are in general agreement with a Ministry of Urban Development (SEDUE) estimate that, nationally, the number of *ejido* plots awaiting legalization in the current *sexenio* came to 2.16 millions (*La Jornada*, 13 April 1989). This means that there were about twelve million people living in illegal plots on *ejido* lands, out of a national population of over 80 millions.[9] The scale of the problem is clearly not insignificant.

Is the illegality of land tenure a problem?

Residents of illegal settlements and the urban popular movement

Seemingly without exception, studies of illegal housing areas have demonstrated that regularization is the residents' most urgent concern. In a Mexico City study of 1970, security of tenure was perceived as the most important community problem by almost one-half of the residents of two squatter settlements surveyed (Cornelius, 1975: 173). A later survey of six settlements in the city confirmed the importance attached to legalization (Gilbert and Ward, 1985: 204–7). More recently, 31 per cent of demand-making activities by settlers in the south of the federal district were found to be directed towards securing legal tenure, compared with 20–22 per cent each for water and sewerage installation (Aguilar, 1988: 42).[10] Other studies tell the same story (Jiménez, 1988; Alonso, 1980; COPEVI, 1977a; van Lindert, 1985; Montaño, 1976).[11]

It is not only individual settlements that display this pattern. A study of the urban popular movement places legalization top of the list of demands of the Unión de Colonos Populares del Valle de México (the main umbrella organization in Mexico City) (Ramírez Saiz, 1986a: 145); it also puts land issues in first place for the national movement, and specifically for the *Coordinadora* (CONAMUP) founded in 1980 (ibid.: 28, 184).

Government officials and representatives of the PRI

Illegal land tenure has a special place in public discussion of the country's urban problems. Mexico City newspapers contain almost daily comment on the subject by federal district *delegados* or their state of Mexico counterparts. They often attribute the lack of services either explicitly or implicitly to the lack of legal tenure. Thus, to take one example from many, in 1987 a spokesman for the Tláhuac *delegación* reported that the illegal status of various settlements was preventing the installation of services (*Metrópoli*, 5 January 1987). As another municipal official put it, 'they won't install services in no man's land' (*La Prensa*, 6 July 1977).

Not surprisingly, the regularization agencies make similar claims. According to a publicity booklet for CORETT, the *ejido* land regularization agency:

> CORETT regularizes [our plots], and many benefits follow. We'll be able to take out bank loans, we'll be able to build our houses well, even start a small business . . . If we *don't* regularize our plots, how are we going to get the services we need so badly? (Mexico, CORETT, nd: 11–14).[12]

Presidential and ministerial statements, and government documents, are usually more circumspect, but deliver the same basic message. In the National Programme for Urban Development and Housing (1984–8) regularization was depicted as providing fair compensation to the original landowners and preventing property speculation. At ceremonies in which the president hands out property titles, legalization has been described as fulfilling government promises to give residents security of tenure, plus the chance to leave a property to their children, and as a means of putting an end to anarchic urban growth (Mexico, Presidencia de la República, 1988a: 715; 1988b: 827).

Officials of the PRI, predictably, echo the government position. Regularization opens the way for service installation and for residents to obtain loans for housing improvements (Mexico, Presidencia de la República, 1987: 267). Interestingly, at the 'First National Meeting of Urban *Colonos*', seemingly an attempt by the CNOP to counter the influence of CONAMUP, Luis Donaldo Colosio Murrieta, head of the PRI's national committee, placed illegality of land tenure second on his list of five fundamental problems for the PRI to tackle in Mexico's cities (*La Jornada*, 29 April 1989).[13]

Whether government ministers and PRI officials really believe that legalization is capable of delivering all they promise is another question. The point is that they consider it to be of sufficient importance in their relations with the community as to merit a prominent place in their public pronouncements. They are not likely to discuss the political significance of legalization in public, although they sometimes come close to doing so, as will be seen. We must, therefore, look elsewhere if we are to unearth the political agenda behind the public message.

The emergence of regularization as a national policy

One of the keys to understanding the political significance of land tensure legalization lies in the timing of its emergence as a major national policy. Legalization of *ejido* lands involves their expropriation, and several expropriations took place for this purpose in Mexico City in 1970.[14] They were carried out by the state of Mexico agency AURIS (the Institute for Urban Action and Social Integration) in the last months of the Díaz Ordaz *sexenio*. In the succeeding administration, under Luís Echeverría, regularization emerged as a national policy, particularly with the founding, in 1973, of CORETT. Initially only an advisory body, CORETT was given the capacity to initiate legal action, including expropriation, together with its own funding, in November 1974.

Most analysts therefore interpret legalization as a response to the problems of rapid urban growth and illegal land occupation in the 1960s and early 1970s. For example, according to Iracheta (1988: 52) 'From 1970 onwards, the Mexican state started to confront the problem of illegality in urban land tenure for the first time.'

However, this was by no means the first time that government agencies had sought to do something about illegal land tenure. The Avila Camacho government was regularizing illegal settlements, mostly on private lands, in Mexico City during the mid-1940s (Azuela and Cruz Rodríguez, 1989: 12),[15] a decade which also saw the beginnings of the regularization of housing areas developing on *ejido* lands (Varley, 1985a).[16]

However, these early measures go largely unremarked, whilst regularization policies in the last two decades have been widely publicized. This suggests that there was a particular significance in the emergence of a national policy in the early 1970s. That regularization could exist without finding a place in government discourse on urban problems for thirty years suggests that illegal settlements were not perceived as significant during those years. That regularization came to the fore in national urban policy in the early 1970s suggests that it was a response to the conditions of the time.

The nature of these conditions has been well documented. At the end of the 1960s, the 'Mexican miracle' of industrial and economic growth with low inflation was beginning to falter, calling into question the model of *desarrollo estabilizador* (Enríquez, 1988). The turning point came when growth in agriculture started to founder (Philip, 1988a: 1–2). Peasant dissatisfaction with the many empty promises of agrarian reform and government policies favouring large-scale commercial agriculture led to a series of rural land invasions during the early 1970s (Sanderson, 1981).

Like their rural counterparts, the urban poor had not received their share of the fruits of growth. Income had been redistributed towards the middle classes; wage levels were falling by the end of the 1960s; and inflation soon started to rise to levels unknown for many years (Hansen, 1974; Ward, 1986; Enríquez, 1988). In addition, the existing model of urban development was clearly in difficulties. Public housing construction was too limited and too costly, and an increasing proportion of the urban poor, their numbers swollen by migration, was having to house itself in illegal settlements. In the *ejidos*, the creation of urban zones had led to a sort of 'administrative limbo'; local authorities used the fact that the process had not been legally completed, meaning that the land still officially belonged to the *ejido*, as an excuse for failing to install services (COPEVI, 1977b: 74; Azuela, 1989b: 121). *Colonos*' petitions for services were passed on from one agency to another with the argument that, since their settlement was illegally founded on *ejido* lands, it fell outside the jurisdiction of the agency in question (Varley, 1989: 166). Thousands of individual conflicts resulted, for example, from *ejidatarios*' selling the same plot to different purchasers. Eventually, these problems ended up on the agrarian authorities' desks.

Nor were these problems limited to *ejido* areas. Conditions in illegal subdivisions of private lands, and subdividers' treatment of plot purchasers, were so bad that a number of 'defence associations' was founded in such areas from the end of the 1960s onwards.[17] In Mexico City, an umbrella organization, the *Movimiento Restaurador de Colonos*, encouraged residents to suspend payments to subdividers until their demands were met (Ward, 1989: 139–41).

Conditions were clearly ripe for what Ward (1986: 18) has called a 'groundswell of public protest in low-income areas of the cities', to which political climate was highly conducive. The upheavals of 1968 and 1971 questioned the durability of the *pax priísta*, and activists from the student movements also sought involvement in the emerging settlement-based movements (Castells, 1982: 271; Ramírez Saiz, 1986a: 44). These organizations filled a gap in the political system. The CNOP had been progressively losing its credibility amongst *colonos*, as a result of widely recognized clientelism, top-down 'organization' of residents and imposition of leaders, and failure to encourage horizontal links with other organizations (Ramírez Saiz, 1986a: 41–2; Cornelius, 1975; Eckstein, 1988). The new movements appearing from 1968 onwards pursued strategies diametrically opposed to those of the CNOP;[18] in particular, links between different areas of types of organization were sometimes formalized in the creation of new umbrella organizations (*Frentes*). The early 1970s, therefore, saw the arrival on the political scene of a major new actor, the independent popular movement (Ramírez Saiz, 1986a: 48).

The response of the incoming Echeverría administration was a populist one, involving, on the one hand, a tolerance of some 'protest outside the established channels' (Castells, 1982: 271) and, on the other, 'a thorough and wide-ranging restructuring of the assorted policies needed to tackle the serious housing problems affecting a wide sector of the population' (García and Perló, 1984: 109). A plethora of different agencies was created to deal with different aspects of the housing crisis (ibid.; Garza and Schteingart, 1978; Ward, 1981).[19] Several of these organizations were briefed to carry out legalization of *ejido* settlements and private lands.

The place of regularization in Echeverría's urban policies can be linked with the role of invasion in the new political movements. The populist response to rural land invasions was a renewed emphasis on agrarian reform; the response to urban invasions was legalization.[20]

Picking off the opposition: invasions, the urban popular movement and legalization

Another clue to the political significance of land tenure legalization can be found in the way in which regularization was targeted at particular types of settlement, namely, invasions, and/or the most conflictive low-income settlements, that is, those in which independent political organizations were active.

Mexico City

Unlike some cities in the north of the country, the capital had not witnessed widespread land invasions since the 1940s. Sales of *ejido* lands had been taking place so rapidly, and on such a dramatic scale, that conflicts were emerging between the various groups involved, particularly in the municipality of Naucalpan.[21] In the conflict of rival interests, those who stood to lose out were the *colonos*, and it is not perhaps surprising that, by the mid-1970s, several Naucalpan *colonias* and an umbrella organization, Naucopac, were active in the Valley of Mexico *colonos* movement (Ramírez Saiz, 1986a: 57). According to a former top official of AURIS, State Governor Carlos Hank González saw 'both the problem and the opportunity' presented by the chaotic development of areas like Naucalpan, in political terms as well as technical 'urban planning' ones (the cost of servicing illegal settlements, and the practical difficulties of doing so). Hank González' response was the creation of AURIS and the expropriation programme of 1970.[22]

During the next few years, the context of illegal land occupation in Mexico City changed, and land invasions emerged with a new vigour in response to the economic problems facing the poor, the problems associated with illegal subdivisions, and Echeverría's populist response to both rural and urban problems. When Echeverría promised to support the urban poor in their efforts to find a home, his words were taken to mean that invasions would be tolerated (Ward, 1986: 67). Two significant invasions which took place in the south of Mexico City at the start of the 1970s underline this point; both followed earlier attempts to invade the same lands. Seven thousand families invaded communal lands of Santo Domingo de los Reyes, the subject of an unsuccessful invasion attempt in 1967, in what has been described as one of the largest invasions in the whole of Latin America (Ward, 1976: 120). Further south, lands belonging to the *ejido* of Padierna were successfully invaded in 1970–71, after several unsuccessful incursions over the previous few years (Varley, 1985c).

These two invasion settlements were the first in the country to be expropriated for legalization under Echeverría.[23] They elicited an urgent response at the highest levels of government. The president toured Santo Domingo by helicopter in November 1971 (Ward, 1976: 122), and his minister of agrarian reform visited Padierna, only to hear his employees receive death threats from the *colonos* (Varley, 1985c: 205). These were not, perhaps, idle threats; the invasions led to several murders, as well as violent clashes between squatters and the police or other government officials. Radical student groups were known to be involved, as were some of the revolutionary groups appearing in these years (ibid.). And there were signs that these were not to be isolated movements. In 1973, Santo Domingo and Padierna were linked in a common organization, the Independent Popular Front (Ramírez Saiz, 1986a: 47).[24]

The first two expropriations carried out in Mexico City by CORETT took place in similar circumstances (Lugo and Bejarano, 1981; Durand, 1983). At the end of 1975, lands belonging to the *ejidos* of Tlalpan and San Bernabé Ocotepec were seized for regularization.[25] Both were also in the south-west of the city, an area of predominantly middle-class housing; and both contributed to the rise of the independent popular movement in Mexico City (Ramírez Saiz, 1986a: 47, 57). Again, radical student groups were involved (Durand, 1983: 98).[26]

It is interesting to compare the government response to these settlements with the reaction to illegal settlements in other parts of the city. Some *ejido* settlements were more than 20 years old; most had developed in a relatively peaceful fashion. While the regularization agencies encountered strenuous opposition from *colonos* in the south-west, settlers in the north of the city were pleading for regularization. Residents of the various settlements belonging to the *ejido* of Cuautepec had been petitioning the agrarian and federal district authorities for regularization since 1970.[27] Action was promised, and the head of the regularization agency FIDEURBE even visited Cuautepec in early 1974 to discuss *colonos*' problems; but nothing came of the visit (*El Día*, 5 March 1974). While the police had to be brought in to help regularization agency officials working in Padierna and San Bernabé Ocotepec, Cuautepec residents saw their pleas for regularization put to the back of the queue.

The political rationale behind regularization in the early 1970s is confirmed by people working for the agencies at the time. The relatively tranquil, co-operative settlements in the north of Mexico City were of little interest to Echeverría's trouble-shooting agencies.[28] The experience they gained in dealing with difficult settlements was highly valued by the administration. Consequently, for example, FIDEURBE representatives were sent to Cuernavaca to advise local officials on their response to the independent organizations which had appeared there, particularly in the radical *colonia* Rubén Jaramillo, where the army was sent in, killing a number of leaders, and arresting many residents, in late 1973.

Chihuahua and Monterrey

By the end of Echeverría's *sexenio*, the cities with most expropriations of *ejido* land were, in addition to the capital, Guadalajara, Mexicali, Tehuacán, La Paz, Monterrey, Chihuahua and Reynosa. In Guadalajara, neither invasions nor independent political movements had been common.[29] It is worth noting, nevertheless, that protests against conditions in illegal subdivisions were beginning to generate a wider response in the early 1970s (de la Peña, 1988; Regalado, 1986). The local authorities took action to restrict the subdividers' activities (Sánchez, 1979); it is not unreasonable to suppose that they would also encourage regularization. The reason for the expropriations in Mexicali, La Paz and Tehuacán remains, for the moment, a matter for speculation. In Reynosa, land invasions were reported to be common at this time, and this may well have been a factor there.[30] There is clear evidence for a link between political movements, invasions and regularization in Chihuahua and Monterrey.

Verbeek (1987) documents the experience of Chihuahua. In 1968, the Communist Party promoted an invasion of *ejido* lands in the north of the city. The formation of *colonia* Francisco Villa gave rise to other invasions, and 'one of the largest and most important urban movements in Mexico, the *Comité de Defensa Popular* (CDP) (ibid.: 93). In addition to the 35 settlements it controlled by 1974, the CDP also included trade unionists and militant students. It had long-term revolutionary goals, but concentrated on labour activism, the foundation of workers' co-operatives, and communal labour for the installation of urban services, with materials provided by the state. *Colonos* acquired water and electricity illegally, and prevented the police from entering their settlements.

The authorities attempted, unsuccessfully, to undermine *colonia* Francisco Villa by offering the squatters other sites, and legalization. When this strategy failed, they tried to drive a wedge between the squatters and the student and trade union elements of the CDP, by providing housing benefits for the *colonos*. One of the first housing projects of the recently formed agency INFONAVIT was completed in Chihuahua in 1972; but the limited scale of such projects left regularization at the forefront of efforts to weaken the CDP. It was intended to create 'a bilateral patron/client relationship between the individual households and the state' (Verbeek, 1987: 98). At first, the settlers rejected regularization, but as settlements became more consolidated, individual concerns tended to replace collective action and political involvement, and 'more and more households were tempted to accept the state's offer of legalization' (ibid.). The CDP had to struggle to survive into the second half of the 1970s.

The case of Monterrey is similar, but here the independent popular movement spanned the whole of the 1970s, and beyond. Invasions here started to gather force in the 1960s; most were organized, in early years, by the PRI (Pozas Garza, 1989). From 1971 onwards, however, a number of major invasions was organized by a group of disaffected CNOP/CTM squatters' leaders and activists from the 1968 student movements (Vellinga, 1989: 161). The largest invasion, in 1973, gave rise to *colonia* Tierra y Libertad, which became the focus for a much broader political movement; a popular front of the same name was founded in 1976.

Like the CDP in Chihuahua, Tierra y Libertad was qualitatively and quantitatively different from many other organizations appearing at this time. The popular front included more than 30 settlements (with over 50,000 residents, known as *posesionarios*), tenant groups, *ejidatarios* and a number of other organizations, such as an independent taxi drivers' union (Pozas Garza, 1989: 71). It developed close links with radical trade unions. The movement's most unusual feature, however, was its policy of 'isolation from official structures', resulting from the Maoist inspiration of university activists (Vellinga, 1989: 168; Castells, 1977: 148). Going further than the CDP, the Monterrey movement rejected all state benefits in order to avoid the co-operation of settlers. The *colonias* had their own schools, a radio station, medical services, an internal police service and co-operative shops. Their independence was generally respected by both the police and the army, although a number of settlers were killed by police in 1976. Government willingness to negotiate with the movement fostered the image of Tierra y Libertad as a 'state within a state', or 'red island' (Vellinga, 1989: 167).

Regularization was one of the government proposals rejected by Tierra y Libertad (Castells, 1977: 147–8; Pozas Garza, 1989: 73). The front was hostile to legalization for economic, ideological and political reasons (Castells, 1977: 148). Economically, it objected to the cost imposed on settlers; the land should be free. Ideologically, it argued that to accept regularization would be to accept housing as a concession from the state, rather than a right, to be extracted from the state through class struggle. Most importantly, in political terms, regularization meant the establishment of an individual relationship with the state, and the consequent disintegration of the movement and settlers' incorporation into the existing political regime.

Eventually, this is what happened. The state was able to exploit internal differences within the movement, using regularization as a lever.[31] Two special land and housing agencies were set up.[32] Predictably, the CNOP and CTM played a key role in promoting the activities of these agencies. Their success may be judged from the fact that, by 1981, the front controlled less than one-fifth of *posesionario* settlements and residents (Vellinga, 1989: 170). In *colonia* Tierra y Libertad, the mainspring of the movement, two groups appeard, with conflicting attitudes towards regularization (Villarreal and Castañeda, 1986: 164–5). The split between these two enabled the governor to play up their differences and undermine the movement by expropriating part of Tierra y Libertad in 1983.

Analysts are unanimous in concluding that the principal aim of regularization was to counter the political influence of the opposition movements with a territorial basis in illegal settlements; as Villarreal and Castañeda (1986: 57) put it, 'to systematically disintegrate forms of organization which are different from those controlled by the state'.

There can be few better illustrations of the political intent behind regularization than the words of a government representative on the occasion of President de la Madrid's visit to Tierra y Libertad to give out the first land titles from the 1983 expropriation:

> in Tierra y Libertad . . . serious problems developed over a period of many years, to the extent that the settlement broke its relationship with the government and nominated its own authorities . . . [but, as a result of legalization, the settlement] changed its relationship with the government of the state and achieved its integration (México, Presidencia de la República, 1985: 178).

In private, government officials may be still more outspoken. The following is a loose transcription of comments by a national CORETT official interviewed in 1989.

> A big limousine – a Gran Marqués, perhaps – enters a low-income neighbourhood. Slowly, it makes its way along the unpaved street, picking its way around the ruts and potholes. One of the local dogs, its midday slumber disturbed, gets up

and growls at the intruder. What is it doing in his neighbourhood? The car keeps moving steadily along the street, and the dog, hackles rising, barks, It runs forward, making a dash for the front wheels of the car, then swerving away, only to renew the attack. The dog's furious barking attracts his fellows from neighbouring streets: they charge across unfenced plots, round piles of bricks and under lines full of washing, and join in the attack on the intruder, yelping and snarling. Then, suddenly, the car stops dead. Startled, the dogs jump back. What should they do? Deprived of their foe, they slink away, tails down, looking foolish. Peace returns to the street.

The *ejido* invades the city . . .

We have seen how regularization serves to demobilize urban popular movements which are a potential threat to the established political system (Varley, 1985c: 303). However, since independent *colonias* are not the norm amongst illegal settlements, what is the relevance of legalization in the majority of *colonias*, which are not formed by invasion, and which are not politically radical?[33]

Regularization is by no means irrelevant in these circumstances. Mele (1987: 26) argues that, rather than demobilizing political activity, regularization entails its remobilization along established channels of demand making. It is a particularly useful strategy, because it prolongs negotiations, for security of tenure and services, between settlers and the state, keeping residents in a dependent position *vis-à-vis* local authorities and the PRI (Mele, 1988: 262).[34]

Regularization therefore plays a conservative role in urban politics. This interpretation is at odds with studies which detect the increasing dominance of urban affairs by a technocratic, urban-planning rationality, with greater emphasis on 'efficiency and delivery of resources' rather than 'traditional forms of mediation such as patron-clientelism and the PRI apparatus' (Ward, 1986: 45, 71–2). It is worth examining this technocratization argument in some detail.

Following the work of Peter Ward (1981, 1986, 1989, 1990), we can sketch a model of three stages in government response to urban demand making. The analysis focuses on the federal district.

The first stage is the period prior to 1970. Until then, Ward argues, there was no formal structure for government–community interaction. Community leaders acted as intermediaries between residents and PRI officials in an informal network of patron–client relationships. In return for recognition of the settlement and some limited service installation and hand-outs (*dispensas*), settlers were mobilized to attend political events under the banners of the PRI, and to vote for the party. This gave the PRI 'direct control over settlement affairs' (Ward, 1989: 149).[35]

The second stage corresponds to Echeverría's presidency, 1970 to 1976. Echeverría espoused a policy of greater political openness (*apertura*), but did so in ways designed to ensure settler loyalty to himself. In an open-door policy, *colonos* were encouraged to take their complaints and petitions to the top. Echeverría did not insist on dealing with only one representative or group from each settlement; on the contrary, he encouraged a proliferation of local bodies. There was also a number of housing, regularization and servicing agencies; each leader could plug in to a different agency, and neither agency nor group could claim exclusive jurisdiction over an area. Bureaucrats and settlers alike were played off one against the other. Community mobilization increased, and although Echeverría's populist tactics were, in some ways, extremely effective, they created chaos at the administrative level (Gilbert and Ward, 1985: 191).

A third stage began with the López Portillo *sexenio*, and continues to this day. In 1977, Hank González, the new *regente* of the federal district, established the first formal structure for government–community interaction, namely, the *Juntas de Vecinos* system. Although modified in subsequent years, the basic features of this system remain intact.[36] It was intended to close the open door of the Echeverría administration. Instead of responding to a multiplicity of residents' organizations, government officials would recognize only community representatives accredited by the *Juntas de Vecinos* (Ward, 1986: 71). López Portillo rationalized the urban planning/developing system, eliminating overlap between competing agencies. Hank González streamlined the federal district's agency structure, and strengthened the role, and, to a lesser extent, the finances, of the 16 *delegaciones* (Ward, 1981: 395). Instead of dealing directly with the agencies, the *Juntas de Vecinos* would channel community demands through the Neighbourhood Council in each *delegación*. Going straight to the top, that is, to the *regente*, was actively discouraged: *colonos*' petitions would simply be redirected to the appropriate *delegado* (Ward, 1986: 71).

For Ward, these changes were symptomatic of a growing technocratization of government response to community demands, a process which is continuing into the 1990s (Ward, 1990: 237). In this context, legalization is no longer 'an end in itself', as in Echeverría's populist manipulation of urban residents, but a 'means to an end', namely, to incorporate *colonos* into the city's tax base to increase revenue, and to extend government control over settlement planning and house building (Ward, 1986: 66, 72; 1989: 144–5). Technocratization implied 'an erosion of opportunities for the PRI to intervene in land regularization issues', and, concomitantly, in local community affairs (ibid.: 150). In other words, 'a conscious effort . . . to make land regularization more efficient, less politicized' (Ward, 1990: 154).

Ward quotes case studies demonstrating how the *Juntas* became 'the principal route for demand making' (Ward, 1981: 395–9). However, other studies conclude that the *Juntas* 'failed . . . to become the main channel for *colonos*' demand-making' (Jiménez, 1988: 29; Aguilar, 1988: 44). Residents' demands are not met through the *Juntas* (Jiménez, 1988: 24); participation is low; and alternative channels for demand making, such as CONAMUP, persist and may be more important than the ineffective official structure (Aguilar, 1988: 45). There are two main reasons for this failure: first, *delegados* encourage direct, informal contact with themselves, side-stepping rather than reinforcing the formal structure for government–community interaction (Jiménez, 1988: 27); second, (some) services, and particularly regularization, are provided directly through central government programmes, and positive results are 'neither formally channelled through the ORCS [*Juntas*] nor attributed to them' (ibid.: 25); for these purposes, 'the participation scheme . . . was irrelevant' (Aguilar, 1988: 45).

As far as *ejido* lands are concerned, it is predictable that attempts to formalize and technocratize government–community interaction will fail, because regularization introduces an agrarian rationality into urban affairs. As Azuela (1989b: 126) argues, it is a 'fundamental fact [that] regularization of land tenure . . . is regulated by agrarian politics, or, more precisely, is an adaptation of the traditional forms of agrarian politics to the new circumstances presented by urban development'. The *ejido* invades the city.

Although regularization started out, under Echeverría, as part of a wide-ranging urban policy package, it soon came to stand alone. Initially, legalization was just one of the briefs of a number of urban development agencies, which were also involved in housing production and improvement, servicing and urban planning.[37] But within a few years, CORETT emerged as the sole national agency for regularization of *ejidos*.[38] The separation of agrarian from urban issues is reflected in CORETT's internal development. Its brief initially included the promotion of new construction, upgrading, and the management of land reserves for planned urban growth (*Diario Oficial*, 8 November 1974), but in practice its activities were confined to regularization and the creation of land reserves; even this function, with important urban planning implications was subsequently lost to another agency (Varley, 1987: 470–72). The loss of CORETT's overtly urban functions underlines its status as an *agrarian* agency.

The agrarian affiliation of the agencies involved in *ejido* regularization leads to a lack of co-ordination between their aims and those of the urban planning sector. For example, seeking an interview in CORETT in 1989, I explained my interest in regularization in terms of international agencies' concern with its role in settlement upgrading and urban development. The official I had approached, whilst willing to assist me, vehemently denied that CORETT had anything to do with housing or urban development. That, he said, was the business of SEDUE (Ministry for Urban Development and Ecology); CORETT simply gave out land titles and ensured that *ejidatarios* received fair compensation for the loss of their land. Conversely, in 1982 I questioned representatives of the federal district servicing agency about their criteria for deciding the order in which settlements would receive water and drainage. Their response made no reference to communities' legal status. Far from being a *sine qua non* for servicing, legalization seemed to be virtually irrelevant.[39]

The agrarian and urban sectors of the bureaucracy have competing interests in the urbanization of *ejido* lands. López Portillo introduced the requirement that each expropriation should be approved by the Human Settlements Ministry (SAHOP, predecessor of SEDUE). This was almost certainly a response to the corrupt practice of overestimating the area to be regularized, for the purpose of illicit land speculation. The potential for conflict introduced by this measure may be judged from the fact that, in a 1981 expropriation from Tulyehualco *ejido*, in the south of the federal district, an area of high land values, the agrarian reform minister apparently sought to push through expropriation of an area twice as large as that eventually expropriated after SAHOP vetoed the original proposal. Agrarian-sector officials presumably resented SAHOP's 'interference' in 'their' territory.[40]

Since the de la Madrid administration, opposition between the two sectors has been heightened by the policy of expropriating *ejido* lands for SEDUE to create land reserves for urban development. Interviews with officials from CORETT and SEDUE confirm the entrenched state of conflict between the two.

In political terms, the agrarian sector includes *ejidatarios* who are members of the CNC and other peasant organizations affiliated to the PRI. Expropriation entails the loss of *ejidatarios*' control over their lands and, if they have not yet finished selling plots, the loss of a lucrative source of income. Not surprisingly, therefore, it frequently arouses fierce opposition in the agrarian communities; and their opposition can constitute a major threat to regularization.[41] *Ejidatarios* are well able to defend their interests, as can be seen in their common practice of taking out injunctions (*amparos*) against expropriation, with or without CNC guidance (Varley, 1985c: 231–5).[42] Even when *ejidatarios* eventually lose the court case (by no means the inevitable outcome), they may succeed in delaying legalization for several years. The significance of this threat may be judged from the authorities' adoption of an unofficial policy to reach an agreement with *ejidatarios* at the beginning of an expropriation, providing for extra compensation over and above the legally stipulated amount.[43]

The agrarian sector therefore struggles to maintain a tight grip on regularization, with the result that the attempt to channel demand-making through a participation structure wedded to the urban bureaucracy is virtually a non-starter for *ejido* settlements, not only in formal terms (expropriation follows the dictates of agrarian law), but also as a result of the agrarian sector's unwillingness to relinquish dominion over an important sector of its territorial base. Urban *ejido* lands are of limited extent when compared with their rural counterparts, but they are the key to political participation by the agrarian sector in urban affairs.

Illegal occupation of *ejido* lands thus locks government response to urban demand-making into patterns associated with the earlier stage of Ward's technocratization model: in political terms, regularization is a reactionary strategy. As in Ward's model, depoliticization of urban demand-making is achieved, but it is achieved not by the replacement of outdated clientelistic practices but by their maintenance and renewal (as in Mele's remobilization thesis). The PRI is far from seeing its opportunities for intervention in the regularization process eroded.

To illustrate this, we may quote a study of recent practices in the outer suburbs of Mexico City, where most current occupation of *ejido* lands is taking place. Although the state of Mexico municipalities do not share the *Juntas de Vecinos* system, they have a similar one in the *Consejos de Colaboración Municipal*.[44]

Moreno Armella (1988: 84–6) analyses the case of La Libertad, an illegal *ejido* settlement founded in 1982 in the municipality of Tultitlán. The municipal planning department at first refused to recognize the existence of the settlement, on the grounds that settlers were occupying agricultural lands, sold to them by *ejidatarios*. Without this recognition, the *colonos* were unable, for three years, to pursue their requests for the installation of services, until they accepted help from their local federal deputy, representing the PRI. She recommended the settlement for recognition by the municipality;[45] this enabled settlers to constitute a *consejo*. However, the elections to this council were won by the opposition. The federal deputy responded to this setback by initiating moves towards legalization. CORETT was brought in, but regularization was held back until the residents affiliated their settlement with the PRI. The municipality then refused to recognize the elected *consejo*. Given that the settlers' first interest was in obtaining title to their land, they held new elections, and the PRI was duly elected into office.

On the basis of such experiences, Moreno Armella (1988: 91–4) proposes a model of the way in which regularization converts land tenure into 'a concrete political problem' which can only be resolved by settlers' incorporation into the existing political system. In the first instance, *colonos* decide to seek installation of services from the municipality. To succeed in this, they need to form a *consejo*, but cannot do so because the existence of their settlement is not recognized (because the lands belong to an *ejido*). Consequently, settlers must take one of two actions: they may approach representatives of an adjacent settlement, already affiliated to the PRI, and ask to be recognized as residents of an extension (*ampliación*) of that settlement; if, however, this strategy fails or is rejected, settlers must seek regularization in order for their settlement to be acknowledged as legitimate. They approach the agrarian authorities, but their petition is initially unsuccessful, because the *ejidatarios* are still selling plots and are therefore unwilling, for the time being, to contemplate legalization. The only option for the *colonos* is to return to square one, and try to get the existence of their settlement acknowledged by the municipal authorities, but in doing so, unless they are prepared to face the consequences of affiliation to CONAMUP, they require the political tutelage of the PRI (Moreno Armella, 1988:93). The PRI will be willing to intervene and seek a new decision from the municipal or state authorities, recognizing the existence of the settlement, and opening the way for regularization and installation of services, but only, of course, after several years co-operation with the official party. . . . The story is a familiar one.

Prospects for the future

The basic premiss of this chapter is that *ejido* land regularization is an important element in the state's repertory of responses to demand-making by the urban poor. It has helped to maintain political stability by demobilizing independent organization in low-income areas, and by remobilizing the urban poor within the limits of political activity prescribed by the existing regime.[46] Legalization of *ejido* lands introduces an agrarian political rationality into urban affairs; in consequence, regularization is a conservative political strategy.

Recent economic and political change may appear to question the continuing validity of this conclusion. There has been a resurgence of the urban popular movement, which has made significant advances in defining a national urban programme, improving its organizational capacity, and materially improving living conditions for at least some of its members (Ramírez Saiz, 1990; Moctezuma, 1990).[47] These advances are linked to the popular response to the destruction wreaked by the 1985 earthquakes, the economic crisis of the last decade, the rise in the political fortunes of the left and the decline in electoral legitimacy of the PRI. Under Salinas de Gortari, the regime has responded by adjusting its corporatist practices, in ways that are discussed elsewhere in this volume.

Does this mean that the days of regularization, at least as described above, are numbered? It may be tempting to respond that they are. Regularization has been portrayed as a reactionary strategy, hindering the technocratization of government response to urban demand-making; and yet technocratization is one of the bywords of the Salinas administration, aiming to convince both external and internal observers of its commitment to rational, technically sound and efficient government. And in a specifically urban context, it has been argued, even before the change of *sexenio*, that 'the state's politics of urban populism . . . is no longer viable' (Pezzoli, 1987: 383) and that the government has lost some of its political and ideological control over low-income settlements (Ramírez Saiz, 1990: 244). Evidence for this argument includes the provision of credit for housing co-operatives affiliated to CONAMUP; the creation of land reserves for urban development; and the formal agreements drawn up between government agencies and earthquake victims or other CONAMUP organizations (ibid.: 245; see also Moctezuma, 1990, and Eckstein, 1988).

The changes taking place at both national and local levels are, clearly, highly significant, but to acknowledge this need not lead us to conclude that regularization is losing relevance or effectiveness. As Eckstein (1988: 274) writes, in a more general context: 'Despite the growing importance of *técnicos* at the national level, the persistence and extension of political bureaucracy on the local level help explain why people . . . have been, from a comparative perspective, quiescent'. And regularization is likely to play a critical role in PRI attempts to reinforce traditional clientelistic responses to demand-making by the urban poor.

Even those observers who argue that Mexican urban populism is losing ground do so somewhat cautiously. Ramírez Saiz (1990: 244) speaks of 'partial' victories for the urban popular movement, and the *beginnings* of a process of change, and Pezzoli (1987: 392) couches his discussion in terms of 'historic *opportunity* and *possibility*', with the outcome far from certain. This caution is not unconnected with regularization. In Pezzoli's federal district case study, 'popular mobilization . . . has fallen before the devisive [sic] tactics of the land tenure regularization process' (ibid.: 394). And CONAMUP's proposals for modifications to the regularization process have been firmly resisted by the government (Ramírez Saiz: 1989: 23).[48]

We may add to this. It is not clear, for instance, to what extent traditional political practices have been discredited amongst the residents of illegal settlements. Electoral reverses for the PRI in the 1988 presidential elections do not necessarily mean that residents are now willing or able to challenge the 'rules of the game' deciding the day-to-day allocation of resources to urban neighbourhoods. The rules of the game have, certainly, been challenged in recent years; but it is worth pointing out, for example, that popular sector mobilization after the 1985 earthquakes was associated with tenants and other groups in the centre of Mexico City, that is, the area suffering most destruction, rather than the inhabitants of peripheral housing areas. In elections to federal district residents' associations, the number of independent settlements has increased since 1980 (*La Jornada*, 29

March 1989), but this is due in part to mobilization in areas worst affected by the earthquakes; otherwise, the same settlement names tend to emerge again and again over the years. As Moctezuma (1990: 44) observes: 'we [CONAMUP] always win the elections in the *colonias where we have been working consistently*' (my emphasis).

There is another reason to be cautious in assessing the significance of recent changes in urban Mexico. It appears that the Salinas administration will try to reinforce traditional modes of response to demand-making by the urban poor. There are indications that Salinas will try to nullify certain advances made by the urban popular movement, and strengthen the PRI's political control of low-income neighbourhoods. For example: the de la Madrid government's provision of credit for 'independent' housing co-operatives features prominently in discussion of CONAMUP's achievements (Ramírez Saiz, 1990: 238; Moctezuma, 1990: 41, 48). However, this was largely the result of efforts by the director of the agency managing the credits (Moctezuma, 1990: 50).[49] It has been reported that, under Salinas, the agency has been directed to provide credit only for organizations affiliated with the PRI.[50]

There are similar reports concerning the regularization agencies. For example, in 1989 the new head (*delegado*) of CORETT in one of the states near Mexico City was said to be holding up the issue of thousands of land titles, for which *colonos* had paid in full, until the president could hand them out in an official visit to the state. This had not previously been normal practice, although actual or symbolic presentation of land titles generally accompanies such visits. When a local official jokingly suggested that, in future, CORETT would only be dealing with the PRI, the *delegado* had replied, seriously, that, in effect, this would probably be the case.

The Salinas government thus appears reasonably confident in its ability to insist on a renewal of clientelistic practices, and on affiliation to the PRI as an essential prerequisite for access to regularization, housing and services.[51]

It is possible, however, that this strategy is ill-advised: its time may have passed, and it may serve to strengthen, rather than weaken, independent political mobilization. The risk implicit in this strategy was visible in local response to the deliberate retention of land titles by CORETT: roundly criticized in the local press, it was attracting opposition from both *colonos* and *ejidatarios*, threatening the success of new *ejido* expropriations in the state.

Nevertheless, in granting or withholding legal tenure, the government has a very strong hand to play in a game whose rules are still widely respected.[52] The strength of the hand depends on the fundamental importance attached by the urban poor to their right to legitimate, peaceful enjoyment of a small house and plot of land, acquired at the cost of many sacrifices. By this same token, however, there are constraints on the state's ability to play this hand. It depends, ultimately, on government willingness to respond to urban development in a *post hoc* fashion, that is, to concede the initiative in urban growth to agents outside the direct control of the urban authorities. It also depends on the continued ability to finance the installation of services in low-income settlements, because, without the prospect of obtaining services, *colonos* are less likely to accept the need for legalization. And ultimately, of course, it depends on the economic viability of self-help housing development on *ejido* lands. If the poor are unable to afford a plot of land, or city governments to install services or if the government, perhaps for ecological reasons, refuses to allow further illegal occupation of *ejido* lands, then, arguably, the offer to provide legal land titles would no longer be effective in the way that it is today. For the moment, however, it seems that regularization still has much to offer as a means of maintaining political stability in urban Mexico.

Notes

1. In Mexico, the process of land tenure legalization is known as regularization. The words 'legalization' and 'regularization' will be used interchangeably in this chapter.
2. Discussed for example in Angel, 1983; Doebele, 1978, 1983; Varley, 1985c, 1987; McAuslan, 1985; Zetter, 1984; and various chapters in Rodwin, 1987.
3. Legalization means that the residents of *ejido* lands have to pay twice for the same plot of land. The process of sale by *ejidatarios* contravenes the Agrarian Reform Law and is therefore illegal (Varley, 1985b). The government agency CORETT (Comisión para la Regularización de la Tenencia de la Tierra) expropriates the *ejido* lands on which illegal housing development has taken place, paying compensation to the *ejido*. It recovers its costs by selling the plots in the expropriated area to their occupants. The benefits enjoyed by *ejidatarios* may, however, be more apparent than real (Varley, 1985c). Often, they have sold lands of little or no agricultural value, and those endeavouring to cultivate their land may have been prevented from doing so by encroaching urban development. Moreover, it is often the *ejidatarios*' leaders (members of the *Comisariado Ejidal*), or people from outside the community (for example, CNC or

Agrarian Reform Ministry representatives) who benefit from land sales, rather than individual *ejidatarios*. And finally, compensation does not always reach (all) those who are entitled to it; even if it does so, its value may have been seriously diminished by inflation as a result of bureaucratic delays. This has served as a stimulus to further land sales (ibid.).

4. The urban poor are not, of course, excluded from the PRI. Associations of urban residents belong to the popular sector, the CNOP; but this branch of the party is both more heterogeneous than the labour or peasant sectors, and more often identified as representing the middle classes, rather than the urban poor (Hansen, 1974: 104).
5. Mexican government agencies are divided by sector, with smaller agencies allocated to a parent ministry, giving its name to the sector in question. Hence, the *ejido* land regularization agency CORETT is part of the agrarian sector headed by the Agrarian Reform Ministry, also closely involved in the legalization process.
6. For example: the failure to sanction *ejidatarios* selling their lands illegally reflects 'a sort of social contract based on the lack of responsibility attributed to agrarian communities, which is symptomatic of the paternalism characterizing official relations with the peasantry' (Azuela, 1989b: 125). Similarly, whilst it might be thought that illegal housing development is a problem best dealt with by local government, regularization is carried out by a federal body, reflecting the centralism of Mexican agrarian policy.
7. This claim was also at odds with a statement by President de la Madrid that over 87,000 plots had received legal title in the capital in the three years to 1985 (*Metrópoli*, 2 September 1985).
8. Schteingart (1989: 135) indicates that Iracheta's figures underestimate the scale of the problem because they ignore areas already legalized by the mid-1980s.
9. Azuela (1989b: 109) reports that there are over ten million people living in illegal plots on *ejido* lands.
10. Given that some of the areas studied were already legalized, the contribution of legalization to demand-making in the illegal settlements is likely to have been far higher.
11. Hiernaux (1986: 125–7) found that the installation of services was residents' highest priority in a survey of various settlements in Tijuana, whereas only 4 per cent of those surveyed gave legalization first place.
12. Similarly, in 1989, the director of the federal district legalization agency announced a programme to regularize a number of areas in the south-east of the city, which would give residents access to 'water, drainage, paving and housing' (*La Jornada*, 29 March 1989).
13. The others concerned the need to control the process of urban expansion, promote community organization for the introduction of basic services, ensure the community of access to housing, education and health care, and draw up a wide-ranging plan of small upgrading projects for low-income areas.
14. Lands which are expropriated first pass into the hands of the regularization agency, and are then sold, plot-by-plot, to residents.

15. Similar measures had already been applied in the state of Puebla. In 1939–40, Maximino Avila Camacho, the state governor, and brother of Manuel Avila Camacho, issued three expropriation decrees to 'create' urban settlements around the city of Puebla (*Periódico Oficial del Estado de Puebla*, 14 November 1939, 20 August 1940, and 13 September 1940); but in at least one case this measure apparently concerned an existing settlement. Moreno Toscano (1979: 161) states that legalization first appeared in 1938–40, under Cárdenas, but does not indicate whether this involved a specific legal process or simply a general tolerance of illegal settlement.
16. This process involved the creation of an *ejido* urban zone, an area set aside to house *ejidatarios*, which could eventually become private property. It could be used to disguise the fact that the area had already been illegally occupied, and urban zones were often created 'to regularize the existing *de facto* situation', though they rarely succeeded in doing so (Varley, 1985a).
17. Illegal subdivision of private lands had been the basic model of low-income housing development in major cities up to and during the 1960s (Sánchez, 1979; Mele, 1984; Gilbert and Ward, 1985; Gilbert and Varley, 1991). It was particularly important to the east of Mexico City, in the municipalities of Nezahualcóyotl and Ecatepec (Guerrero *et al.*, 1974; COPEVI, 1977a). Ninety per cent of illegal settlements in this area lacked services by 1970 (García, 1979: 44).
18. They sought to involve people from a wide range of bases and deliberately fostered links between different groups, such as *colonos*, workers, tenants, students and peasants (Ramírez Saiz, 1986a: 49).
19. The new policies did not necessarily involve an equal commitment to funding the improvement of housing conditions. Schteingart (1989: 145–6) notes that in the 1970s housing agencies satisfied less than 10 per cent of effective demand; support for self-help housing was especially limited. Regularization is a cheap way of making it look as though the government is doing something about the problems of housing the urban poor.
20. In 1971, the new Agrarian Reform Law was passed, the first time since 1942 that a major revision of the agrarian legislation had been carried out. At the same time, the Agrarian Department was converted into the Agrarian Reform Ministry, headed by one of Echeverría's closest collaborators, Augusto Gómez Villanueva.
21. By 1970, three-fifths of the Naucalpan population were resident on *ejido* lands (Varley, 1989: 132). For an example of the conflicts arising in the area, see Varley (1985a: 84). Benítez (1975: 41–51) provides a colourful account of local *ejidatario* leaders' mafioso-style behaviour. This reflects the power structure established by agrarian law and the *ejido*'s place in the political system (Azuela, 1983, 1989b; Hinojosa Ortiz, 1983: 23–4).
22. The importance attached to regularization can be judged by the way in which Hank González ensured the programme's success. AURIS employees were sent to camp out at the offices of the head of the Agrarian Department until he consented to the expropriations, rushed through in

record time. Special compensation deals were struck with *ejidatarios* (Varley, 1985c). Interestingly, presidential approval for the expropriations was granted in the very last days of the Díaz Ordaz administration; the difficult relationship between Hank González and Echeverría has been noted by Ward (1986: 81).

23. Santo Domingo lands were expropriated in late November 1971 on behalf of INDECO (the National Institute for Community Development and Popular Housing) (*Diario Oficial*, 4 December 1971). The Padierna expropriation, on behalf of the federal district urban develpment and regularization agency FIDEURBE, took place at the end of 1973 (*Diario Oficial*, 4 January 1974).
24. The alacrity of government response may also be related to the threat the invasions posed to the development of luxury housing in another part of Padierna, with many wealthy and highly influential residents.
25. The expropriation of San Bernabé Ocotepec lands was overthrown by a legal action undertaken by the *ejidatarios*, and had to be repeated in 1981.
26. It was rumoured that government interest in San Bernabé was not entirely unconnected with the fact that Echeverría's own house was in the area.
27. Information from Cuautepec files in the offices of the agrarian delegate to the federal district, Mexico City.
28. The description of INDECO as a 'trouble-shooting agency' comes from an interview with the agency's former director by Peter Ward; information on FIDEURBE is from an interview with its former director by the author of this chapter.
29. There was, however, a certain emphasis on invasion in the early 1970s. The expropriations of the Echeverría administration included a large area invaded in the *ejido* of Tetlán.
30. Some other cities witnessing the growth of independent community organizations, such as Tepic and Acapulco, also received attention from INDECO and CORETT in the early 1970s.
31. Ramírez Saiz (1986a: 51) observes that regularization, the government policy with the most direct impact on the urban popular movement, has elicited contrasting responses. Some have argued that regularization incorporates settlements into the land market, driving out the original settlers. It should, therefore, be rejected. But others point to the vital role played by security of tenure in mobilizing *colonos* and argue that regularization is a legitimate individual demand (ibid.: 181).
32. FOMERREY was set up in 1973, to relocate settlers to site-and-service projects or to regularize existing settlements. *Plan Tierra Propia* was established in 1979 by a state governor committed to eliminating the 'red island'. Like FOMERREY, *Tierra Propia* was aimed chiefly at independent settlements, but it concentrated on the older *colonias*, whose residents would be unimpressed by the offer of relocation (Villarreal and Castañeda, 1986: 51–7).
33. Ramírez Saiz (1989: 21) argues that the urban popular movement should not be associated with land invasions: since the late 1970s, it has been agreed that the condition necessary for successful independent invasions do not exist in Mexico.

34. There is a well-documented tendency for political activism to fall away sharply once *colonos*' immediate demands are fulfilled (Cornelius, 1975: 197; Gilbert and Ward, 1985: 206; Ramírez Saiz, 1986a: 210; Castillo, 1986: 350–51; Regalado, 1986: 138).
35. Two 1970s studies provide the classic accounts of co-optation and clientelism in low-income settlements: Eckstein, 1988 (first published 1977, with fieldwork in 1967–8 and 1971–7); and Cornelius, 1975 (fieldwork in 1970).
36. See Jiménez (1988, 1989). Each block elects a representative (*Jefe de Manzana*) who participates in a residents' association for the area. This association sends a representative to the Neighbourhood Council (*Junta de Vecinos*) for the *delegación* in which it is located. There are sixteen *delegaciones*, and, therefore, Neighbourhood Councils; each sends a representative to the Federal District Consultative Council (*Consejo Consultivo*).
37. The agencies operating in Mexico City were INDECO and FIDEURBE, mentioned above, and AURIS, which had survived the change of *sexenio* in the state of Mexico.
38. The president of CORETT's Administrative Council was the head of the Agrarian Department, and members included representatives of agencies such as FONAFE (the National *Ejido* Investment Fund) and the CNC (*Diario Oficial*, 8 November 1974).
39. See also Aguilar (1988: 44). In fact, many settlements had received services years before they were legalized (Varley, 1987: 475).
40. The length of time it took for an expropriation to be achieved increased dramatically under López Portillo (Varley, 1985c: 225–7). Could it be that this was, at least in part, a product of foot-dragging by the agrarian authorities, in response to the loss of some of their influence over *ejido* lands' expropriation?
41. This opposition is sharpened by the knowledge that compensation is well below the urban value of the expropriated lands, and that it is often delayed for considerable periods, losing value in a context of rapid inflation (Varley, 1985c: 253–5).
42. *Ejidatarios* in semi-urban areas have been moving out of agricultural occupations since at least the 1940s and transferring their lands to urban uses. This might be expected to deprive them of the support of the CNC and related organizations. In practice, urban *ejidatarios* are still quite capable of enlisting their support, and, for example, making effective use of the media to publicize their grievances (Varley, 1985c: 82; see also Calderón Cockburn, 1987).
43. Information from interviews with Agrarian Reform Ministry and CORETT officials, April 1989.
44. Gilbert and Ward (1985: 196) argue that the state of Mexico system for 'citizen participation' is broadly similar to that of the federal district, except for the lack of resources available to the municipal president.
45. The federal deputy also served as guarantor for *colonos*' down-payments for services installation (Moreno Armella, 1988: 86).

46. As noted above, the remobilization argument is drawn from the work of Patrice Mele (1987).
47. The resurgence of CONAMUP is recent years contrasts with a much more pessimistic scenario in the early-to-mid-1980s (Prieto, 1986: 80–83).
48. Organizations in the federal district have argued that land titles should come directly from the Agrarian Reform Ministry, and not through CORETT (Ramírez Saiz, 1989: 18).
49. The director convinced the World Bank to fund the programme and found a way of circumventing the difficulty of providing credit for groups of people who were unable to offer land titles as security.
50. Information from interview with the former director of the agency concerned, April 1989.
51. It would be unwise to make too much of the anecdotes on which this suggestion is based. Nevertheless, it is supported by observations made by other analysts. Ramírez Saiz (1990: 245) notes that only the strongest independent movements have been able to achieve access to government resources and that access to services continues to be linked with affiliation to the PRI: 'In short, clientelist practices persist'.
52. For example, the argument that an area cannot receive services unless it is legalized is a persuasive one, appealing to a technical rationality; the law forbids the government to collect taxes in illegal settlements on *ejido* lands, but needs this revenue to finance installation of services. Such arguments are widely accepted by *colonos* (Varley, 1987: 472).

Part IV

CRISIS, RESTRUCTURING AND RESPONSE

10· INTELLECTUALS AND THE STATE IN THE 'LOST DECADE'

*Sergio Zermeño**

In what ways have relations between Mexican intellectuals and the state changed during the past decade of crisis, neoliberalism and *neocardenismo*?[1] Prior to the economic recession of the 1980s, critical thought was closely identified with the political imagination of the 1968 student movement. It held that economic growth did not necessarily bring about a reduction in social inequalities nor a more democratic political system. The problem required political rather than technical solutions. New areas for democratic participation had to be opened up with the goal of limiting the state's capacity to arbitrarily implement policies favouring the privileged classes and their transnational partners.

Three main currents with diverse strategies emerged in the aftermath of the repression at Tlatelolco in 1968.[2]

Firstly, there was the radical tendency which argued for a revolutionary assault upon the state. This path led to Mexico's own secret war in which the army and police wiped out the guerrilla organizations and far-left groups.[3]

Secondly, thousands of students went out to rural villages and poor urban neighbourhoods to put into practice the Maoist mass-line strategy. The principal proponents of this strategy were Línea Proletaria (LP) and Organización de Izquierda Revolucionaria-Línea de Masas (OIR–LM).[4]

* I would like to thank Aurelio Cuevas, Julio Labastida, Salvador Martínez della Rocca, Sara Gordon, Marina Fe and Neil Harvey for their comments and criticism, some of which were in total disagreement with the arguments presented in this chapter.

Thirdly, a less socially oriented current emphasized gradual democratization of the system through party political activity and electoral struggle. Most of the political prisoners from 1968 who regained their freedom in the Echeverría administration (1970–76) belonged to this current. Its main forces were the Partido Comunista Mexicano (PCM), Partido Mexicano de los Trabajadores (PMT) and Punto Crítico. They participated actively in the struggles of independent unions in the 1970s but abandoned this sphere for parliamentary politics following the political reform of 1977 which provided them with legal recognition. In 1981 the PCM was dissolved when it merged with smaller leftwing groups to form the Partido Socialista Unificado de México (PSUM). In the abrupt transition from oil boom and parliamentary reform to debt crisis and economic stagnation, the PSUM constituted a space of convergence for intellectuals and the political left.

The reformist path

It was this third current which became the most privileged form of political activity in the 1980s. How did this happen and how, out of this convergence, did there emerge by the early 1990s intellectuals who embrace the neoliberal policies of President Salinas and others who support *neocardenismo*? The latter is surprisingly less well nourished by the intellectual left.

The repression of 2 October 1968 and 10 June 1971[5] and the massacre of the guerrilla movements, the sweet taste of democratic opening, increased public spending for the universities, and the 1977 political reform were all factors which contributed to the ascendancy of the reformist current. On the international scene, a similar combination was occurring. Following on the military defeat of guerrilla movements in Chile, Argentina and Uruguay, we saw the rise of Eurocommunism with its relativization of the working class as the central agent of social change and of the place of revolution as the privileged path to socialism. Journals such as *Zona Abierta*, *Ruedo Ibérico*, *El Viejo Topo*, *Pasado y Presente*, and authors such as Bozal, Claudin, Coletti, Bobbio, Paramio, Pereyra and Perry Anderson became influential, both in Europe and Latin America.

In addition, as I have argued elsewhere, in Mexican political culture there is a strong tendency towards 'bureaupolitics'; that is, the search for influence at the heights of the political system which neglects the task of building collective indentities at the grassroots (Zermeño, 1990).

Until the early 1980s, therefore, the strengthening of the formal arena of politics (the party and parliamentary system) was inseparable from the social question. Here was a concrete programme of political action which held that economic growth ought to lead to greater equality. The problem was one of gaining control of the decision-making process in order to implement socially progressive policies.

The new intellectuals and the end of the utopia of 1968

An alarming element of the crisis decade is that it was strong enough to smash into pieces the founding principles of the reformist programme. Instead we must now admit that economic and social policy are increasingly formulated independently of the political sphere of parties, Congress, trade unions and popular movements. The great hope of gradual change and political reform, inherited from Eurocommunism, appears to have been frustrated. The numerous parties and currents are represented in a Congress which is unable to force any modification of economic policies which exclude 80 per cent of the population from the opportunity to achieve some degree of social and cultural development. One of the country's foremost intellectuals, Héctor Aguilar Camín, confirmed this when he stated (1989:29):

> I do not think that democracy alone will solve all of Mexico's problems. Mexico could become a democratic society tomorrow and hold fair elections but that would not in any way create the million jobs a year which its young people need. During the administration of Miguel de la Madrid (1982–8) we saw how it is possible to have social austerity with greater political opening and democratic tolerance.

Does this mean that, in a country like Mexico, all forms of political participation only serve to provide a stable context for increasing polarization and poverty? Are not the formal spaces of political democracy the exclusive domain of privileged actors who belong to the world of the integrated and some leaders who stand out from the world of the excluded, with little or no effect on the decisions taken by the state's *núcleo duro*, or central core? It is this central core of the state apparatus which formulates both macro-economic policy and the more *ad hoc* responses to the social crisis.

If this is true then we must consider three implications: a) that there is a wide gulf between the political sphere and the state's *núcleo duro*; b) that there is a second gulf between the political sphere and the world of the excluded which we can see in the lack of communication between social movements and their political 'representatives'; and c) that we are witnessing a growing separation between an ever-smaller integrated sector and an ever-larger excluded sector, which is not unique to Mexico but can probably be generalized to most of Latin America. In addition, the integrated may at least make their demands known within the political sphere (despite their limited impact), while the excluded enjoy no such access.

We do not lack information about the conditions in which the poor live, but this information is also interpreted for us by the reporter, the television camera, the specialist or the calculating discourse of the *núcleo duro*. We never hear the interpretation of the real actors of the excluded population. When leaders manage to incorporate themselves into the political system, their links with the grassroots are distorted, tending to undermine those elements which give continuity and coherence to the defence of social identities.

The *núcleo duro*, the integrated and the excluded

The political configuration of the 1980s, and the new role occupied by the intellectuals, can be summed up in the following way: a) the dominant *núcleo duro*, made up of the central core of the state apparatus and the top levels of the bureaucracy: the president, the economic cabinet, state security agencies, leaders of state-controlled unions and some university chancellors; b) domestic and foreign private entrepreneurs, financiers and traders; c) the mass media, particularly the monopolistic position enjoyed by television; d) intellectuals recruited from all political tendencies, most of them curiously from the left, who have put themselves at the service of the *núcleo duro* in exchange for only limited influence but much personal prestige.[6]

Let us consider the integrated sector, that is, the middle classes who make up 25 per cent of the population. This is the sector which, since 1968, has been most consistent in articulating demands for democratization, pluralism and choice in cultural and consumption patterns. It has given life to the modern democratic will, which now competes with a national popular will rooted in paternalistic authoritarianism, without fully displacing it. The latter, with its legacy of mass politics, still finds support among the excluded majority in rural and urban areas. The crisis and the neoliberal response have increased the numbers of excluded for whom neoliberal ideology has only contempt, a situation which puts at risk the legacy of Mexico's political stability.

In the integrated sector, leaders and organizations fight for representation and positions of influence in Congress, political parties, bureaucracy, universities, consultancies, newspapers and television. Above we have bureaupolitics, and below we have social anomie and atomization. Between the two, where we might hope to find consistent and organized identities, there is only empty space. Consequently, for the excluded there is little point to the impassioned speech of an opposition deputy in Congress or the negotiations and confrontations of the integrated with the president. The real issue is nearer home: when will urban services such as drainage and drinking water be installed? Unable to operate at this level, parties, including the Partido Revolucionario Institucional (PRI), appear to be inside the system and hence divorced from reality. In this way, the rationalizing zeal of the 1980s has led to the dismantling of the populist state and its replacement with an exclusionary state.

Neocardenismo

The end of the populist state does not, however, mean the end of a populist relationship with the state. The dismantling of corporatist institutions that linked state and society gave rise to another cleavage in the political system. The excluded, who have weak ties to parties and the bureaucracy, move easily from a demand for the introduction of drinking water in their neighbourhood to expressing political support for Cuauhtémoc Cárdenas. The almost complete lack of a tradition of party activity makes this a prodigious act. The excluded tend not to value the liberal, representative dimension of democracy but, rather, the participatory, substantive aspect which is given by unmediated relations with executive power. The phenomenon of *neocardenismo* can be understood as the emptying by the president and the PRI of their ritual content, which transfers their centrality to a new leader.

In societies such as the Mexican one, where the absence of intermediary identities constantly generates new leaders, the most important mechanism for achieving stability is precisely the similarly constant destruction of independent organizations. Through imprisonment, assassination, division and co-option, local forms of authority are destroyed. What is left is the highly centralized, hierarchical and disciplined bureaucracy behind an unquestioned leader.

We are currently seeing a rapid growth and expansion of alternative orders. This partly results from a weakening of bureaupolitics as a mechanism of governability. The modernization process, presented as the voluntary act of rational social planners, undermines bureaupolitics. When repression is not accompanied by co-option, exclusion becomes a reality for leaders as well as the base. Economic stagnation in the 1980s removed much of the material bait for co-option, but also provided the neoliberal regime with the perfect opportunity to expel from the state not only large numbers of low-level functionaries, but also all those leaders of the PRI who could be accused of inefficiency, populism, cronyism and corporatism.[7]

At the same time, it appears that in just six years the lines of communication between the state and the PRI were broken. While high-level bureaucracy looked for solutions to the economic crisis, the party took care of organizing consensus. The two contradictory roles of all capitalist states (that is, accumulation and redistribution) now correspond to different actors: namely, the government and the party. This became apparent in 1982 when the PRI's presidential candidate, Miguel de la Madrid, clashed with the leader of the Confederación de Trabajadores de México (CTM), Fidel Velázquez. The distancing of government and party was also reflected in the displacement of the older, traditional political élite from the leading positions in the state by the new group of young technocrats. The restructuring of the regime, however, did not simply respond to these internal struggles. It was *neocardenismo*, at first timidly proclaiming itself to be a democratizing current, which eventually split the PRI in two.

The party and the government

From the moment that the party and the government failed to recognize their differences there emerged insurmountable problems. In the people's mind, Carlos Salinas de Gortari, the neoliberal modernizer, was incompatible with the figure of the president.[8] The PRI had remained submissive throughout the administration of Miguel de la Madrid, unable to distance itself from the government and its austerity policies. The principal architect of these policies was Salinas and his nomination only served to deepen the party's legitimacy crisis which resulted in the electoral débâcle of July 1988.

The PRI tried to continue functioning as a transmission belt for the implementation of government policy and the recruitment of top-level bureaucrats. If it is true that historically the PRI formed the basis of the Mexican political system, then *neocardenismo* represents the rupture of most of this system from the state's economic policy apparatus. In this way the government neglected the use of co-option, its traditionally privileged mechanism of political control.

Given that co-option had provided such a useful service to the regime, it is surprising that the *neocardenista* movement grew so rapidly and was able to weaken its effectiveness. Moreover, towards the end of the de la Madrid administration there emerged a nascent alliance between large segments of the excluded and integrated sectors. The latter included not only students and university faculty but also leaders of the opposition and even important figures of the political establishment. This was, and continues to be, a delicate issue for the government and Salinas has sought to rectify it as quickly as possible. For a short time there appeared the possibility of a radical alliance between the excluded and the integrated with a distinct and coherent identity. The earthquakes of September 1985 partly destroyed the walls of exclusion, providing the marginalized with some degree of collective identity. The student movement of 1986–7 similarly pointed in this direction but it was *neocardenismo* which finally provided the opportunity for an alliance of integrated and excluded.

The intellectuals

Then came the clever idea. If there are neither money nor jobs to hand out, let us invent a new way to separate the intellectuals from the people. The president threw open the doors of the National Palace and invited all and sundry to negotiations, to *concertación*. Intellectuals, scientists, politicians, artists, representatives and leaders of almost any interest group, elected or self-appointed, received invitations to attend this or that round-table, popular consultation, consultative council, or to preside over prize-giving ceremonies. Their faces and names were publicized on the front pages of national newspapers and projected on the television screen or in the many other areas reserved for the cult of self-admiration. Some intellectuals were made not only the object of publicity but also its very promoters, hosting popular television shows or receiving generous government support for their prestigious magazines or specially created newspapers.

At the same time, despite the rhetoric, the system of interest representation only concerns itself with social problems in exceptional circumstances. In this way election results have nothing to do with the real living conditions of voters. Similarly, the attempt to modernize the political system through free and fair elections runs parallel to the consolidation of an exclusionary state. The neoliberal reformers call on everyone to be more politically modern by participating in parliaments, unions, parties and universities, but what has winning the elections got to do with controlling state power? Where is the relationship between the aparatus of consensus and that most secretive apparatus of policy-making? It is one thing for people to participate but it is an entirely different thing for this participation to result in concrete solutions to specific problems. Even less likely is the possibility of achieving control over the general direction of government policy.

This system of representation and public recognition has been able to function on very limited resources. It has not, however, been able to hide the social effects of austerity measures. Despite the drastic spending cuts in education, health, nutrition and job creation, the regime, concerned with its image, decided to create some new agencies amid great publicity. As a result, the budgets for health and social security were reduced by 30 per cent in the period 1982–4 alone, but an agency was set up to attend extreme cases of poverty, headed by renowned intellectuals and politicians, but which perhaps carries out its functions with barely 1 per cent of the cuts in the above-mentioned areas. Subsidized milk and *tortilla* vouchers are handed out but the shelves of CONASUPO shops are almost bare.[9] Expenditure on education fell from 4 per cent to 2 per cent of gross national product (GNP) between 1982 and 1986 while for the same period the salary of a university lecturer was cut by a third. In 1988 the government's youth programme CREA (Consejo Nacional de Recursos para la Atención de la Juventud) was dismantled after struggling to survive continual cuts and in its place an Olympic medallist was appointed head of a sports council and a prominent intellectual named president of an arts council, neither of which will reach more than one in a thousand young citizens. Of course, both of these personalities appear more than once a week in the press and on television at inaugurations, accompanied by the president, and at events such as the recovery of the pre-Hispanic jewels stolen from the Museum of Anthropology, the finals of the Davis Cup and on Sunday-evening television programmes hosted by intellectuals. Meanwhile, guaranteed prices for agricultural products are replaced by 'realistic' ones in line with the international market, and for the dissenters the government sets up a deputy ministry to negotiate the implementation of agrarian neoliberalism.

The former leftwing intellectuals who have been seduced by neoliberal ideology also need a discourse which allows them to enter and exit the National Palace by the front door. They feel anguished by the crisis of development and the accompanying sensation of the defeat of intellect, science, technology and human will in the struggle to create a more just society. The ideologies of modernization are therefore more in tune with the intellectual rather than the pessimism inspired by a quick survey of current social conditions and trends. It is difficult to accept that there may be no promised land of progress and development, at least in the terms espoused by Western ideology; namely, the infinite appropriation of nature and its technical conversion into commodity form.

This contrast between the modern, rationalist conceptual frameworks in which we were formed and a future which corresponds less and less to these basic assumptions is reflected in the separation of science (the university) from society and nature. On the one hand, modern intellectual activity finds institutional expression and order at the service of high technology and political power. On the other, society tends towards disorder, disorganization and anomie.[10] We are living through a conservative reaction which separates intellectual activity from popular needs and aspirations. What arguments do the former left intellectuals turn to in justifying their incursion into the field of bureaupolitics in the age of neoliberalism? How was it that, despite the existence of a political alternative in the shape of *neocardenismo*, the bureaucratic mechanism won out once more? The following sections deal with the new faith of intellectuals in the neoliberal path to economic development and political democracy.

Faith in the world beyond

According to the ideology of dependent neoliberalism, solutions to the country's problems are not to be found within our borders. They can only come from outside. The development crisis is universal and we form part of a single world economy whose codes of practice we must respect. Any autonomous moves to reverse the exclusionary effects of neoliberal policies will only lead to financial ostracism and a consequent increase in inflation, poverty and social disorder. Alone we can do nothing, nor should we attempt to do anything. There is an almost religious faith in a superior being, the transcendental power of the world beyond.

In this respect, it is worth citing Rolando Cordera (1989:3):

> The process of global restructuring which began in the 1970s, which Mexico thought it could bypass thanks to its oil reserves, has clearly shown that in Mexico, France or Brazil, not to mention Venezuela, Poland or China, globalization affected all without mercy and without distinction of race, creed or mode of production, although some might come off better than others. Attempts to find short-cuts or ways to relaunch independent national economies have been unsuccessful and, moreover, have not lasted, even in the case of large and complex economies such as the French during the first Mitterrand government. To modernize, reconvert and link up industries to the world economy also presupposes national design of trade policies in the search for economic integration through diversified international relations. These aims cannot be achieved without modernization and industrial reconversion. But this does not seem possible without the winding up of product lines or even the closure of entire plants.

Before commenting on this argument, let us turn to a second, closely related element of neoliberal ideology.

Faith in future progress

There is a constant movement towards scientific and technical progress. Any attempt to operate independently of the rules of the world economy, it is argued, holds us back in perpetual underdevelopment. But if we continue sending a team of wise financiers to negotiate our trade flows and debt repayments with the world beyond, if we only maintain internationally competitive industries, then change will come automatically. Economic growth will modernize our companies and prepare them to participate in the third scientific–technological revolution.

Let us temper this modernizing euphoria and remember that this inevitable arrival of progress from our insertion into the world economy is not about the simple production and exchange of commodities, but about human and social conditions. The faith of neoliberal ideology in progress could lead to the argument that a mechanized, agro-industrialized and globalized economy is a healthy economy, even though three-quarters of the nation's population live in a state of complete anomie and poverty.

Consider some figures describing the Mexican economy in 1989.

Industrial production increased by 4.9 per cent and manufacturing by 6 per cent in the period between January and May in comparison with the same period in 1988. In the first four months the trade balance was positive due to manufacturing exports and higher prices for oil. Inflation for the same period was only 9.3 per cent, and the public deficit had been cut by 60.4 per cent since the first half of 1988.[11] At the same time, however, we learn that in the three months from April to June 1989 the government's modernization programme meant the dismissal of 71,140 workers and the closure of 13 companies.[12]

Dramatic examples of this divorce between healthy economic figures and social anomie abound, and the rural sector is no exception. In Brazil the government promoted sugar production for export to help pay for industrialization. Its success meant the displacement of thousands of peasant families engaged in subsistence agriculture who became seasonal labourers or migrated to shanty towns (Lingart, 1989). In Mexico, it has been shown that in the central Bajío region approximately one million jobs, or 30 per cent of the region's total, were lost between 1960 and 1983 due to the replacement of maize cultivation with broccoli, cauliflower and other fruits and vegetables destined mainly for export. Given that almost all the in-bond assembly plants employ exclusively young women, it is difficult to accept the argument that the unemployed peasantry will be reabsorbed by these new plants.[13] As Harvey points out (Chapter 7, this volume):

> The economic crisis has severely affected the production of basic grains in Mexico, exacerbating a longer-term trend towards dependency on food imports. The SARH budget as a share of public spending declined from 5.1 per cent in 1983 to 4.7 per cent in 1984, remaining the same in 1985, falling to 4.2 per cent in 1986, 3.7 per cent in 1987 and 2.7 per cent in 1988. Guaranteed prices for staple crops such as maize fell in real terms by 41 per cent between 1981 and 1988, forcing many poorer peasants to abandon cultivation. The shortfall has meant a steady increase in grain imports from 4.5 million (m) tonnes in 1985 to 5.2m in 1986, 6.6m in 1987, 5m in 1988 and a record 9m in 1989.

It can be argued that international trade is not inherently negative. What can be criticized, however, is the ideology of dependent neoliberalism which, in its fascination with accountancy, values only monetary flows in this process of exchange and forgets about the living conditions of those affected by industrial reconversion or those forced to produce a specific crop at a given moment simply because international prices are favourable.[14] Economic modernization increasingly expropriates entire social groups and populations which have no control over the productive systems on which their subsistence depends (see Chesneau, 1988; and Partant, 1983).

The fallacious nature of the model is revealed by its inability to guarantee that the social sacrifices of today will be rewarded with progress tomorrow. This is because social equality, one of the fundamental goals of humanism, is not intrinsic to neoliberalism but has to be reincorporated into it through ideological intervention. Although the issue of poverty is presented as something external to the economic model, the government refers to its eradication as one of its main policy goals. It must demonstrate that the steps being taken are designed to redress the disruptive effects of the model itself. For this task the intellectuals are indispensable.

Faith in the virtuous poor

The *núcleo duro* does not speak of poverty as a consequence of its policies but as something dynamic and positive. The culture of poverty possesses an intrinsic capacity for organization which must be carefully linked up to modernization so as not to lose its economic virtue. At a PRI-organized seminar, Carlos Tello stated that 41 million Mexicans, half the total population, cannot meet their basic needs and around 17 million of these live in conditions of extreme poverty (*La Jornada*, 13 July 1989). Arturo Warman (1989:v), speaking at the inauguration of a forum on extreme poverty, claimed that:

> The poor in Mexico are not only productive, they are also creative and inventive. They develop new products which make use of unsuspected resources and techniques. The popular markets are a testimony to this constant innovation. But this is seen most clearly and vigorously in the social networks which help the poor survive when the statistics appear to be so much against them: the strengthening of the family as a unit which combines maximum efficiency and the reduced waste of resources; the human networks that supply the services that society cannot, from the care of old people and children to the complex chains which allow millions of workers to migrate and

return; the villages and neighbourhoods where collective goods are exchanged without profit and loyalties are formed, providing identity, security and a sense of belonging; all these things illustrate the creativity of the poor to build human relationships based on collaboration, the prime expression of solidarity. The productive, creative and collaborative character of our poverty allow us to consider it not only as a series of shortages, but also as a potential source of development.

Poverty, however, is not a folkloric element of traditional societies but is part of our modernity. According to Chesneau (1988:65):

> Modernization advances simultaneously in opposite directions around two antagonistic but inseparable ideas: there is modernity in prosperity and success and there is modernity in failure, in the oceans of misery which surround pockets of prosperity. Both are as modern as each other and the classical distinction between 'traditional societies' and 'modernizing societies' has lost all meaning.

This modern poverty proliferates among extreme levels of social disorder. Informal employment and the black economy are not the seedbeds of popular entrepreneurship as Hernando de Soto would like but are instead marked by the absence of solidarity, extremely hierarchical structures of power, the most merciless forms of exploitation, the absence of job training and its associated workplace discipline, and the survival of the fittest. For its part, to invoke the extended family as a model of solidarity in the preservation of humanistic morality is to employ a stereotype which is increasingly inapplicable to the urban poor. On the contrary, it is not difficult to find broken homes, absent or alcoholic fathers and the 'super-mother' who takes on multiple roles and feels guilty because she cannot provide her children with the harmonious image of family life publicized in television commercials by Manolo Fábregas (*tener una familia así . . .*). The children then turn to different forms of blackmail which they extend to the rest of society, their schools and other institutions. Another example is given by the high rate of pupils who drop out of school before completing their secondary education. For every thousand pupils who finished secondary school in 1981 there were 184 who did not. By 1988 this figure has risen to 238.

Popular youth is also stereotyped as an integrated subculture, with its own authentic production of rock music, fashion and values. This was how it was portrayed by CREA, for example. Unfortunately, the reality is less comforting. The young and the excluded are instead caught up in unemployment, ignorance, police repression, drugs, a total lack of options and, in extreme cases, violence and delinquency. Religion, community and neighbourhood solidarity are similarly being weakened. The discussion is therefore between poverty as virtue or poverty as anomie.

Faith in negotiated peace

The negotiation of social problems, or *concertación*, is the most delicate point of the dominant discourse. The term *concertación* has invaded all public speeches in Mexico today and provides the basis for determining adherence or opposition to the regime. It involves the use of just two juxtaposed images: a) a vision of gradual change, pacted between the country's public and private institutions in a way that will lead to the harmonious modernization of the economy and the political system, and which will eventually allow for the formal expression of the plurality of interests and positions in Mexican society; and b) an image of chaos, violence, suffering, hunger and despair, the product of confrontation. We need not dwell on the examples of El Salvador, Nicaragua, Argentina and, more recently, Venezuela and Peru because television has brought them into our homes with abundant detail.

This is a clever trick, not unlike those of the 1960s, except for the fact that what was then given a negative connotation is now held up as positive and vice versa. If, for the intellectual left, revolution was preferable to reform, the opposite is now true. In a full-page statement disguised as comradely advice a representative group of intellectuals fiercely criticized the radical positions of the newly formed Partido de la Revolución Democrática (PRD) (Adrián de Garay *et al.*, *La Jornada*, 3 May 1989):

> The attitude of not accepting dialogue with the government by adopting a position of intransigent confrontation has had the effect of reducing support of some sectors for the PRD. To insist on polarizing and catastrophic postures demonstrates, at the very least, a lack of seriousness in using to the full all the available channels for achieving gradual and negotiated changes.

One of the signatories of this statement was more explicit when he wrote elsewhere not of 'reform or revolution' but of 'democracy or revolution' (Salazar, 1989:vii–ix):

> The revolutionary myth which has permeated socialist thought and action underlies a particular form of political practice. This form, with many variations, assumes that the resolution of social contradictions necessarily follows from their radicalization and the polarization of social forces. As a result, this approach privileges the moment of confrontation, open struggle and complete rupture, while undervaluing processes of negotiation, pacts and accords. Most of the processes of true democratization in modern states have been handled in regulated and civilized ways through reforms agreed upon by the majority of political actors and social forces. Revolutionary politics, by contrast, with its drama, emotional energy and extraordinary spirit, is diametrically opposed to democratic politics: the latter implies that we dedramatize, secularize, rationalize politics, in a word, modernize it.

On the one hand, we have an image associating revolution with catastrophe, irrationality, violence, suffering, death, disorder and underdevelopment. On the other, we have the idea of *concertación* associated with images of peace, democracy, order, communicative interaction, rationality and modernity. This is nothing more than the production of ideological stereotypes and such notions rightly correspond to a class of organic intellectuals who, in order to maximize their efficiency, declare themselves to be neutral and independent of the system of domination with whose legitimation they have been entrusted.

Revolution, *concertación* and identity

Each of these stereotypes can be turned upside down. The idea of revolution, for example, also has positive social and political values: acting collectively, building common identities and knowing one's enemies. These values do not necessarily lead to confrontational politics. The emergence and development of social movements, far from recalling the revolutionary myth of a fight to the death, can instead lead to something very different, namely, the creation of spatially limited but consistent collective identities; for example, urban neighbourhoods, rural villages, municipalities, regions, union branches and peasant associations. Such natural boundaries can provide continuity and an organizational basis for popular struggles.

The idea of peaceful, democratic *concertación* can also be turned around to reveal that the enormous energy put into negotiations and pacts can easily end up as nothing more than bureaupolitics. This negative outcome involves not only the co-option of leaders, but, more significantly, the destruction of collective identities among the excluded. *Concertación* can therefore lead to co-option above and despair below, an effective device in maintaining the gulf between the integrated minority and the excluded mass.

If democracy alone cannot provide solutions to injustice, backwardness and unemployment, then what we must aim for is the reconstruction of social identities and the tempering of the feverish activity in the distant heights of the political system. For if political democracy cannot solve the country's social problems, the following statement by the intellectual critics of *neocardenismo* (*La Jornada*, 3 May 1989) appears as nothing less than the impudent posturing of the co-opted:

> As members of the Partido Mexicano Socialista (PMS) we believe it necessary to follow a reformist and gradualist path, to use the narrowest of possibilities, to maximize negotiations in the struggle for democratic change. This does not in any way imply abandoning our principles but does mean that we recognize the difficult and complex obstacles to achieving them. We also believe that the vote of 6 July 1988 was a vote for democratic change through peaceful, legal and institutional means. Not to interpret it in this way, in the name of revolutionary dogma, is to squander not only our credibility but also the hopes of a large part of the population who demonstrated on that day just how far behind the old doctrines have been left.

We can say, perhaps, that in Latin America the struggle for political democracy is an issue which concerns integrated minorities from the most modernized regions and sectors, which aim to increase their influence through the formal, institutional channels of the political system. The vote for Cuauhtémoc Cárdenas in July 1988 was more a case of support for a leader than for representative democracy. Consider the high abstentionism in state elections in 1989, and that in

Chihuahua the PRI could win with the support of just 16 per cent of eligible voters. At the same time, what is lacking is the democratization of social conditions; that is, the delicate, gradual and negotiated task of building and rebuilding solid and consistent grassroots collective identities. It is here that negotiations can be a positive element.

Without wishing to deny the presence of social movements which achieve some degree of representation in the political system, we should note that most of the leaders have little in common with grassroots identities and do little to promote them, mainly because bureaupolitics leaves them little time to do so. But the problem is not solely with the political sphere. For even in an institution such as the national university, with its declared vocation to address social problems, there are few attempts to build bridges with the world of the excluded. There are some exceptions, such as in medicine, agronomy, architecture and, to a lesser degree, the social sciences, but very few research projects make solid links with popular groups and much less do they lead to concrete proposals to improve their conditions.

Yet we do not even need to go off campus. Within the very heart of the university, lecturers' and students' associations have lost their way, and lost their members' interest, despite a three-year struggle to redefine the future goals of higher education. Here too, academics and students neglected identity for strategy and were seduced by *concertación*, closed meeting rooms and special commissions, in this case the Comisión Organizadora del Congreso Universitario (COCU). If this happens among the integrated groups whose education facilitates democratic participation and which, in this case, follows hard on an extended period of mobilization, then what can we expect of the excluded groups immersed in poverty and with little formal education?[15]

We may conclude that in polarized societies such as ours, the effective political participation of most ordinary people is practically nil. When collective action begins to worry the regime, the bureaupolitical mechanism, combined with repression, quickly dismantles its organizational expression and, with it, its specific identity. This is why leaders and intellectuals look upwards to the apex of the system where power is concentrated, apparently the only point where they can hope to influence policy. In their courtship of power, however, they unwittingly reproduce the negative legacy which they claim to be combatting.

Although this appears like a vicious circle, it should not cause us to lose hope, initiative and imagination in the task of democratizing society. The other path only serves to conceal growing inequalities with a thin veil of negotiated peace. This veil can be torn apart, however, because when everything appears under control, dramatic alternatives suddenly spring up from the world of the excluded. Consider the case of Peru. Just at the moment when all the parties had taken up their places in the political and institutional system, the guerrilla movement Sendero Luminoso announced a total break with what it called the opportunism of the integrated. In this context, the following passage from the critics of *neocardenismo* (*La Jornada*, 3 May 1989) is symptomatic:

> The leadership of our party (PMS) clearly made the right decision in joining the PRD. So far, however, it does not appear to have understood the seriousness of this step. Instead it has abandoned the gradualist path taken following the 1977 political reform. This explains in large part the unfortunate resurgence of the sectarian left which we thought had been overcome. Mexico, with its problems does not need this. On the contrary, it needs a renovating and modernizing left which is prepared for the challenges of the times.

In the past two decades, and particularly in the crisis years, the dynamics of change in Latin America have been signalled by new categories. The positions of left or right are no longer as relevant as those of 'integrated' or 'excluded' and 'above' or 'below'. Yet this is normal in a society which is becoming poorer and more polarized, where anomie and stagnation spread and walls are built to separate the worlds of the excluded, the integrated and the dominant.

Notes

(*translation by Neil Harvey*)

1. The term *neocardenismo* refers to the political movement which emerged in 1988 in support of the presidential candidacy of Cuauhtémoc Cárdenas. Its ideology is opposed to the government's neoliberal policies which are considered a betrayal of the Mexican Revolution. It is not a homogeneous movement, however, but is made up of diverse and sometimes opposing currents within the *neocardenista* party, the Partido de la Revolución Democrática (PRD), which was formed in May 1989.
2. On the repression of the 1968 student movement see Zermeño, 1978.
3. The most important were the Movimiento Armado Revolucionario

(MAR), Fuerzas Revolucionarias Armadas del Pueblo (FRAP), Unión del Pueblo, Partido de los Pobres, Liga 23 de Septiembre and Enfermos.

4. The mass-line strategy sought to build popular bases of support for revolutionary change. Among the most important experiments was the organization of working-class neighbourhoods in Comités de Defensa Popular (CDP) in Chihuahau and Durango (see Chapter 8 in this volume for a discussion of the latter case). In the countryside, the mass-line approach was used in the formation of peasant co-operatives in Chiapas, Nayarit, Sonora and Coahuila. It was also influential in some branches of the miners' and steel workers' union, the Sindicato Nacional de Trabajadores Mineros, Metalúrgicos y Similares de la República Mexicana (SNTMMSRM).
5. On 10 June 1971 a student demonstration in downtown Mexico City was violently broken up by armed thugs with the acquiescence of the police.
6. Intellectuals are made into celebrities by constant publicity in the press and on television where they appear at this or that prize-giving ceremony, which is both extremely popular with the media and highly economical for the coffers of public and private agencies.
7. Similarly, during the long reign of Porfirio Díaz (1867–1911), a technocratic élite created an ideology of modernization to exclude other groups from power and tighten its grip over the state apparatus. As Cardoso and Faletto (1969) noted, in an enclave economy based on the extraction and export of minerals and oil, such control assures a hegemonic position over the economy and privileged access to finance. The political power which this implies can, however, be suddenly destroyed if the exclusion of competing élites goes too far. This applies as much now as it did in 1910–11.
8. In October 1987 the PRI announced that the head of the Planning and Budget Ministry (Secretaría de Programación y Presupuesto – SPP), Carlos Salinas de Gortari, would be its candidate in the 1988 presidential elections.
9. Compañía Nacional de Subsistencias Populares (CONASUPO) is a state-run system designed to provide basic food items for low-wage groups at subsidized prices.
10. It is for this reason that, at the time of the university reform, the majority of scientists and intellectuals favour a university which is separated from social problems, a producer of high technology and aloof from popular culture.
11. 'Informe sobre la situación económica y las finanzas públicas del segundo semestre de 1989: Secretaría de Hacienda y Crédito Público y Secretaría de Programación y Presupuesto', *La Jornada*, 16 August 1989.
12. Andrea Becerril, *La Jornada*, 14 August 1989.
13. See the study cited by Beatriz Johnston in *Proceso*, 712, 25 June 1990:35.
14. Partant (1983) reminds us that one fallacy of this model is that if Third World countries began to approach the consumption levels of the industrialized world, the result would be an almost immediate destruction

of the biosphere and of humanity. The per capita energy consumption of Ruanda, for example, is 1,100 times less than that of the United States.

15. Maybe it is for this reason that the Church base communities, which are politically barred from participating in bureaupolitics, have been able to make remarkable advances in the construction and maintenance of collective identities.

11· MODERNIZATION AND CORPORATISM IN GOVERNMENT–LABOUR RELATIONS

Ilán Bizberg

Economic crisis and restructuring

The Mexican state has traditionally adopted the role of the main agent of development. The state established the foundations for economic growth and promoted favourable conditions for industrialization through its economic policies, subsidies and the protection of national industry. In addition, private capital investment has generally followed up and depended upon public investment, while the state bailed out companies that went broke in order to prevent unemployment and created jobs through the expansion of its own firms and public administration.

These policies, together with an increase in the buying power of the urban population and an expansion of public education and health services, corresponded to a nationalist and populist ideology that considered that the aim of the regime was to achieve economic development accompanied by social justice. The state not only sought to be the main agent of economic development, but also a mediator to prevent the social inequalities which arise with any process of development. For as long as public spending continued to increase significantly, the population felt that the state was actually carrying out this function.

The 1982 crisis considerably eroded the state's capacity in each of these areas. Since then, the state has become less able to finance development and the integration of more people into the modern sectors of the economy. Instead there has been occurring a greater degree of exclusion. If we take into account the fact that over 800,000 young people enter the job market each year, the exclusion of more and more Mexicans from economic development is far more serious than suggested by official employment and social security statistics.[1]

Up until 1982 income from oil exports and foreign loans allowed the government to use a significant proportion of gross domestic product (GDP) in public expenditure. During the administration of Miguel de la Madrid (1982–1988), public spending was reduced from 17.5 per cent of GDP in 1981 to 13.3 per cent in 1985 (Trejo Reyes, 1987:175). Since reductions were to be permanent, government spending would have to come under a rationalization programme. The impossibility of returning to the government's pre-1982 income levels implied important changes in the state's economic role. Public intervention would have to be more efficient and private capital would have to be stimulated.

Government spending has traditionally been based on an economic deficit. In 1982 this deficit reached 16 per cent of GDP and by 1985 had been cut back to 8.2 per cent (Trejo Reyes, 1987:175). In order to respond to the immediate problem of servicing the foreign debt, de la Madrid began to reduce and rationalize subsidies in an effort to eliminate the inefficiencies generated by state paternalism. The government also felt it necessary to attract local and foreign capital to substitute state investment and overcome the lack of access to foreign currency. All this implied the reduction of excessive protectionism and the opening up of the economy to the rest of the world with the goal of making domestic industry more efficient.

These implications were recognized in the government's discourse. Immediately upon taking office, de la Madrid declared that populism had been overtaken by circumstances. Realism was constantly invoked by the government as its guiding principle, seeming to bury the populist project which had been followed since the mid-thirties. De la Madrid proposed that the state withdraw from the most modern sectors of the economy in order to concentrate its reduced resources on the most backward sectors and regions, together with the construction of the necessary infrastructure for modernization. In sum, it was recognized that the financial crisis of the state was not momentary but that the role of the state as the main agent of development had reached its limits.

These changes, which may appear as mere adjustments to increase efficiency, amount in reality to an economic transformation of the country's development model. This situation implies serious tensions for a regime such as the Mexican one in so far as its legitimacy has traditionally rested on the state's ability to act as an agent of development. Consequently, the formal political arena, that is the electoral sphere, will have an increased importance as a source of legitimacy. Furthermore, as Sennett (1990) has argued, authority based on paternalism is inherently unstable since solutions to social problems are demanded directly from the paternalistic regime.

The way in which the de la Madrid government chose to tackle the economic crisis through a new modernizing project (which has been continued by the Salinas administration since 1988) has had important implications for a political system based on corporatist relations between the state and popular organizations. Firstly, the new economic model and its ideology alienate groups which are still within the corporatist apparatus and feel directly threatened. These groups will increasingly turn to parties and groups that argue that economic reform demands not the reduction of the state but, on the contrary, the recuperation of state-led development. Secondly, there are also tensions arising from the incompatibility between corporatism and economic modernization. Thirdly, there are pressures which originate in sectors which have developed outside the channels of corporatist control.

In this chapter we will mainly focus on the first two tensions, since they are directly related to the implications of the current economic project. If the government is not able to control them, these two pressures on the political regime may inhabit economic modernization. Our main hypothesis is that economic modernization requires a transformation of the relationship between the state and popular organizations, especially labour unions. In the long run, as a consequence of this change in labour corporatism, the modernization of the economy will demand a change of the political regime.

The traditional role of corporatism

Most authors who have analysed the significance of corporatism in Mexico, especially in relation to trade unions, argue that it laid the basis for industrial development (see Middlebrook, 1982; Roxborough, 1984; de la Garza, 1988; Bizberg, 1990). This was due to the stability which corporatism lent to the regime and therefore the relative predictability of its economic policies and development project. Moreover, corporatism also provided very favourable conditions for industrialization. On the one hand, workers' salaries were kept low during the take-off phase. Bortz found that between 1939 and 1946 real wages declined, recuperated slowly between 1946 and 1952 by 8 per cent and then grew rapidly during what has been called the phase of stabilized development until 1976 (cited in Aguilar Camín, 1988). On the other, the corporatism of rural organizations allowed the cost of agricultural products to be maintained at a low level and permitted a net transfer of capital from the rural to the urban areas (Reynolds, 1973).[2]

Reyna (1974) has argued that union corporatism is intimately related to a government policy that, in the aftermath of repression of strike action by railwaymen in 1958–59, favoured strategic sectors of labour. In a situation where strikes are legal, corporatism prevented a wage drift from these sectors to the rest of the working class. Corporatist control also helps explain why the organized peasantry did not pursue the wage rises seen in the urban areas. State control over social groups explains how it was possible to implement a model of development that, as Lustig (1975) demonstrated, was not only accompanied by profound income inequalities, but required them.

Since the financial crisis of 1976 only union corporatism can explain how and why the labour sector has accepted a reduction of real minimum wages from 101.3, in that year, to 63.4 in 1985.[3] Even though industrial wages have behaved somewhat better (the rate of increase has been higher than that for the legally-fixed minimum wage), they have also suffered a considerable loss. This despite the fact that salaries in some of the most modern and dynamic firms have been partly compensated by non-wage benefits. These went from 30.6 per cent of total salary in 1975 to 34 per cent in 1985.[4] It is also evident that the signing of the Economic Solidarity Pact in November 1987 would have been considerably more difficult to achieve in the absence of corporatist relations between the unions and the state. At the very least it would have required some degree of recovery in real wages, as happened with the (unsuccessful) stabilization plans implemented in Brazil and Argentina.

Corporatism has not only been important for industrial development, but has also acted as an effective means of electoral control. Unions have provided the ruling Partido Revolucionario Institucional (PRI) with an important source of supporters. It is well known that the majority of the statutes which regulate the internal life of official unions include the obligation to affiliate to the party to which one's union is affiliated, generally the PRI. The fact that defiance of this obligation can be penalized, although this has been uncommon, implies a strong pressure either to vote for the PRI or to abstain. This control has been particularly strong in relation to workers in geographically isolated sectors, such as the oil industry, mining and steel manufacturing, sugar growing and primary school education.

Nonetheless, corporatist control over the working class has not been based solely on coercion, but also on exchange. Until 1982, even when salaries were falling or growing very slowly, there were mechanisms to distribute income indirectly. Social benefits were distributed through a variety of channels: the Compañía Nacional de Subsistencias Populares (CONASUPO), a government body which controls the prices for basic food items by buying directly from producers and selling at subsidized prices in mainly urban areas; the continuous expansion of social security services as well as the services given directly by some state firms such as Petróleos Mexicanos (PEMEX); the creation during the Echeverría administration (1970–1976) of the Instituto del Fondo Nacional para la Vivienda de los Trabajadores (INFONAVIT), which oversees the construction of housing for workers; and the Fondo Nacional para el Consumo de los Trabajadores (FONACOT), a loan system to help workers and employees purchase furniture. In general terms social expenditure had been growing almost continuously until 1982. It began decreasing considerably thereafter (Ward, 1986).[5] Workers in the most strategic sectors, who are organized in industry-wide unions, received higher wages and other benefits in comparison with the rest of the working class.[6]

The unions of the largest public enterprises are all crucial members of the corporatist pact with the state. These are found in PEMEX, the Comisión Federal de Electricidad (CFE), Ferrocarriles Nacionales de México (FNM), Teléfonos de México (TELMEX), Mexico City's central administration, the Ministry of Agriculture and the country's most important steel plants; namely, Altos Hornos de México and Siderúrgica Lázaro Cárdenas–Las Truchas. All these enterprises and sectors have high rates of unionization. While the average national rate is between 18 per cent and 25 per cent, it is 57 per cent in the oil industry, 79 per cent in the railway industry and 98 per cent in the central administration. In each of these, workers are organized in large national unions. The smallest is the telephone workers' union with 27,000 members, while the largest is the teachers' union with over 800,000. Together, the workers in these unions represent 35 per cent of the country's total unionized work force.

Consequently, the control of these unions has been fundamental in assuring political and economic stability during the period of rapid industrialization, but especially so during the economic crisis of the 1980s. In the administrations of López Portillo and de la Madrid, wage policy was in principle established by the annual setting of minimum wages on January 1. However, this was backed up by negotiations with the larger unions, usually with those of Altos Hornos de México and the Mexican Electrical Workers' Union, held in early March to renew their respective collective contracts. The control wielded by unions and leaders over workers' demands was rewarded by economic concessions and political prerogatives, the paradigmatic case being that of the oil workers. In 1977 and 1980 important concessions were given to the Sindicato de Trabajadores Petroleros de la República Mexicana (STPRM). In 1977, due to the government's urgent need to expand its oil exporting capacity, PEMEX had to resort to private companies for perforation of new oil–wells. In order to neutralize union opposition the latter obtained 40 per cent of the perforation contracts; the union could, in return, transfer the contracts to other companies. In 1980 something similar happened with contracts for the transportation of crude oil (Alonso and López, 1985).

All this was not only advantageous for the union leaders but also benefited the workers. It allowed them to obtain a variety of benefits, such as improved access to housing, union stores, hospitals and scholarships. Moreover, all of the large unions have had considerable control over hiring mechanisms. This has also benefited workers as, in some enterprises, particularly PEMEX, they could even sell the job vacancies if nobody was recommended. These unions have also had considerable control over job mobility. The teachers' union, for example, can influence or even decide the appointment of inspectors and heads of state schools. It naturally rewards its most loyal members with these posts.

The political pressures against economic modernization

The financial crisis of the economy since 1982 and the modernization project which has been adopted as a result demand greater efficiency from public enterprises where precisely those unions who formed the heart of the corporatist pact are located. After more than 50 years of corporatism the accumulated power of these unions is one of the main obstacles to reorganizing state–controlled enterprises and sectors, such as education. Any change is considered by the unions as an attack on their acquired rights.

The transformation of industry and corporatism, which began with de la Madrid, meant that the political rationality which had underpinned state–labour relations would have to give way to economic rationality. This implied the removal of many types of inefficiencies through a restructuring of certain enterprises, the dismissal of excessive personnel in some of them and in central administration, and the reduction of union economic prerogatives and workers' privileges. All this meant a confrontation with politically strategic unions.

From the start of the de la Madrid administration, the government began to reduce the prerogatives and concessions enjoyed by the STPRM. A year after the change in administration, the new Law of Public Works, drawn up by the Ministry of Planning and Budgets (Secretaría de Programación y Presupuesto, SPP), was promulgated in January 1984. It declared that no public contract could be granted without prior open competition. This eliminated the two most important concessions granted to the union in connection with the perforation of oil wells and the transportation of crude oil (Alonso and López, 1985). In December of that year the government stopped paying the 2 per cent of the total cost of the contracts granted to private capitalists which the union used to receive for its social benefit fund (Cruz Bencomo, 1989).

In response to these measures, the union began its counter-attack. In December 1984, at its XVIII national convention, the union symbolically added the adjective revolutionary to its name. The following year members were encouraged to vote not for the PRI but the Partido Socialista de los Trabajadores (PST). In January 1986 the general secretary, José Sosa, used the occasion of the annual meeting of the STPRM leadership with the President to declare that 'if PEMEX sinks, you sink, and everybody else sinks, the county too will have no confidence in those that flatter you'. Sosa was referring not only to the director of PEMEX but also to the future President, Carlos Salinas de Gortari, who was at that time head of the SPP and who had been behind the 1984 Law of Public Works. The presidential elections of 6 July 1988 clearly revealed the position of the oil union leaders towards de la Madrid and his successor. Salinas lost in almost all the districts where the STPRM was strong.[7] Despite this, the union's candidates for the Chamber of Deputies and the Senate were all elected (Cruz Bencomo, 1989:28).[8]

Once in office the new administration had to confront a new offensive by the STPRM, including strike threats if the government attempted to privatize parts of the oil industry.[9] Salinas responded almost immediately by imprisoning the union's main leaders on charges of corruption and possession of fire-arms. That these leaders were corrupt and possessed guns was well known but the government chose to use these charges as a pretext for their arrest. Either the de la Madrid administration did not consider itself strong enough or the offensive of the STPRM had not been so open to warrant such a confrontation.

The fact that the Salinas government was successful in replacing a strong union leadership with another set of leaders beholden to the new administration, and that this occurred in one of the most important national unions, does not necessarily mean that the state will not face future acts of resistance against new measures. Union leaders will still attempt to uphold their legitimacy by demonstrating some degree of autonomy from the government.

The declarations on the modernization of the steel industry made by leaders such as Napoleón Gómez Sada, general secretary of the Sindicato Nacional de Trabajadores Mineros, Metalúrgicos y Similares de la República Mexicana (SNTMMSRM), and Angel Olivo Solís, general secretary of one of the largest confederations, the Confederación Obrera Revolucionaria (COR), should be understood in this light. While accepting the closure in 1985 of the country's oldest steel mill in Monterrey, Gómez Sada stated that it could lead to political and social conflict. Olivo Solís criticized the same decision more harshly: he declared that the historical alliance between the state and the workers was being endangered (Rubio and Veloquio, 1986:33).

Whether it is costly union privileges or low levels of efficiency, the government will have to confront the unions directly due to the latter's control of single collective contracts and their capacity to influence economic reforms. For example, they can block a decision to relocate a plant, to permit the entry of private capital and can obstruct decentralization of decision making.

In the case of private firms the problem is different. The government aims to stimulate industrial restructuring in order to attain international competitiveness. Although, in theory, the need for consensus between workers and management in plant reorganization is acknowledged, most studies show that it has generally been imposed through coercion. Most restructuring has aimed at radically reducing operational costs and many firms have achieved high levels of international competitiveness by these means.[10]

In some cases, such as the car industry, the preferred strategy has been plant relocation. Since 1987 its traditional trade deficit has been reversed. Car exports have also helped the industry compensate for the dramatic fall of sales on the domestic market during the economic crisis (Hernández Cervantes, 1987). The new auto plants have been mainly located in the north of the country, allowing them to establish new industrial relations, based on greater internal flexibility, something that would have been unthinkable in the older plants where the unions are very strong. In the northern plants, by contrast, the unions have little say with respect to job specification and decisions over work processes. At the same time, the promotion system based on seniority is replaced by one based on qualifications. These new relations also permit greater external flexibility: unionized workers are substituted by temporary, often non-unionized personnel, weakening the unions' bargaining position when faced with the threat of lay-offs. Finally, all of the new plants pay their workers considerably less than the older plants in the centre of the country (Arteaga, 1985; Carrillo and García, 1987; de la Garza, 1989).

We will discuss later the consequences and limitations of such a strategy. For the moment we want only to mention that the fact that private capital can weaken union power with the government's blessing will surely have consequences for the corporatist relationship. The largest confederations, such as the CTM (Confederación de Trabajadores de México), the CROM (Confederación Regional Obrera Mexicana), the CROC (Confederación Revolucionaria de Obreros y Campesinos) and the COR (Confederación Obrera Revolucionaria), mainly bring together unions in private firms. These unions are severely affected by economic modernization because they base their power over workers on very rigid controls of working conditions. They have a paternalistic and clientistic relationship with the workers which is founded upon highly specific job specification, tight control of internal mobility within plants and jurisdication over lateness, vacations and sick leave.

It is clear, therefore, that the leaders of official unions are faced by a double pressure which makes them resist the restructuring process.

On the one hand, union members exert pressure to defend acquired rights. On the other, modernization policies directly threaten the economic and political prerogatives of the union bureaucracy. The large confederations of unions located in small and medium-sized firms would be ready to accept, to a certain degree, a reduced role in determining internal conditions within particular firms as long as they continued to have authority and obtain the associated political benefits. This means that, even though modifications to collective contracts imply reduced prerogatives for affiliated unions, and consequently a shift in the control mechanisms wielded by the large confederations, these latter are not necessarily weakened politically (or even economically). By contrast, in the case of the large industry-wide unions, changes in collective contracts inevitably imply the loss of some economic benefits and political power.

We must also take into account changes in the electoral sphere, particularly greater pressure for true voting figures and the tendency in urban areas of voters to identify union leaders with the most discredited sectors of the PRI. This means that political posts traditionally held by PRI-affiliated unions are no longer guaranteed. In July 1988 all of the labour leaders that ran as PRI candidates for the Chamber of Deputies were defeated. Gamboa Pascoe, leader of the Federation of the Federal District, the largest single federation in the CTM, was also defeated in his bid for one of the capital's Senate seats. Even though Salinas obtained second place in Mexico City with 27 per cent of the vote, behind Cárdenas who won 49 per cent, the PRI came third in the elections for senator. This suggests that even some PRI supporters did not vote for Pascoe.

Finally, given that the ideology of revolutionary nationalism was rejected by the Salinas government but adopted by the *neocardenista* opposition, it is possible that official union leaders might turn to other parties, as happened in 1988 when the STPRM decided to back Cuauhtémoc Cárdenas and the FDN. For many workers and government employees the modernization policies are seen as a threat to their acquired rights and even their jobs. They consider that the *neocardenistas* more authentically represent the original project which gave life to the PRI. Briefly, it could be said that the PRI seems to have emptied itself not only of its original project, its ideology and its discourse, but also of its supporters.

The incompatibility between corporatism and modernization

The contradictions between economic modernization and corporatism are not all due to the obstacles posed by corporatist relations for the restructuring process,[11] nor the fact that corporatism is less efficient in carrying out its traditional tasks.[12] There is also a contradiction with the new forms of labour organization seen in other countries and in some Mexican firms. These forms clash with the centralized, hierarchical and rigid forms of decision-making upon which corporatism is based. The new forms of labour organization are based upon the active participation of workers. They require union organizations that act less as mediators between management and work force, and more as a safeguard of basic conditions. This means that the union is accepted as legitimate and, in some cases, even necessary in maintaining stable industrial relations, although with clearly defined functions.

For this reason, it is necessary to study the effect of corporatism at the micro-level, the level that determines what enterprises may or may not do. In the first place, state intervention has tended to homogenize industrial wages and benefits and labour relations, with the exception of strategic industries. Although this was necessary at the start of industrialization and continues to be so in disadvantaged sectors and regions to prevent extreme inequalities, economic modernization requires differentiation. Those enterprises in the most dynamic economic branches and those geared towards export markets have to be able to offer workers higher wages or create systems which link salaries to productivity and quality. This has not been possible in Mexico where the state has traditionally required business and unions to submit their contracts to the Ministry of Labour for revision. During the administrations of López Portillo and de la Madrid, even official unions accused the Ministry of Labour of imposing maximum wage rises on companies which had agreed on higher settlements with their respective unions. Several strikes were called in response to the government's decisions. This forced some of the most dynamic and productive firms to avoid wage rise limits by increasing their non–wage benefits.

Another element of rigidity is related to the process of collective bargaining. Labour legislation requires unions to announce their intention to go on strike and gives the labour authorities the power to reject either the strike call or determine if the strike is legal or not once it has started (sometimes they can rule that a strike is illegal even before it starts). As a result, the labour authorities have usually been able to manage conflicts within the two legal instances relating to the negotiation of collective contracts: the negotiation of the contract itself and the negotiation of salaries;[13] there were practically no conflicts apart from these two issues. However, this is also changing with economic modernization. Since 1985 conflicts occur more frequently due to contract violation and modifications caused by the reorganization of firms.

A direct consequence of the restriction of the causes of conflict is that, prior to collective bargaining, workers' demands and problems simply accumulate. Sometimes the salary negotiations are used to express other grievances, leading to demands for excessive wage rises, which allows the union to negotiate the real cause of conflict under the table.[14]

This situation is inevitable when conflicts cannot be solved at the moment in which they arise due to the restricted nature of the contract. It is also usually true that these conflicts cannot be dealt with at the place in which they occur either and require the intervention of a union official. In most cases not even the union branch delegate has the power to solve the problem. Any union demand for new conditions will therefore have to wait until the next negotiation of the collective contract. As a result there is limited flexibility in working conditions and in the organization of production. This can discourage modernization of the enterprise and hinder its capacity to adapt to market fluctuations.

These legal obstacles for the expression of labour conflicts lead both labour and business to view each other as antagonistic parties. The union considers that its function is to obtain concessions, usually described as conquests that are wrested from the firm. Any change in the rules of the game is resisted even though, on some occasions, a demand from the workers could be advantageous for the firm and vice versa. In addition, because any solution to a conflict has to wait for a formal round of negotiations, problems sometimes express themselves spontaneously outside of union channels, frequently in an individual form and in some cases in anomic manner (such as sabotage, absenteeism, low productivity, very rapid turn-over and even accidents), but also in collective forms (illegal strikes and stoppages). Industrial relations are thus considered in terms of power conflicts rather than interest conflicts.

The fact that collective bargaining is the only way in which conflicts can be solved and demands met enhances the paternalism of management. Company administrators are not inclined to respond to any demands from the workers. Instead, they try and pre-empt their expression by granting concessions. Amongst supervisors and foremen, direct negotiations are always rejected, preferring to resort to union representatives and formal negotiations where they tend to impose their solution.[15]

An industrial relations system based almost exclusively on collective bargaining also intensifies a general characteristic of unionism which is even more pronounced in the Mexican case: the centralization of union power. On the one hand, an emphasis on negotiation tends to emphasize those problems which can be foreseen on a long-term basis, such as salaries, benefits and promotion criteria. This clearly strengthens the centralization of power since formal negotiations are carried out by union officials. On the other hand, the fact that the main function of Mexican unionism has been one of achieving political control has enhanced the paternalistic and clientelistic relationship between leaders and workers. Consequently, unions have been able to reward their most loyal members and punish those who are disloyal. This explains why Mexican unions are above all interested in those benefits which can be channelled through the union apparatus, for example, hiring mechanisms, the promotion system, leave of absence, scholarships and housing.

By contrast union leaders show little interest in any sort of agreement over work organization. Any agreement aiming to increase productivity and quality or which tries to link wages to these two factors requires constant and close surveillance at the work place. This implies the decentralization of union power because discussions regarding the labour process require a union structure with departmental delegates who have the authority to negotiate problems as and when they arise. This structure would allow the workers to decide upon the best form of action without having to channel everything through the union.

The traditional industrial relations that we have described are being attacked on various flanks. On the one hand, the homogenizing interventionism of the state is being challenged. Some of the most dynamic firms are trying to evade the government's wage policies. Additionally, as a result of restructuring, there are more and more conflicts which fall outside the scope of collective contracts, thereby weakening the mediating role of the Ministry of Labour.

On the other hand, paternalism and clientelism of union leaders and managers are under attack from workers demanding a greater say in the organization of the production process. At the same time, the new forms of labour organization, together with the new industrial relations that they require, are based on the decentralization of decision-making and greater worker participation.

Conclusions

Two main conclusions can be drawn from the above discussion. Firstly, society advances more rapidly than the state apparatus, evading, where possible, governmental and union control. Secondly, Mexican corporatism is a homogenizing, centralized, hierarchical and inflexible structure. The tendency of modernization is towards flexibility and heterogeneity. However, modernization does not only demand the dismantling of corporatism, as most recent studies emphasize, but also the introduction of new forms of industrial relations which are being established in those domestic firms which are internationally competitive. In the long term these new industrial relations will spread to the rest of the economy as a result of the opening of the Mexican economy to the world. Furthermore, they are based on participatory and consensual forms of decision–making.

Nevertheless, there is strong resistance to the establishment of new industrial relations. While, mainly for political reasons, the state continues to require corporatist control of unionism, it will not be able to do without its power to control the legal recognition of unions and strikes, the monitoring of collective contracts and will have to keep in power union leaders loyal to the state, even though they lack legitimacy. Although there are many reasons why corporatism is incompatible with modernization, it is not inevitable that it will end. There is a real possibility that the government will try to install a form of neo-corporatism.

A neo-corporatist strategy would aim to preserve the corporatist structure but would remove some of the prerogatives of the strongest unions and, where necessary, replace some of their leaders. This option depends on a degree of economic recovery in the short or medium-term which would allow the government to recover its spending capacity and with it a degree of legitimacy for itself and the corporatist system. Nevertheless, we do not believe that this is feasible because, in the first place, a large segment of society has developed outside of the corporatist organizations and has also found in the electoral arena new spaces for political expression. On the other hand, some of the most dynamic firms are increasingly more autonomous from traditional corporatist control and often negotiate independently of the Ministry of Labour and official unionism. In addition, unions in these enterprises face radical changes: the workers are younger, better educated and better qualified than their predecessors; they often come from urban areas and in many cases are second-generation workers. As a result they express demands that differ from those of the old working class and they tend more readily to reject traditional mechanisms of union control, that is, paternalism and clientelism.

Furthermore, many of the unions in the more dymanic enterprises have gone through some experience of independent unionism such as the Unidad Obrera Independiente (UOI), Línea Proletaria (LP) and others. This means that official unionism has been obliged to adopt a less corporatist and localistic attitude, while also having to maintain a greater degree of autonomy with respect to the large confederations. Official unions have been forced to take on the same forms of action as those developed by independent unionism.

It has also been pointed out by most recent studies of the Mexican labour movement that economic restructuring tends to undermine the working class. Undoubtedly, both government and business interests are tempted to try and weaken unionism. From this perspective flexibility would necessarily mean the marginalization of unions and, in some cases, their disappearance. There would be a direct relationship between company management and the workers in which the present unions (conceived of as a factor of rigidity) would be substituted by company unions.

Flexibility, however, does not necessarily imply the eventual disappearance of unions. A comparison of industrial relations in Germany with those existing in Mexico illustrates this situation. In contrast to Mexico, where collective contracts regulate labour relations within the plants in a very detailed manner, in Germany co-management has allowed for labour conditions to be defined through *ad hoc* agreements. The plants' internal organization permits greater flexibility but the dismissal of workers is strictly determined by the collective contract and is subject to precise procedures and obligations. While in Germany there co-exists a high degree of internal flexibility with relatively high job stability, in Mexico there exists low internal and external flexibility (Dombois, 1986).

In those countries which have chosen a development strategy which includes total flexibility, external as well as internal, there is debate as to the limits of this model in comparison with the advantages of the Swedish and German models where flexibility is only internal. Analysts have argued that total external flexibility can lead company management to neglect the importance of effective long-term planning. If they miscalculate or if the market for their products shrinks, they simply dismiss part of their work force. Where there is less external flexibility, firms have to try and foresee possible changes in market conditions. This means that in the long run they acquire a greater capacity to adapt to market fluctuations and implies the development of a more intelligent entrepreneurial class. Judging by the economic success of countries like Germany and Sweden, it is possible that external rigidity does not necessarily constitute a greater obstacle to economic modernization, and may even imply the contrary (*Le Monde*, 1 November 1988).

On the other hand, the tendency to take advantage of economic crisis and reconversion in order to weaken unionism fails to take into account that, where unions have a strong tradition, they may be important actors in the negotiation process. Any agreement designed to raise productivity and quality cannot be effectively pursued unless it is also accepted by the unions. The existence of company unions which are weak and unrepresentative does not guarantee the absence of conflict. This may be a favourable strategy in the short term, but in the long term faces the type of problems that have appeared in some of the plants that were re-located in northern Mexico. Even though union life here is practically non-existent, it does not prevent tensions and conflicts from emerging in a more spontaneous and often strictly individual manner. Not even collective action can be prevented, as demonstrated in 1988 by the large number of spontaneous conflicts in northern auto plants (Carrillo and García, 1987).

Finally, neither of the options we have mentioned, neo–corporatism and total flexibility, comply with the new types of work organization being applied in many of the areas in which Mexican companies will have to compete. Even though these forms of organization considerably reduce the role of unions, relegating them to watching over salary and dismissal conditions and excluding them from decision-making over working conditions, they do not eliminate the unions.

In countries where unions have been traditionally weak, new methods of organization have been established by a direct relationship between the manager and the workers, through different ways of stimulating the participation and discussion of labour and production problems between workers and administrators. This is the case of Japan, where the introduction of quality circles and of other total quality methods has been based on the attitude of the Japanese population towards work, an attitude rooted in their family traditions (Drancourt, 1989:59–85).

In other countries, where unionism has traditionally been strong, the new forms of organization (even the same Japanese quality methods as well as others to make work organization more flexible) have been established with the agreement of the unions. In some cases where unionization is voluntary, as in France, workers simply ignore their unions' indecision and accept these methods. In countries like Mexico, where unionization is obligatory, the implementation of a new method of work organization would need the agreement of the union. In this case, the new industrial relations would demand representative and legitimate unions in which the workers are able to represent themselves. This would probably be the easiest way to overcome workers' resistance towards these methods. In enterprises where there is no union it would probably be necessary to organize one to show that there is no intention of hurting the workers' basic conditions. This is essential because confidence is at the root of a method that demands active worker participation.

This type of work organization will have to confront resistance from managers and union leaders. The former are used to having exclusive authority over the organization of production. The latter will feel that more participatory schemes inevitably affect the centralization of union power and undermine the paternalistic and clientelistic practices upon which corporatism in Mexico is based.

Notes

1. Between 1980 and 1986 the decline in employment in the manufacturing and construction sectors was only 2.8 per cent and 2.7 per cent respectively. However, in those sectors which conceal underemployment, the decline was far greater: 5.3 per cent in commerce, 11.5 per cent in services, 24.3 per cent in non–specified activities and 4.6 per cent in agriculture. Nonetheless there was an important increase in the number of Mexican workers from all sectors who were covered by the social security system (Instituto Mexicano de Seguro Social, IMSS). This can only mean that the government has been stricter in obliging businessmen to include their employees in the social security institutions.
2. Reynolds argues that this transfer continued until at least the end of the sixties.
3. This wage index has 1978=100 as its base year (Trejo Ryes, 1987:96).

4. Elaborated on the basis of data in INEGI, 1975 and 1985.
5. According to Ward, the percentage of social expenditure fell from 25 per cent in 1975 to 13 per cent in 1985. During the administration of López Portillo (1976–1982), the decrease was probably due to the concentration of public spending in industry, as revealed by the rapid growth in oil investment after 1978. The proportion of gross national product (GNP) dedicated to public social expenditure reached a peak of 9 per cent in 1976 before beginning its descent to just 6 per cent in 1983. The percentage of public expenditure on education and health services reached a maximum in 1980 of 17.5 per cent and 1.4 per cent respectively.
6. For a comparison between the salaries and economic benefits in these strategic sectors and the rest of manufacturing industry, see Bizberg (1986).
7. This was possible thanks to the characteristics that the oil workers share with the teachers, although the latter are even more important because their union extends throughout the country. The geographical concentration of the oil union members and the absence of representatives from opposition parties to watch over electoral procedures made it possible for the union to exert strict control over the individual vote.
8. Cuauhtémoc Cárdenas, the candidate of the Frente Democrático Nacional (FDN), won in the primarily oil enclaves of Coatzacoalcos, Poza Rica and Minatitlán in the state of Veracruz, and Salamanca in the state of Guanajuato.
9. This referred to privatization without the same offer of compensation for the union as it had received in 1977 and 1982.
10. According to a study carried out by one of the largest banks, Banco Nacional de México (BANAMEX), this strategy is not feasible in the long run. Eventually, high levels of productivity and quality will be the most important factors in increasing competitiveness: 'The cost of labour, at present our main comparative advantage, will become less and less important in relation to global costs. At the same time, real wages in Mexico will approach those paid in other countries. For this reason, an important aspect of national policy should be to improve and modernize the productivity and quality of human resources' (Alduncín Abitia, 1989:75).
11. Besides the reasons already mentioned, there is also the fact that corporatist control of unions limits the government's ability to fully regain business confidence since this control allows it to change the rules of the game at will.
12. Besides the functions already mentioned, corporatism is less and less efficient in mobilizing the PRI vote. Only agrarian corporatism continues to be relatively effective, although it too, like the national teachers' union, has come under pressure from opposition parties in some northern areas.
13. Mexican labour law stipulates that negotiations to revise collective contracts should take place every two years, while salaries should be renegotiated every year.

14. This issue, as well as others included in this section, have been extensively discussed in Bizberg, 1990.
15. This situation is being challenged in the largest and more complex plants, where the productive structure separates workers (particularly the more skilled workers) from power centres. In some of these enterprises there is greater flexibility and decentralization of decisions and problem solving. If this were not so, production would be continuously hindered.

12· WOMEN'S WORK AND HOUSEHOLD CHANGE IN THE 1980s[1]

Sylvia Chant

Querétaro and the Mexican crisis

Querétaro is capital of the state of the same name and lies on the eastern edge of the Bajío about 200kms north of Mexico City (see Map 12.1). Founded originally in 1445 and coming under Spanish control in 1531, it became an important agricultural and mining centre in colonial times, and from the 1960s onwards emerged as one of the leading industrial cities of the republic.

Querétaro's current prominence as a major modern manufacturing centre arises from its strategic position in the geographical core of Mexico, good transport and communications, abundant natural resources, and in particular its proximity to Mexico City; nearness to the capital has made it one of the most attractive intermediate cities for firms induced out of the overcrowded Federal District by incentives offered under successive programmes of industrial decentralization implemented in the last 30 or so years (Chant, 1984; see also Aguilar-Barajas and Spence, 1988). Many firms in Querétaro are subsidiaries of foreign companies, including Singer, Gerber, Black and Decker, Carnation, Clemente Jacques, Massey Ferguson and Ford. The first multinational located in Querétaro in 1956 set a precedent for other factories to move onto the city's large, cheap, well-planned greenfield sites (Selby, 1979).

Between 1960 and 1980 the share of the economically active population employed by the primary sector fell from 39.7 per cent to only 7.5 per cent against a rise of 24.5 per cent to 38.2 per cent in the secondary sector, that is, mainly manufacturing. Industrial expansion

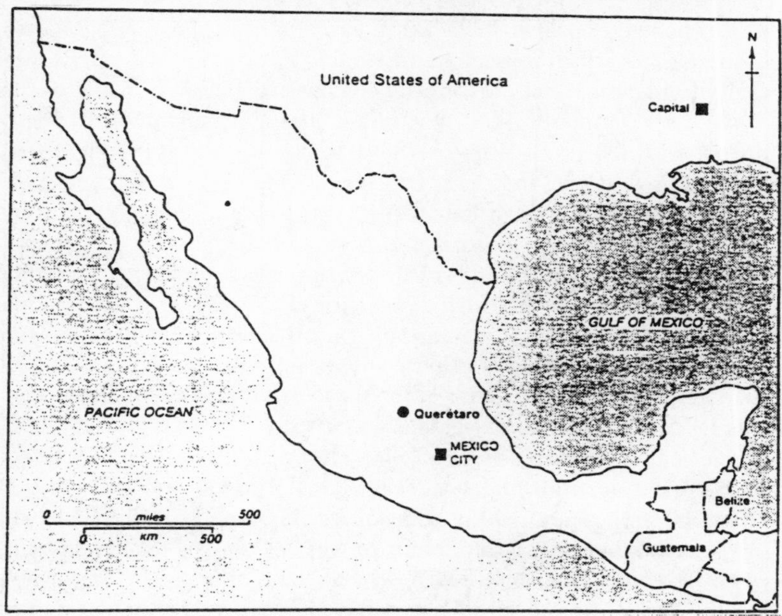

Map 12.1 Mexico: Location of Querétaro

was accompanied by massive rates of demographic growth, with the city's population almost doubling between 1960 and 1970 from 75,000 to 140,000, doubling again by 1980 to nearly 300,000 inhabitants, and reaching around 450,000 by 1985 (Gobierno Constitucional de los Estados Unidos Mexicanos/Gobierno del Estado de Querétaro, 1986). Much of this growth resulted from in-migration from rural areas in other parts of the state, or from neighbouring states such as Guanajuato and Michoacán.[2]

Rapid demographic growth placed severe pressure on existing housing stock with the result that by the early 1980s around one-third of Querétaro's population had been forced to house themselves in one of ten irregular self-help settlements around the edge of the city.[3] Three of these settlements, namely Bolaños, Los Andadores and Las Américas, formed the basis of the author's survey (see Map 12.2).

After two decades of high growth, however, in the 1980s Querétaro's economy plunged into drastic decline as a result of national crisis. Since much of the city's industry was dependent on imported components, shortages of hard currency meant that many factories

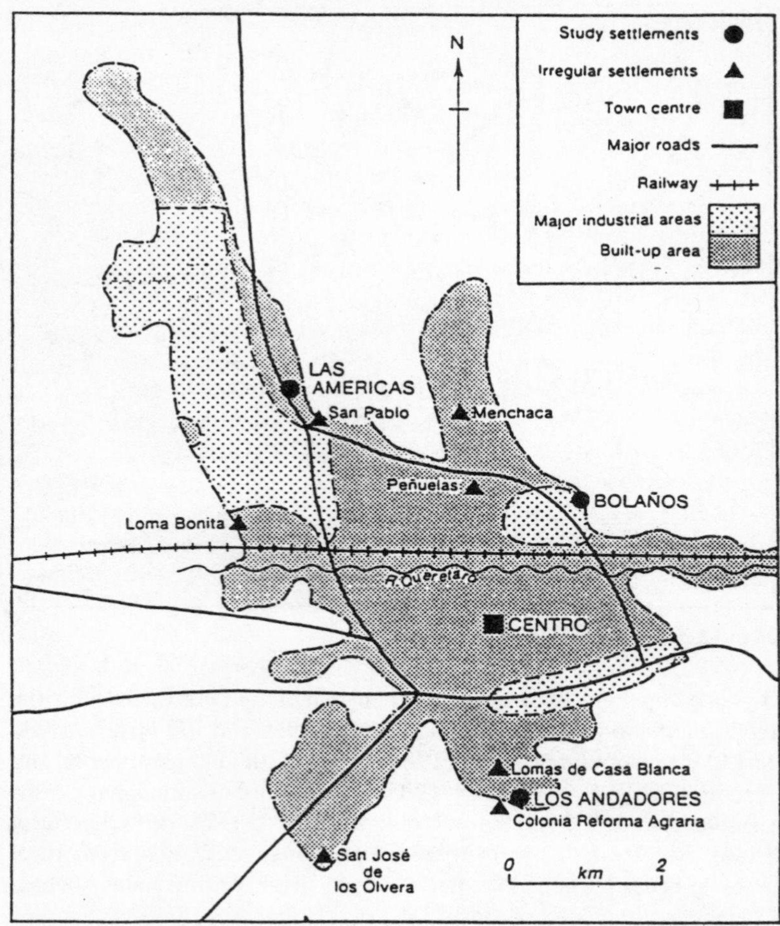

Map 12.2 Querétaro: low-income neighbourhoods and study settlements

could not continue operating on a regular basis, and in some cases shut down. The Carnation factory, for example, had to lay off around half its workforce in the latter part of 1982 because production was almost entirely based on imports, including powdered milk, which the company could not afford; by December 1982 industry in Querétaro was working at only 20 per cent of its installed capacity, and between 1982 and 1983 around 25 per cent of the industrial workforce lost their jobs (Chant, 1984). In addition to widespread losses in employment, wages in industry in the country as a whole fell by about one-third between May 1982 and November 1985 (Gilbert, 1989:159–60). It is against this background of deteriorating employment opportunities and falling real wages that we must evaluate the changing survival strategies of low-income households. While some commentators, for example, Roberts (1990) have argued that the Mexican crisis hit middle-income groups most severely, there is no doubt that there were also serious consequences for the poorest groups in society.

Household survival and economic crisis: perspectives from the literature

Before going on to examine the specific responses of households in Querétaro to economic recession, it is useful to consider the findings of two other longitudinal studies of a similar type: first, the work of Mercedes González de la Rocha (1988) on economic crisis, women's work and domestic reorganization among low-income groups in Guadalajara, western Mexico, in the 1980s; and second, the work of Caroline Moser (1989) on responses of poor urban households in Guayaquil, Ecuador, to recession and structural adjustment over the period 1978–88. González de la Rocha's work is obviously more relevant to the present study in terms of both area and timing; although Guadalajara has a more diverse industrial base than Querétaro, with a plethora of small-scale enterprises that have probably kept more of a lid on open unemployment, on the whole it appears that the effects of increased poverty have been broadly similar.

Ninety-five of the 100 households interviewed by González de la Rocha in 1982 were re-traced and re-interviewed in 1985, and again in 1987, although her 1988 article concentrates mainly on the changes between 1982 and 1985. The principal findings of her research are as follows:

- households increased in size between these two periods, particularly through the incorporation of other kin;
- related to this, while nuclear households were in the majority in both years, by 1985 they had declined at the expense of increasing proportions of both extended and multiple family households;[4]
- there was an increase in the number of wage-earners in households, particularly among women aged 15 years or more, and among boys under fourteen.

Partly as a result of this last factor there was a decrease in household dependency (worker: consumer) ratios.

Looking at these findings in more detail, household size among Guadalajara's urban poor increased from an average of 6.58 to 6.97 members during the three-year interval, and in some respects is associated with the de-nuclearization of household units. Nuclear households fell from 80 per cent of the sample in 1982 to 74.7 per cent in 1985 (González de la Rocha, 1988:211–12). At the same time the average number of workers per household rose from 2.13 to 2.69 (ibid.:212). Although there is no way of telling from her article whether female labour-force participation increased in those households which had become extended in the period – an association which is particularly strong in the case of Querétaro as will be discussed later – it appears that households with women aged 15 years or more working rose from 63 per cent of the earlier sample to 79 per cent in the later one, and the labour-force participation of female heads (by which she refers both to female heads and spouses) increased from 38 per cent to 46.7 per cent. Younger women were playing an important role in taking over domestic duties from mothers who now went out to work.

Other relevant changes in household survival strategies discovered by González de la Rocha relate to household expenditure and consumption. Although there was a drop in real wages of the order of one-third, and the real salaries of male heads declined by 35 per cent, there was actually only an 11 per cent fall in real per capita household income for those in the survey, largely because families were deploying more members into the labour force. Nevertheless, cuts in most parts of the family budget were inevitable. Although people had tried to protect food consumption, they were eating less in the way of protein, and in per capita terms expenditure on food had dropped by 13 per cent. Very few households were saving money and less was being spent on education and health (ibid.:216–19).

Moser's (1989) findings over a longer time span in Guayaquil, Ecuador, reveal strong similarities. Although Ecuador is poorer than Mexico, with substantially greater numbers of people in rural areas, as an oil producer its economy has suffered in similar ways to that of Mexico during the last 15–20 years. High rises in public spending in the 1970s at the expense of a mounting external debt were followed by drastic cuts in the subsequent decade associated with the oil price shocks of 1982 and 1986–7. As in Mexico, a massive stabilization programme was initiated in 1982–3, with severe curtailment in wage rises and public expenditure (see Moser, 1989).

At grassroots level, poor households of the neighbourhood Barrio Indio Guayas in the port of Guayaquil, Ecuador's second major city, have responded to recession in much the same way as has Guadalajara. The principal effects noted by Moser are also increased numbers of workers in each household, with many women amongst new workers, and modifications in consumption patterns. Moser observes that the proportion of households with only one wage-earner fell from nearly one-half to one-third of all households in the period 1978–88. At the same time, those households with three or more workers rose from one-fifth to one-third of the total, and women's labour-force participation increased from 40 per cent to 52 per cent. With respect to consumption, as in González's study, people were eating less in the way of high protein and/or nutritious foodstuffs such as milk, fish and fresh fruit juice, were eating smaller portions, and had fewer meals a day (many people began to omit supper for example). In addition Moser observed a disturbing rise in domestic violence, particularly over cash and in households where women were not contributing to household income and thus having to ask husbands for bigger handouts. Although an increase in marital conflict was not mentioned by González de la Rocha, she does note that the poor in Guadalajara are more 'tired and worn' and have less time to relax than they used to (González de la Rocha, 1988:220).

Many of the changes identified in both the above cities are also found in Querétaro to a greater or lesser degree.

Household survival strategies in Querétaro 1982/3–1986[5]

Family size

As in González de la Rocha's study in Guadalajara, the average size of household units in Querétaro also increased over three to four years, but by an even bigger margin, from 6.8 in 1982–3 to 7.6 in 1986. However, this former figure derives from the wider questionnaire survey of 1982–3 and it is important to bear in mind that the sub-sample selected for interview in 1986 from the earlier survey had slightly different characteristics, with an average size in the earlier period of seven persons.[6] Even then, this was still a larger increase (8.6 per cent) than in Guadalajara (6 per cent) (González de la Rocha, 1988:211).

Larger household size in Querétaro, as in Guadalajara, is accounted for mainly by the incorporation of new members: over one-third of the households which had been nuclear or one-parent in 1982–3 converted to extended formations in 1986 (see Table 12.1).

In fact, although 65 per cent of households selected for the 1986 survey had been non-extended in 1982, this figure dropped to 40 per cent by the latter period (see Table 12.2). Quite apart from its influence on household size, the transformation of household structure in itself appears to be an extremely important feature of change in the years of recession, with a marked de-nuclearization of both male- and female-headed units.

Numbers of workers and dependency ratios

Along with the small increase in average household size, mean numbers of workers within households had also risen slightly, if only in absolute tems. In the larger questionnaire survey in Querétaro in 1982–3 the average number of workers per household was 1.6, and in the sub-sample 2.1. In 1986 the average had risen to 2.3. Using the latter figure as the more accurate of the two for direct comparisons, the increase in numbers of workers is far less than that calculated by González de la Rocha, around 10 per cent as against 65 per cent. The slightness of the increase is even more apparent when set against household size and numbers of dependants. Although González de la Rocha (1988:213) found that one waged worker supported only 2.59 household members in 1986, compared with 3.09 in 1982, in Querétaro in 1986 one worker was still supporting an average of 3.3 persons in each household, only fractionally less (under one decimal point) than in 1982 (see Chant, 1984). What explains the fact that the poor in Querétaro have not significantly increased their numbers of workers?

One reason is probably that many schoolchildren in Querétaro, especially in female-headed one-parent units, had already been working part-time in 1982–3 and were accordingly registered as workers in the earlier survey. However, by 1986 some of these former part-time adolescent workers had left school, moved into full-time jobs and were thus bringing in higher wages (see below). With greater financial returns from these individuals, there was obviously less need to send other members out to work. It does seem also that parents are holding on to children for longer. Aside from the fact that many in their late teens and early twenties are still single and thus living at home, it appears that a significant number, over one-third, are staying with their

Table 12.1: Changes in household structure in Querétaro 1982–3–1986

Original structure 1982–3	Stayed same	Changed to:	Structure by 1986 Nuclear	One-parent	Male-extended	Female-extended	Total in 1986 Original-losses + additions = total
Nuclear	****		n/a		***	*	8 − 4 + 2 = 6
One-parent	**		*	n/a		**	5 − 3 + 0 = 2
Male-extended	***		*		n/a	*	5 − 2 + 3 = 6
Female-extended	**					n/a	2 − 0 + 4 = 6
Net gain or loss of household type			−2	−3	+1	+4	

Source: Household Questionnaire Survey, Querétaro, 1986.

Table 12.2: Households selected for 1986 survey in Querétaro according to structure in 1982–3 and 1986

Category of household structure	Structures of households in 1986 sample as they were in 1982–3	Structures of households in 1986 sample
Nuclear	40% (8)	30% (6)
One-parent	25% (5)	10% (2)
Male-extended	25% (5)	30% (6)
Female-extended	10% (2)	30% (6)
Total	100% (20)	100% (20)

Source: Household Questionnaire Survey, Querétaro, 1986
NB. Numbers in brackets refer to numbers of cases.

parents(s) on marriage. Although a total of six sons and daughters from five households in the sample formed their own independent units with spouses during this period, a further four, from four different households, got married but continued living at home; in another case a son and his wife returned and in another case, even though a daughter had left home, the father of a female head moved in instead. The retention of older children on marriage is one of the most important factors accounting for extension of households in the sample and in part represents a drive to keep income earners within the family.

The same argument about existing workers receiving higher wages by 1986 also applies to adult female income earners; although some women had entered the labour force over the previous three years, some had also moved into higher-paid jobs during that period and/or had businesses or activities which were more consolidated and making reasonably healthy profits. It is interesting to note, for example, that the gap between female and male average earnings had narrowed slightly. While in 1982–3 average female earnings were only 40 per cent of men's, these had risen to 58 per cent by 1986, mainly as a result of changes in the nature of women's employment as opposed to improvements in remuneration in their former jobs, although there were a few exceptions. As such, increased earnings of women and young household members probably provides a partial explanation for the relatively small rise in numbers of income earners within households.

Changes in employment

Looking at these change in women's employment in more detail, exactly 50 per cent of the female heads and spouses in the sub-sample of 20 households had been working in 1982–3. While this had risen only to 55 per cent (or 60 per cent if one includes a woman working on an occasional unpaid basis in her husband's photographic business) by 1986, the seemingly small overall change masks a great deal of actual movement: a large proportion, around one-third, of those working in 1986 were in fact new to the labour force, and correspondingly some of those working in 1982–3 had left by the latter period (see Table 12.3) for various reasons. This last group consisted of three women. One left work because of sickness (Guadalupe S.), one because she was replaced by a male worker in her husband's small manufacturing enterprise when the household lost its extended component (Berta), and one because of a combination of inability to delegate domestic work to daughters and because the woman's husband was jeered at by neighbours for letting his wife 'out on the streets' (Gloria R.). In contrast, four new women had taken up work, and three had changed their jobs. Two of this last group were female heads of household (Ana and Socorro) who had moved from part-time/casual work in domestic service and garbage-picking respectively in 1982–3 to better-paid positions as municipal roadsweepers by 1986. Opportunities for women in the municipal cleaning department are the direct result of a programme for equal opportunities in public employment promoted by the incoming state governor, Mariano Palacios Alcocer, in 1985.

Despite the relatively small overall rise in women's labour-force participation, it is evident from Table 12.3 that the kinds of jobs in which women were represented in 1986 tended to be of a more 'formal' nature than those in the sub-sample in 1982–3. In the earlier period, for example, 40 per cent of workers had been domestic servants, a further 40 per cent in home-based commerce or small-scale domestic manufacturing, and only 20 per cent in the formal sector. By 1986, alternatively, out of the overall total of 12 workers, 45 per cent were in formal jobs in registered public- or private-sector enterprises, 33 per cent in a home-based business or self-employment, there was only one domestic servant and only one unpaid worker in a family business. As for men, there had been little change in employment. Eight out of eleven male heads of household were in the same jobs as in 1982–3: most of these had their own businesses or were employed in construction, one who had previously been a master builder, however, could only find work as a general labourer and two had been made redundant from factory jobs in the interim (one remained unemployed, while the other had found clerical work). Regarding instances where households had become female-headed, one husband had died (that of María del Refugio) and the other (Paula's husband) had left to work in the United States. The male head of household that became attached to a former one-parent family (Francisca) was a soldier. Basically, however, there had been much more change in female than in male employment, an issue which is critical to understanding shifts in household structure between the early and mid-1980s.

Purchasing power, consumption and savings

Having reviewed some of the major changes in household size, composition and income-generating strategies, it is also important to

Table 12.3: Women's work and household structure in Querétaro 1982–3 and 1986

		1982–3			1986		
	Name of woman	Labour-force participation	Job	Household structure	Labour-force participation	Job	Household structure
Women entering labour force	María Asunción	X	–	Nuclear	√	Shop owner	Male-extended
	Josefina	X	–	Nuclear	√	Office cleaner	Male-extended
	Guadalupe Ramírez	X	–	Male-extended	√	Factory worker	Male-extended
	Laura	X	–	Nuclear	√	(Unpaid) worker in family business	Nuclear (paid domestic help)
Women in same job	María del Refugio	√	*Tortilla* maker	Male-extended	√	*Tortilla* maker	Female-extended
	Paula	√	School-dinner lady	Nuclear	√	School-dinner lady	Female-extended (*de facto*)
	Cruz	√	Own breakfast business	One-parent	√	Own breakfast business	One-parent
	Guadalupe Ramírez	√	Hotel kitchen assistant	One-parent	√	Hotel kitchen assistant	Female extended
	María Uribe	√	Domestic servant	Male-extended	√	Domestic servant	Male-extended

Women changing jobs	Socorro	√	Domestic servant	One-parent	√	Municipal roadsweeper	Female-extended
	Ana	√	Garbage-picker	One-parent	√	Municipal roadsweeper	One-parent
	Francisca	~	Factory redundancy	One-parent	√	*Tortilla* maker	Nuclear
Women leaving work	Gloria R.	√	Domestic servant	Nuclear	X	–	Nuclear
	Berta	√	Paid worker in family business	Male-extended	X	–	Nuclear
	Guadalupe S.	√	Domestic servant	Female-extended	X	(sick)	Female-extended
Housewives	María Trejo	X	–	Male-extended	X	–	Male-extended
	Lourdes	X	–	Nuclear	X	–	Nuclear
	Rosa	X	–	Nuclear	X	–	Nuclear
	Doña Lupe	X	–	Nuclear	X	–	Male-extended
	Gloria C.	X	–	Female-extended	X	–	Female-extended

Source: Household Questionnaire Survey, Querétaro, 1986.

consider modifications in patterns of expenditure, which in many respects depend on changes in the former group of variables. Between the second half of 1982 and 1986, consumer prices rose by 981 per cent, whereas the daily minimum wage rose by only 573 per cent. However, average per capita income (based on earnings) of households in Querétaro in 1986 was 6,037 pesos, compared with 563.7 in 1982–3; thus an increase in the order of 971 per cent has actually meant that households have almost managed to maintain their relative earning capacity. Overall, household income fell by 11 per cent. Nonetheless, it is important to remember that by 1982, wages had already lost about one-third of their purchasing power from the mid-1970s and we must therefore briefly take into account modifications in consumption practised by households in the sample.

Changes in consumption

Unfortunately detailed data on expenditure and consumption, such as those collected by González de la Rocha, were not gathered in the present project; households were asked merely to comment on the way in which the crisis had most affected them. Nonetheless, there were several general similarities, most of which involved a reallocation of resources away from long-term to short-term reproduction. For example, as in Guadalajara, the key objective on people's minds was to satisfy immediate consumption needs such as food; although one or two of the poorest households no longer buy meat, most had tried to ensure that some protein, eggs for instance, was included in one of the daily meals. In virtually every other respect people were cutting corners. In Bolaños, for example, where households have no piped water and still have to rely on costly deliveries by tanker, people were washing clothes less frequently. Few people had invested money in housing improvements, despite the fact that general servicing levels had improved in all three settlements. Expenditure on shelter was regarded as a luxury which should wait until such time as people began to feel more secure in their jobs and earnings, especially with inflation running at over 80 per cent in 1986 (see also Chant, 1984; Ch. 7 on the effects of inflation on building materials). Several households had also stopped saving money; long-term perspectives which had been the prerogative of the more privileged households in 1982–3 had now been replaced by a much more day-to-day approach to survival. In 1982–3 nearly half the 244 households in the questionnaire survey were able to put aside small amounts of cash each week;

by 1986 this had dropped to one-third of the families in the sub-sample, partly because household income was insufficient in many cases to cover more than the very basic necessities (food, clothing, rates, service charges and so on), and partly because people were highly sceptical about the utility of saving money when inflation could so easily erode its value, even in a high-interest bank account. (In 1982–3 most people [55 per cent] had saved money at home or in the local tanda [an informal rotating credit arrangement among groups of neighbours in the community], and only 45 per cent of households in a savings association or bank.) On average, saving households in 1986 had 30 per cent more earnings per capita than non-savers.

To sum up the situation thus far, households in Querétaro have responded to economic crisis by introducing a series of changes in patterns of household composition, expenditure and income-generating strategies, the main changes being increased rates of female labour-force participation which have turned single-earning units into multiple-earning households, and a conversion of household composition from nuclear to extended formations. Analysis of the data suggests that households which have either maintained or encouraged the entry of women into the workforce, or extended their households or, as is usually the case, both, have been most successful in combatting economic crisis. Before going on to look at the relative success rates of different household structures in terms of earning power and income levels, it is necessary to consider briefly the issue of links between female labour-force participation and family form.

Female labour-force participation: family structure and economic crisis

Somewhat surprisingly few studies of household survival strategies have made specific note of the correspondence between women's employment and household composition and headship, even though *a priori* one might imagine important links between the two. Given the sexual division of labour common in most societies, and certainly apparent in Mexico, women's central position in household reproduction would suggest that any movement into the labour force, especially if it involves working outside the home and/or full time, is extremely likely to rebound upon the organization of the domestic unit, either in terms of altering internal divisions of labour of existing members, or by incorporating new members to free up women for economic activity. I have stressed elsewhere the critical importance of recognizing the role of household structure in influencing female labour-force participation (e.g. Chant, 1985, 1987, 1991), and the present study appears to confirm the significance of the ties between them.

In brief, earlier research in Querétaro and in two other Mexican cities, León and Puerto Vallarta, in 1986 has indicated that household structure and female labour-force participation are intimately interrelated (see Chant, 1984, 1991). On the one hand, household structure plays a critical role in influencing the likelihood of women entering the workforce, that is, it plays a major part in shaping labour supply. One set of reasons here relates to practical aspects of household divisions of labour. Nuclear households, especially with young children, for example, are those least capable of releasing women into the workforce because the adult female in the unit is needed for domestic labour and childcare. In extended households, on the other hand, the common existence of other female kin members, often mothers or mothers-in-law, or adolescent nieces, sisters, cousins and so on, means that female spouses may discharge some, if not most, of their routine reproductive labour to other people in the family unit. To a certain extent this also applies to nuclear households at more advanced stages of the life-cycle when adolescent daughters often take over a large share of their mothers' responsibilities in the home.

Another critically important set of issues however, relates to ideological aspects of household organizations, especially women's personal freedom in familial decision-making. Low rates of female labour-force participation in nuclear households, for example, appear to derive not only from the practical difficulties associated with going out to work, but also from the fact that men in these units, often through their position as chief or only breadwinner, have much more control over determining whether their wives work than either units characterized by multiple earners (generally extended households) or where women head their own households. It is not only economic necessity, therefore, that influences whether women work or not in female-headed households, for example, or whether there are other people in the family unit who can help out with housework and childcare as in extended households, but also the issue of whether women are free to take the decision to work, a phenomenon obviously most characteristic of women-headed households (see Chant, 1984, 1987, 1991). Certainly in 1982–3 many women mentioned how husbands could, and often would, veto any suggestion they might make to go out to work, even if it was technically possible for them to take a job; for example, there were teenage daughters in the family or the wife only wanted to work part-time and/or from home. This was most evident in nuclear households which had the lowest proportions of women in work than any other household type. Household structure, then, for a combination of pragmatic and ideological reasons, can often play a major role in enabling or restraining women's involvement in the labour force.

At the same time, it is important to recognize that the decision of a given household unit to mobilize the labour power of secondary household earners may itself be a catalyst for modifications in family structure; that is, households may alter their membership deliberately to promote the labour-force participation of wives. In Mexico this virtually always means extension of the household unit through the incorporation of in-laws or blood relatives. While households in a situation of economic crisis may well become extended for other reasons as well, such as the need for kin to combine economic resources as a means of retaining workers (by asking sons' and daughters' spouses to come and live in the family home), or through inability to buy land or build shelter and so on, the role played by women's movement from home to workplace should not be underestimated as a major factor accounting for the conversion of parent–child households into extended units.[7] Indeed, of the six households in the sample which became extended between 1982–3 and 1986, half did so as a direct corollary of women's labour-force changes in that period (María Asunción, Josefina and Socorro, see Table 12.3), two were where women had been working in the same job since before 1982 (Paula and Guadalupe Ramírez), and only one where the woman remained a housewife and the principal objective of extension was to retain a key male earner (Doña Lupe).

Looking more closely at the inter-relationships between women's work and household structure during the crisis years, of the 20 households in the 1986 Querétaro sub-sample, a total of 70 per cent (14) had experienced some change in household structure and/or the workforce position of the adult woman (whether entry or withdrawal from the labour force, or a qualitative shift in job status) within the three years between 1982–3 and 1986 (see Table 12.3). In nine of these fourteen cases, women's changing employment characteristics had been in some way related to adjustments in domestic arrangements, and of these, six were linked directly to alterations in family structure, two to movement through the life-cycle, and in the remaining case, where the help that might otherwise have been provided by kin was substituted by paid domestic service. Thus in over two-thirds of the households which had experienced changes in household composition and/or female employment between 1982–3 and 1986 there was a strong link between the two variables. Obviously a sample as small as this does not lend itself easily to generalizations, but an attempt is made below to pinpoint the main sources of changes and articulations of links.

Linkages between changes in women's work and changes in household structure

Regarding the six households where women's labour-force entry, withdrawal or job change was associated with a shift in family structure, three changes in female employment followed on from modifications in household structure; in two, changes in household structure came about as a result of women's entry into the labour force, and in one, both events were planned to coincide.

The three cases where changes in women's employment arose from modifications in household structure included: that of Berta who was forced to withdraw from the family toy-making business when the household became nuclear in 1984 following the move of her husband's niece to Mexico City; that of Francisca, the female head who had remarried in 1984 and instead of taking up an offer to go back to her previous factory job, which had been the original intention after her redundancy during the earlier period of interviewing, had decided it was not necessary now there was a man's wage coming in, and remained at home making *tortillas* for local sale; that of Socorro, another female head who in 1982 had been surviving on the basis of casual domestic service jobs. Following the extension of the household with the arrival of her elderly father in 1985 who took on most of the domestic chores, Socorro was able to move into full-time formal employment as a municipal roadsweeper.

Of the two women whose labour-force participation had prompted a change in household structure, the shift was in both cases from nuclear to extended. Josefina who had entered the labour force after her husband had been made redundant now has living with them her newly married daughter-in-law, who does most of the domestic labour. Paula, who while actually starting work in 1980, has filled the gap left by the departure of husband as a migrant labourer to the United States in 1982 with a sister who is now in charge of most of the housework.

Finally, there is María Asunción, presently setting up a grocery business with her husband Antonio's redundancy money. Here the couple consciously decided to extend their household, inviting a niece to come and help out in the home while María gets the business off the ground. In recognition of the help the niece was to give, Antonio actually offered to pay her a small wage in addition to providing school expenses. Although payment was flatly refused, this gesture indicates the real economic value that household extension can bring to low-income families.

Overall, the four positive changes in women's employment identified here, that is, a move into the labour force or an upward shift in job status, have been associated with the transformation of a nuclear or single-parent unit into an extended structure; conversely, negative changes, namely labour-force withdrawal or retreat into a home-based informal occupation, have been associated with the change of a single-parent or extended household into a nuclear unit (see also Table 12.3).

Moving on to consider the two cases where women's changing labour-force participation had been linked to progress through the life-cycle and to a stage where non-extended units come to approximate extended units through the existence of adolescent or young adult daughters, one, Guadalupe R., has gone into full-time factory work and delegated the bulk of her domestic duties to two teenage daughters. The other, Ana Piña, has been able to move from informal garbage-picking and petty commerce into municipal roadsweeping now there is only one child, a daughter of 14, still at school; she is old enough to fend for herself. Two sons, previously schoolboys with part-time jobs, now work full time.

The final case where women's entry into the labour force is associated with changes in domestic arrangements is that of Laura. Since her family moved to a flat above her husband's photographic business, Laura has begun to help out part time on an unpaid basis in the studio and enlisted the help of a daily domestic to make it easier for her to do so.[8] In time she expects to become much more involved in the business.

In all the above three cases, women have only been able to sustain a move into the labour force through passing some of their reproductive responsibilities on to a daughter or on to outside help, the same kind of process which occurs when families convert conventional extended formations.

Non-linked changes in women's work and household structure

However, not all households experiencing changes in household structure and female employment between 1982–3 and 1986 demonstrate similar relationships. In five cases a change in female employment or family structure, but not both, had occurred during the crisis years. Three of the women in question had experienced changes in household structure, and two in workforce participation. One of the two latter interviewees, Guadalupe S., had withdrawn from the labour force because of damage to her arm; here the household was already extended and the existence of other earners has largely compensated for the loss of her own contribution. The other, Gloria R., spouse in a nuclear household, had worked briefly in 1982 as a domestic servant, but found it impossible to manage domestic work both inside and outside the home, especially as her daughters were not felt to be sufficiently mature to be left in charge. She had since resumed her role as full-time housewife.

In two of the three cases in which changes in household structure had not apparently affected women's employment, women were already working in 1982–3 and had the same occupations in 1986. One woman head of an extended unit, María del Refugio (see Table 12.3) had been widowed during that time. Nonetheless, in employment terms, widowhood meant very little for María who had worked for most of her married life; her husband's weak liver had prevented him undertaking any major physical activity and he had been out of work frequently. The other woman, Guadalupe Ramírez, was head of a non-extended unit in 1982 whose married son had brought his wife to live with the family in 1985 who, within a year, had given birth to a baby girl. Although there is no direct link here, the arrival of a daughter-in-law has been extremely beneficial to Guadalupe, where three out of her four children are working full time and she herself is temporarily laid off, on half-pay, with a work injury. With her daughter-in-law now doing the bulk of the housework, extension in this case could conceivably be interpreted in part as a delayed reaction to female labour-force participation.[9] In the remaining case, the formerly nuclear household of Doña Lupe has recently become extended with a daughter-in-law and grandchild. Neither women is permitted to work by her husband, but nor is it particularly necessary with four adult male workers in a family of only eight persons.

Summing up, family extension occurred in situations where two out of three women had already been working in 1982 and continued to do so (Paula and Guadalupe Ramírez, see Table 12.3). In only one case had the conversion from nuclear to extended happened in a household where the adult woman was a full-time housewife (Doña Lupe). Of those women who had withdrawn from the labour force, one belonged to a nuclear unit which could not cope with the strain of releasing her from reproductive work (Gloria R.), and the other to a household of multiple earners, which made it possible for her to retreat to the home (Guadalupe S.). In many respects the issue of time is very important here, especially in the two cases where households with women who were already working became extended. Although there was no direct or explicit acknowledgement of links between labour-force participation and changes in household membership made by interviewees, it is entirely possible that working women's need for domestic assistance makes it more likely that their households will eventually become extended than those households where women are full time in the home, even if it does not happen immediately.

No changes in work or household structure

Finally, what of the six cases where there had been no change in household structure or female labour-force participation? In two instances, women belonging to a female-headed one-parent and a male-headed extended unit respectively were working in the same occupations in both periods. In another, the female head of an extended unit had died and been replaced by her daughter; neither woman worked because there were several other earners in the household. Of three women not working in either 1982–3 or 1986, two belonged to nuclear households and one to a male-headed extended unit. This latter household consisted of 13 members where there were three adult male workers and an adult female worker. The woman worker in question was the spouse's sister, meaning that in this instance most of the childcare and domestic labour of the household unit fell to the spouse instead.

Although it is obviously difficult to pick out general tendencies and factors from such a wide variety of experiences represented by the 20 households, the main ones apparent are, first, that in order to cope with positive changes in female labour-force participation, households usually have to make some adjustments on the domestic front, either by becoming extended or substituting the labour generally provided by female heads or spouses with the labour of daughters or paid help; when that assistance is unobtainable, it is rare that women's labour-force participation can be sustained. A second, and related point is that this is most often the case in nuclear households, hence Berta's and Gloria's withdrawal from the labour force (see Table 12.3). During the crisis it has been largely imperative that women keep working or take up a job, unless there are very good reasons for not doing so, as in the few (four) extended households in the sub-sample where the existence of at least two other household members in work, usually men, meant that income levels were relatively sound.[10] In turn, nuclear units which are less well-equipped to accommodate women's labour-force participation are likely to be less able to protect income levels. Evidence that nuclear households find it difficult to release women into the labour force is largely borne out by breaking down women's workforce involvement according to household structure: whereas both female heads of one-parent units worked, as did two-thirds of female heads of extended units (four out of six) and female spouses in male-headed extended households (four out of six), only one out of six women spouses worked in the nuclear units (or two if Laura, the unpaid casual worker with domestic help, is included) (see also Table 12.3); alternatively, considering the issue from the angle of the sex of head of household, 75 per cent of all female heads in Querétaro worked, compared with only 42 per cent of spouses in male-headed families.

Do these differences in female labour-force participation between households affect in any major way the poor's ability to shoulder the increased economic pressures imposed upon them by national recession? Does, for example, the inflexibility or resistance of nuclear units to the labour-force participation of wives place these households at a significantly greater disadvantage than those in which women's remunerated work is an increasingly feasible, accepted and integral part of household survival strategies? Certainly the data seem to suggest that this may be the case.

While we have already considered general trends in household income and employment at the beginning of the chapter, it is now necessary to break down the analysis in such a way that different types of household structure may be compared. Since the object of the analysis is to consider the effects of structure on survival strategies, categories of household in 1982–3 are compared with like categories in the later period, rather than looking at individual household trajectories. Comparisons in structures between the two time periods are based, as far as is possible, on the specific conditions of the 1986

Table 12.4: Household size in Querétaro between 1982–3 and 1986 according to household structure

Household structure	Household size 1982–3	1986	Percentage change
Nuclear	5.6 (8)	7.0 (6)	+25%
One-parent	5.8 (5)	4.0 (2)	−31%
Male-extended	8.6 (5)	8.1 (6)	−6%
Female-extended	11.5 (2)	8.8 (6)	−23.5%
All households/average	7.0 (20)	7.6 (20)	+8.5%

Source: Household Questionnaire Survey, Querétaro, 1986; sub-sample 1982–3 Household Survey. NB. Numbers in brackets refer to number of cases.

sample in 1982–3, rather than on the larger survey. For example, overall averages of household size, numbers of working members and so on are calculated on the basis of the 20 households in the 1986 survey in their configurations in 1982–3 to give more accurate comparisons.

Household survival strategies 1982–3–1986; the influence of household structure

Family size, numbers of workers and dependency ratios

While average family size increased from 7 to 7.6 between 1982–3 and 1986 overall, the only type of household which actually increased its membership was the nuclear unit (see Table 12.4). All other household structures actually experienced an overall decline in membership within their categories. Increased size of nuclear units was either the result of new births or because those which became extended between 1982–3 and 1986 and were thus taken out of the nuclear category in the latter period had been slightly smaller than those which remained. Conversely, in extended units decline in size is above all due to the fact that households which converted between 1982–3 and 1986 were obviously nuclear and single-parent units in the former period (see also Table 12.1). Recently extended households are somewhat inevitably smaller than those which have been extended for some time; over the years kin tend to be incorporated in an incremental manner, with births to young newly-weds and so on. However, even those households which remained extended during the

Table 12.5: Numbers of workers and dependency ratios in Querétaro according to household structure 1982–3–1986

Household structure	No. of workers 1982–3	No. of workers 1986	Dependency ratio 1982–3	Dependency ratio 1986
Nuclear	1.5	1.7	1:3.7	1:4.1
One-parent	2.0	2.0	1:2.9	1:2.0
Male-extended	2.4	3.0	1:3.6	1:2.7
Female-extended	4.0	2.2	1:2.9	1:4.0

Source: Household Questionnaire Survey, Querétaro 1986; sub-sample 1982–3 Household Survey.
N.B. Figures rounded up to nearest decimal point.

whole period also declined in size from an average of 10.3 to 9.6 members, partly as a result of deaths in a couple of instances and partly because, as already mentioned, there were a few cases where sons and daughters formed independent households of their own in the intervening years and one or two already had children, meaning that when they moved out household size dropped considerably. Single-parent households became smaller still between the two time periods, possibly because the larger ones among this group in 1982–3 (and *ipso facto* those possibly less likely to be able to rely on a single female wage) became extended by 1986.

Regarding changes in numbers of workers and dependency ratios, that is, worker: non-worker, we noted earlier that overall there had been only marginal changes. However, breaking these down by family structure we find that in single-parent units and male-headed extended households, the number of workers relative to household size has risen substantially in the group as a whole, thereby reducing dependency in these structures (see Table 12.5).

In nuclear household units on the other hand, while there was a marginal increase in workforce participation, each worker was actually supporting a greater number of dependants in 1986 than in 1982–3 (see Table 12.5). This also applied to female-headed extended households which, although having slightly lower dependency ratios than nuclear households in 1986, actually had fewer workers than in 1982–3 in both absolute and relative terms. In part this could be attributed to the fact that one male-headed extended household had become female-headed through death (automatically reducing the

Table 12.6: Mean per capita earnings in Querétaro according to household structure 1982–3–1986

Household structure	Per capita earnings 1982–3 (pesos)	Per capita earnings 1986 (pesos)	Percentage increase
Nuclear	585.6	5,022.0	758%
One-parent	579.8	9,250.0	1495%
Male-extended	516.9	6,075.0	1075%
Female-extended	387.3	5,776.0	1391%
Total	563.7	6,037.0	971%

Source: Household Questionnaire Survey, Querétaro 1986; sub-sample 1982–3 Household Survey.
* Mean per capita earnings are calculated by summing the wages of all members with an income-generating activity in the household and dividing by household size. As such, the figures show the amount of income actually generated by households on a per capita basis. This is not necessarily equivalent to the income which actually ends up in the household budget for the use and benefit of all household members.
N.B. Figures rounded up to nearest decimal point.

number of income-earners given that the woman herself had worked in the earlier period as well),[11] but it could also be due to the fact that family extension between 1982–3 and 1986 has actually arisen in female-headed units where women were already working but did not incorporate domestic assistance until fairly long after they had entered the workforce. As such, the incorporation of relatives has not actually resulted in additions to the paid household workforce, but to its unpaid reproductive element, most probably as an attempt to sustain the position of those already in employment. This helps to explain the lack of any notable deterioration in household welfare.

Household income

Indeed, considering per capita household income (earnings) it appears that female-headed extended households have not suffered from their relative rise in dependency ratios; if anything, they have improved substantially their financial position since 1982–3 (see Table 12.6).

The most interesting set of figures from Table 12.6, however, is that while nuclear households in 1992–3 were, in terms of wages per capita at least, the most well-off category of household, by 1986 they were the poorest by a substantial margin, earning only just over half that of female-headed single-parent units, and less than 90 per cent of that of female-headed extended units. These figures tend to suggest that households which have either deployed women into the labour force or extended their membership, or, as is usually the case, both, have been able to cope with recession more adequately than nuclear families. Indeed, if we recall that consumer prices rose by 981 per cent between late 1982 and 1986, then non-nuclear households have actually managed to increase their potential purchasing power between these dates, whereas each member of a nuclear unit now has only four-fifths of previous income at their potential disposal.

Another very interesting finding is that female household headship is not the apparent sentence to relative poverty that it was in the early 1980s. In terms of per capita household earnings in 1982–3, women-headed households in general, that is, extended and non-extended units, were poorer than their male counterparts, with only 90 per cent of the per capita earnings of male-headed households: 515.6 as against 571.1 pesos; but this balance has now changed. Members of women-headed units now have greater earnings per capita (6,644 pesos) than male-headed units (5,596 pesos), meaning that the situation has more or less reversed: earnings of male-headed households are only about 48 per cent of those of female-headed structures.[12] Moreover, in terms of actual disposable income, that is the amount of earnings that ends up in a pool for the benefit of the family in general, differences are even more marked. As noted in several other studies (for example Benería and Roldán, 1987; Dwyer and Bruce, 1988; Huston, 1979; Quiroz *et al.*, 1984), women tend to devote more of their wages to household use than to personal expenditure. As a result, with more women tending to work in female-headed households, disposable per capita income in male-headed units is only 67 per cent of that in female-headed households, and nuclear households alone have only 62 per cent of the average per capita income of women-headed households. In some senses then, the Mexican crisis seems to have turned the tables on male-headed households, especially nuclear structures, where women's labour power is not likely to be mobilized for the labour market and where there is often a rather arbitary sub-optimum use of household income-generating resources (see also Chant, 1984, 1985).

Women's labour-force participation in Querétaro 1982–3–1986

Before concluding this chapter, it is useful to consider briefly the major characteristics of female labour-force changes in Querétaro between the early and mid-eighties. Since slightly more female heads and spouses seem to be working than previously, and those that are working are in comparatively better-paid jobs, does this indicate that there has been some improvement of women's position in the local economy, at least relative to that of men? How can that be explained, and what implications may it have for women's position within their households?

We noted earlier that among the women in the survey there has been a tendency for female workers to move away from low-paid informal jobs such as domestic service and into a wider range of formal jobs including working for the municipality, in factories, offices and so on, albeit generally at a semi- or unskilled level. Mainly as a result of this, the gap between average female and male earnings has narrowed from a difference of 60 per cent to 42 per cent. Certainly it cannot be explained by greater parity of remuneration within the occupations traditionally held by both sexes. For example, women industrial workers in 1982–3 were earning 75 per cent of male wages, but this had dropped to 64 per cent by 1986,[13] and in self-employment, that is home-based commerce, production and so on, men were still earning two to three times as much as women in the latter period. Nor can it be explained by a rise in earnings within exclusively female activities such as domestic service; pay here was still only about one-third of that in formal employment. Thus, the relative rise of women's earnings in general has to be accounted for by their movement into new areas of work, rather than an increase in wages or occupational status in their traditional and/or former branches of employment.

However, explaining these changes in women's labour-force participation in the space of three to four years of economic recession is extremely difficult, not least because of the small size of the sample. One attempt, for low-income women in Mexico City, has been made by Lourdes Benería and Martha Roldán (1987:49) who have noted similar tendencies in female employment in the course of the 1980s. They argue that increased movement of women into the workforce can be attributed to two main sets of factors, classified respectively as supply and demand, on the premiss that it is not only economic need within households which has prompted women's labour-force participation in the last few years, here designated as a supply factor, but also the requirements of the wider economy. The two crucial demand factors identified by Benería and Roldán are, first, that employers facing declining profits need to exploit cheaper sources of labour to reduce wage costs; the employment of women is particularly relevant to the expansion of labour-intensive *maquila* (assembly) production carried out in the home on contract from large firms; second, that the widespread recruitment of women in multinational enterprises, both in Mexico and elsewhere, is beginning to have a trickle-down effect in the sense that Mexican employers are now beginning to imitate the example of their foreign counterparts (ibid).

On the supply side, the two most important factors identified by Benería and Roldán in releasing women into the labour force are first, that women's work outside the home is becoming more acceptable generally, although the authors do not really provide an explanation. Most probably, it is a knock-on effect from their second designated supply factor, namely, that in the course of the recession, women's income has become an increasingly vital component of household survival strategies. Although their discussion revolves mainly around homeworking they do stress that there is no reason to believe that the same strategy does not apply to work outside of the home (ibid:49).

Although Benería and Roldán are undoubtedly correct in identifying household economic needs as critical in explaining rising numbers of female household members in the labour force, it is also important to note this so-called supply factor is very much exogenously determined; were it not for economic recession at a national level, would the supply of female workers necessarily be the same? Moreover, with respect to their point about the relaxation of traditional mores surrounding the labour-force participation of married women, to what extent is this aspect of social change an inevitable response to strategies designed by households to accommodate more pressing financial stringency – again largely shaped by national crisis? In other words, Benería and Roldán's attribution of the above two processes to the supply side of the labour market may not be entirely appropriate. This apart, the evidence from Querétaro suggests that other supply factors, whose origins are perhaps less easily attributed to external circumstances, are essential in determining the relative success of individual households in riding out the crisis, especially that of household structure.[14] In Querétaro certainly, rising numbers of extended units have undoubtedly in some cases facilitated and in others been prompted by an upward trend in women's employment, although other elements obviously come into this.

For instance, although women's move into the labour force is often a catalyst of household change, the crisis has also given rise to modifications in household structure for other reasons; the fact that just over one-third of households in the sample became extended between 1982–3 and 1986 is not due to women's labour-force participation alone. One such reason is an all-round increase in poverty and the necessity and/or desirability for low-income people to pool resources. In Socorro's case, for example, her father was too old and too poor to continue to live alone and thus needed to come and live with his daughter, even if at the same time his incorporation within the household has allowed her to move into a full-time formal sector job, thereby boosting family income. The rise in household extension, then, is to some extent motivated by the poor's need to join forces in times of increased hardship. Indeed, only one household in the entire sample reverted to a nuclear form from an extended unit; and the only other household which became nuclear was a former one-parent unit where a widow had remarried (see also Table 12.1).

However, in addition to the fact that household extension has been very important in pushing women into new types of work, whether by design or default, a small niche has certainly also been opened up at the level of demand through the state government's equal opportunities programme in public services. So far this phenomenon does not seem to have extended to the private sector in Querétaro. Benería and Roldán argued that firms would increasingly take on women as a means of keeping wage costs low, and indeed the small amount of evidence on industrial pay in Querétaro suggests that remuneration of women workers has fallen behind that of men in the period 1982–3–1986. None the less, there are no major signs yet of a generalized feminization of Querétaro's workforce, a fact borne out by a survey of industrial employers conducted by the author in 1986, where on average only 21.7 per cent of the workforce in 14 manufacturing firms was female, compared with a figure of 28.3 per cent (as per the census) for the city as a whole (see Chant, 1991). In part the lack of any notable increase of women working in and/or for factories may be due to differences in industrial structure between the cities: in Mexico City, which has a wide range of industries, many of which are labour-intensive, women tend to be taken on increasingly as homeworkers, whereas the more restricted range of industrial establishments in Querétaro, predominantly large-scale, capital-intensive manufacturing plants, is perhaps less likely to lend itself to domestic sub-contracting or piecework arrangements, which tend to use female labour.

Aside from state policy, then, there are few employer-related demand factors in evidence to explain women's changing work patterns in Querétaro. Women in this city still have more restricted access to formal sector jobs than men, and their general position within the employment hierarchy does not seem to have altered substantially; although they are now employed in increasing numbers by the public sector, roadsweeping is still a very low-grade occupation. It is also important to note, however, that it is not only formal employment which accounts for higher wages; some self-employed women with substantial, long-standing and/or regular businesses, for example their own shop or catering enterprise, are making quite reasonable incomes.

In accounting for women's greater involvement and remuneration in Querétaro my main conclusion on the basis of the evidence is that the women are pushing themselves, and various members of their household, harder in order to cope with economic crisis; poor women acting on their own account are the main architects of observed changes in work patterns, rather than any substantial shift at the level of demand. One of the most effective ways for women to cushion their families against recession is to enter the labour market personally; there is obviously more scope to control one's own income than to commandeer the wages of another. In order to do this, women not only appear to be looking harder for full-time employment and/or putting several hours into their own business, but also, and in order to best achieve this, exploiting existing reserves of reproductive labour within the household unit, for example using daughters and/or sons for domestic work, or, and to make domestic arrangements run smoother still, absorbing the labour power of kin and extending their households.

Conclusions and implications

In conclusion, the mobilization of women's earning capacity, generally through a change in household structure or the use of extant reproductive resources within the domestic unit, normally daughters, appears to be one of the critical strategies developed to shield families from the more deleterious effects of Mexican economic recession in the early to mid-1980s, notwithstanding that several households recognized that obviously no matter what they did they could not solve the national crisis through their own efforts alone. Many were acutely aware that major improvements in their situation would not come about unless significant measures were taken by the state over national debt, political corruption, the diversion of public funds into overseas private bank accounts, and the amount of the nation's trade and industry under multinational control. As such most respondents realized that the crisis could not be overcome indefinitely by a unilateral mobilization of resources at the household level, even if they had done their utmost to maximize earning power.

Having said this, shifts in women's workforce involvement and flexible approaches to household composition have served some households quite well, with most success apparent where households have not only maintained or encouraged women's labour-force participation but also moved away from a restrictive nuclear family model. The association between female labour-force participation and the de-nuclearization of household units in Querétaro has been more than incidental and confirms the existence of very fundamental links (see also Chant, 1991). In the absence of evidence to support the idea that growth and change in female work are derived primarily from the needs of Querétaro's employers during the crisis, with the possible exception of the state and municipal government, one is left to conclude that this is owed to low-income women themselves, who have pushed further towards the front-line against poverty in the city via a considerable restructuring of household labour-supply patterns. The immediate consequences of this trend appear to be that those households exploiting the earning potential of adult women are best able, in a material sense at least, to face up to crisis. Indeed female heads of household, who have had traditionally greater freedom to move into areas of work prohibited to women with male partners, now appear to have overtaken the earning levels of their male counterparts. However, what the longer-term and/or non-material consequences might be are open to question. In concluding, therefore, I would like to raise a series of points relating to the likely implications of observed shifts in survival strategies for low-income households and especially their female members in Mexico in the 1990s.

- Recession was identified by some women as having brought with it a series of personal benefits. This was especially true of women who had entered the labour force for the first time since marriage or their first child, as a result of economic crisis. While in 1982–3, as mentioned earlier, men tended to resist letting their wives out to work, this resistance seems to have eroded quite substantially in the relatively short period up to 1986. Going out to work was regarded in some respects as a triumph in terms of gaining personal independence and reducing reliance on men, as well as contributing to a greater sense of purpose, power and status within the household, and enabling greater influence and control over household expenditure. Moreover, despite the fact that few women had been able to abandon their domestic duties entirely, they felt freer than they had done and welcomed the break in routine provided by a job, especially where most of the housework could be passed into the capable hands of adult female kin. Those women whose entry into the workforce had been eased by extension of the household unit were the most positive about work, appreciating not only the practical assistance provided by female kin, but also the company of other adults in the home. This is not to say, however, that the transition to greater female labour-force participation was necessarily smooth. In most cases women had still had to ask their husbands for permission, and husbands were not keen on their wives working in environments where men were also working. Some men still displayed a staunch resistance to the question of any type of female employment. Doña Lupe, for example, mentioned that both her husband and son refused categorically to let either her or her daughter-in-law work. Whenever the women ventured to suggest that they might do something, even in the home, to make a little money, the response was an indignant *Qué es lo que les hace falta?* (What is it you need?), as if the men were not providing enough. Lupe felt that many men still did not want their wives to work because it made them feel less like men (*se sienten menos hombres*). Having said this, for a number of women economic hardship had opened doors to increased personal status and better relationships with their partners. At the same time, however, while positive trends in female labour-force participation and current shifts towards more flexible household structures may in some respects be making for a more egalitarian division of labour and allocation of power and status between the sexes, it must also be recognized that this may not necessarily endure into the next generation. In certain households, particularly nuclear units, women's labour-force participation has only been accommodated by passing the burden of domestic labour and childcare on to daughters. Older daughters in particular may be cast prematurely into full-time domestic and mothering roles which have serious implications for their own futures. Research carried out by the author in León and Puerto Vallarta (Chant, 1991), by González de la Rocha (1988) in Guadalajara and by Moser (1989) in Guayaquil, would seem to indicate that older daughters may have to neglect their education or even leave school altogether in order to cope with increased loads of domestic work. With less education and job experience, it is entirely conceivable that young women may be seriously disadvantaged in the labour market in future and accordingly have no option other than to comply with more traditional roles when they form their own households. In this respect, potential for substantial shifts in gender roles and relations among the poor in Mexico may be rather limited. A key task of future research will be to examine what happens to these young women, and their own daughters and granddaughters.

Another related point here is that even in extended households, where daughters tend to be spared domestic responsibilities through their being taken on by female kin, the fact is that it tends almost invariably only to be female kin who assume the conventional tasks of the female head or spouse. Although some men take on a little domestic labour when their wives go out to work, and boys often do so in non-extended one-parent units, on the whole the primary responsibility for reproductive tasks is still seen to lie with women.

- While it appears that some women in Querétaro have managed to move into better-paid, more formal jobs, these still seem to be of lower status and to be lower paid than men's. Regarding the state programme of equal opportunities for women and the corresponding rise in female recruitment in the public sector, the general feeling was that this was tokenism, meaning no real improvement in women's general access to work, range of employment, pay or job status. Indeed many non-working women commented that without education they could still probably do no better than get jobs as domestic servants and consequently there was little point in going out to work. Inequality of access to jobs also tends to signal a continued, if reluctant, reliance on male income. Socorro, for example, despite having secured work with the muncipality, still felt it might be worthwhile to accept an offer of marriage from a widower, Alejandro, for whom she had little real affection. At the time of the last interview, she was actively weighing up the material benefits of entering a union which would mean her eldest son could continue studying and the family would at long last have a stereo, colour television and so on, goals that she could not possibly hope to meet through her own efforts. Although women's employment opportunities may well expand in the light of current economic programmes in Mexico that include opening up the economy to greater foreign investment, especially in the sphere of multinational in-bond manufacturing production (the *maquiladora* sector), this will undoubtedly only occur at the expense of their continued existence as a more exploitable source of labour accepting low wages for high productivity in monotonous un- or semi-skilled assembly jobs. As such, gender inequalities in employment are unlikely to disappear, even if growth in jobs means that more women have access to an independent source of income.

- While the crisis years have witnessed a de-nuclearization of household units, there is still very much in evidence a normative ideal of nuclear households. Single parents are often shunned by neighbours as moral deviants and extended households viewed as lacking the resources to establish independent homes. Nuclear households are, of course, those which most readily lend themselves to a sexual division of labour consonant with patriarchal norms of male breadwinner–female housewife (Chant, 1985, 1991). Nevertheless, with the increasing formation of non-nuclear units, especially those proving more economically viable than conventional nuclear families, it may be possible that such households will become less stigmatized in social terms, and along with that bring about greater acceptance of flexibility in gender roles and relations. This apart, household structure is of course an inherently dynamic entity through its association with the life-cycle, and it will be interesting to see whether households choose, or indeed are able, to retain a broad-based extended membership in the next ten years or so. Further longitudinal research on this front would be extremely useful.
- Households in the course of the recession have used progressively more of their own resources to combat increased structural poverty. The success of the poor in riding out the crisis has been due largely to efforts from the bottom up, and scope for further stretching of household labour supply is undoubtedly limited, just as Caroline Moser (1989:159) has noted that there is only so much more work women in Guayaquil can take on in the home, the workplace and in the wider community in order to keep increased poverty from

the door. Moreover, as González de la Rocha (1988:220) has argued, if the current administration is unable to sustain full economic recovery, the next group of members to be plucked out of the home and sent to work will be adolescent daughters. What this implies for the satisfactory execution of essential reproductive household tasks is potentially critical. If there is no one capable of looking after jobs in the home on an adequate and/or full-time basis anymore, it is difficult to imagine how households will experience anything but the crudest and most vulnerable existence. It must also be noted that since young girls, especially those with limited education, are likely to earn least in terms of wages, more household members may be pushed into the labour force over time with ever-diminishing returns, a fact already evident in Querétaro, with women earning less than men but still being counted on to provide an indispensable source of family income. At some point, then, the buck must stop. The key question for the future is at what point a line may be drawn where poor households shift efforts away from exploiting their own resources to demanding that the state provide them with more satisfactory and dignified means of survival.

Notes

1. The research for this chapter is based on two periods of fieldwork in Mexico in 1982–3 and 1986. The earlier fieldwork was carried out as part of a doctoral research programme on women, housing and family structure in Querétaro funded by an ESRC postgraduate studentship linked to the ODA-financed research project directed by Drs Alan Gilbert and Peter Ward in the Department of Geography, University College, London, entitled 'Public intervention, housing and land use in Latin American cities'. The second piece of fieldwork was undertaken as part of a wider comparative project on urban labour markets, women's work and low-income households in Puerto Vallarta, León and Querétaro funded by a Leverhulme Trust Study Abroad Studentship. In the earlier project, interviews were held with 244 low-income households in Querétaro (see Chant, 1984); in the latter, 20 households from the earlier survey were retraced and interviewed in-depth to discover changes that had occurred over three-and-a-half years of economic crisis. Further information about the projects and fuller discussion of the issues covered in the chapter may be found in Chant (1991). An earlier version of this chapter was presented as part of the Mexico seminar series at the Institute of Latin American Studies, University of London, 9 May 1990.
2. In 1982–3, 58 per cent of the 244 women households heads and spouses in the Querétaro survey were recorded as migrants.

3. 'Irregular settlements' are areas of self-help housing in which initial occupation of land is illegal. They generally house low-income people, are the most common form of popular housing in Mexico and may be classified into three main types:

   - Squatter settlements, which arise out of invasion of either public or private land.
   - Low-income or clandestine subdivisions, where land is sold off illegally for residential development by owners or agents who not only lack planning permission but who also fail to provide official minimum levels of services and infrastructure.
   - *Ejidal* urban settlements, where agricultural communities on state-owned land sell plots to urban settlers with no entitlement to do so. Tenure is awarded to the urban inhabitants once a presidential decree makes possible expropriation.

   Regarding the communities selected for the present study, Bolaños and Las Américas fit this last category of settlement. Los Andadores on the other hand was an illegal subdivision promoted by government officials for personal political and pecuniary motives (see Map 12.2).
4. González de la Rocha (1988:212) defines extended households as those which consist of one conjugal unit and additional members which do not constitute a second conjugal unit, and multiple households as those consisting of two or more conjugal units.
5. For clarification, the term 'household survival strategies' refers broadly to the ways in which low-income households organize their production and consumption activites in order to guarantee the maintenance of members. The term 'livelihood strategies' is also used (e.g. Clarke, 1986; Radcliffe, 1986). Sarah Radcliffe (1986:30) defines household livelihood strategies as the 'decisions, actions and goals of household members which ensure their reproduction'. Another term is 'household work strategy', defined by Ray Pahl (1984:20) in connection with his discussion of pre-industrial households in England as a method for making 'the best use of resources for getting by under given social and economic conditions'. However, Gerry Rodgers (1989:20) cautions against indiscriminate use of the term strategy, especially in situations of economic crisis, observing that: 'the term strategy may itself be misleading, implying a well-worked out plan for the allocation of family labour resources. While this may sometimes be accurate, it is probable that the strategy will more often consist of attempts to obtain additional income by any means available'.

   'Women's work' here refers to income-generating activity, notwithstanding that non-remunerated labour carried out by women in the home should also be recognized as work. 'Household structure' is a term which embraces two major constituents of household form: sex of the household head and household composition. Sex of the household head refers to whether the position of head of the family unit is occupied by a woman or a man. The convention used in the present study is that all households headed by couples are male-headed and only those where women do not have a resident male partner as a result of divorce, separation, widowhood and so on, as female-headed. Household composition describes whether membership of the family unit consists of parent(s) and children or other types of relative as well, such as sisters, aunts and cousins. In Querétaro the four most common types of household unit, and those included in the survey are:

- Nuclear families (male-headed): couple and their children.
- One-parent families (female-headed): mother without partner and children.
- Male-headed extended families: core nuclear unit with additional relatives, for example, in-laws, siblings of head or spouse living in household on same basis as parents and children, that is, sharing living expenses, eating together and so on, as distinct from nuclear-compound households where shared residence does not include shared consumption (see Brydon and Chant, 1989:136–7).
- Female-headed extended families: core one-parent unit and additional relatives, as in male-headed unit.

6. The sub-sample selected for the 1986 survey in Querétaro was based on slightly different proportions of the four main types of unit represented in the 1982–3 questionnaire survey. In 1982–3, 68.5 per cent of households were nuclear, 9 per cent one-parent units, 18 per cent male-headed extended and 4.5 per cent female-extended (see Chant, 1984). Selection of households for the 1986 survey was made to accord broadly with these relative proportions of different structures as they were in 1982–3, but in order to compensate for small sample size it was necessary to include greater percentages of less common household types, such as female-headed extended and one-parent units (see Table 12.2); as it was, several households had changed structure anyway.
7. Establishing and analysing the nature of linkages between changes in women's labour-force participation and household structure is inevitably problematic. Although in many instances explicit aknowledgement of links was made by interviewees, and a relatively short space of time elapsed between women's entry into the workforce and change in household structure (less than 12 months for example), it is rare that there is only one factor involved in accounting for change in either variable.
8. Laura is not counted as a worker in the 1986 sample generally because she was only helping out on a very occasional basis, besides receiving no remuneration. However, her example still provides a useful point of reference, especially as she intends to play a larger part in the family business in the future.
9. In addition to the value of having a full-time houseworker to execute the reproductive tasks of so many income generators, it is also likely that Lupe's son did not want to leave his mother. Many elder sons in female-headed households feel it is their duty to support the family. As such it is likely that Lupe's daughter-in-law was incorporated for a combination of reasons, including the fact that it meant her husband could remain with his mother.

10. The average size of this particular group of extended households is 11.3 persons with a mean of 3.3 working members.
11. Inevitably small sample size inflates the significance of such changes.
12. It is interesting that data presented in Molly Pollack's study of urban poverty in Costa Rica between 1971 and 1982 show that women-headed households here have also tended to improve their position relative to male-headed units among the poorest classes. Notwithstanding an overall decline in women-headed units from 20.2 per cent to 15.7 per cent of the national total during the period under consideration and that the former are generally more prevalent among the poor, in 1971 male-headed units constituted 52.8 per cent of destitute households in Costa Rica, and women-headed households 47.2 per cent, whereas by 1982 women were only 37.1 per cent of this category, and men 62.9 per cent. In poor households (those classed as an intermediate group between the destitute and non-poor) similar trends occurred, with women-headed households here falling from 24.7 per cent to 17.7 per cent of the total and male-headed households rising from 75.3 per cent to 82.3 per cent. Thus although the proportion of women-headed units in non-poor households also declined from 18.1 per cent to 13.8 per cent in the same period and men increased their share in this latter category from 81.9 per cent to 86.2 per cent, relatively speaking the increase of the latter in the best-off group was small (+5 per cent) compared with that of +10 per cent in destitute groups and +7 per cent in poor households.
13. Figures for gender differences in earnings in 1982–3 are drawn from the wider questionnaire survey of 244 households. The appearance of a closing gap may again be due partly to the very small size of the sample in 1986. Comparisons between weekly earnings of female and male industrial workers in 1986 are made on the basis of only one woman and two men. However, data gathered from a survey of employers in Querétaro bear out the fact that women factory workers almost invariably have lower average wage levels then men, partly as a result of segregation into unskilled and/or low-status jobs (see Chant, 1991: Ch. 3).
14. Benería and Roldán (1987) do in fact identify in another part of their book the way in which certain kinds of family unit facilitate the labour-force participation of women, noting for example that in young extended households 'counting on help from resident adult relatives for housework and industrial homework was fundamental in the work strategies of the majority of wives' (ibid.:31). They also go on to identify that degrees of assistance depend on a whole series of more specific factors, such as the sex of the kin in question, whether the relative(s) are from the wife's or husband's side of the family, reasons for co-residence and so on. Male relatives on the husband's side, for example, tend not to take on any domestic activities at all, whereas sisters, aunts and mothers do. However, the authors do not discuss at any length the general effects exerted by household structure as a major supply variable, and to what extent household structure undergoes modification as a result of women's entry into the workforce.

BIBLIOGRAPHY

Aguilar, Adrián Guillermo (1988) 'Community participation in Mexico City: a case study', *Bulletin of Latin American Research*, 7, 1: 33–46.

Aguilar-Barajas, Ismael and Spence, Nigel (1988) 'Industrial decentralisation and regional policy' in Philip, George (ed.) *The Mexican Economy*: 183–228.

Aguilar Camín, Héctor (1988) *Después del milagro*, Mexico: Cal y Arena.

——(1989) 'Lectura de la democracia mexicana', interview with José Agustín Ortiz Pinchetti, *Nexos*, 137 (May): 27–36.

Aguilar Valenzuela, Rubén and Zermeño Padilla, Guillermo (1989) 'De movimiento social a partido político. De la UNS al PDM' in Alonso, J. *El PDM. Movimiento regional*, Guadalajara: Universidad de Guadalajara.

Alduncín Abitia, E. (1989) *Expectativas económicas de los líderes empresariales*, Mexico: Banco Nacional de México.

Alonso, A. and López, C. R. (1985) 'El sindicato de trabajadores petroleros y sus relaciones con el Estado, 1970–1985', México: El Colegio de México.

Alonso, J. (ed.) (1980) *Lucha urbana y acumulación de capital*, Mexico: Ediciones de la Casa Chata.

Altshuler, Alan *et al.* (1988) *The future of the automobile*, *Report of the MIT International Automobile Programme*, London: Allen & Unwin.

Angel, S. (1983) 'Land tenure for the urban poor' in S. Angel, R. W. Archer, S. Tanphiphat and E. A. Wegelin (eds) *Land for Housing the Poor*, Singapore: Select Books: 110–42.

Anguiano, Arturo (1975) *El estado y la política obrera del cardenismo*, Mexico City: Era.

Ankerson, Dudley (1984) *Agrarian Warlord. Saturnino Cedillo and the Mexican Revolution in San Luis Potosí*, DeHalb: Northern Illinois University Press.

Arreola Ayala, Alvaro (1985) 'Atlacomulco: la antesala del poder' in Martínez Assad, C. (coord.) *Municipios en conflicto*: 75–132.

Arroyo Alejandre, Jesús (1986) 'Emigración rural de fuerza de trabajo en el occidente-centro de México: una contribución de información básica para su análisis', *Cuadernos de difusión científica*, 6, Guadalajara: Universidad de Guadalajara.

Arteaga, A. (1985) 'Innovación tecnológica y clase obrera en la industria automotriz' in Gutiérrez Garza, E. *Reestructuración productiva y clase obrera*, Mexico: Siglo XXI/UNAM.

Aziz Nassif, Alberto (1985) 'La coyuntura de las elecciones en Chihuahua' in Martínez Assad, C. (coord.) *Municipios en conflicto*.

Azuela, A. (1983) 'La legislación del suelo urbano: ¿ auge o crisis?' in Sociedad Interamericana de Planificación (ed.) *Relación Campo-Ciudad: La Tierra, Recurso Estratégico para el Desarrollo y la Transformación Social*, Mexico: Ediciones SIAP: 514–31.

——(1989a) 'El significado jurídico de la planeación urbana en México. Diez años de legislación' in Garza, Gustavo (ed.) *Una década de planeación urbano regional en México, 1978–1988*, Mexico: El Colegio de México.

——(1989b) *La Ciudad, la Propiedad Privada y el Derecho*, Mexico: El Colegio de México.

——and Cruz Rodríguez, M. S. (1989) 'La industrialización de las colonias populares y la política urbana del DDF, 1940–1946', *Sociológica* 9.

Bailey, John, Dresser, Denise and Gómez, Leopoldo (1990) 'Balance preliminar de la XIV Asamblea del PRI', *Perfil de la Jornada*, 26 September.

Banco de México (1989) *Boletín de Economía Internacional*, XV/1, (January–March), Mexico City.

——(1990) *The Mexican Economy in 1990. Economic and Financial Developments in 1989: Policies for 1990*, Mexico City.

Barberán, José, Cárdenas, Cuauhtémoc, López Monjardín, Adriana and Zavala, Jorge (1988) *Radiografía del fraude: análisis de los datos oficiales del 6 de Julio*, Mexico: Editorial Nuestro Tiempo.

Barkin, David (1987) 'The end to food self-sufficiency in Mexico', *Latin American Perspectives*, 14, 3: 271–97.

Bartra, Armando (1985) *Los herederos de Zapata: movimientos campesinos posrevolucionarios en México*, Mexico: Ediciones Era.

——(1989) 'Prólogo al libro de Gustavo Gordillo: Estado, mercados y movimiento campesino', *Pueblo*, Year 12, 144/5, (May–June): 25–30.

——(1990) 'La organización de productores rurales como una alternativa de poder regional', paper given at the conference on 'People, State and Nation in Mexico', University of Texas at Austin, (April).

Bartra, Roger (1989) 'Changes in political culture: the crisis of nationalism' in Cornelius, Gentleman and Smith (eds) *Mexico's Alternative Political Futures*.

Benería, Lourdes and Roldán, Martha (1987) *The Crossroads of Class and Gender: Industrial Homework, Subcontracting and Household Dynamics in Mexico City*, Chicago: University of Chicago Press.

Benítez, F. (1975) *Viaje al Centro de México*, Mexico: Fondo de Cultura Económica.

Benjamin, Thomas (1989) *A Rich Land, A Poor People. Politics and Society in Modern Chiapas*, Albuquerque: University of New Mexico Press.

Bennett, Douglas C., and Sharpe, Kenneth E., (1985) *Transnational Corporations Versus the State. The Political Economy of the Mexican Auto Industry*, Princeton: Princeton University Press.

Best, Edward (1987) *US Policy and Regional Security in Latin America*, London: International Institute of Strategic Studies.

Bizberg, Ilán (1986) *La clase obrera mexicana*, Mexico: SEP.

——(1990) *Estado y Sindicalismo en México*, Mexico: El Colegio de México.

Blackhurst , Richard, Marian, Nicholas and Tumlir, Jan (1977) *Trade Liberalization, Protectionism and Interdependence*, GATT Studies in International Trade, 5, Geneva.

Bortz, Jeffrey (1988) *El salario en México*, Mexico: Fondo de Cultura Económica.

Brydon, Lynne and Chant, Sylvia (1989) *Women in the Third World: Gender Issues in Rural and Urban Areas*, New Jersey: Rutgers University Press/Aldershot: Edward Elgar.

Buchanan, J. M. *et al.* (1980) *Toward a Theory of the Rent-seeking Society*, Texas: A & M University.

Buci-Glucksmann, Christine (1978) *Gramsci y el Estado (hacia una teoría materialista de la filosofía)*, Mexico: Siglo XXI.

Buzan, Barry (1983) *Peoples, States and Fear. The National Security Problem in International Relations*, London: Harvester Wheatsheaf.

Calderón Cockburn, J. (1987) 'Luchas por la tierra, contradicciones sociales y sistema político. El caso de las zonas ejidales y comunales en la Ciudad de México (1980–1984)', *Estudios Demográficos y Urbanos*, 2: 301–24.2

Cammack, Paul (1988) 'The "Brazilianization" of Mexico?' *Government and Opposition*, 23, 3 (summer): 304–20.

Cardoso, F., and Faletto, E. (1969) *Dependencia y Desarrollo en América Latina*, Mexico: Siglo XXI Editores.

Carmona Amorós, Salvador (1982) 'Comentario' in *Perspectivas del sistema político mexicano*, Mexico: CEN del PRI: 40–43.

Carrillo, J. and García, P. (1987) 'Etapas industriales y conflictos laborales: la industria automotriz en México', *Estudios Sociológicos*, 14 (May–August).

Castañeda, Jorge (1990) 'Salinas' international relations gamble', *Journal of International Affairs*, 43, 2, (winter) : 407–22.

Castells, Manuel (1977) 'Marginalité urbaine et mouvements sociaux au Mexique: le mouvement des "posesionarios" dans la ville de Monterrey', *International Journal of Urban and Regional Research*, 1: 145–50.

——(1982) 'Squatters and politics in Latin America: a comparative analysis of urban social movements in Chile, Peru and Mexico' in H. Safa (ed.) *Towards a Political Economy of Urbanization in Third World Countries*, Delhi: Oxford University Press: 249–82.

Castillo, J. (1986) 'El movimiento urbano popular en Puebla' in Castillo, J. (ed.) *Los movimientos sociales en Puebla II*, Universidad Autónoma de Puebla, Departamento de Investigaciones Arquitectónicas y Urbanísticas, Instituto de Ciencias (DIAU–ICUAP): 201–360.

Castro Martínez, Pedro (1990) 'México y la política comercial estadunidense 1982–1988', *Foro Internacional*, 30, (January–March): 481–96.

Cawson, A. *et al.* (1990) *Hostile Brothers: Competition and Closure in the European Electronics Industry*, Oxford: Clarendon Press.

Centro de Derechos Humanos 'Fray Francisco de Vitoria' (1990) Informe sobre los derechos humanos en México. Periodo: diciembre 1989–noviembre 1990', Mexico City.

——'Miguel A. Pro' (1990) 'Informe sobre derechos humanos, 1989', *Christus* (Mexico City), 634 (April): 45–57.

Chabat, Jorge (1990) 'Los instrumentos de la política exterior de Miguel de la Madrid', *Foro Internacional*, 30 (January–March): 398–418.

Chant, Sylvia (1984) '"Las Olvidadas": a study of women, housing and family structure in Querétaro, Mexico', Ph.D dissertation, Department of Geography, University College London.

——(1985) 'Family formation and female roles in Querétaro, Mexico', *Bulletin of Latin American Research*, 4, 1: 17–32.

——(1987) 'Family structure and female labour in Querétaro, Mexico' in Momsen, Janet and Townsend, Janet (eds) *Geography of Gender in the Third World*, London: Hutchinson: 277–93.

——(1991) *Women and Survival in Mexican Cities: Perspectives on Gender, Labour Markets and Low-income Households*, Manchester: Manchester University Press.

Chesneau, Jean (1988) 'La modernité-monde', *Les Temps Moderns*, 43, 503 (June): 63–77.

CIA, Directorate of Intelligence (1989) *OECD Trade with Mexico and Central America*, US Government, Washington.

Clarke, Colin (1986) 'Livelihood systems, settlements and levels of living in "Los Valles Centrales de Oaxaca", Mexico', Research Paper 37, School of Geography, University of Oxford.

Colmenares Páramo, David (1990) 'Los cambios en la economía mundial y su impacto sobre la economía mexicana' in Alzati, Fausto (coord.), *México en la economía internacional: ensayos sobre la modernidad nacional*, Mexico City: Diana, 77–111.

Comisión Mexicana de Defensa y Promoción de Derechos Humanos, AC (1990) 'Casos representativos de presuntas violaciones a los derechos humanos en México (julio 1988–febrero 1990)', Mexico City.

Concha Malo, Miguel *et al.* (1986) *La participación de los cristianos en el proceso popular de liberación en México*, Mexico: Siglo XXI.

Contreras, Ariel José (1985) *Mexico 1940: industrialización y crisis política*, Mexico: Siglo XXI.

COPEVI (Centro Operacional de Vivienda y Poblamiento) (1977a) *Investigación sobre Vivienda II: la producción de vivienda en la Zona Metropolitana de la Ciudad de México*, Mexico: COPEVI.

——(1977b) *Investigación sobre Vivienda III: las políticas habitacionales del estado mexicano*, Mexico: COPEVI.

Cordera, Rolando (1989) 'Los dolores del ajuste', *Cuadernos de Nexos*, 9 (in *Nexos*, 136) (April): 3.

——and Tello, Carlos (1981) *México: la disputa por la nación*, Mexico: Siglo XXI.

Córdova, Arnaldo (1973) *La ideología de la Revolución mexicana: la formación del nuevo régimen*, Mexico: Ediciones Era.

Cornelius, Wayne (1975) *Politics and the Migrant Poor in Mexico City*, Stanford: Stanford University Press.

——(1988) 'Las relaciones de Estados Unidos con México: fuentes de su deterioro, 1986–87', *Foro Internacional*, 29 (October–December).

——Gentleman, Judith and Smith, Peter (eds.) (1989) *Mexico's Alternative Political Futures*, La Jolla: Center for US-Mexican Studies.

——(1989) 'The dynamics of political change in Mexico' in Cornelius, Gentleman and Smith (eds) *Mexico's Alternative Political Futures*.

CORETT (Comisión para la Regularización de la Tenencia de la Tierra) (nd) *CORETT y los Vecinos*, Mexico: CORETT.

Cotteret, Jean Marie and Emeri, Claude (1973) *Los sistemas electorales*, Barcelona: Oikos Tau.

Craig, Ann (1983) *The First Agraristas: An oral history of a Mexican agrarian reform movement*, Berkeley: University of California Press.

Cruz Bencomo, M. A. (1989) 'El quinismo, una historia del charrismo petrolero', *El Cotidiano*, 28 (March–April).

de la Garza Toledo, Enrique (1988) *Ascenso y crisis del estado burocrático autoritario*, Mexico: El Colegio de México.

——(1989) *La crisis del corporativismo en México*, Mexico: Fundación Friedrich Ebert.

de la Peña, Guillermo (1988) 'Movimientos sociales, intermediación política y poder local', paper presented to 46th International Congress of Americanists, Amsterdam (July).

Departamento de Servicios de Teleinformática (1987) Informe sobre la prestación de servicios de valor agregado proporcionados en el extranjero através de las redes públicas de datos que se encuentran interconectados con Telepac de México (February).

DGT (1985) 'Programa de Desarrollo Integral de la Telegrafía', (December).

——(1988a) 'Evaluación del Programa Nacional de Comunicaciones, 1984–8', (January).

——(1988b) 'Programa Omega: documento para discusión', (February).

di Palma, and Whitehead, Laurence (1986) (eds) *The Central American Impasse*, London: Croom Helm.

Doebele, W. (1978) 'Selected issues in urban land tenure' in H. B. Dunkerley (ed.) *Urban Land Policy: Issues and Opportunities*, Washington: World Bank and Oxford University Press: 63–110.

——(1983) 'The provision of land for the urban poor: concepts, instruments and prospects' in S. Angel, R. W. Archer, S. Tanphiphat and E. A. Wegelin (eds) *Land for Housing the Poor*, Singapore: Select Books: 350–74.

Dombois, R. (1986) 'La empresa transnacional – nivelador transnacional de condiciones de trabajo', paper presented at the International Conference on Qualification and Change in Enterprise, Landesinstitut Sozialforschungsstelle, Dortmund.

Dornbusch, Rudiger (1988) 'Mexico, stabilisation, debt and growth', *Economic Policy*, (October): 231–83.

——(1990) 'Mexico's economy at the crossroads', *Journal of International Affairs*, 43, 2 (winter): 313–26.

Drancourt, M. (1989) *L'économie volontaire*, Paris: Odile Jacob.

Drucker, Peter (1986) 'Dramatic changes in the world economy', *Foreign Affairs* (spring).

Durand, J. (1983) *La Ciudad Invade al Ejido*, Mexico: Ediciones de la Casa Chata.

Dwyer, Daisy and Bruce, Judith (eds) (1988) *A Home Divided: Women and Income in the Third World*, Stanford: Stanford University Press.

Eckstein, Susan (1988) *The Poverty of Revolution: the State and the Urban Poor in Mexico*, Princeton: Princeton University Press.

——(1990) 'Formal versus substantive democracy: poor people's politics in Mexico City', *Mexican Studies/Estudios Mexicanos*, 6, 2 (summer): 213–39.

Enríquez, R. (1988) 'The rise and collapse of stabilising development' in Philip, George (ed.) *The Mexican Economy*, London: Routledge: 7–40.

Esponda de Torres, Blanca (1982) 'Comentario' in *Perspectivas del sistema político mexicano*, Mexico: CEN del PRI: 27–30.

Equipo Pueblo (1986) *Llegó la hora de ser gobierno*, Mexico: Equipo Pueblo.

Escobar, S. D. (1987) 'Rifts in the Mexican power elite' in Maxfield and Anzaldúa (eds) *Government and the private sector in contemporary Mexico*, La Jolla: Center for US–Mexican Studies, UCSD: 65–88.

Esteinou, J. (1988) 'The Morelos satellite and its impact on Mexican society', *Media, Culture and Society*, 10.

Ethier, Diane (1990) 'Introduction: processes of transition and democratic consolidation: theoretical indicators' in Ethier, D. (ed.) *Democratic Transition and consolidation in Southern Europe, Latin America and Southeast Asia*, London: Macmillan: 3–21.

Fagen, Richard and Tuohy, William (1972) *Politics and Privilege in a Mexican City*, Stanford: Stanford University Press.

Falcón, Romana (1984) *Revolución y Caciquismo en San Luis Potosí, 1910–1938*, Mexico: El Colegio de México.

Foweraker, Joe and Craig, Ann (eds.) (1990) *Popular Movements and Political Change in Mexico*, Boulder, Colorado: Lynne Rienner Press.

Fowler Salamini, Heather (1978) *Agrarian Radicalism in Veracruz, 1920–1938*, Lincoln: University of Nebraska Press.

Fox, Jonathan (1989a) 'Towards democracy in Mexico?', *Hemisphere*, 1, 2 (winter): 40–55.

——(1989b) 'Time to cross the border: paying attention to Mexico', *Radical America*, 22, 4, (1 September).

——and Gordillo, Gustavo (1989) 'Between State and Market: the Campesinos' Quest for Autonomy' in Cornelius, Gentleman and Smith (eds), *Mexico's Alternative Political Futures*.

Gaceta de la Reforma Politica, 1, 1977, Mexico

Gamboa Villafranca, Javier (1988) 'La estructura sectorial del Partido Revolucionario Institucional en la lucha política electoral 1987–1988' in *Las elecciones en México*, compiled by the Facultad de Ciencias Políticas y Sociales, UNAM.

Gándara Mendoza, Leticia (1976) 'La evolución de una oligarquía: el caso de San Miguel el Alto, Jalisco' in Martínez Saldaña, T. and Gándara Mendoza, L. *Política y sociedad en México: el caso de los Altos de Jalisco*, Mexico: INAH.

García, B. (1979) 'La acción del estado en tierra y vivienda: el caso de Izcalli Chamapa (AURIS)', dissertation, el Colegio de México, Mexico.

——and Perló, M. (1984) 'Estado, sindicalismo oficial y políticas habitacionales: análisis de una década del INFONAVIT' in J. A. Alonso *et al. El Obrero mexicano 2: Condiciones de Trabajo*, Mexico: Siglo XXI: 94–133.

García, Emilio (1989) 'El movimiento campesino, hoy', *Pueblo*, 12, 144/5 (May–June): 19–20.

Garza, Gustavo and Schteingart, Marta (1978) *La Acción Habitacional del Estado en México*, Mexico: El Colegio de México.

Garza, Humberto (1984) 'Desequilibrios y contradicciones de la política exterior de México', *Foro Internacional*, 24, 4 (April–June): 443–57.

GATT (1989) *International Trade: Annual Report, 1989*, GATT Secretariat, Geneva, Vols I and II.

Gereffi, Gary (1990) 'Big business and the state: East Asia and Latin America compared', *Asian Perspectives*, 14, (spring–summer): 5–29.

Giddens, Anthony (1980) *The Class Structure of the Advanced Societies*, 2nd edn, London: Unwin Hyman.

Gilbert, Alan (1989) 'Housing during recession: illustrations from Latin America', *Housing Studies*, 4, 3: pp. 155–66.

——and Varley, Ann (1991) *Landlord and Tenant: Housing the Urban Poor in Mexico*, London: Routledge.

——and Ward, Peter (1985) *Housing, the State and the Poor: Policy and Practice in Three Latin American Cities*, Cambridge: Cambridge University Press.

Gillespie, Charles (1990) 'Models of democratic transition in South America: negotiated reform versus democratic rupture' in Ethier, D. (ed.) *Democratic Transition*: 45–72.

Gil Villegas, Francisco (1988) 'Opciones de política exterior: México en el Pacífico y el Atlántico', *Foro Internacional*, 29, 2 (October–December): 262–87.

Gledhill, John (1988) 'Agrarian social movements and forms of consciousness', *Bulletin of Latin American Research*, 7, 2: 257–76.

——(1991) *Casi Nada: A study of agrarian reform in the homeland of cardenismo*, Austin: University of Texas Press, Institute for Mesoamerican Studies on Culture and Society, Series, no. 4.

Gobierno Constitucional de los Estados Unidos Mexicanos/Gobierno del Estado de Querétaro (1986) *Plan Querétaro*, Querétaro.

Gómez Tagle, Silvia (1987) 'Los adjetivos de la democracia', *Revista Argumentos*, *1*, *1*, Mexico: Universidad Autónoma Metropolitana–Xochimilco.

——(1990a) *Estadística de la Reforma Política, 1977–1988*, 1, Mexico: El Colegio de México.

——(1990b) 'Entre la razón y la fuerza: el Tribunal de lo Contencioso Electoral en 1988', *Estudios Sociológicos*, 7, 22 (April).

González, Luis (1972) *Pueblo en vilo. Microhistoria de San José de Gracia*, Mexico: El Colegio de México.

González-Arechiga, Bernardo and Barajas Escamilla, Rocío (compil.) (1989) *Las maquiladoras: ajuste estructural y desarrollo regional*,

Tijuana: El Colegio de la Frontera Norte and Fundación Friedrich Ebert.

González de la Rocha, Mercedes (1988) 'Economic crisis, domestic reoganisation and women's work in Guadalajara, Mexico', *Bulletin of Latin American Research*, 7, 2: 207–3.

González Gutiérrez, Carlos (1988) 'México en el Congreso de EU: La inmigración', *Foro Internacional*, 29, 2 (October–December): 236–62.

Gordillo, Gustavo (1987) 'Estado y movimiento campesino en la coyuntura actual' in González Casanova, Pablo and Aguilar Camín, Héctor *México ante la crisis*, 2, 3rd edn., Mexico: Siglo XXI: 295–311.

——(1988) *Campesinos al asalto del cielo: una reforma agraria con autonomía*, Mexico: Siglo XXI/Universidad Autónoma de Zacatecas.

Grindle, Merilee S. (1977) *Bureaucrats, Politicians and Peasants in Mexico: a Case Study in Public Policy*, Berkeley: University of California Press.

Guerra, M. T., Monroy, M. B. and Ríos, H. (1974) 'Tierra, especulación y fraude en el fraccionamiento Nuevo Paseo de San Agustín', mimeo.

Haber, Stephen (1989) *Industry and Underdevelopment. The Industrialisation of Mexico, 1890–1940*, Stanford: Stanford University Press.

Hamilton, Nora (1982) *The Limits of State Autonomy: Postrevolutionary Mexico*, Princeton: Princeton University Press.

Hansen, Roger (1974) *The Politics of Mexican Development*, Baltimore: Johns Hopkins Press.

Hardy, Clarissa (1984) *El estado y los campesinos: la Confederación Nacional Campesina*, Mexico: Nueva Imagen/CEESTEM.

Harvey, Neil (1988) 'Personal networks and strategic choices in the formation of an independent peasant organisation: the OCEZ of Chiapas, Mexico', *Bulletin of Latin American Research*, 7, 2: 299–312.

——(1990a) 'Peasant strategies and corporatism in Chiapas' in Foweraker, J. and Craig, A. (eds) *Popular Movements and Political Change in Mexico*: 183–98.

——(1990b) 'Corporatist strategies and popular responses in rural Mexico: state and opposition in Chiapas, 1970–1988', Ph.D thesis in Government, University of Essex.

Heller, Claude (1990) 'Tendencias generales de la política exterior del gobierno del presidente Miguel de la Madrid', *Foro Internacional*, 30, (January–March): 380–97.

Heller, Michael (1990) 'The politics of telecommunications in Mexico', D.Phil thesis, University of Sussex.

Henderson, Jeffrey (1989) *The Globalisation of High Technology Production: Society, Space and Semi-conductors in the Restructuring of the Modern World*, London: Routledge.

Hernández Cervantes, H. (1987) 'Retos y perspectivas de la reconversión industrial' in *La reconversión industrial en América Latina*, 1, Mexico: Fondo de Cultura Económica.

Hernández, Luis (1990) 'De la coronación de la dama a los tiempos nuevos', *El Cotidiano*, 34 (March–April): 53–9.

Herrera Zúñiga, René and Chavarría, Manuel (1984) 'México en Contadora: una búsqueda de límites a los compromisos en Centroamérica', *Foro Internacional*, 24, 4 (April–June): 458–83.

Hiernaux, D. (1986) *Urbanización y Autoconstrucción de Vivienda en Tijuana*, Mexico: Centro de Ecodesarrollo.

Hinojosa Ortiz, J. (1983) *El ejido en México: análisis jurídico*, Mexico: Centro de Estudios Hisóricos del Agrarismo en México.

Hurrell, Andrew (1986) 'The quest for autonomy: the evolution of Brazil's role in the international system, 1964–1985', D.Phil thesis, Oxford University.

Huston, Perlita (1979) *Third World Women Speak Out*, New York: Praeger.

Ibarra, Eduardo (1985) 'Pormenores de un proyecto unitario para 1982', *Nueva Antropología*, 7, 27.

IMF (1989) Direction of Trade Statistics, Washington, DC.

INEGI (1975) *Estadística industrial anual*, Mexico: INEGI.

——(1985) *Estadística industrial anual*, Mexico: INEGI

——(1988) *Estadísticas del Comercio Exterior de México*, Vol. 12, Aguascalientes.

——(1989) *Avance de información económica: industria maquiladora de exportación* (May), Aguascalientes.

——(1990) *Mexico: Economic and Social Information*, 1, 1 (September–December).

Iracheta, A. (1988) 'Los problemas del suelo y la política urbana en la Zona Metropolitana de la Ciudad de México' in R. Benítez Zenteno and J. Benigno Morelos (eds) *Grandes problemas de la Ciudad de México*, Mexico: Plaza y Valdés Editores: 47–95.

Jiménez, Edith (1988) 'New forms of community participation in

Mexico City: success or failure?', *Bulletin of Latin American Research*, 7, 1: 17–31.

——(1989) 'A new form of government control over colonos in Mexico City' in Gilbert, Alan (ed.) *Housing and Land in Urban Mexico*, La Jolla: Center for US-Mexican Studies: 157–72.

Kate, Ten and de Mateo, Venturini (1989) 'Changing structure of protection during the eighties', *Comercio Exterior* (April).

Kennedy, Paul (1971) *The Middle Beat. A Correspondent's View of Mexico, Guatemala and El Salvador*, Columbia University: Teachers College Press.

Knight, Alan (1985) 'The Mexican Revolution: bourgeois? nationalist? or just a "great rebellion"?', *Bulletin of Latin American Research*, 4, 2: 1–37.

——(1986) *The Mexican Revolution*, Cambridge, 2 vols: Cambridge University Press.

——(1990a) 'Mexico's elite settlement: conjuncture and consequences', paper given at the workshop on elite settlements and democratization, Panajachel, Guatemala, publication forthcoming.

——(1990b) 'Historical continuities in popular movements' in Foweraker and Craig (eds) *Popular Movements and Political Change in Mexico Boulder, Colorado*: 78–102.

Krauze, Enrique (1976) *Caudillos culturales en la Revolución Mexicana*, Mexico: Siglo XXI.

——(1987) *Lázaro Cárdenas: General Misionero, Biografía del poder* 8, Mexico: Fondo de Cultura Económica.

Laclau, Ernesto (1985) 'New social movements and the plurality of the social' in David Slater (ed.) *New Social Movements and the State in Latin America*, Dordrecht: FORIS Publications, Holland: 27–42.

Lajous, Roberta (1987) 'La agenda bilateral entre México y Estados Unidos', *Foro Internacional*, 27, 3 (January–March).

Linck, Thierry and Santana, Roberto (coords) (1988) *Les paysanneries du Michoacán au Mexique*, Toulouse: CNRS.

van Lindert, P. (1985) 'Mudarse en Chihuahua: la movilidad residencial de la población con ingresos bajos' in W. Hoenderdos (ed.) *Migración, empleo y vivienda en la ciudad de Chihuahua, Chihuahua*: Desarrollo Económico del estado de Chihuahua AC: 51–60.

Lingart, Robert (1989) *Le sucre et la faim*, Paris: Minuit.

Loaeza, Soledad (1987) 'El Partido Acción Nacional: de la oposición leal a la impaciencia electoral' in Loaeza, S. and Segovia, R. (eds) *La vida política en la crisis*, Mexico: El Colegio de México.

——(1988) *Clases medias y política en México*, Mexico: El Colegio de México.

Looney, Robert (1985) *Economic Policymaking in Mexico: Factors Underlying the 1982 Crisis*, Durham: Duke University Press.

Lowenthal, Abraham (1987) *Partners in Conflict: The United States and Latin America*, Baltimore: Johns Hopkins University Press.

Loyola Díaz, Rafael (1990a) 'La liquidación del feudo petrolero en la política moderna, México 1989', *Mexican Studies/Estudios Mexicanos*, 6, 2 (summer): 263–97.

——(coord.) (1990b) *Entre la guerra y la estabilidad política. El México de los 40*, Mexico: Editorial Grijalbo.

Lugo, M.L.G. and Berjerano, F. (1981) 'La acción del estado, el capital y la formación de las colonias populares, en la transformación urbana de las tierras ejidales en las delegaciones de Magdalena Contreras y Tlalpan: el caso de la colonia popular Miguel Hidalgo', dissertation, Universidad Iberoamericana, Mexico City.

Luna, M., Tirado, R. and Valdés, F. (1987) 'Businessmen and politics in Mexico, 1982–1986' in Maxfield and Anzaldúa (eds) *Government and the private sector in contemporary Mexico*, La Jolla: Center for US–Mexican Studies, UCSD, 13–43.

Lustig, Nora (1975) 'Distribución del ingreso, estructura del consumo y características del crecimiento industrial', *Comercio Exterior*, 29, 5 (May).

Madrazo, Jorge (1985) 'La reforma política y la legislación electoral en las entidades federativas' in González Casanova, P. (coord.) *Las elecciones en México: evolución y perspectivas*, Mexico: Instituto de Investigaciones Sociales/UNAM.

Márquez, Enrique (1987) 'Political Anachronisms: The *Navista* movement and political processes in San Luis Potosí, 1958–1985' in Alvarado, A. (ed.) *Electoral patterns and perspectives in Mexico*, Monograph series no. 22, La Jolla: Center for US–Mexican Studies, UCSD.

Martínez Assad, Carlos (coord.) (1985) *Municipios en conflicto* Mexico: Instituto de Investigaciones Sociales/UNAM.

——(1985) 'Nava: de la rebelión de los coheteros al juicio político' in Martínez Assad, C. (coord.) *Municipios en conflicto*: 55–74.

Martínez Saldaña, Tomás (1976) 'Formación y transformación de una oligarquía: el caso de Arandas, Jalisco' in Martínez Saldaña, T. and Gándara Mendoza, L. *Política y sociedad en México: el caso de los Altos de Jalisco*, Mexico: INAH.

Martínez Vázquez, Víctor Raúl and Anselmo Arrelanes, M. (1985) 'Negociación y conflicto en Oaxaca' in Martínez Assad, C. (coord.) *Municipios en conflicto*.

Maxfield, Sylvia (nd) 'Bankers' alliances and macro-economic policy patterns in Mexico and Brazil', unpublished paper, Yale University.

——(1989) 'International economic opening and government–business relations' in Cornelius, Gentleman and Smith (eds) *Mexico's Alternative Political Futures*: 215–36.

——and Anzaldúa, Ricardo (1987) *Government and the Private Sector in Contemporary Mexico*, La Jolla: Center for US–Mexican Studies, UCSD.

McAuslan, P. (1985) *Urban Land and Shelter for the Poor*, London: Earthscan.

McCarthy, Kevin and Burciaga Váldez, R. (1986) *Current and Future Effects of Mexican Immigration in California*, Santa Monica: California Round Table, Rand (R–3365–CR).

Medina, Luis (1978) *Historia de la Revolución Mexicana, 1940–1952. Del cardenismo al avilacamachismo*, Mexico: El Colegio de México.

Mele, P. (1984) 'Los procesos de producción del espacio urbano en la ciudad de Puebla', *Documento de Investigación* 1, Instituto de Ciencias, Universidad Autónoma de Puebla.

——(1987) 'Croissance urbaine, illegalité et pouvoir local dans la ville de Puebla (Mexique)', paper presented to the annual conference, Institute of British Geographers (January).

——(1988) 'Cartographier l'illégalité: filières de production de l'espace urbain de la ville de Puebla (Mexique)', *L'Espace Geographique*, 4: 257–63.

Méndez, Luis and Quiroz, Othon (1990) 'Organización obrera: nuevos rumbos, ¿nuevas perspectivas?', *El Cotidiano*, 36 (July–August): 47–56.

Mertens, L. (1986) *Employment and stabilisation in Mexico*, International Labour Organisation, World Employment Research Programme, Working Paper 10, Geneva.

Mexico, Presidencia de la República (1985) *Las Razones y las Obras: Gobierno de Miguel de la Madrid. Crónica del Sexenio, 1982–1988. Segundo Año*, Mexico: Presidencia de la República.

——(1987) *La Razones y las Obras: Gobierno de Miguel de la Madrid. Crónica del Sexenio 1982–1988. Cuarto Año*, Mexico: Presidencia de la República.

——(1988a) *Las Razones y las Obras: Gobierno de Miguel de la Madrid.*

Crónica del Sexenio 1982–1988. Quinto Año, Mexico: Presidencia de la República.

——(1988b) *Las Razones y las Obras: Gobierno de Miguel de la Madrid. Crónica del Sexenio 1982–1988. Sexto Año*, Mexico: Presidencia de la República.

Meyer, Jean (1976) *The Cristero Rebellion. The Mexican People Between Church and State*, Cambridge: Cambridge University Press.

Meyer, Lorenzo (1990) 'The United States and Mexico: the historical structure of their conflict', *Journal of International Affairs*, 43, (winter): 251–71.

Middlebrook, K. (1982) 'The political economy of Mexican organised labour, 1940–1973', Ph.D thesis, Harvard University.

Ministerio das Relaçoẽs Exteriores (1975) *Resenha de Política Exterior do Brasil*, Brasilia, Divisão de Documentação (March).

Moctezuma, P. (1990) 'Mexico's urban popular movements: a conversation with Pedro Moctezuma', *Environment and Urbanization*, 2: 35–50.

Moguel, Julio (1990) 'Programa Nacional de Solidaridad, ¿para quien?', *El Cotidiano*, 38 (November–December): 23–7.

Montano, J. (1976) *Los pobres de la ciudad en los asentamientos espontáneos*, Mexico: Siglo XXI.

Moreno Armella, F. (1988) 'Política y territorio: la presencia del poder político institucional en el proceso de expansión del Area Metropolitana de la Ciudad de México' in A. Iracheta Cenecorta and A. Villar Calvo (eds) *Política y movimientos sociales en la Ciudad de México*, Plaza y Valdes Editores: 77–95.

Moreno Toscano, A. (1979) 'La "crisis" en la ciudad' in P. González Casanova and E. Florescano (eds) *México, hoy*, Mexico: Siglo XXI: 152–76.

Moser, Caroline (1989) 'The impact of recession and structural adjustment policies at the micro-level: low-income women and their households in Guayaquil, Ecuador' in UNICEF (ed.) *Invisible Adjustment*, Vol. 2, UNICEF Americas and Caribbean Regional Office, New York: 137–162.

Murphy, R. (1988) *Social Closure: the Theory of Monopolisation and Exclusion*, Oxford: Clarendon Press.

NACLA (1975) 'Hit and run: US runaway shops on the Mexican border', *Latin America and Empire Report*, 9, 5 (July–August).

O'Connor, James (1988) *Accumulation Crisis*, Oxford: Basil Blackwell.

OECD (1988) *The newly industrialising countries: challenge and opportunity for OECD industries*, Paris: OECD.

Ojeda, Mario (1976) *Alcances y límites de la política exterior de México*, Mexico: El Colegio de México.

——(1986) *México. El Surgimiento de una política exterior activa*, Mexico DF: SEP Cultura.

Orlando Espíritu, Jorge (1984) 'Evaluación de las elecciones locales durante 1983', *Nueva Antropología*, 7, 25 (October).

Pahl, Ray (1984) *Divisions of Labour*, Oxford: Basil Blackwell.

Palomares, L. and Mertens, L. (1987) 'Programmable automation and new work contents: experiences of the electronics, metal engineering and secondary petrochemicals industries in Mexico, and evolving skill profiles and new technology in the Mexican electronic industry', Mexico City: International Labour Organisation.

Panizza, Francisco (1990) 'The paradoxes of democratic consolidation in Latin America', paper presented at Joint Sessions of European Consortium for Political Research, Bochum (April 1990); forthcoming as 'Las paradojas de la consolidación de la democracia en América Latina', *Cuadernos de CLEAH*, Montevideo.

Partant, François (1983) *Le fin du développement*, Paris: Maspero.

Pastor, Roberto (1990) 'Salinas takes a gamble', *New Republic*, 10–17 September: 27–32.

——and Castañeda, Jorge (1988) *Límites en la amistad: México y Estados Unidos*, Mexico: Editorial Joaquín Mortiz.

Pellicer de Brody, Olga (1972) *México y la revolución cubana*, Mexico: El Colegio de México.

——(1977) 'La oposición en México: el caso del henriquismo' in *Las crisis en el sistema político mexicano (1928–1977)*, Mexico: El Colegio de México.

Pérez-Escamilla, J. R. (1987) 'Telephone policy in Mexico: recent experience and perspectives', paper presented in the workshop on Mexico's Telecommunications Options in the World Service Market, University of California at San Diego, 13–14 November.

Pezzoli, Keith (1987) 'The urban land problem and popular sector housing development in Mexico City', *Environment and Behaviour*, 19: 371–97.

Philip, George (1988a) 'Introduction' in Philip, George *The Mexican Economy*: 1–6.

——(1988b) *The Mexican Economy*, London: Routledge.

Pozas Garza, M. de la A. (1989) 'Land settlement by the poor in

Monterrey' in Gilbert, Alan (ed.) *Housing and Land in Urban Mexico*. 65–77.

Prieto, A. M. (1986) 'Mexico's national *coordinadoras* in a context of economic crisis' in Carr, Barry and Anzaldúa Montoya, Ricardo (eds) *The Mexican Left, the Popular Movements and the Politics of Austerity*, La Jolla: Center for US–Mexican Studies: 75–94.

Purcell, Susan Kaufman (1975) *The Mexican Profit-sharing Decision: Politics in an Authoritarian Regime*, California: University of California Press.

——(1990) 'US–Mexico relations: an optimistic view', *Journal of International Affairs*, 3, 2 (winter): 423–9.

——and Purcell, John (1980) 'State and society in Mexico: must a stable polity be institutionalized?', *World Politics*, 32, 2: 194–227.

Quiroz, Teresa, Osorio, Rodolfo, Carmen, Violeta, and Vásquez, Rita (1984) 'La mujer en Costa Rica y su participación política-económica en el desarrollo del país', *Avances de investigación* 51, Instituto de Investigaciones Sociales, Univerisidad de Costa Rica, San José.

Radcliffe, Sarah (1986) 'Gender relations, peasant livelihood strategies and migration: a case study from Cuzco, Peru', *Bulletin of Latin American Research*, 5, 2: 29–47.

Ramírez Saiz, Juan Manuel (1986a) *El movimiento urbano popular en México*, Mexico: Siglo XXI.

——(1986b) 'Reivindicaciones urbanas y organización popular. El caso de Durango', *Estudios Demográficos y Urbanos*, 3.

——(1989) 'Efectos políticos de la proposición y puesta en práctica del programa urbano del Movimiento Urbano Popular (MUP)', paper presented at the research workshop, Popular Movements and the Transformation of the Mexican Political System, (29–31 March), La Jolla: Center for US–Mexican Studies (mimeo).

——(1990) 'Urban struggles and their political consequences' in Foweraker, Joe and Craig, Ann (eds) *Popular Movements and Political Change in Mexico*: 234–46.

Redclift, Michael (1987) *Sustainable Development: Exploring the Contradictions*, London: Methuen.

Regalado, J. (1986) 'El movimiento popular independiente en Guadalajara' in Tamayo, Jaime (ed.) *Perspectivas de los movimientos sociales en la región Centro-Occidente*, Mexico: Editorial Línea: 121–57.

Rello, Fernando (1986) *El campo en la encrucijada nacional*, Mexico: SEP, Foro 2000.

Rendón, Teresa and Escalante, Roberto (1989) 'Neoliberalismo a la mexicana: su impacto sobre el sector agropecuario', *Problemas de Desarrollo*, 19, 76 (October–December): 115–45.

Reyna, José Luis (1974) 'Control político, estabilidad y desarrollo en México', *Cuadernos del Centro de Estudios Sociológicos*, 3.

Reynolds, C. W. (1973) *La economía mexicana: su estructura y crecimiento en el siglo XX*, Mexico: Fondo de Cultura Económica.

Reynolds, David (1989) 'Rethinking Anglo–American relations', *International Affairs*, 65, 1 (winter): 89–111.

Rico, Carlos (1989) 'Una vuelta a la montaña rusa. Relaciones Mexico-Estadounidenses después de la posguerra y desafíos del futuro inmediato', *Foro Internacional*, 29, 3 (January–March): 387–404.

Roberts, Bryan (1990) 'Economic crisis, social change and political reform in Mexico', seminar paper presented at the Institute of Latin American Studies, University of London, 14 March.

Robinson, Linda (1988) 'Peace in Central America?', *Foreign Affairs*, 66, 3.

Robles, Rosario and Moguel, Julio (1990) 'Agricultura y proyecto neoliberal', *El Cotidiano*, 7, 34 (March–April): 3–12.

Rodgers, Gerry (1989) 'Introduction: trends in urban poverty and labour market access' in Rodgers, Gerry (ed.) *Urban Poverty and the Labour Market: Access to Jobs and Incomes in Latin American Cities* , Geneva: International Labour Office: 1–33.

Rodríguez Cabo, F. (1935) Report of Federal Labour Inspector, 30 September 1935, in *Archivo General de la Nación*, Mexico City, Presidentes, Lázaro Cardenas, 533.4/12.

Rodwin, L. (eds) (1987) *Shelter, Settlement and Development*, Boston: Allen & Unwin.

Romero Miranda, M. A. (1991) 'Elecciones: nueva situación geopolítica', *El Cotidiano*, 39 (January–February): 14–20.

Ross, Stanley R. (1982) 'Los profetas de la ruina, los analistas de crisis y la estabilidad política mexicana' in *Perspectivas del sistema político mexicano*, Mexico: CEN del PRI: 17–26.

Roxborough, Ian (1984) *Unions and Politics in Mexico: the Case of the Automobile Industry*, Cambridge: Cambridge University Press.

——(1988) 'The economic crisis and Mexican labour' in Philip, George (ed.) *The Mexican Economy*: 110–28.

Rubio, R. and Veloquio, F. (1986) 'La respuesta obrera a la modernización', *El Cotidiano*, 17 (July–August).

Salazar, Luis (1989) 'La democracia y la idea de la revolución, *Cuadernos de Nexos*, 10 (in *Nexos* 137), (May): vii–ix.

Salinas de Gortari, Carlos (1982) *Political Participation, Public Investment and Support for the System: a Comparative Study of Rural Communities in Mexico*, La Jolla: Center for US–Mexican Studies, UCSD.

——(1989) *Primer informe de gobierno*, Mexico: Presidencia de la República, 1 November.

——(1990a) 'Reformando al estado', *Nexos*, 148: 27–32.

——(1990b) 'Segundo informe de gobierno', *La Jornada*, 2 November.

Sánchez, M. (1979) 'Le phenomène des fractionnements populaires à Guadalajara, Jalisco, Mexique', Ph.D dissertation, Ecole des Hautes Etudes en Sciences Sociales, Paris.

Sanderson, Steven E. (1981) *Agrarian Populism and the Mexican State: the Struggle for Land in Sonora*, Berkeley: University of California Press.

Sarmiento, Sergio (1989) 'El movimiento campesino y el Congreso Agrario Permanente', *Pueblo*, 12, 144/5 (May–June): 21–3.

Saragoza, Alex M. (1988) *The Monterrey Elite and the Mexican State, 1880–1940*, Austin: University of Texas Press.

Sartori, Giovanni (1976) *Parties and Party Systems: a Framework for Analysis*, Vol. 1, Cambridge: Cambridge University Press.

Sassen, Saskia (1990) 'US immigration policy toward Mexico', *Journal of International Affairs*, 43, 2 (winter): 369–83.

Schryer, Frans (1980) *The* Rancheros *of Pisaflores: the History of a Peasant Bourgeoisie in Twentieth-century Mexico*, Toronto: University of Toronto Press.

Schteingart, Marta (1989) *Los Productores del Espacio Habitable: Estado, Empresa y Sociedad en la Ciudad de México*, Mexico: El Colegio de México.

SCT (1981) 'Evaluación económica del sistema de satélite doméstico mexicano' (November).

Selby, Robert (1979) 'Women, industrialisation and change in Querétaro, Mexico', Ph. D dissertation, Department of Anthropology, University of Utah, Michigan: Ann Arbor.

Senett, R. (1979) *Autoritée*, Paris: Fayard.

Sklair, Leslie (1989) *Assembling for Development: the* Maquila *Industry in Mexico and the United States*, Boston, MA: Unwin Hyman.

Smith, Peter (1979) *Labyrinths of Power: Political Recruitment in Twentieth-century Mexico*, Princeton: Princeton University Press.

Spalding, Rose (1981) 'State power and its limits: corporatism in Mexico', *Comparative Political Studies*, 14, 2: 139–61.

Stoddard, Elwyn R., (1987) Maquila: *Assembly Plants in Northern Mexico*, El Paso: University of Texas.

Tamayo, Jaime (nd) 'Los movimientos populares y el proyecto neocardenista: la influencia del nuevo "nacionalismo" en la política mexicana", Guadalajara: Centro de Investigaciones sobre los Movimientos Sociales (unpublished).

TELENALES (1987) 'Análisis de la productividad telegráfica', (September).

TELMEX (1983) 'Cuarta reunión de planeación corporativa: Memoria 1983'.

——(1987a) 'Autoevaluación 1986 y perspectivas a 1987'.

——(1987b) 'Estadísticas básicas telefónicas, Dirección de servicios a clientes'.

——(1987c) 'La infrastructura para la RDSI en México', Dirección de Planeación (August).

——(1987d) 'Octava reunión de planeación corporativa: Memoria 1987 (September).

Therborn, Goran (1980) *The Ideology of Power and the Power of Ideology*, London: Verso.

Thorup, Cathryn L., *et al.* (1987) *The US and Mexico: Face to Face with New Technology*, Overseas Development Council, US–Third World Policy Perspectives no. 8: New Brunswick.

Tirado, R. (1990) 'Los empresarios y la política: presente y perspectivas', *El Cotidiano*, 35 (May–June): 54–8.

Trejo Reyes, S. (1987) *El futuro de la política industrial en México*, Mexico: El Colegio de México.

UNECLA (United Nations Economic Commission for Latin America) (1989) *Statistical Yearbook for Latin America and the Caribbean, 1988*, Santiago de Chile.

US International Trade Commission (1988) *Imports under Items 806.30 and 807.00 of the Tariff Schedule of the United States, 1984–87*, Washington, DC.

Varley, Ann (1985a) 'La zona urbana ejidal y la urbanización de la Ciudad de México', *Revista de Ciencias Sociales Humanidades*, 6: 71–95.

——(1985b) 'Urbanization and agrarian law: the case of Mexico City', *Bulletin of Latin American Research*, 4, 1–16.

——(1985c) 'Ya somos dueños: ejido land development and regularisation in Mexico City', Ph.D dissertation, University College of London.

——(1987) 'The relationship between tenure legalization and housing improvements: evidence from Mexico City', *Development and Change*, 18: 463–81.

——(1989) 'Settlement, illegality and legalization: the need for re-assessment' in Ward, Peter (ed.) *Corruption, Development and Inequality: Soft Touch or Hard Graft?*, London: Routledge: 156–74.

Vásquez, Pilar (1990a) '¿Habrá final feliz en el conflicto de la Ford?', *El Cotidiano*, 34, (March–April): 61–4.

——(1990b) 'El telefonista sostiene su apuesta: revisión contractual 1990', *El Cotidiano*, 35 (May–June): 66–71.

Vaughan, Mary Kay, (1990) 'Women school teachers in the Mexican Revolution: the story of Reyna's braids', *Journal of Women's History*, 2, 1, (Spring): 143–68.

Velázquez Zárate, E. (1988) 'La verdad electoral en los sótanos de San Lázaro', *Pueblo*, 11, 139 (October): 2–6.

Vélez-Ibáñez, Carlos G. (1983) *Rituals of Marginality. Politics, Process and Cultural Change in Central Urban Mexico*, 1969–1974, Berkeley: University of California Press.

Vellinga, Menno (1989) 'Power and independence: the struggle for identity and integrity in urban social movements' in Schuurman, F. and Van Naerssen, T. (eds) *Urban Social Movements in the Third World*, London: Routledge: 151–76.

Verbeek, H. (1987) 'The authorization of unauthorized housing in Ciudad Chihuahua, Mexico' in O. Verkoren and J. van Weesep (eds) *Nederlandse Geografische Studien*, 37: Spatial Mobility and Urban Change, Geografisch Instituut, Rijksuniversiteit te Utrecht: 89–102.

Villarreal, D. R. and Castañeda, V. (1986) *Urbanización y Autoconstrucción de Vivienda en Monterrey*, Mexico: Centro de Ecodesarrollo.

Wallace, William (1977) *Foreign Policy and the Political Process*, London: Macmillan.

Waltz, Kenneth N. (1979) *Theory of International Politics*, Reading, Massachusetts: Addison Wesley.

Ward, Peter (1976) 'In search of a home: social and economic characteristics of squatter settlements and the role of self-help housing in Mexico City', Ph.D dissertation, University of Liverpool.

——(1981) 'Political pressure for urban services: the response of two

Mexico City administrations', *Development and Change*, 12: 379–407.

——(1986) *Welfare Politics in Mexico: Papering Over the Cracks*, London: Allen & Unwin.

——(1989) 'Political mediation and illegal settlement in Mexico City' in Gilbert, Alan (ed.) *Housing and Land in Urban Mexico*: 135–55.

——(1990) *Mexico City: The Production and Reproduction of an Urban Environment*, London: Belhaven Press.

Warman, Arturo (1976) *Y venimos a contradecir. Los campesinos de Morelos y el estado nacional*, Mexico: Ediciones de la Casa Chata.

——(1989) 'Persistencia de la pobreza', *Cuadernos de Nexos*', 8 (in *Nexos*, 135) (March): v–vi.

Whitehead, Laurence (1981) 'On "Governability" in Mexico', *Bulletin of Latin American Research*, 1, 1: 27–47.

——(1986) 'Debt, diversification and dependency: Latin America's international political relations' in Middlebrook, Kevin and Rico, Carlos (eds) *The US and Latin America in the 1980s. Contending Perspectives on a Decade of Crisis*, Pittsburgh: Pittsburgh University Press: 87–126.

——(1987) 'La perspectiva económica de México: sus implicaciones para las relaciones entre el Estado y los trabajadores', *Foro Internacional*, 28, 2 (October–December) 165–95.

——(1989a) 'Political change and economic stabilisation: the Economic Solidarity Pact' in Cornelius, Gentleman and Smith *Mexico's Alternative Political Futures*.

——(1989b) '"Tigers" in Latin America?' *Sciences*, 505, special issue edited by Peter Gourevitch 'The Pacific Region: Challenges to Policy and Theory', (September): 142–51.

Wilkie, James (1973) *The Mexican Revolution: federal expenditure and social change since 1910*, Berkeley: University of California Press.

Woldenberg, José (1988) 'La negociación político-social en México', in González Casanova, Pablo and Cadena Roa, Jorge (coords.) *Primer informe sobre la democracia: Mexico 1988*, Mexico: Siglo XXI and Centro de Investigaciones Interdisciplinarias en Humanidades, UNAM: 188–208.

World Bank (1979) *Special study of the Mexican economy: major policy issues and prospects*, Washington, DC.

——(1981) *Mexico: development strategy, prospects and problems*, Washington, DC.

Zepeda Patterson, Jorge (1986) 'No es el mismo agrario que agrio, ni comuneros que comunistas, pero se parecen' in Jaime Tamayo (ed.) *Perspectivas de los movimientos sociales en la región Centro-Occidente*, Mexico: Editorial Línea: 323–77.

——(1987) 'Michoacán antes y durante la crisis o sobre los michoacanos que no se fueron de braceros', *Relaciones*, 8, 31: 5–24.

Zermeño, Sergio (1978) *México: una democracia utópica*, Mexico City: Siglo XXI Editores.

——(1990) 'Crisis, neoliberalism and disorder' in Foweraker and Craig (eds) *Popular movements and political change in Mexico*, Boulder, Colorado: 160–80.

INDEX

divided factions over this issue, such as the Frente Popular de Zacatecas and the Unión Popular Revolucionaria Emiliano Zapata.

Cárdenas can do little to match the material resources which Salinas can offer popular movements, but the PRD is in a position to give more political space to the movements within the party, a major complaint of many movements, although doing so would create another set of problems. Should the party decide on this, it may well be possible for Cárdenas to keep within the coalition movements such as the CDP which will go on making *convenio* agreements with the government, while insisting that this has not compromised them politically. The CDP leadership claims that it wants to remain within the Cárdenas fold and build a united democratic front. What it requires is the freedom to make its own internal political decisions and to have a voice in the making of coalition decisions to which all members will be bound.

Julio Moguel makes the interesting observation that the critique of corporatism, a central theme throughout the development of the PRD, has influenced the exclusion of popular movements (*El Cotidiano*, July–August 1989: 20–23). He argues that basing membership and the structure of organization on the individual citizen may work well in the electoral arena but the absence of sectoral representation and 'organic political currents' within the PRD results in a lack of contact with the many popular organizations. This issue was of considerable concern throughout the formation of the PRD and during its [illegible]

[illegible]